SAVING THE NATION

SAVING THE NATION

Economic Modernity in Republican China

MARGHERITA ZANASI

The University of Chicago Press • Chicago and London

Margherita Zanasi is associate professor in the Department of History at Louisiana State University.

The University of Chicago Press, Chicago 60637
The University of Chicago Press, Ltd., London

Printed in the United States of America
15 14 13 12 11 10 09 08 07 06   1 2 3 4 5

ISBN-13 (cloth): 978-0-226-97873-4
ISBN-10 (cloth): 0-226-97873-7

Library of Congress Cataloging-in-Publication Data

Zanasi, Margherita.
Saving the nation : economic modernity in republican China / Margherita Zanasi
p. cm
Includes bibliographical references and index.
ISBN 0-226-97873-7 (cloth : alk. paper)
1. China--Economic conditions–1912–1949. 2. China--History--Republic, 1912–1949.
3. China--Rural conditions. I. Title.
HC427.8.Z36 2006
330.951′04--dc22

2005032848

∞ The paper used in this publication meets the minimum requirements of the American National Standard for Information Sciences—Permanence of Paper for Printed Library Materials, ANSI Z39.48-1992.

For my parents, Marisa and Domenico Zanasi,

with love

CONTENTS

ACKNOWLEDGMENTS

This project has benefited from the help and support of many people, and I am greatly indebted to them all. During my research in both the ROC and the PRC, I received the kind help of Professors Zhang Xianwen, Chen Hongming, Chen Qianping, and Cai Shaoqing of Nanjing University. Thanks also to Professors Chen Sanjin and Wang Shuhuai and to Shen Huaiyu, Li Yuping, and Lin Qiunrong at Academia Sinica, who spent much time talking and discussing my work with me. I am also grateful to the archivists and personnel at the Nanjing Second Historical Archives. I want to especially thank Deputy Director Ma Zhende, Director of Research Guo Biqiang, and all the personnel in the reading room for their generous help during my three visits to the archives. I also want to extend a special thanks to the personnel at the Economic Archives of the Modern History Institute at Academia Sinica, at the GMD Party History Committee, at the Taiwan National Archives, at the Center for Chinese Studies, and at the Shanghai Municipal Archives, who offered precious help in the research stage of this book.

This book would not have been possible without the financial support of the Pacific Foundation, China Times Foundation, the Center for Chinese Studies in Taibei, Taiwan, and an An Wang Postdoctoral Fellowship from the Fairbank Center for East Asian Research at Harvard University.

I would also like to extend a special thanks to my graduate adviser at Columbia University, Professor Madeleine Zelin, whose support during these many years has proved crucial for the completion of this book. I am also grateful to Professor Andrew Nathan, who, when I was a graduate student and this book was in its dissertation stage, was always very generous with his time and advice. Professors Carl Riskin, Richard Lufrano, and Michael Tsin, members of my dissertation committee, offered valuable comments that proved crucial for revising the dissertation into a manuscript. I wish to thank Professor Ramon Myers, of the Hoover Institute, for inviting me to participate in the dissertation workshop on Republican China and for his valuable insights on my research. I am also greatly indebted to Chen Kan, who generously shared his memories of his father, Chen Gongbo, and allowed me access to his personal papers.

During the years this book was in the making, Professors Parks Coble, Paul Cohen, Prasenjit Duara, David Strand, Susan Burns, and Edward Rhoad, at one stage or another, have offered valuable support, help, and advice. Thanks also to the anonymous reviewers who read the manuscript so carefully and suggested revisions that greatly improved this book. I am grateful to my editor at the University of Chicago Press, Alex Schwartz, for his support of this book and the care he has taken with its production, and to Pamela Bruton for her careful editing of the manuscript.

I am greatly indebted to the many friends who have supported and encouraged me. I will never be able to fully repay the friendship of Maria Tucci, Robert Gotlieb, Robert Cornfield, Andre Schimd, Ned Walsh, and Yu Ning. My husband, who has stoically stood by me through good times and bad, deserves my special thanks. Finally, it would be unforgivable not to thank Micia, Macchia, and Nero for napping on my desk and books with such inspired determination.

ABBREVIATIONS

AMO	administrative mass organization
CCC	Cotton Control Commission
CCP	Chinese Communist Party
CDFC	China Development Finance Corporation
CIFRC	China International Famine Relief Commission
FRC	Flood Relief Commission
GFII	General Federation of Italian Industry (Confederazione generale dell'industria italiana)
GMD	Nationalist Party (Guomindang)
GMDPHC	Guomindang Party History Committee
NEC	National Economic Council
NFC	National Finance Commission
NHA	National Historical Archives
NRA	National Revolutionary Army
NSHA	Nanjing Second Historical Archives
PRC	People's Republic of China
RNG	Reorganized National Government
ROC	Republic of China
SIC	Silk Improvement Commission

INTRODUCTION

Economic modernity is so closely associated with modern nationhood that it is impossible to imagine a modern nation without a modern economy. If pressed to define a "modern economy" and to describe its connection to nationhood, however, most people would probably be unable to do so. Until recently, Marxist and structuralist narratives appeared to offer a direct and self-evident answer to these questions. They traced the emergence of nations to the development of modern technologies and to socioeconomic forces whose basic elements were railways, industries (industrialization generally being considered the basis for development and modern nationhood), and a bourgeoisie. These narratives have come to be questioned, however, as new works have demonstrated that different nations have achieved industrialization following different paths based on different socioeconomic elements.[1] In addition, the notion that ideas of nation precede nation building has become widely accepted. It is the idea of what constitutes a modern nation that leads nation builders to shape national institutions and a national economy, and not vice versa.[2] Finally, the meaning of economic modernity has been subjected to different interpretations and is constantly changing. The industrial modernity of seventeenth- and eighteenth-century England hardly seems modern by today's standards. Adam Smith's theory of the natural laws of the market and their absolute self-regulatory power is modern only in the historical sense of the term but not in its popular usage.[3] For a while, socialist and fascist movements, which questioned liberal economic theories and called for a state-regulated economy, claimed to be the epitome of modernity, but eventually these movements became associated with images of backwardness. Today what constitutes economic modernity remains vague as information technology and service industries become increasingly important vis-à-vis the industrial sector. The relationship between nation and economy is also increasingly unclear, as it becomes virtually impossible even to define a "national" economy in the current process of globalization.

Crucial questions thus come to the fore: What kind of relationship does, in fact, exist between notions of modern nationhood and modern economy and what does it mean to be economically modern in different historical periods, in different geographical regions, and under different sociopolitical circumstances? In addition, how do ideas of economic modernity influence nation building? How do they shape the institution of the state and the sociopolitical foundation of the nation? These questions are particularly relevant for understanding the history of modern China. Since the mid–nineteenth century, Chinese leaders have pursued different nation-building projects inspired by different ideas of economic modernity and modern nationhood. Late Qing officials, who favored mercantilist policies in their attempt to modernize China's economy and to resist growing Western imperialism, were concerned with the effects of economic reforms on China's identity. Marxist-Leninist notions of socioeconomic justice played an important role in the development of the vision of a modern Chinese nation and in the nation-building effort of the Chinese Communist Party (CCP). Today's Communist leaders struggle to justify the coexistence of the new capitalist economy with an authoritarian (Communist, if only in name) state. Thus, for more than a century, Chinese leaders have pondered what it means to be economically modern and how this modernity affects China as a modern nation.

The issue of economic modernity and its role in nation building assumed particular importance for the Nationalist Party (Guomindang, GMD) during the Nanjing Decade, that is, the ten years from the establishment of the Nationalist government in Nanjing in 1927 to full-scale war with Japan in 1937. After the demise of the imperial system in 1911 and more than a decade of civil war among provincial military strongmen (warlords), the GMD, having successfully reunified a large portion of the country under its leadership, appeared poised to begin the long-postponed project of transforming China into a modern republican nation. These ten years were crucial for the GMD, not only for consolidating its power but also for defining the political nature of its rule and of the new Chinese nation at large. The Nationalists, however, were deeply divided on crucial nation-building issues. What was the meaning of economic modernity and what was its role in China's nation building? What model of development would fit China best? How could China pursue economic modernization (at the time overwhelmingly identified with Western economic trends) while maintaining a distinctive identity? What would be the relationship between state and private economy (in other words, what would be the socio-economic base of the new nation)?

These questions tore the party apart and generated intense struggle among its leaders. The most significant of these confrontations was the one between Jiang Jieshi (Chiang Kai-shek), the GMD's all-powerful military leader, and the political group that rallied around Wang Jingwei, a senior civilian party leader who had been closely associated with Sun Yat-sen (the founder and leader of the party until his death in 1925) since Sun's early revolutionary activities against the Qing in the late nineteenth century. The two leaders disagreed on what kind of nation the Nationalists were to build. Inspired by Prussia and Germany, Jiang favored an authoritarian militarist model and subordinated the economy to the military needs of the nation. The Wang group (the focus of this book) favored a *minzu* (national and nationalist) economy as the foundation of China's modern nationhood and consequently advocated economic reforms as the only effective means of nation building.

Building China's *Minzu* Economy

At the center of the Wang Jingwei group's nation-building vision was the idea of *minzu* economy developed by Wang and his closest associate, Chen Gongbo. Originally a member of the CCP, Chen had joined the GMD in 1925. Chen had received a master's degree in economics from Columbia University, and as the economist of the group that rallied around Wang, he became the most important theoretician and most vocal supporter of the Wang group's program for economic nation building, writing extensively on China's economic situation, its problems, and their solutions.[4] Chen's role in developing the idea of *minzu* economy and in implementing reforms aimed at achieving it makes him particularly important to this study.

The term "*minzu* economy" (*minzu jingji*) can be loosely translated as "national economy" although in Wang's and Chen's conception it assumed a more specific meaning since it did not refer simply to the sum of the economic elements located inside China's borders. It specifically referred to the ethnically Chinese socioeconomic forces that were not involved with foreign economic interests, distinguishing these ethnically Chinese economic elements from foreign businessmen operating in China and the Chinese working with them. According to Wang and Chen, this *minzu* group was an anti-imperialist force and constituted the foundation of the modern

Chinese nation. For this reason, Wang and Chen believed that the government should mobilize them in its nation-building effort. Their ultimate goal was, in fact, the *minzu* industrialization of China. Like most Chinese at the time, Wang and Chen believed that only a modern economy (and industrialization was widely considered the ultimate form of economic modernity) could generate a modern nation. They also believed that China's industrial system needed to be *minzu* in nature. This meant that it should not only be the expression of a modernizing *minzu* socioeconomic elite but also achieve two main goals. The first goal was to transform China into a highly unified and centralized "economic unit" (*jingji danwei*). This transformation (and not military action as Jiang Jieshi maintained) was the only way, Wang and Chen argued, to solve one of the main problems faced by China at that moment, namely, the disunity generated by recalcitrant provincial leaders who would not yield to Nanjing's authority and by the Communists in their rural bases. The second goal was to achieve autarky in order to resist the escalation of Japanese imperialism, the most pressing threat facing the government and China as a whole. An economy that was not autarkic would be dependent on Japan and would thus reinforce Japan's grip on China rather than help China assert its national independence. Wang's and Chen's plan was thus based on the idea that while the modernity of a nation rested on the modernity of its economy—that is, industrialization—this industrialization needed to be national(ist) (*minzu*) in nature. There could be no nation without a modern economy and no modern economy that was not national(ist). Economic modernity was thus the ultimate goal of nation building and, at the same time, a weapon for nationalist assertion against internal and external enemies.

The Wang group's nation-building program was firmly rooted in the reformist legacy of Sun Yat-sen, developing, and often reinterpreting, some of the themes that had characterized Sun's political program. It thus represented a main trend of Nationalist political and economic thought and for this reason was widely supported by prominent Nationalist leaders. Among them was Song Ziwen, a longtime leader of the GMD, his family having been close to Sun both politically and personally for decades: Song's sister, Song Qinglin, had married Sun. Song, who had a bachelor's degree from Harvard and a doctorate in economics from Columbia, had been the financial wizard of the party since the 1920s and was one of the most powerful political actors in the Nanjing government.[5] Since the establishment of the Nanjing government in 1927, Song had consistently opposed Jiang's military priorities and, sharing the civilian reformist approach embodied by Wang, had attempted extensive economic reforms. When Wang came to head the Nanjing government during the years of the Wang-Jiang coalition cabinet (1932–35), Song became one of his main supporters.

The Wang group's nation-building program also echoed one of the main themes of the Self-Strengthening Movement, a late Qing reform movement (1870s–90s) aimed at strengthening China against both domestic rebellion and Western imperialism. The idea was that economic modernization was key to China's national assertion and anti-imperialist struggle and that the reform-minded economic elite were to play an important role in it. For this reason, the platform proposed by the Wang group also ensured support from such reform-minded businessmen as Chen Guangfu, the founder and director of the Shanghai Commercial and Savings Bank (*Shanghai shangye chuxu yinhang*).

The support of Song Ziwen and Chen Guangfu was crucial to the realization of the Wang group's nation-building program. When Wang and Chen, together with other members of the Wang group, joined the government at the time of the Wang-Jiang coalition cabinet (1932–35), Wang became the new chairman of the Executive Yuan (1933–35) and Chen Gongbo became the minister of industry (1932–35). In spite of their prominent positions in the cabinet, Wang and Chen probably would have been unable to implement their reform plan without Song Ziwen's and Cheng Guangfu's support. Because of Song's support, the National Economic Council (*quanguo jingji weiyuanhui*, NEC)—established by Song Ziwen in 1931 as the highest economic planning unit of the Nanjing government—became the main vehicle for the realization of their reforms. Chen Guangfu became an active member of the NEC and played an important role in financing its reform initiatives. The history of the NEC suggests that the Wang group's program had the potential to create a broad alliance within the GMD and to develop a socioeconomic base in support of the party. Ultimately, however, Jiang defeated his political opponents at the end of the Nanjing Decade and imposed his military vision of modern nationhood on the government and on the country as a whole.

The confrontation between the two ideas of nation embodied by Jiang and Wang did not find a final resolution in the Nanjing Decade but reemerged during the years of the Japanese occupation of China. Wang, along with some of the leaders who had rallied around him in the 1930s, including Chen Gongbo, established a Nationalist government in Nanjing in collaboration with the Japanese occupying forces. At the end of the war Wang and Chen were considered the two most infamous Chinese collaborators, *hanjian* (literally, "betrayers of the Chinese people"), and little memory remained of their prewar efforts in nation building. This amnesia was not just the result of a natural hostility against collaborators in the postwar period; it was also rooted in the apparent impossibility of making sense of the contradiction between Wang's and Chen's 1930s nationalist reforms and their 1940s collaboration. Their decision to collaborate with the Japanese can be understood only in light of their experiences during the Nanjing Decade. Full war with Japan put Wang's and Chen's ideas of economic nation building to the test. Because they believed that China had not successfully completed economic nation building, and thus lacked the highest form of power (the power of a modern nation), they believed that war with Japan was destined to end in total defeat. The only way that China could survive was to strengthen its economy; only then could it resist Japan. The national economy, Wang and Chen believed, should be defended at any cost, even if that meant compromising with the invading forces. They feared that if Japan were allowed to control the national economy, China would lose any hope of regaining its independence one day. It was, once again, the two leaders' opposition to Jiang's vision of China and their consequent understanding of how to defend the nation that played an important role in their decision to abandon Chongqing, the seat of the Nationalist government at that time, and to collaborate. The Japanese invasion, therefore, proved to be a moment of truth for Wang's and Chen's notions of China's modern nationhood, revealing the contradictions and limits of these views in a dramatic and tragic way.

Cold War Historiography and Party History

This book presents an image of a Nationalist government deeply divided, debunking the prevalent interpretation that it was a monolithic political entity, firmly under the leadership of Jiang Jieshi and representing a unified view of nationhood. This latter interpretation has mostly been the result of Cold War historiography, which tended to project back to the prewar period the radicalization of Chinese politics into two blocks, the GMD and the CCP, a radicalization that came to characterize Chinese history only after 1945. Because it was invested in constructing an image of Jiang (and his staunch anticommunism) as the longtime and paramount leader of Nationalist China, Cold War historiography depicted the Wang group (and other political opponents of Jiang, such as Hu Hanmin, who was a party elder and, after Jiang and Wang, the third most important GMD leader after the death of Sun Yat-sen in 1925) as rather marginal to the political destiny of the GMD and China as a whole. This approach, which has proved surprisingly persistent, reduces the political choices faced by Chinese political leaders in the Nanjing Decade to two main lines: communism or a vaguely defined anticommunist program embodied by Jiang.[6] This reading does not do justice to the political complexity of the GMD and to the historical significance of the Nanjing Decade in twentieth-century China.

In this simplified reading of the Nanjing Decade, the rivalry between Wang and Jiang is too often reduced to a struggle for personal power, devoid of significant political implications.[7] In reality, as this book reveals, this rivalry was based to a large extent on important differences in their visions of nation building and modern nationhood. After 1927 most GMD leaders shared some broad political notions, including an anti-Communist bent and a strong belief in a one-party system, political centralization, and a high degree of control over the economy.[8] This wide political framework, however, left room for controversies and disagreements. These differences were rooted in long-standing problems in the party. Since its early days, the GMD, like its predecessor, the Revolutionary Alliance (*tongmenghui*), depended on an alliance among a broad range of political groups.[9] Even after 1924, when Sun Yat-sen attempted to centralize the party and to impose a unified political line—outlined in his lectures on Three People's Principles (*sanmin zhuyi*)—the party remained divided. During the reorganization in 1924, while preparing for the Northern Expedition (1926–28, the military campaign launched by the GMD against provincial warlords and aimed at unifying China under its rule), Sun added a military apparatus to the GMD, which had, until then, been a strictly civilian political organization. Jiang became the head of the new Huangpu (Whampoa) Military Academy (*Huangpu junxiao*), established to train the new Nationalist modern army (the National Revolutionary Army, NRA) and, in keeping with the practice of most Chinese warlords, used this position to build a base of personal followers, whom he later promoted to high positions in both the military and the political organizations of the GMD.[10] The introduction of warlord practices into the Nationalist Party, represented more than Jiang's personal ambitions and expressed a wider political culture that was predominant in China at the time. Jiang's power in the GMD greatly increased during the Northern Expedition. Even after 1928 Jiang continued to represent the GMD's new strand of military nation building and actively maneuvered to establish himself, and the military, at the head of both party and government. Jiang's relations with Wang and other civilian leaders such as Hu Hanmin became increasingly tense. Wang wanted the military to be strictly subordinated to the GMD's civilian political leadership and was eager to refocus the party on Sun's legacy of economic reform. The uncertainty of the GMD's political line in the Nanjing Decade was, therefore, a direct consequence of the reorganization of the party in 1924 and the resulting political ambiguities it created between the GMD's military and civilian leaders. In other words, the reorganization in 1924 had given the party the military might it needed to return to power, but it had also sown the seeds for its transformation from a political to a military organization.

The lively debate on the Chinese discourse on nationhood and national identity that has emerged recently in the field of modern Chinese history, bringing to light the coexistence of different visions of nation building and modern nationhood in the Republican years, has done much to break the dichotomy imposed by Cold War historiography.[11] Prasenjit Duara, for example, has introduced the idea of "bifurcated history," arguing that alternative visions of national reconstruction emerged parallel to that promoted by the GMD.[12] He convincingly argues that the Nationalist idea of the Chinese nation as a highly centralized and totalitarian entity was challenged by other groups, such as the federalists, who did not subscribe to the GMD's narrative of a highly centralized nation.[13] Duara thus questions the apparent inevitability of the passage from empire to nation, as realized by the Nationalists under the leadership of Jiang Jieshi. Historian John Fitzgerald adds to the debate by tracing the formation of the Nationalist discourse on the modern state. In doing so he clarifies the process by which the Nationalist idea of nation building came to be defined vis-à-vis alternative narratives, became hegemonic at their expense, and ultimately shaped long-lasting political institutions.[14]

Both Duara and Fitzgerald, however, assume that, because the GMD was highly centralized, it represented a unified political line. But even if centralization was indeed the goal of the GMD leaders, the party remained deeply divided until full war with Japan erupted. We can understand this apparent contradiction when we consider that no leader wanted centralization to happen under the control of his opponent. For Wang, centralization under Jiang Jieshi meant not only Wang's personal political marginalization but also moving the country along what he believed was the wrong path to nationhood. The feeling was reciprocal. Jiang opposed the centralization of the Nanjing administration until late 1935, when he finally defeated Wang. Only at that point was Jiang sure that centralization would occur under his own control. It was, after all, the very idea of the necessity of a highly centralized party and national political system that encouraged the factional struggle within the GMD. Because there was no administrative channel for expressing or negotiating political disagreements, the GMD leaders knew that if they could not dominate the entire party and government, their political voice would be lost forever. The struggle between the two nation-building strands that divided the Nationalists in the Nanjing Decade would thus determine the identity of the nation they were intent on creating.

Toward What Kind of Nation? A Crucial Crossroad

The confrontation between Jiang Jieshi and the Wang group was of particular importance to the future of China. Their viewpoints not only represented important political trends that had developed since the turn of the century but also revolved around issues that remain fundamental today. During the Nanjing Decade, in fact, certain long-term trends came to a head, as the first opportunity to create a modern Chinese nation presented itself.

In this context, Jiang Jieshi came to represent the most progressive expression of the militarist trend that had emerged in the wake of the fall of the empire. Jiang admired the Prussian and German examples of militarist national modernity and combined militarism with the nationalist spirit of the GMD. His outlook was thus fundamentally national and nationalist, going against the prevalent regionalist nature of warlordism. Because of his military priorities, Jiang favored the development of a military-oriented heavy industry, a priority that can be traced back to early Self-Strengthening reforms aimed at modernizing and strengthening the Chinese army vis-à-vis foreign imperialism and domestic rebellions.[15]

The Wang group instead built on alternative political and socioeconomic trends that can also be traced back to the late Qing and the early Republican years, as illustrated by an analysis of the reforms the Wang group carried out through the NEC. To fully understand the nation-building program of the Wang group, in fact, it is important to go beyond its intellectual dimension and to observe how the idea of China's *minzu* economy translated into reforms and how these reforms affected the socioeconomic landscape of China. Based on this consideration, this book bridges discourse analysis and socioeconomic and political history to show how, borrowing the words of historian Michael Tsin, "nationalism actually works in practice, that is, how it actually exercises its forces beyond the realm of consciousness."[16] This approach brings to light, for example, that the Wang group identified the industrial economy that had emerged in the coastal areas around the treaty ports as China's *minzu* economy. The NEC's reforms thus formalized into government policies the idea—that had begun to take shape at the turn of the century—that the center of China's modern identity was no longer the rural hinterland but its coastal urban economy. The autarkic development of this *minzu* economy became an attempt to reorient the coastal industries away from Japan and to integrate them with China's rural economy, which was to serve as its supplier of raw materials as well as new privileged market. This plan would have deeply changed the socioeconomic structure of the country at the time since it would have displaced the rural elite (identified as "backward" and as obstacles to economic modernization) and allowed both the state and the coastal industrial elite to access rural resources at the expense of the local elite. The NEC's reforms thus met with the fierce opposition of the village gentry, who resisted being marginalized in the new economic nation. These reforms also opposed a contemporary trend of economic modernization and nation building that continued to focus on the village as the source of modern China's identity—a trend not just pursued by the Communists under Mao Zedong's leadership but also popular within the Nationalist camp. Finally, these NEC reforms took an approach that was diametrically opposed to Jiang's. Jiang, in fact, not only favored heavy industry over consumer industry but also located his industrial center in the hinterland, thus marginalizing the emerging private industry in China's modern economy.

In addition, an analysis of the NEC reforms reveals that the Wang group appropriated joint state-private (*guanshang*) economic reform patterns initiated in the late Qing and combined them with worldwide corporativist trends. Because of the nation-building function they assigned to economic development and their wish to mobilize China's *minzu* economic forces, the Wang group organized the economic administration of the state along corporativist lines, centered on a system of controlled economy (*tongzhi jingji*). These corporativist organizations came to institutionalize, at the national level, the informal networks of cooperation between reform-minded industrialists and local authorities that had developed since the Self-Strengthening period. Tension, however, arose between a wish to support the development of the private industrial economy and the idea of a strong interventionist state actively engaged in nation building. In this context, the Wang group struggled to strike a balance between state control and supporting the private sector, rather than marginalizing it in the new modern economy as Jiang wanted.

In addition to absorbing reform trends that emerged at the turn of the century, the Wang group's vision of nation building also addressed issues that were at the center of the Chinese discourse on the nation and were thus an object of concern across political lines. The idea of a *minzu* economy, for example, reflected a tension between socialist notions of social change (as a means for modernization) and nationalist aspirations. This tension informed the political platform that Sun Yat-sen presented at the time of the party's reorganization in 1924 (the Three People's Principles). It was at this time that, under pressure from his Soviet adviser, Sun inaugurated a period of cooperation with the CCP based on the shared goal of reunifying the country. The CCP identified the *minzu* socioeconomic groups as the basis of the joint CCP-GMD political enterprise and limited the target of the

Communist class struggle to a small portion of the Chinese capitalist class (those who collaborated with imperialist interests) in order to allow the pursuit of a temporary nationalist goal and to justify its alliance with the GMD. In other words, the 1924 *minzu* political platform imposed a nationalist agenda on the socialist revolution (in this respect it was in keeping with the current Soviet international policy).[17] The idea of China's *minzu* socioeconomic basis became a shared CCP and GMD heritage and remained part of the Chinese political discourse through the twentieth century. Rejected by Jiang, who, departing from Sun's legacy, was not concerned with social change and the relationship between state and society at large, it became the main concept of the Wang group's nation-building program. In 1942 it was also reappropriated by Mao Zedong as the pivotal idea of his *New Democracy* (*Xin minzhu zhuyi*), the political platform that successfully supported the CCP through the early 1950s.[18]

It is commonly believed that the GMD finally lost the country to the CCP in 1949 due to its inability or unwillingness to carry out significant political and economic reforms and its inability to ultimately gain significant support in society.[19] The question arises of whether a final success of the civilian and reformist GMD led by the Wang group would have been able to establish a different kind of Nationalist government than the one established by Jiang. Would a reformist Nanjing government have led the country in a different direction and to a different destiny? In other words, the outcome of the confrontation between two different nation-building strands in the 1930s, by silencing the GMD's most vital and successful reformers, influenced the terms, if not the result, of the GMD's struggle against the Communists in the postwar years. This consideration becomes even more salient because one of the main reasons for the Communist victory was the success of the political platform outlined in 1942 by Mao Zedong in *New Democracy*, which focused on the importance of the *minzu* economy to China's destiny and thus ensured the CCP the support of the broad socioeconomic alliance that had been at the center of the Wang group's program. In addition, the Wang group's plan for the removal of the rural elite and the village "middlemen"—a group identified by the CCP as the "local bullies" and targeted in their land reform campaign—would have shown a commitment to social and economic change in the village that could have counteracted, at least in part, the Communist land reform propaganda.

The question also arises of how the NEC's reforms speak to today's China. Contemporary Chinese leaders are also trying to strike a balance between maintaining a certain degree of political and economic control while fostering the private economy: the same balance that the Wang group tried to strike. Today's leaders, like Wang and Chen in the 1930s, also try to promote national unity in an economic environment in which social differences are deepening, group interests are becoming increasingly differentiated, and provinces are seeking greater autonomy. In addition, once again, the coastal private economy is leading the modernization of the country, bringing a new cosmopolitan flavor to China. In this context, today's leaders struggle to balance global modernity with the defense of what they believe, or claim, to be China's identity (as elusive and controversial a notion now as it was in the 1930s).

Many of the problems faced by the Wang group in the 1930s were dormant under Jiang's and the Communist authoritarian regimes. These problems are now reemerging, although in different historical circumstances, as some of the most important issues that any Chinese government needs to address for successful economic development and modernization. In other words, today, as in the 1930s, Chinese leaders are struggling to define the model of economic modernity that they believe can best serve China (and their political goals) while reformulating the connection between the economy (increasingly capitalist) and the nation (still politically authoritarian). For Chinese leaders today, the question of the relationship between economic modernity and nation is, therefore, just as crucial as it was for their predecessors in the 1930s.

China and Fascist Modernity

One of the main characteristics of the nation-building vision of the Wang group is that it combined domestic reformist trends with worldwide trends. Although corporativist and productivist trends reached China from a variety of sources, representing their wide range of manifestations and levels of radicalism, Wang Jingwei and Chen Gongbo appeared to have been particularly attracted by the Italian Fascist model of nation building and economic modernity.[20] Italian Fascism was centered on autarky and the two correlated notions of corporativism (devised to mobilize a country's economic forces) and productivism (an expansion in economic production aimed, as explained in more detail in chapter 2, at achieving autarky and counteracting socialist ideas of wealth redistribution). In the early 1930s, Il Duce, as the Italian Fascist leader Benito Mussolini liked to be called, appeared to have succeeded in transforming Italy into a strong and modern nation. Looking from abroad, Italy appeared to prosper under the new Fascist regime, although the prosperity of the 1920s was not necessarily the result of Fascist policies, and in the 1930s the international economic depression as well as Mussolini's stress on autarky and mobilization of the economy in support of his military exploits posed a severe strain on the economy.[21] Mussolini, however, eager to be recognized as a world leader and to export his Fascist model to other countries, actively publicized his regime abroad. Italian movies vaunting the achievements of fascism were shown in Shanghai's theaters, Italian planes soared acrobatically in its skies, and new courses in corporativist law were inaugurated at the University of Shanghai under the patronage of the Italian Fascist government.[22] Chen Gongbo became a close friend of Galeazzo Ciano, who was Mussolini's son-in-law and the Italian consul in Shanghai at the time.[23] Chen, like most Nationalist leaders of the time, was very conscious of Mussolini's reforms, which were often discussed in local newspapers.[24] The NEC leaders invited Italian experts from the Fascist regime to help with their economic reforms.[25]

The historiographical debate on the influence of fascist thought on the Nationalist regime in the 1930s has been marked by deep disagreement. Focusing on Jiang's Blue Shirts and New Life Movement, historians Lloyd Eastman and Frederic Wakeman have argued that both were manifestations of a Chinese form of fascism (more specifically, according to Wakeman, "Confucian fascism"), although with certain limitations and ambiguities.[26] On the other hand, focusing on the same movements, historian William Kirby argues that they were only superficial manifestations of Jiang's authoritarian aspirations and superficial reflections of direct German influence. Kirby thus concludes that we should not label them fascist.[27] More recently, political scientist A. James Gregor, in his survey of fascist influences in China, has also argued against calling the Nanjing government fascist.[28] This discordance of opinions is mostly a result of the difficulty of reaching a satisfying definition of what constituted the worldwide political movement called fascism in the interwar years. In spite of the wide historiographical debate, a valid definition of fascism has only recently begun to emerge.[29] Historian Zeev Sternhell explains that the difficulty in providing a satisfactory definition of fascism is due to its heterogeneity and to the fact that it was, in his words, "a political idea which is already ambiguous enough." However, Sternhell points out, we are met with the same problem even when discussing democracy and socialism. "There is obviously no single example in history that corresponds to a 'model' or 'ideal type' . . . of democracy, socialism, or communism. Much the same applies to fascism. Italy in the twenties or thirties could not claim to be an 'ideal' fascist state any more than the Parti Populaire Français (PPF), the British Union of Fascists, or the Legion of the Archangel Michael was an ideal fascist party." In short, according to Sternhell, fascism is "a universal category with regional and cultural variations."[30]

The question remains, however, of whether fascism was specifically a European trend arising from the experience of World War I. Sternhell downplays the importance of the Great War as the catalyst for the development of fascism, describing it as "one of the byproducts of the crisis of Marxism and the crisis of liberalism."[31] In this way, fascism emerges as a phenomenon that goes beyond the European experience of the Great War, being rather the result of a much wider crisis of political and economic models that were at the basis of the international system.[32] In this sense, fascism constituted a reaction against both capitalism and communism and was an attempt to combine aspects of both in order to create a better, and dialectically more modern (since it was the product of the synthesis of capitalism and socialism), political and economic model. Non-European countries experienced the same crisis, and although their local perspectives shaped their perceptions, they still participated in the same transformation of the political and economic scene.

Chinese leaders, in fact, did not attempt to apply the Italian Fascist model—or a more vaguely defined European fascism—in its entirety. Rather, they selected the aspects that resonated most with their political vision and with China's own circumstances. One of the local factors that brought Wang Jingwei and Chen Gongbo to embrace fascism (especially autarky and a controlled economy) was the escalation of Japanese aggression. It is impossible to overstate the impact of Japan's imperialism—military, political, and economic—on China's nation-building effort. Its impact imposed serious limits on the Nationalist government's reform effort, in terms of both time and direction. In 1937 every reform project had to be curtailed as China swiftly succumbed to Japanese occupation. Even before 1937, the problem of Japan loomed so large over Chinese political and economic life that it deeply informed the country's political discourse. There was no aspect of Chinese political life that did not have to come to terms with Japan's ambitions.[33] Resistance against Japan inspired Wang and Chen to create a vision of an autarkic and controlled Chinese economy and thus played an important role in their progressive slide toward fascism. On the other hand, Japanese economic imperialism in China—especially the presence of Japanese factories on Chinese soil—led the two leaders to formulate autarky in the distinct framework of the development of the *minzu* economy. Chinese autarkic policies thus came to differ from the Italian because of their different goals. While in some countries, such as Germany and Japan, autarky became the justification for the aggressive building of self-sufficient empires, in others, such as China, it became a weapon for resisting foreign imperialism and economic dependency.

Fascism has also been linked to the European bourgeoisie and a specific socioeconomic environment characterized by "widespread unemployment, an impoverished middle class, a terrorized petit bourgeoisie." Because of these elements, fascism in Europe came to constitute "a rebellion against bourgeois society, its moral values, its political and social structures, and its way of life" and developed into a mass movement.[34] The fact that socioeconomic conditions were different in China from those in Europe did not prevent fascism from developing but did determine its characteristics as a political movement. Reacting to the same crisis of liberalism and socialism that had inspired its European counterpart, China developed its own brand of state fascism in the 1930s, but Chinese fascism never became a mass movement.[35]

The diversity of fascist manifestations within the GMD, while stressing once more the depth of the political division within the party, also illustrates the local characteristics of Chinese fascism. GMD leaders did not just imitate Italy or Germany; they adopted, and adapted, what resonated with their personal political experiences, their political and intellectual development, and their aspirations to participate in global modernity. Jiang, for example, favored a German-style militarist form of fascism because it appealed to his own military background and political vision. Wang and Chen, however, because of their focus on the economy, were particularly attracted to the Italian Fascist model of nation building (it is for this reason that Italian fascism serves in this book as the main source of comparison). In Fascist Italy, for example, corporativism had not developed at the expense of private business as it had in Germany. On the contrary, the corporations came to be dominated by private industrial interests. The Italian corporativist model, because it was based on an alliance between state and industry, particularly appealed to Wang's and Chen's notion of *minzu* economy.[36]

As discussed above, the anti-imperialist characteristics of Wang's and Chen's nation-building project, together with its emphasis on the economy, resonated with a wider movement of reconstruction initiated in the late nineteenth century. Wang and Chen believed that their reform would finally end the crisis that had plagued China for almost a century. In other words, they felt that they were adopting the most modern political and economic tools available at the time to save China from a predicament whose origins were to be found in its recent past.

National Reconstruction: A Brief Historical Background

The Chinese discourse on economic reconstruction can be traced back to the second half of the nineteenth century, a time when domestic rebellion and foreign aggression brought government officials to focus on strengthening China. The Self-Strengthening reforms relied on a combination of educational, military, and economic initiatives aimed at modernizing the country vis-à-vis foreign imperialism. Major personalities of this movement, such as Zeng Guofan and Li Hongzhang, while establishing new arsenals, sponsoring translation bureaus, and introducing Western-style military training, also focused on the development of joint state-private business enterprises. Zhang Zhidong, who gave the Self-Strengthening Movement its basic principle of "Chinese learning as essence, Western learning for practical use" (*Zhongxue wei ti, Xixue wei yong*), generally shortened to "Chinese essence and Western practices" (*tiyong*), advocated grafting Western modern technology into the Chinese political context. Zhang announced "saving the country with business" (*shiye jiuguo*) as one of his main reform strategies. Thus, the notion that economic development constituted an important tool for state building (most Qing reformers in that period thought in terms of the state rather than the modern nation) and modernization originated in the late nineteenth century.

The widespread perception that the Qing dynasty, because of its foreign Manchu origins and its "feudal," nonmodern political nature, was unable and unwilling to enact any significant reform or to fight foreign imperialism was one of the most crucial motives for the 1911 revolution. The task of reconstruction was assigned to the new Republic, which was supposed to be politically modern and directly representative of the interests of the Chinese nationality. The Republic, however, did not live up to these expectations. The Yuan Shikai presidency was unable to transform China into a modern nation as many Chinese had hoped. Although Yuan did attempt a number of domestic reforms designed to strengthen the Chinese state, they had little time to yield results (Yuan ruled for only four and half years) and were forgotten soon after his death.[37] In addition, Yuan had spent most of his career as an official of the Qing dynasty. Although he had been a reformer—and had been involved in the Self-Strengthening reforms—he was deeply ambivalent about the idea of nation. Yuan felt that the Beijing government could restore order in China and firmly establish its control over the nation only by reviving the political legitimacy represented by the empire. Therefore, shortly before his death, Yuan planned to make himself emperor. By attempting to restore the imperial system and perpetuating some form of imperial rituals, the Yuan Shikai presidency poignantly reveals the difficulty of abandoning the familiar imperial model and launching into the uncertain waters of republican politics and modern nationhood.[38]

With the death of Yuan, the country fell into political disintegration and warlordism. It was only in 1927, toward the end of the Northern Expedition, that China was brought again under a certain amount of unified leadership by the GMD, raising hopes that those nation-building reforms that had been postponed for so long would finally be realized. High expectations gave birth to a plethora of reform agencies all over the country. A foreign observer visiting China in 1936 commented that China "is alive with the discussion of her problems. . . . [T]he welter of experimental *hsien* [*xian*, counties], welfare centers, model villages, committees, commissions, and bureaux for reconstruction which cover the whole country . . . represent no less than the scaffolding in the building of a new society."[39] The author of this comment, George Taylor, a former lecturer at the Central Political Institute in Nanjing, was struck by the drive for reform that pervaded all of China during the Nanjing Decade. The movement for national "reconstruction" (*jianshe*)—the term privileged at the time to indicate a wide range of reforms aimed at strengthening and modernizing the country—appeared to be forging ahead with inexhaustible enthusiasm. Most of these agencies, no matter what their primary focus, regarded the economy as a crucial aspect of national reconstruction. For example, Liang Shuming and James Yen, two of the most prominent reformers of the Republican years, although working primarily in political (the development of local governments) and educational reform, respectively, included in their programs different forms of economic cooperative societies.[40] The number of journals dedicated to economics—such as *Reconstruction* (*Jianshe*), *Chinese Village* (*Zhongguo nongcun*), *Research in Chinese Economy* (*Zhongguo jingji yanjiu*), and the English-language *Nankai Social and Economic Quarterly*—increased dramatically.

It soon became clear, however, that many obstacles still lay in the path of nation building. Although the GMD government in Nanjing enjoyed recognition as China's official national government, it was unable to control large areas of the country. In addition, as argued above, internal disagreement made unified decision making impossible. Finally, the Nanjing government had to face increasing Japanese aggression. Japan's aspirations for China dated back to the turn of the century but had become increasingly threatening since 1931. At this time Japan invaded Manchuria and established it as a nominally independent state, Manchukuo. This maneuver, however, could hardly disguise the de facto colonization of the region. In the following years the Japanese army came to control China's northeast while continuing to push south. In 1932 the Japanese army attacked Shanghai, the economic and cultural heart of the Chinese Republic. Although an agreement was reached that pushed the Japanese back to their previous positions, the feeling grew among the Chinese that Japan was planning to incorporate China into its empire. Between 1931 and 1937, growing Japanese aggression remained a central problem in Chinese politics, leading to one crisis after the other and becoming pivotal to the discourse on nation building.[41] Between Japanese attacks—September 1931 on Manchuria and January 1932 on Shanghai—China's political system fell into total chaos. Two cabinets fell in short succession. Lengthy and acrimonious negotiations were carried out in Shanghai, where leaders of the GMD met repeatedly to discuss ways to restore stable governance.[42]

The Shanghai talks led to the establishment of the Wang-Jiang coalition government (January 1932–December 1935), which was based on the two leaders' shared perception that China needed time to complete nation building before engaging Japan militarily. The Wang-Jiang cabinet was launched on the political platform of *an'nei rangwai* (pacify the domestic front while resisting on the external front). This cabinet reversed the approach of its short-lived (January 1–28, 1932) predecessor, led by Sun Ke, the son of party founder Sun Yat-sen. Sun and his foreign minister Eugene Chen (Chen Youren) had announced their intention to be more determined toward Japan by breaking off official relations and mounting vigorous military opposition. Unfortunately, lacking the support of both military and party leaders, the Sun cabinet was unable to take any kind of action and collapsed when the Japanese army attacked Shanghai in January 1932.[43] The *an'nei rangwai* coalition of Wang and Jiang, however, did not bring unity to the Nanjing government. Although Wang and Jiang agreed on the necessity of postponing war with Japan to gain time to strengthen China, they fiercely disagreed on how to go about the latter task. For Wang it meant giving absolute priority to economic nation building. Jiang, instead, interpreted *an'nei* as military pacification of both insubordinate provincial leaders and the CCP. The new cabinet, therefore, represented only one stage in the protracted political confrontation between Wang and Jiang.

My evaluation of the Wang-Jiang coalition differs from that of the historian So Wai-chor. In his important book on the Wang group, So argues that Wang decided to join the government in 1932 only to gain personal power. Once in Nanjing, So contends, Wang catered to Jiang's requests, virtually ending his long opposition to Jiang. So even ends his book on the Wang group (which he calls the GMD Left although soon after 1927 the Wang group had begun to move to the right) in 1931, arguing that, after that date, Wang sold out to Jiang and, later, to the Japanese. In this way, So depicts Wang as a collaborator even before 1940.[44] Instead of using Wang's and Chen's political record in the 1930s to understand the 1940s (the approach I use in this book), he uses the *hanjian* reputation the two leaders had gained in the war years to explain their participation in the Wang-Jiang coalition. In other words, So takes 1932 as the turning point in the history of the Wang group, while I regard the 1930s as a continuation not only of the Wang group's opposition to Jiang but also of its attempt to restore the GMD to civilian leadership and to return to what Wang believed to be the original platform of Sun Yat-sen.

The Wang Jingwei Group before 1932

The history of the Wang group highlights the profound disunity of the Nationalist leadership during the Nanjing Decade. In 1927, once the GMD had entered the lower Yangzi Valley during the final stages of the Northern Expedition, Jiang, at the head of the advancing NRA, established a second Nationalist government in Nanjing to compete with the existing Nationalist base in Wuhan led by Wang Jingwei. By inaugurating a new national government in Wang's absence, Jiang not only gained personal control over the new central government but attempted to cut off Wang and the rest of the civilian leadership, which had strongly dominated the Wuhan government. Cooperation with the Communists, who had been allowed to join the party since 1923, soon became a bone of contention between the two competing governments. In April 1927, Jiang purged the Communists from the GMD. Wang strongly opposed Jiang's move but eventually he also repudiated the policy of cooperation with Communist members and declared it a serious mistake that was due to a misunderstanding of Sun Yat-sen's original policy. Disagreement between the two leaders, however, persisted. Jiang began curbing leftist influence within the party by suppressing mass organizations and anti-imperialist activities. During this de-radicalization process, social and economic reforms were also abandoned. This reversal was the main focus of criticism from the Wang group.[45] Wang denounced the backlash that had started in Nanjing and endorsed reconstruction policies, mass organization, and anti-imperialism as crucial components of the GMD's political program.[46]

These persisting political differences ultimately led to a second major confrontation between the Wang and Jiang groups in 1929. At that time, the Wang group, in opposing Jiang's attempt to control the party and the government, advocated a return to the spirit and policies formulated by Sun Yat-sen in 1924. They formed an organization that became known as the Guomindang Reorganization Comrades Association (*Guomindang gaizu tongzhihui*), generally called the Reorganization Group (*gaizupai*). Chen Gongbo took most of the initiative on this occasion since Wang was abroad. Chen was undoubtedly Wang's most loyal associate, because of shared political beliefs and an often-declared personal loyalty. For this reason, although the two Nationalist leaders often disagreed on important issues (as became clear at the time of the Reorganization movement and, later, on the issue of collaboration with the Japanese), Wang and Chen most often fought on the same political side.[47] Wang derived much political prestige from his early cooperation and friendship with Sun Yat-sen, but Chen showed, on many occasions, a theoretical and political initiative surpassing Wang's. His articles on the role of the GMD and the CCP in China's economics and politics became very influential, although they did not always meet with Wang's approval.[48]

The final confrontation between the Reorganization Group and Jiang took place at the Third Party Congress, held on March 15, 1929. The political tide turned on Wang and Chen at the congress. The two leaders, along with other Reorganization members, were expelled from the GMD.[49] After the 1929 debacle, Wang attempted to form various alliances with warlords and other groups who challenged Jiang from the periphery. However, it was not until the inauguration of the Wang-Jiang coalition government in January 1932 that the Wang group was able to return to Nanjing.

The group of Nationalist leaders who rallied around Wang Jingwei has generally been called either the left wing of the GMD (the GMD Left) or the Reorganization Group. By 1932, however, Wang Jingwei was firmly anti-Communist and hardly a leftist. At the same time, Wang had stopped directly advocating party reorganization. Therefore, neither appellation is an adequate description of Wang's political group from 1932 on. For this reason, I refer to the Nationalist leaders who rallied around Wang simply as the "Wang group."

Chapters and Content

In the first part of this book, I focus on the intellectual foundation of the nation-building project initiated by Wang Jingwei and Chen Gongbo. Chapter 1 explores the two leaders' understanding of China's crisis, their notion of economic modernity, and their development of the idea of *minzu* economy as the foundation of the nation. This chapter also traces the connection between Wang's and Chen's political platform and worldwide fascist trends, stressing how the two leaders' support of autarky and economic control was rooted in their experience of China's circumstances in the changing regional and world environment. Wang and Chen appropriated the language and logic of fascism because they believed fascism could help them make sense of, and deal with, China's crisis. This chapter also demonstrates that Wang and Chen, rather than just imitating Western trends, selected only the aspects of fascism that resonated with their own ideas of China's problems and their solution.

Chapter 2 explains the productivist policies of the GMD and how they affected its rural policies. I discuss these issues at length because, in the 1930s, the rural village came to be regarded as a crucial aspect of China's crisis. As this chapter illustrates, the questions of how to reform the village and what role rural China should be assigned within a new modern China became key issues in a heated debate among reformers of all political persuasions. In this context, the village became a major site of political confrontation not only between the GMD and the CCP but also between the Wang group and Jiang Jieshi.

In part 2 I show how notions of modern nationhood and nation building shaped the institutions of the Nationalist state and the reforms launched by the Nanjing government. Chapter 3 details how disagreements among the higher echelons of the Nationalist leadership over these issues fragmented the government administration into political "fiefs," each responding to different GMD groups and pursuing different reform agendas. In this chapter, Jiang Jieshi emerges as a formidable opponent of the GMD civilian leaders, who believed that economic reforms were crucial for creating a modern Chinese nation. This chapter explores Song Ziwen's attempt to reform China's finances and economy and his conflicts with Jiang's military priorities. The chapter outlines Song's reform agenda, which came to resemble Wang's and Chen's, and his strategy to overcome a stalemate created by the factions in Nanjing that blocked the implementation of reforms. It also describes how Song established the National Economic Council and how, with the inauguration of the Wang-Jiang coalition cabinet, the NEC became the main vehicle for the realization of the Wang group's program. Chapter 4 discusses how Wang's and Chen's idea of *minzu* economy led the NEC leaders to embrace corporativism. The NEC thus became a corporativist organization, merging worldwide fascist trends with reform practices initiated in the Self-Strengthening period. NEC corporativism, in fact, institutionalized the joint state-private economic reform pattern initiated in the late Qing. This chapter examines how the NEC leaders attempted to establish a constructive relationship with the *minzu* economy—which they identified with the Jiangnan industrial elite—and to oppose Jiang's desire to marginalize this group in the Nationalist reconstruction effort.

In part 3 I examine how the idea of *minzu* economy was translated into actual reforms, abandoning the intellectual realm and coming to terms with the economic and social realities of the day. This section is concerned mostly with the reforms carried out by the Cotton Control Commission (CCC), a committee of the NEC. Chapter 5 explores CCC reforms in rural areas: their goals, their potential to change the socioeconomic structure of the Chinese village, and the problems these reforms met. Chapter 6 shifts the focus to CCC reforms in urban areas, reforms designed to modernize the production and management of industrial plants. This chapter traces the final political demise of the Wang group, a turn of events that allowed Jiang to eliminate the NEC and to set up an economic agency (the Natural Resource Commission, *ziyuan weiyuanhui*) that reflected his view of China's economic modernity.

Chapter 7, which by itself constitutes part 4, functions as an epilogue. It is here that I address the collaborationist period. This chapter emphasizes the deep impact of the intellectual constructs of nation building on the political life of Republican China; it highlights how different visions of nation led to two dramatically different defensive strategies after the eruption of full war with Japan. The disagreement between Wang and Chen, on the one side, and Jiang Jieshi, on the other, over the political and economic nature of modern China (a disagreement that had characterized the years of the Wang-Jiang coalition) contributed to the establishment of two different Nationalist governments, each claiming to embody the legacy of Sun Yat-sen and, consequently, to be the only legitimate GMD government. Both regimes declared themselves to be following the correct path for saving China and to possess the secret to postwar nation building.

Envisioning Modern China PART I

【壹】

CHAPTER 1

China's *Minzu* Economy

When Wang Jingwei entered the coalition government with Jiang Jieshi in January 1932, he was determined to reverse the course of action taken by Jiang and shift the government's attention from military toward economic nation building. At the time of the Shanghai negotiations in late 1931, Wang had made his position very clear. On that occasion, during an interview with the press, he stated: "My position on the solution of the present situation is not similar to those who want to use military force. . . . I believe that only with reconstruction is it possible to unify [the country]."[1] Wang thus denied Jiang's use of military force as a legitimate tool for nation building (reconstruction). He firmly maintained this position throughout his years in the government and did not hesitate to openly and forcefully attack the military strategy adopted by Jiang: "The policy of attempting to bring about national unification by armed force—subsequent to the establishment of the present regime at Nanking [Nanjing]—has been a failure, and it is the realisation of this very plain fact which has led me to advocate the policy of unification by reconstruction."[2] As Wang explained, military force had failed in the two most important goals of nation building: national unification (against warlords, centrifugal regionalist trends, and Communists) and anti-imperialism. Although Japan was rarely mentioned in Wang's speeches, as Japan was very sensitive to direct anti-Japanese proclamations by any Chinese government official, his references to imperialism were obviously targeted at the escalation of Japanese imperialism, which had generated the protracted governmental crisis leading to the formation of the Wang-Jiang cabinet. Attempting unification by military means, Wang warned, only meant "wasting men and money upon military adventurers, and especially fratricidal struggles between factions whose common aim should be the building-up of their country into a powerful and prosperous State."[3] Military action would also fail in resisting foreign imperialism if not used within a wider context of nation building and international politics. "To repel imperialism, we cannot use only the military. We have to focus all our energies—military, political, diplomatic, industrial, and economic—on the anti-imperialist struggle."[4] Departing from Jiang's military strategy, Wang was determined to base the new cabinet's approach to nation building on economic reforms. As Wang explained in 1934, the new administration was aiming "at attaining national solidarity [as an essential part of nation building] by the evolutionary method of economic reconstruction."[5]

Wang's statement on evolution and economic nation building testifies to the complex roots of Wang's and Chen's plan. Influences included a reform legacy initiated by the Self-Strengthening Movement, a Marxist-Leninist understanding of evolutionary history and of imperialism, Fascist international trends, the slow-brewing crisis of liberalism around the world, and the deepening of the international economic depression that marked the 1930s. The Chinese discourse on the nation, in fact, was very much engaged with themes that went beyond China's own circumstances. As historian Rebecca Karl has convincingly argued, since the early years of the twentieth century Chinese intellectuals had read the Chinese situation in a global context.[6] In the 1930s this discourse was even more globally engaged. In an attempt to shed light on China's new crisis, political and economic journals constantly published articles on the situation of other countries that were supposedly experiencing circumstances similar to those in China. In addition to coloring Chinese intellectuals' readings of China's problems, worldwide trends also appeared to offer the most modern and effective political and economic tools for solving them.

Late Qing officials placed Western imperialist pressure on China within a mercantilist framework (mercantilism and its stress on the balance of trade were in the mainstream of economic thought at the time), and they devised strategies to defend China based on mercantilist ideas.[7] Wang's and Chen's plan for nation building, instead, reflected the deep changes in the political and economic thought of the interwar years, marked by the growth of antiliberal ideas. We cannot forget, however, that China was indeed integrated into the world economy and directly experienced, and reacted to, problems and changes in the international system. As discussed in detail later, China was directly affected by the emergence of protectionist policies (especially those adopted in countries such as the United States and Great Britain) and autarkic empires (such as the German and the

Japanese). These changes in the international environment convinced Chinese leaders that they needed to keep up with the transformations that were taking place all around their country. In this context, Wang and Chen came to perceive mercantilism and free trade as obsolete and Fascism as the epitome of modernity. As had been the case with earlier reformers, Wang and Chen believed China's crisis to be an aspect of the global struggle for the survival of the fittest, and they wanted to transform China into a modern nation to better equip it to survive. The intellectual and economic tools they had available were, however, new.

An Evolutionary Approach to National Reconstruction

Social Darwinist theories had been influential in China since the prominent late Qing intellectual Yan Fu first translated portions of Thomas Huxley's *Evolution and Ethics* in 1898. Social Darwinism became an important element of the Chinese discourse on history and on the country's current circumstances. The depth of its impact was such that it soon began to influence the nature and goals of modernizing reforms. Among the Chinese intellectuals and reformers who embraced and propagandized evolutionary ideas was Liang Qichao—at the time a young intellectual and reformer, destined to become one of the most influential figures in Chinese modern history. Liang incorporated these ideas in his influential writings and also adopted them in the formulation of the reform program he sponsored with the late Qing official Kang Youwei (the Reform Movement of 1895–98).[8] The evolutionary notion of history embraced by Liang and many other intellectuals was subsequently reinforced by the spread of Marxist-Leninist ideas in China after the success of the Bolshevik revolution. Setting aside the issue of class relations (a notion crucial to the original Marxist-Leninist formulation), Liang turned historical materialism into, in Arif Dirlik's words, "a version of evolutionist theory based on technological progress."[9] In this evolutionary scheme, which came to be widely adopted by Chinese of all political creeds, a country would climb a ladder of progress in three stages—tribal, feudal, and national—each dependent on a different economic system—agricultural, commercial, and industrial, respectively.[10] This combination of social Darwinism and historical materialism generated the notion that modern nationhood (the ultimate evolutionary stage) was the real form of modernity and the source of power for all countries involved in the international environment, where the strong colonized the weak and, in doing so, erased their identity. These ideas inspired Wang Jingwei's and Chen Gongbo's notions of how to survive Japanese imperialism.

In his 1934 English-language book, *China's Problems and Their Solution*—which aimed at propagandizing the Wang-Jiang administration to Western powers so as to win their sympathy and support for China's cause—Wang declared that China was

> sick . . . suffering from . . . a weak heart, and a tumorous growth. . . . The weak heart refers to the political and financial strength of the National Government, while the tumorous growth stands for foreign invasion and occupation of the Chinese territory. These being the pathological conditions of the patient, it is obvious that the service of a surgeon to perform . . . the removal of the tumor [is] not yet needed, for the patient is not strong enough to stand the shock to the system. . . . [T]he first thing necessary is to build up the invalid's strength. . . . Then, with heart and body and mind all functioning more normally, the question of a surgical operation might be discussed if, indeed, by that time the cankerous growth had not disappeared of its own accord, as does sometimes happen when the patient's powers of resistance are stimulated.[11]

The idea was that China (the sick body), in order to recover its "national vitality," needed to heal its financial and political heart, the very foundation of modern nationhood, before a successful military resistance to Japan (surgery to remove the "cankerous growth") could be waged. Moreover, a healed and stronger China might not even need surgery after all and might naturally shed Japanese aggression merely by virtue of its health. In other words, modern nationhood was the ultimate source of power and could be obtained only by reconstructing the very foundations of the nation. For Wang, it was only when China had regained its "national vitality" that peace with Japan could be achieved "and become firmly established, on the foundation of equality."[12] Expounding on this theme, Wang—borrowing from the holistic imagery of traditional Chinese medicine (a common rhetorical device in China's traditional political discourse)—explained how to revive that strength. As with a medical patient, China needed to find a cure to solve the problem at its root (*zhiben*) rather than attend only to its superficial symptoms (*zhibiao*), as Jiang Jieshi's military approach did. The latter strategy would lead the patient to sure disaster.

Chen shared Wang's view but more clearly anchored China's national "vitality" in the economy. The economy, he argued, was the very foundation of every nation because "regardless from what point of view [one approaches nation building], there is no way to escape economic relationships. . . . [A country's] political system is a reflection of its economy."[13]

Only changes in the economic structure, therefore, could lead to changes in the political system. Because the economic structure of a country constituted its foundations and the main motor of its evolutionary process, the advancement of a country was determined by changes to its economy, and each stage was tied to a different stage of economic development. Following Liang's periodization, Chen represented history as a process in which nationalities (*minzu*) progressed (*jinbu*) up a ladder of evolution (*yanjin*), each stage depending on a specific economic system: tribal (agriculture), feudal (commerce), and national (industry).[14] Chen thus concluded that the most advanced nationalities (*jinbu minzu*) had reached the status of "nation" because their economy had industrialized. It was this advanced political and economic status that gave them power vis-à-vis the "backward" nationalities that lagged behind in the global evolutionary competition. If China wanted to catch up, it needed to transform itself into a "nation" by transforming its economy into a modern industrial system.[15] Like Wang, therefore, Chen believed that national power relied primarily on a country's ability to reach the top of the evolutionary ladder by industrializing and becoming a "nation."

The economic reform plan promoted by the Wang group was therefore entrusted with the revolutionary (and evolutionary) task of changing the Chinese economic structure. This meant not only its transformation into an industrial system but also, Chen argued, the transformation of China into "a whole economic unit [*jingji danwei*]."[16]

The Nation as an Economic Unit

National unification had been a concern of Chinese intellectuals and political leaders since the early twentieth century. At that time, the predominant view was that the Chinese people lacked national consciousness, each pursuing his or her personal interest at the expense of the interests of China as a whole. Liang Qichao complained that the Chinese were like flying ducks, while Sun Yat-sen compared them to a "sheet of loose sand," lamenting their lack of national consciousness.[17] While in Guangdong in the mid-1920s, preparing for the Northern Expedition, Sun had made national unity one of the most important goals of the newly reorganized Nationalist Party. In this area, as in many others, Sun's legacy to the party was ambiguous. The Northern Expedition appeared to signal that military unification was indeed Sun's preferred solution to China's disunity—or at least the one he believed had some chance to succeed. At the same time, most of his writings focused on political and economic issues, without expounding much on the goals of the new Nationalist army.

This ambiguity was reflected in the disagreement between Wang and Jiang on how unity should be achieved. On the one hand, Wang stated, "We must know that a nation is really unified only when it has achieved economic unification. This is the goal of the so-called national reconstruction movement. This is the necessary task for saving the nation."[18] For this reason the goal of the government, Wang argued, was "the attainment of that national unity which the government believes will depend upon the development of productive enterprises, agricultural and industrial."[19] This was the only solution to China's current fragmentation, Wang argued, as proved by the fact that "efforts to unify the country by force were unsuccessful." Therefore, the "policy of the Government today is to bring about national unity by economic reconstruction."[20] On the other side of the party, Jiang rebutted, "Germany's powerful precedent must be our model." The German example advocated by Jiang was one of vigorous military unification followed by the establishment of a military regime relying on a strong, military-oriented heavy industry. "No matter what the nation, the revolution needs first to regulate [*zhengli*] the military. [It needs] first to seek military unification and progress."[21]

Chen stood firmly on Wang's side and, as the most vocal member of the Wang group on economic matters, he further elaborated the idea of economic unification. Economic unification, he argued, was the most effective way to achieve national unity, a goal that not even political measures such as the calling of a parliament or the promulgation of a constitution could achieve. "Only the economy constitutes the foundations of unification. During the last twenty years of domestic chaos, [we] have repeatedly tried [to achieve unification] through political [or military] ... means. However, in spite of the fact that the central government [nominally] rules over the entire country, today people are still debating why China cannot be unified. From this we can see that the claim of unification is only superficial."[22] Going back to the economic evolutionary theme, Chen identified unity with modernity. "A nation cannot be divided. If it is, it does not constitute a nation anymore. A nationality also cannot be divided. If it is, it does not constitute a nationality anymore."[23]

Wang's and Chen's obsession with unity reflected a common preoccupation of both GMD and CCP leaders, who perceived political and economic decentralization to be divisive and thus a manifestation of "feudalism" and "backwardness."[24] This formula was effectively summed up by the Marxist Zhang Tingfei: "Only that which unifies is progressive; division means reaction."[25] In this vein Chen argued that China could achieve nationhood only by overcoming its regionally based economy, which kept it in a feudal economic and political mode. "If [China's] feudal economy does not break down one day, China will never be able to become a modern-style nation-state [*jindaishi de guojia*]."[26] Chen held China's regionally based economic structure responsible for the persistence of warlordism, which he considered the most palpable sign of feudalism. "Old warlords go and new come. This is because our infant industry cannot set itself free from its small-scale, rural character."[27] "I personally wonder why . . . center and provinces appear to have no relationship at all. The simple answer is that there are very few economic contacts [between the two]."[28]

Chen's accusations of feudalism were not just targeted at warlordism but extended to all centrifugal regionalist tendencies that kept the initiative for economic reforms decentralized. In the 1930s, China was as divided economically as it was politically. Most of the economic reforms that had taken place since Self-Strengthening were carried out at the local level by diverse and often competing groups. The country was fragmented by rebellious provinces, which managed the local economy with protectionist policies in competition with neighboring provinces. At the same time provincial governments, especially those close to coastal areas, attempted to achieve mercantilist Self-Strengthening goals by encouraging the growth of the local export industry, which resulted in linking the local economy with the international market rather than with other provinces.[29] This dependency on the international market was encouraged by the disruption of communications in the interior as a result of protracted civil war. It was also helped by declining production in the hinterland, caused by the widespread rural economic crisis. It was thus easier and less costly to import raw materials from abroad than to undertake the risk of having them shipped from the interior. A mill owner in Shanghai, for example, would pay more for grain grown in Shanxi than for grain imported via Seattle in the United States.[30] In addition, domestic crops were unpredictable and of lower quality than the imported variety, making them unreliable and unsatisfactory supplies for manufacture.

At the level of political discourse it was federalism that posed the most serious threat to Nanjing because it was armed with both the military power of the warlords who supported it and a strong political and reformist agenda. In the early 1920s the idea of a federalist state had gained the support of prominent personalities, such as Hu Shi and Li Dazhao, as well as provincial leaders in Hunan, Yunnan, and Guangdong. The main leadership of both the GMD and the CCP, however, consistently criticized federalism as a concession to fragmentation and "feudalism." As historian John Fitzgerald has cogently argued, the stress of Nationalist and Communist leaders on political centralization was a consequence of their identification of nation with state and, in turn, of state with party.[31] Both parties took inspiration from the same Marxist-Leninist theories of "democratic centralism," as well as the role of the party as the guardian and controller of the state during the period of the dictatorship of the party, or, in Leninist terminology, the dictatorship of the proletariat. Although the GMD never used this Leninist terminology, it had adopted the idea of party authoritarian supervision of government and nation during China's transformation from feudalism to a full-fledged modern republic. In this context, the three stages of the Republican revolution devised by Sun—military, tutelage, and democracy—required a role for the party very similar to that envisioned by Lenin. The ideological foundations of this notion had its roots in Sun Yat-sen's 1924 idea of "partyfying the masses" (i.e., transforming the masses into party members), which he perceived as a way to bring the entire society under the unifying umbrella of the ideology expressed in his Three People's Principles (*sanmin zhuyi*) and to achieve the ultimate unity between party and nation.[32] This was part of his vision of "governing the state, and nation, through the party" (*yi dang zhi guo*), or, rather, as in a later formulation, his vision that he would "build the nation through the party" (*yi dang jian guo*).[33]

In fact, federalism was not incompatible with the establishment of a unified Chinese nation, as Nationalist and Communist intellectuals argued, but as Fitzgerald highlights, federalism represented "an alternative reading of national unity."[34] Chen Jiongming, the warlord of Guangdong and one of the most prominent leaders of the federalist movement,[35] was concerned as much as Chen Gongbo and Wang Jingwei with national unity and perceived China's domestic political struggle as the cause of foreign imperialist aggression. In 1932, at the time of the Manchuria and Shanghai crises, he wrote, "We know there is no other way to save the country than by uniting the 400 million people of the five major ethnic groups. . . . When there is rebellion within a country, foreign aggression will follow."[36] He had, however, a different idea of what constituted national unity. While he favored the elimination of local armies as well as the establishment of a system of open governmental finance to combat corruption—both goals very much supported by Chen Gongbo and Wang Jingwei and the majority of civilian reformers in the GMD—his plan for national salvation included abandoning the GMD's one-party rule and establishing a federal government "based on the democratic principles of federalism." He advocated "ridding [the Chinese people] of totalitarian rule, and constructing a new nation based on the principles of democracy."[37] The debate over federalism was, above all, a debate over the role of state, party, and social groups in the country's political and economic life. Most supporters of federalism perceived it as a political system that would ensure the participation of elites in local government. "Guangdong people rule Guangdong" (*yue ren zhi yue*) advocated Chen Jiongming, who had inspired Zhang Tingfei's remarks on division and reaction.[38] Chen Jiongming's statement implied a conception of a modern Chinese state that was deeply different from Chen Gongbo's because it included local political, economic, and financial autonomy. As an example he advocated fiscal reform that included "separat[ing] the finance of the central and local governments."[39] This view went directly against Chen Gongbo's idea that a modern economy should form an "economic unit."

For Chen Gongbo the unity of the *minzu* economy was not just a matter of geographical and administrative centralization. It also needed to be the expression of a unified socioeconomic alliance, which was to form the social foundation of the new Chinese nation. This attempt at creating an alliance with social groups in society, finding a social base for political legitimacy, and defining the social composition of the modern nation had already characterized the political life of the GMD in Guangdong, as poignantly described by historian Michael Tsin in his study of the Nationalist rule in Guangdong in the years 1900 to 1927.[40] This task became an even greater imperative in Nanjing when the GMD had finally risen to the status of national government.

It was in the context of defining the GMD social base that Chen, in his attempt to distinguish his ideas from Jiang's conservatism while at the same time distancing himself from the Communists, came to share the political ambiguity of interwar fascism. His persistent revolutionary rhetoric, his invocation of Marxist-Leninist ideas, and his denial of class struggle resonated with the fascist intellectual trends that were sweeping throughout Europe at the time.

Mapping the *Minzu* Economy: The Socioeconomic and Revolutionary Base of the GMD

Chen Gongbo began to formulate the idea of a *minzu* socioeconomic alliance during the crisis experienced by the GMD Left (as the Wang political group was called at the time) after Jiang Jieshi's abrupt and bloody 1927 attack on the Communists and the GMD's mass-organization activities. At that time, the members of the GMD Left experienced a deep identity crisis, instigating a heated debate on the political nature of the two parties, CCP and GMD, and their role in the Chinese revolution. Opposing Jiang's attempt to curtail anti-imperialism and mass movements from party and government, Wang Jingwei argued that they were actually essential for keeping alive the GMD's political character as established by Sun Yat-sen.

This disagreement with Jiang also focused on the social base of the GMD. Wang opposed Jiang's and Hu Hanmin's idea that the GMD represented the entire Chinese population but criticized the Communists because they targeted their mass movement only at the proletariat for the purpose of instigating class struggle. The GMD, instead, Wang argued, represented all the masses that were oppressed by "warlords and bureaucrats." Wang thus avoided recognizing the concept of class struggle while maintaining the idea of the exploitation of the masses.[41] Chen was not ready to accept Wang's formula, which he argued was too inclusive and condemned class struggle.[42]

In his 1927 *What Does the Guomindang Represent?* (*Zhongguo Guomindang suodaibiao de shi shenme?*), Chen argued that the GMD's political base rested on China's revolutionary classes, which included the peasantry, the working class, and the petite bourgeoisie but excluded the high bourgeoisie. Answering the criticism of a certain Jing Pu, who asserted that class conflict did not exist in China, Chen insisted that classes and class struggle did exist and that the weakness of the GMD to date had been the product of its failure to achieve sufficient class consciousness to take a proper stand in this class struggle.[43] To further strengthen his argument in favor of the socialist revolutionary nature of the GMD leadership, Chen reminded his readers that the aim of the Nationalist revolution, as stated by Sun Yat-sen, was not to establish a capitalist state but rather to prevent the rise of the bourgeoisie. More specifically, the goals of the Nationalist revolution were, according to Chen, not only anti-imperialism but also the realization of the Principle of People's Livelihood (*minsheng zhuyi*). The latter was ultimately a socialist goal, which implied state intervention, restriction of private capital, and the building of state capital.[44] These were traits of the Nationalist revolution that were not in agreement with the interests of the high bourgeoisie and that thereby excluded the possibility of alliance. Chen thus attempted to restore a class dimension to Wang's vague formulation and preserve, to a degree, the revolutionary credentials of the GMD Left.

It was not enough for Chen to distance himself from the conservative leaders of the party. He also needed to differentiate his group from the current Communist political line. Because Chen wanted both to preserve the principle of class struggle and to give priority to Nationalist goals, he came to so qualify class struggle as to make it meaningless. He argued that while class struggle did exist in China, it was not of the "so-called scientific" kind (*suowei kexue zhuyi de jieji douzheng*) touted by the Marxists because, in China, industrialization had not yet occurred and the industrial high bourgeoisie was still underdeveloped.[45] For these reasons, China's situation was characterized only by a random class struggle (*shehui jieji de hunzheng*). By using the idea of "random" class struggle, Chen wanted to maintain a degree of revolutionary rhetoric while removing class struggle from the focal point of his political program.

This view of "random class struggle" was first developed by Sun Yat-sen as one of the main ideas in support of his Principle of People's Livelihood. At the time of its formulation in 1924, Sun had been facing a problem similar to Chen's. He was caught between, on the one hand, his Soviet allies' wish for the GMD to collaborate with the CCP and present at least a façade of socialist commitment and, on the other hand, his own desire to give priority to national political and social unity.[46] He thus declared his Principle of People's Livelihood to be a definitively socialist goal. At the same time, however, he argued that class struggle was not, as Marx had argued, a necessary tool of historical change, crucial for the passage from one politico-economic stage to another. It was instead a disease that could occur in times of change. The occurrence of class struggle was the result of a lack of intervention on the part of states which had failed to supervise their countries' political and economic transitions appropriately. The transformation of a country from rural to industrial and from industrial to Socialist, Sun argued, could be achieved without passing through this painful stage. In China, for example, industrialization had not yet taken place and the bourgeoisie was not significantly developed. Therefore, China was experiencing only a "random" class struggle. Under these circumstances, the GMD, committed to the creation of a socialist society, would be able to supervise the transition to socialism (as embodied in the Principle of People's Livelihood) and to ensure its smooth and nonviolent success while actually promoting solidarity among social groups.[47] The idea of random class struggle and of the importance of class struggle in China's political development became a central issue of the Nationalist political discourse and the focus of heated controversies. Chen Gongbo's 1927 interpretation came to symbolize the position of the GMD Left and was embraced by other leaders of the Wang group.[48]

Chen and Sun had found themselves in the same difficult position as the European Fascist intellectuals who had tried to maintain the revolutionary nature of socialism while pursuing nationalist goals. The prominent Italian economist and official of the Fascist regime Felice Guarnieri, for example, attempted to solve the same ideological contradiction. His stated goal was to find "a fundamental solidarity of interests between capital and workers without, for this reason, confining class struggle to 'the old rusty tools of history.'"[49] As a former socialist leader who came to embrace fascism, the Frenchman Jean Allemane stated in 1919 that the Fascists "have the duty of enlightening the working class concerning its real interests and showing it that they are identical with those of the nation."[50] The ideological acrobatics of Sun and Chen in this area, therefore, were not the result of a lack of political sophistication. Rather, they were a reaction to a dilemma faced by many other leaders around the world who, concerned with modernity and national power, adopted socialist modernity to realize their nationalist goals.

Having played down the class issue, Chen proceeded to further de-demonize the Chinese high bourgeoisie by applying the distinction the CCP had used at the time of the First United Front. He divided the bourgeois elements into two groups along Nationalist lines: those who supported foreign imperialism and those who did not.[51] The "national [*minzu*] bourgeoisie" opposed imperialism. It thus participated in the nationalist revolution and should be part of the GMD class base. Those groups in the high bourgeoisie who collaborated with imperialism hindered the revolution and should not be included in the GMD's class base.[52] A Chinese cotton mill owner could either be or not be included among the ranks of the *minzu* bourgeoisie depending on whether he collaborated with Japanese bankers and entrepreneurs. If he did not, Chen considered him as contributing to the development of a *minzu* economy and thus to China's nation building. In that case, although belonging to the high bourgeoisie, his interests coincided with those of the Nationalist revolution. Because Chen's idea of nation was based on economic evolutionary determinism rather than on socioeconomic relationships between classes, the building of Chinese capital, whether state or private, always carried nationalist significance, as long as it was "national" in its ownership and nationalist in its goals.[53] These random bourgeois elements, even if allowed to survive because of the national(ist) (*minzu*) nature of their work, would not pose a threat to China's future, because, Chen argued, the GMD's rule would prevent them from developing into a full-fledged high-bourgeois class. Here too, the centralized party state was critical. In a manner reminiscent of the Leninist idea of the "dictatorship of the proletariat," the party would lead the country's transformation into an industrialized nation in a "greenhouse" artificial environment. The idea of the nature and duties of the modern state was borrowed from socialist and communist theories but, as in European fascism, was made to work in favor of a nationalist agenda.

Chen's redemption of *minzu* capital and bourgeois elements testifies to how far he had come since his earlier writings on imperialism in China. In 1924, although he had already abandoned his affiliation with the CCP, Chen's analysis of China's predicament vis-à-vis imperialism closely echoed the manifesto of the CCP. At that time Chen was at Columbia

University writing his master's thesis on the communist movement in China, in which he stated,

> [Since the Opium War,] during eighty years of increasing foreign power, China has become a *de facto* colony of stronger nations. . . . Foreign capitalists also occupy many mines, they have established factories in Shanghai and Tientsin [Tianjin], and drive the Chinese workers with whips in the mines and factories as their productive slaves. . . . One of the disastrous effects is the rise in the cost of living. Three hundred millions of peasants tend to become paupers, tens of millions of handicraftsmen gradually become the proletariat.[54]

By 1927 Chen had softened his position, avoiding mention of exploitation of the proletariat and shifting his focus to nationalist goals, thus paving the way for the formulation of the plan adopted by the Wang-Jiang coalition in 1932. His idea of a *minzu* socioeconomic alliance, although still echoing revolutionary themes, replaced the proletariat with the nation as the main revolutionary category.

This shift, from proletariat to nation, was particularly successful in those countries, such as Germany, Italy, and China, that felt threatened by neighboring nations. In Germany Hitler exploited the common feeling that the Treaty of Versailles was the result of French and English hostility against Germany and that these two countries continued to try to keep Germany weak. The payment of war indemnity, the demilitarization imposed on Germany at Versailles, and finally the French and Belgian invasion of the Ruhr in 1923 fed the growing revanchist feelings in the country and helped Hitler's ascent to power.[55] In Italy Mussolini also used the feeling of international injustice to foment nationalism among the Italians. The themes of the defeat at Caporetto during World War II and of the recovery of Fiume—a prosperous city of the Austro-Hungarian Empire that, despite its vicinity to the new 1914 Italian border, had been left to Austria at Versailles—were very much at the center of national public attention. Especially after the spectacular short-lived takeover of the city by Gabriele D'Annunzio on September 12, 1919, Fiume became a symbol of Italian Fascist revanchism.[56]

In China, the crescendo of Japanese aggression (a much more threatening reality than the loss of Fiume was for Italy) imposed national priorities on the country's political life at the expense of issues of social justice and class struggle. Wang's and Chen's defensive (anti-imperialist) nationalism, even if not revanchist nationalism (the survival of the nation as a whole increasingly appeared more urgent than the return of Manchuria to

China), became, with national unity, the most important goal and found its expression in the autarkic nature of their plan for developing China's *minzu* economy.

Moving toward Autarky: The Four Great Necessities of the People

As for the idea of *minzu* economy as a whole, its autarkic nature was the result of a complex elaboration of current trends, both international and more specifically Chinese. With "more specifically Chinese" I also refer to notions that had already gone through a process of assimilation and adaptation to Western trends but had become highly integrated in Chinese discourse. By the 1930s, arguably the years of greatest internationalization of China's political life until the 1990s, it was impossible to define a trend as completely Chinese in its essence. This was the case with one of the main tropes used by Chen Gongbo to make his case for autarky: the Four Great Necessities of the People (*minsheng sida xuyao*)—food, clothing, shelter, and means of travel (*shi, yi, zhu, xing*).

A firm believer in the importance of Sun Yat-sen's thought as a source of political legitimacy and inspiration for Nationalist reforms, Chen once again returned to one of the main ideas of Sun's Principle of People's Livelihood. In this principle Sun had placed the welfare of the people at the very core of nation building, an argument he reiterated in his *Fundamentals of National Reconstruction* (*Jianguo dagang*):

> The primary requisite of reconstruction lies in the people(s) livelihood [*minsheng*]. In reference to the four great necessities of the people—food, clothing, shelter and means of travel [*shi, yi, zhu, xing*]—the government should, in cooperation with the people, strive to develop agriculture to feed them; to develop the textile industry to meet their clothing requirements; to work out a large-scale housing project to furnish them with better living quarters; to improve and construct roads and canals to facilitate their traveling.[57]

Sun had borrowed classical images of the four basic economic functions of Chinese society and of the paternalistic responsibilities of traditional government to explain the duties of a Socialist and interventionist state that was very different from its pre-1911 predecessors. Because Sun had used it in his political platform, the trope of the Four Great Necessities of the People (food, clothing, shelter, and means of travel) became quite popular in 1930s China and became one of the tropes of political legitimacy favored by the Nationalists. Wang Jingwei echoed Sun in arguing that the goal of reconstruction was the building of a society and economy in which the Chinese people would live happily in peace and have their needs for clothing, food, living conditions, and travel satisfied.[58]

Chen also relied on this trope, although he adroitly modernized Sun Yatsen's idea by substituting consumption (*yong*) for means of transportation (*xing*)—a more fitting combination for an autarkic plan focusing on scarcity of supplies and the people's need for consumption. Chen took the notion of the Four Great Necessities of the People one step further and linked it to national defense rather than to domestic prosperity and stability. In this way, he took a formula that Sun had used mostly to express the GMD's concern for socioeconomic justice (the Four Great Necessities of the People were the foundation of the Principle of People's Livelihood) and used it to legitimize autarkic policies. China's growing economic dependency on Japan became, for Chen, a direct threat to the Four Great Necessities of the People, and hence a threat to the basic subsistence of the Chinese people and the survival of the nation.[59] According to his data, Chen explained, China spent more than 736, 509, 911 custom taels (approximately 47, 5167, 684. 51 Chinese silver dollars)[60] buying basic products, such as oil, cotton, rice, cereals, and wood. This showed that China was growing increasingly dependent on foreigners for its own subsistence. Foreign imperialism was gnawing at the very foundation of the country (*guoben*), leading it to its destruction. "Let's just look at the fact that we depend on foreign people for clothes, food, housing, and consumption [*yi, shi, zhu, yong*]. . . . How can a nationality [*minzu*] support its life [*zihuo*] in such a situation?"[61]

Chen used this trope to create a powerful image, evocative of national disaster. Sun had built his Four Great Necessities of the People on classical economic ideas, especially the notion of "state finance and people's livelihood" (*guoji minsheng*) and China's basic economic functions traditionally identified as the economic foundation (*guoben*) of China. According to the political theory of the Mandate of Heaven,[62] when the *guoben* was shaken, the entire country would experience a period of misery and destruction. Chen's suggestion that China had already reached the point of losing control over its basic needs, leaving them in the hands of foreigners, effectively conveyed a sense of China's extreme weakness and the urgency of the national question. Chen thus tapped the traditional discourse on the economy and national (or, rather, imperial) crisis while also directly referring to Sun's Principle of People's Livelihood as his source of political legitimacy. The basic economic functions that allowed the Chinese people to survive were in danger. The imperialist threat reached directly to the lifeblood of the nation. The only way to overcome this crisis, Chen argued, was to adopt autarkic policies aimed at making China self-reliant and breaking its dependency on Japan. In this way China could regain control over its resources and ensure the survival of its people. If this was not accomplished, Chen warned, China would perish. "Let's close our eyes and think. In case something happened to China, isn't it the case that we would have no alternative but to wait for death?"[63]

Chen's autarkic plan found confirmation in the usually more cautious statements of Wang. Wang reiterated the idea that the goods needed for the fulfillment of the people's basic needs were at the core of national defense and, for this reason, needed to be controlled by the Chinese state. He bemoaned the harmful effects of increasing imports, which were disrupting China's economic productive forces and creating a serious emergency that could be solved only by state regulation. He thus advocated the "establishment of some control over foodstuffs and other raw materials." "Centralized food control," he claimed, discussing China's wheat production, "is closely related to the solution of questions relating to the present harmful effect of foreign wheat imports on the native wheat market."[64]

Jiang Jieshi also utilized the trope of the Four Great Necessities of the People, defining it as the most important aspect of China's own "independent" economic thought.[65] Like Chen, Jiang also linked the idea of People's Livelihood to national defense: "National plans for the support of the people are plans for the People's Livelihood. But since this livelihood must also be protected, plans for livelihood become plans for the national defense."[66] The similar rhetoric, however, cannot blind us to the marked differences between the two leaders. Jiang thought in terms of militarization of the economy. He supported his view by revisiting what he described as one of the most positive characteristics of China's "independent" economic thought: a practice started by Guan Zhong, prime minister of the state of Qi from 685 to 643 BC. Jiang argued that Guan's most famous policy was the conscription of farmers. Jiang explained that Guan's "policy was to organize the farmers and give them military training, and by this means he made the entire population of Ch'i [Qi] potential soldiers. The People's Livelihood and national defense were thus provided for simultaneously."[67] This strategy was so successful, Jiang pointed out, that Qi eventually conquered all the other rival states.

Jiang's predilection for stressing historical continuity and tradition differed from Chen's rhetoric. Chen never invoked proofs of an alleged Chinese essence or unchangeable characteristics in support of his policies. His reliance on the past went only as far back as Sun Yat-sen, whom he considered the source of political legitimacy for the GMD and the nation as a whole. Chen actually strove to sound consistently revolutionary, in spite of the increasingly conservative nature of his thought. On the other hand,

Jiang invoked traditional values in support of a plan that was inspired by very modern ideas of military totalitarianism. Differences between the Jiang and the Wang group could not have run deeper, although their opposing political lines could both be traced back to Sun Yat-sen and, as stated before, to the ambiguity of the political legacy he left to the GMD after the 1924 reorganization. In a wider context, both political lines also reflected contemporary global antiliberal trends. The three leaders—Wang, Chen, and Jiang—agreed on autarky and were all equally responsible for the government's abandonment of the mercantilist policies that had inspired the Self-Strengthening reforms.

From Self-Strengthening to Autarky

Under the growing pressure of foreign imperialism, influential Chinese intellectuals and officials of the late Qing period, such as Zheng Guanying, identified the strength of the West with its economic power. Borrowing the example of Great Britain's colonization of India, Zheng argued that the English built their empire through commerce and used military force only to protect it. For this reason, he argued, China had now to face a new state of affairs and adapt to the ways of the system in which it was integrated. This system was characterized by international exchange and commerce, in which each country focused only on gaining profits, based their power on trade, and used their armies to protect it.[68] Zheng believed that in this situation China had to engage in a trade war (*shangzhan*) with the West as the only effective way to resist imperialism. The goal was to reverse China's unfavorable balance of trade, which he perceived as the key to the country's weakness.[69] Late Qing official Ma Jianzhong (1845–1900) was the first to include this Self-Strengthening approach within a systematic mercantilist theory. Ma linked domestic aspects of the Chinese economy to its balance of trade. Introducing the idea of a monetary standard, he suggested that China unify its currency system and adopt the gold standard in order to harmonize with the rest of the world and help China's commerce.[70]

These Self-Strengthening mercantilist strategies were reflected in the direction taken by the plethora of reconstruction projects initiated at the local level at that time. Many local governments promoted the manufacturing of goods destined for export in an effort to redress their unfavorable balance of trade.[71] This approach rested on the assumption that China was part of a system of free trade, as Zheng Guanying had pointed out. It soon became clear, however, that that was not really the case. Because of the Unequal Treaties—a series of treaties imposed on China by Western powers and Japan, which aimed to open the country to foreign economic interests—the Chinese government was unable to control customs duties, foreign enterprises within its territory, and large portions of its own taxation system, all essential elements for carrying out protectionist action against foreign powers. Although when pressing China to open its door to foreign goods, the foreign powers had rhetorically touted the "civilized" and "progressive" nature of international free trade, they had not played by these rules. Instead, they had imposed severe limitations on China's ability to act in the international market on an equal footing. Moreover, the Chinese government embraced the basic policies of the international free-exchange market system just when that very system was showing signs of crisis. Protectionist barriers went up all around Europe and the United States as early as the years before World War I.[72] Sun Yat-sen reacted to this situation. Following these new protectionist trends, he argued that the modernization of China required the end of cosmopolitanism and the free-trade regime because they served the interests only of the most productive economies. They suited economies in expansion, such as those of Great Britain and the United States, but did not suit China.[73]

As historian Karl Polanyi argues, the dissolution of the world economic system—its transformation from a free-exchange system to a system of autarkic units—had been in progress since 1900 and was responsible for the explosion of World War I in 1914.[74] In the 1930s, however, the common perception was that the Great War had taught a fundamental lesson: national power rested in a country's ability to control natural resources in order to keep its productive apparatus working and feed its population in times of war and peace. Felice Guarnieri, the architect of Italy's autarkic policies, argued that autarky sprang from "the need to be self-sufficient" (*bastare a noi stessi*) and from the need to "ask the state to set up the appropriate defensive measures aimed at ensuring the country full economic independence."[75] Based on this perception, a new wave of colonial expansion emerged, led by countries like Germany, Italy, and Japan that perceived direct control over natural resources and markets to be vital not only for the expansion of their industrial economies but also for national survival, since importation of supplies could suddenly be interrupted by unfriendly nations.

Along with many mainstream thinkers of the day, Chen also believed in the lesson taught by the war and noticed its influence on the world economy. "In Europe during the war, regardless of how many soldiers the Soviet Union was able to rely on or how powerful Germany's offensive apparatus was, the Soviet Union ended up with a revolution and Germany was defeated. . . . In reality the outcome [of the war] was still due to the fact that the Soviet Union and Germany did not have enough grain."[76] In his article

"An Independent Economic Control System" ("Geju de tongzhi jingji") published in September 1934, Chen argued again, "During the European war, defeated Germany, as well as the victorious powers, all deeply felt the lack of raw materials. . . . It is for this reason that after the war they all sought national autarky [*zizu*]. . . . This so-called national autarky means that, regardless of whether in war or in peace, all the goods needed must not be sought abroad."[77]

In China protectionist trends became more acute with the expansion of the Great Depression, which began to be severely felt in China by 1932. China's strongest industries, such as silk and tea, which relied heavily on exports, suddenly lost most of their markets in the West while also losing the opportunity to expand in East and Southeast Asia because of Japan's growing influence in the region. At the same time, China's economy was gradually being forced into a bilateral trade relationship with Japan that resembled the trade relations between many colonized, or satellite, countries and other imperialist powers around the world.[78] Aiming at building an autarkic empire, Japan wanted to pull China into its regional "Co-prosperity Sphere," in which China, together with Korea and Taiwan, would serve both as markets for Japanese manufactures and as suppliers of raw materials in support of Japan's industrial production. From the turn of the twentieth century the Japanese government was actively involved in promoting and supporting Japanese firms in their trade with China by means of special loans and the easing of foreign exchange regulations. As Peter Duus has argued, "From the 1890s onward, the Japanese government made a concerted effort to promote the growth of the China trade as part of a larger policy of expanding Japanese exports in world markets."[79] In 1898 Ito Hirobumi stated: "Among the other countries confronting our own, there is none that surpasses us in proximity to China, in close access to its ports, and in convenience of navigation. It must be said that our country occupies the best position with respect to the China trade. If we take good advantage of the position to carry on trade, it will not be at all difficult to make our country the central source of supply of goods for all ports both in the north and south of China."[80] The volume of Japan's China trade, which surpassed trade with its formal colonies, testifies to Japan's interest in China as a privileged market and supplier of raw materials. By the 1930s Japan was relying heavily on China to feed Japanese markets and its industries' hunger for raw materials.[81] The fear of many Chinese that Japan's plans were to "industrialize Japan and agriculturalize China" (*gongye riben, nongye zhongguo*) was certainly not unjustified.[82]

Although China had experienced imperialism before, Japan imposed a different kind of economic stranglehold. While other foreign powers, such as Great Britain and France, had been happy to control China's tariffs and open up access to its markets and resources, they never aimed at confining China into one economic sphere and subordinating its economy to that of a colonial metropole. Although Japan was not seeking the outright colonization of the Chinese mainland, the level of economic control it sought was colonial in all senses.[83] In this environment, Chen became aware that the international economic environment had changed deeply. At the same time, like most other Chinese leaders and intellectuals, he could not refrain from interpreting the new situation as a development of the colonial trends initiated in East Asia in the previous century. Chen believed that what China was facing at the moment was a more acute version of the struggle that began with the Opium War.[84] The world, Chen argued, had come to be divided into two groups of countries: the powerful, that is, the countries that relied on autarkic and controlled economies (nationalist economies), and the weak, that is, dependent economies that were not autarkic and consequently fell victim to imperialist powers. "Since World War I, autarkic policies have become a creed in every country, and petty nationalist economies [*xiayi de guojia zhuyi jingji*] have reached their height. Under these circumstances, those countries that still adopt a free economy will inevitably become the victims of the economies of petty nationalist [*xiayi de minzu zhuyi*] countries."[85]

In this passage, Chen used terminology that had developed in China since the late nineteenth century, when Liang Qichao had criticized Han (anti-Manchu) nationalism, which he called petty nationalism (*xiaominzhu zhuyi*), for being narrowly linked to the idea of race. Against this petty nationalism, Liang advocated a great nationalism (*daminzu zhuyi*), which would be based on the notion of a cosmopolitan China in which non-Han people also had a place.[86] Liang's position on issues of race, however, remained ambiguous and complicated, and his thought was not always faithful to the idea of great nationalism.[87] It was Liang's attempt to distinguish between positive and negative forms of nationalism that was echoed in the writings of later intellectuals, including Chen. In revisiting Liang's differentiation, Chen abandoned the idea of race adopted by Liang and argued that petty nationalism (*xiayi minzu zhuyi*) was an economically defined aggressive nationalism that motivated imperialist countries to infringe upon the autonomy of other countries. That race also played a role in the German and Japanese imperial discourse was so marginal for Chen that he never discussed it.

Wang and Chen felt that in this hostile international environment, marked by the rise of "petty nationalisms," China was in danger of becoming completely dependent on Japan and even colonized outright. There was now a struggle between China and Japan over who would control China's resources. If China lost, Japan would employ China's own resources to build its strength and use this newly found strength to colonize China. If instead China won, Japan would become weaker and China stronger, reversing the unbalanced power relationship between the two neighbors.

Wang and Chen were aware of the growing military component of Japanese aggression. Yet, in keeping with their commitment to economic strengthening as the key to national independence, they rarely expounded on the development of the Chinese military. We can speculate that they did not need to worry on this point since Jiang was already attempting to monopolize most of the resources of the Nanjing government in support of the development of the military. They also probably feared that advocating any kind of military buildup would inevitably reinforce Jiang's position in the government. In addition, Wang, more than Chen, continued to believe in the efficacy of international mechanisms of collective security (*jiti anquan*), embodied in the League of Nations. In 1932, when the Wang-Jiang cabinet was established, the League was still intent on investigating the Japanese presence in Manchuria, and the Chinese trusted that the League would decide in their favor. Even as late as 1937, in spite of the League's failure to check Japan's expansion into Manchuria and restore the region to China, Wang was still arguing that China needed to trust the League. During the time he spent in Europe, Wang claimed, he had come to the realization that, although the system had its weaknesses, it was still the only way to preserve peace worldwide. Wang assured his readers that this feeling was shared by most of the European nations. They, Wang explained, realized that the problem with the League lay not with the system itself but with its member nations, which had not been willing to make the appropriate effort to yield power to the League. Wang had pinpointed the League's major problem: its inability to gain authority over the national states that were its members. He remained blind, however, to the seriousness of this limitation and insisted that it was now the moment to make the system work and avoid war at all costs. Nations should prepare for war, he argued, but only as a deterrent, as a way to discourage unwanted aggression: "Working energetically to prepare for war and supporting the collective security system are two tasks that have to be carried out at the same time. They seem to be in contradiction, but in reality they are consistent with each other." The Nanjing government, therefore, should "work hard to construct China into a modern nation" and resume working through diplomatic channels to solve its international problem. "This policy is the path that we must follow to save China."[88]

National economic reconstruction thus remained for Wang and Chen the only effective weapon for national unification and resistance against Japanese imperialism, two goals they perceived as the essence of China's modern nationhood. Both goals could be achieved only through an incisive and far-reaching state intervention at all levels of the economy. At that time, however, the Nanjing government was far from being able to perform such a task, as Chen and Wang were fully aware. It was for this reason that their plan included one more requirement: the adoption of a controlled economy (*tongzhi jingji*). As Chen explained, "Economic control makes a nationality an economic unit. For this reason if we discard the nation, it is not even possible to talk of economic control."[89] And again, in "An Independent Economic Control System," he expounded, "Economic control comes from policies of national autarky. It comes from basic national [*minzu*] survival. If we abandon the nation [*guojia*] and nationality we cannot even discuss economic control. . . . Economic control is the means for a nation or a nationality to reach autarky."[90] Supporting a controlled economy, Wang echoed: "Talking of national emergencies, none is more serious than our economic emergency. But if the economic situation is brought under centralized control, and the agricultural, industrial, and commercial enterprises of the country readjusted, then most of our economic problems can be solved."[91]

Toward Economic Control

As in the case of Chen Gongbo, many leaders around the world closely related autarky to the expansion of both agriculture and industry since domestic production had to be sufficient to meet all the needs of the nation. This need, in turn, justified the government's intervention in the economy for the sake of the ultimate mission of national survival.[92] Paradoxically, the rise of autarkic markets created a crisis in the domestic economy of many countries, requiring their governments to adopt new development policies. A country that was unable to rely on imports and exports needed centralized management of the economy to regulate demand and production, boost production of those goods that were needed for economic development but not naturally developing in the country, adjust customs duties, and regulate taxation. Although Chen appeared to consider these recent autarkic developments as a deterioration of the international system, he argued that it was absolutely necessary for China to adapt to them. It was not, he argued, an ideal state of affairs, being actually the result of petty nationalist movements around the world. Adapting to these changes was, however, a matter of life or death for China. Not doing so would amount to "virtual suicide." Identifying World War I as the crucible of the political and economic changes that were sweeping the world, Chen wrote:

> When the [Versailles] peace conference opened, all countries focused on economic recovery. Other problems such as demobilization, paying back war debts, . . . , were all related to [economic] recovery. If a country wanted to recover [its economy] it had no other choice but [to increase] production. . . . At that time the policy of economic control did not exist because there was no need for it. But later the policy of autarky [*zizu*] brought about a series of economic crises. A country which wanted to repay its debts or force production of those goods that [it needed for self-sufficiency but] were not naturally developing had to raise a protective wall of customs duties. Goods from abroad could not enter the country and the spirit of [liberal economic] harmonization was already lost. At the same time domestic goods could not leave the country, leading to an unsound situation. Factories were forced to close down, workers lost their jobs, the economy stagnated, purchasing power dropped, prices kept falling while life became increasingly difficult. . . . Production limitations and customs wars are remedies to the problems created by postwar autarkic policies. Since national autarky policies are in vogue, it has been discovered that laissez-faire policies not only endanger and harm industries but also shake the foundations of a country [*guoben*]. If a government cannot make an overall plan balancing production and demand, we cannot even discuss autarky. The result would be a virtual suicide. These are the origins of economic control.[93]

Chen argued that economic control was needed even more in China than in other countries. In fact, overall productivity was so low that China, far from reaching self-sufficiency and becoming a modern nation, was increasingly at the mercy of foreign powers. "China is threatened by foreign countries but it does not have any defense worth talking about. It has not even started a defense industry. . . . No doubt this state of affairs is not enough to rank as a modern nation [*jindai guojua*], and we cannot even discuss conditions for survival. This is why . . . I advocate economic control."[94] For this reason, Chen argued, autarky had to be the first goal of China's nation building, while economic control was the urgently needed means for achieving it. "So-called nation building [*liguo*] means survival; the most reliable means for survival is, definitely, autarky. . . . If we want to reach this goal, I cannot see any better way than adopting the policy of economic control."[95]

The idea of a controlled economy was popular worldwide in the interwar years. It implied a high level of centralization under the leadership of the government, which planned economic development strategies and implemented them down to the level of grassroots economic activities. The idea was originally inspired by Marxist economics, but it had also been employed, to a limited degree, by anticommunist regimes during the war effort and while they were attempting to lead their countries out of the 1930s Great Depression. This was the case in the United States, where President Franklin Delano Roosevelt, inspired by the ideas of British economist John Maynard Keynes, began a series of new policies, known as the New Deal, that placed the state at the head of economic enterprises aimed at economic welfare and recovery. The New Deal was perceived by many as smacking of socialism, although it simply empowered the state with a higher level of economic initiative. Other anticommunist governments, such as the German and the Italian, which were already hostile to liberalism and liberal capitalism, embraced planned economy more overtly and to a fuller extent. These governments, while hoping to maintain a free-market system, wanted to be able to manipulate both producers and consumers and make them pursue nationalist economic goals. These regimes distrusted classical liberalism, which they came to perceive as unable to control the selfish interests of individuals. Like other fascist leaders, Mussolini believed that the unregulated thirst for profit encouraged by capitalism was the main cause of World War I. He also believed the liberal economy to have reached a phase of "inhuman supercapitalism" in the years following the world war. In this phase, private enterprises had become "inflated," overstepping the capacity of humans to produce and consume. So while in the earlier stages of capitalism "it was spirit which controlled matter," in the current situation it was "matter which curbed and molded the spirit."[96] This "inhuman capitalism" relied, according to Mussolini, on unlimited consumption and on standardization of products and consequently of human nature. Moreover, supercapitalism needed to manipulate the state in order to survive since it operated outside the framework of a balanced system of supply and demand. For this reason, it was becoming increasingly influential over the state, threatening to completely overtake it. Mussolini argued that, if "undisciplined," supercapitalism would transform itself into a type of "state capitalism." Therefore, he was absolutely convinced that the state needed to intervene in every aspect of the economy. Individual interests needed to be "disciplined" by the state and their energy channeled toward the realization of the interests of the nation as a whole. As Mussolini stated, this new form of economy was "no longer economy aiming at individual profit, but economy concerned with collective interests."[97] It was on this theoretical basis that Il Duce justified the establishment in Italy of a system of *dirigismo economico* (economic dirigisme).

Although China's experience with capitalism was dramatically different from that of Europe, the idea of "disciplining" capitalism resonated with the Nationalist objective of preventing its full-fledged development (a policy that was an integral part of Sun's thought and of the idea of *minzu* economy). Above all, however, the notion of controlled economy appealed to Nationalist leaders and economists because of its nation-building and anti-imperialist potential. Fang Xianting (also known as H. D. Fong), who was a prominent economist and the director of research at the prestigious Economic Institute of Nankai University and adviser to the Nationalist government, argued that "economic control, largely an offspring of the post-war mal-adjustments within an erstwhile 'cosmopolitan' economy, has assumed an increasing importance in proportion to the progress of post-war nationalism and, more specifically, fascism."[98] The authoritarian nature of China's economic institutions was justified, in Fang's eyes, by the need to reassert state power (economic and political control) at the expense of imperialist forces and local clusters of "feudal" power. Thus, it was ultimately nationalist goals that required the Chinese state to take upon itself the burden of controlling the economy and leading China to independence.[99]

China's departure from liberal political and economic ideas was also noted by a second prominent economist of the Economic Institute, D. Z. Xu (T. C. Hsu). In 1934 Xu observed that since the end of World War I Chinese economic thought had shifted from the "laissez faire doctrine and individualistic theories of the 18th and 19th centuries" to Socialistic collectivism and planned economy. This change, he commented, reflected changes in the politico-economic thought of the West itself: "The Great War had totally discredited the theory of individualism. With the success of the Bolshevik revolution in Russia and the rise of Fascism in Italy, politics and economics have become inseparable. A study of the postwar constitutions in Europe will reveal the fact that all these constitutions embody a new politico-economic doctrine of collectivism quite different from the old individualistic doctrine."[100] Bolshevik Russia and Fascist Italy, in the eyes of most Chinese intellectuals, seemed to offer the same economic model, in which the role of the individual was diminished to enable the state to exercise more power and more control over society. By the 1930s most of the GMD's leaders had embraced the idea of economic control, including Minister of Finance Song Ziwen, who was generally considered to be the staunchest representative of private capitalism in China. Jiang Jieshi was also convinced that this was the new direction in which the world was moving and argued that free industrial and commercial competition in Europe and America had ended—a change that was "particularly apparent after the First World War."[101]

Conclusion

Chen Gongbo's idea of a *minzu* economy rested on tropes and themes that constituted the basic elements of the Chinese discourse on the nation and nation building in the 1930s and went beyond the boundaries of Nationalist political and economic thought. They were, in fact, also fundamental to Mao's *New Democracy* political platform. The concept of *minzu* economy was employed by different political groups for different political agendas. In *New Democracy,* Mao Zedong used it to combine class struggle and anti-imperialism, while Chen and Wang used it to express a unified socioeconomic alliance. For both Chen and Wang, however, the economy was intrinsically linked to nationalist goals and, consequently, *minzu* in nature. Because of their ubiquity in Communist rhetoric, such formulas as a *minzu* socioeconomic alliance and People's Livelihood (*minsheng*) have generally been considered by historians to be mostly propaganda refrains devoid of real political meaning. In prewar China, on the contrary, they offered a common language for the conceptualization of crucial nation-building issues and were the source of heated controversy.

The idea of a *minzu* economy, that is, an economy not compromised by foreign imperialism, as opposed to a "comprador" economy ("comprador," *maiban,* was a negative term used at the time to identify merchants involved with foreign economic interests), was so deeply rooted in the Chinese discourse on the modern nation that it is still used in Chinese historiography. Post-Mao Chinese historiography uses this term to identify the portion of the Chinese industrial economy of the late Qing and Republican years that theoretically was not compromised by foreign imperialism. The *minzu* industrial economy (the center of the 1930s idea of *minzu* economy) is today identified with the origins of China's modern economy and nation.[102] Although Chinese historians generally rather formulaically criticize it for its bourgeois nature, the *minzu* industrial economy emerges today as the beginning of China's economic modernization (the "sprouts" of China's industrial capitalism) and, as such, the origins of China's modern nation.[103]

The *minzu* economy that formed the core of Chen's plan for nation building and that was adopted by the Wang group borrowed creatively from such common tropes as *minzu* and *minsheng* to gain political legitimacy. Chen's plan was, however, highly controversial because of its almost exclusive focus on the economic foundations of the nation, its highly centralized notion of economic development, and its reversal of prevailing mainstream mercantilist practices. Chen's and Wang's idea of *minzu* economy and their decision to move toward autarky created a series of thorny problems, involving a redefinition of the revolutionary goals of the GMD and the social base of the new nation, the organizational and interventionist capacity of the state, and the relationship between central and local government (centralization versus federalism).

Although the formula for economic nation building promulgated by Chen and Wang appeared, at first glance, rather simplistic and highly rhetorical, its realization actually required important choices for the new cabinet. It was mostly the conceptual categories used to express it that were alien to Western observers. As Philip Jaffe, a commentator on Jiang Jieshi's *China's Destiny and Chinese Economic Theory,* lamented: "This is an example of the unscientific and inexact reasoning that characterizes this book. . . . [It] can hardly be regarded as the product of scholarly or scientific analysis."[104] The same kind of criticism was directed against most of the Chinese economic and political writings of this period. Although Jiang's writings, as well as those of most Chinese political leaders, including Wang and Chen, were often aimed at political, rather than "scientific," goals, thus deserving in part these kinds of criticism, these negative reactions represent a failure to understand tropes and language that differed from those prevailing in the United States and many European countries. The attempt to find sources of legitimacy that were both universally modern and yet transmittable within the Chinese political rhetoric of the time often led to images that obscured the real nature of the issues at hand. In practice, however, Chen's and Wang's writings were not just exercises in rhetoric. The definition of the nation's socioeconomic basis (*minzu jingji*) and goals (national unification and autarky) determined the shape and direction of the reforms carried out by the Wang-Jiang cabinet, as well as the strategy they offered for solving crucial problems.

貳

CHAPTER 2

The Rural Question: Identity, Modernity, and Peasants in China's Industrial Development

The autarkic nature of the *minzu* economy proposed by Wang Jingwei and Chen Gongbo touched on one of the major controversies in the Chinese discourse on the nation: the role of the rural economy and of the peasants in China's modernization. Developing an autarkic industrial system required a remapping of the economic landscape of the country and a rearrangement of its hierarchies. The coastal industrial economy would be forced to look inward to the rural hinterland for supplies of raw materials and markets, reversing its current reliance on the international market. At the same time, the rural village—in the 1930s still considered by many the repository of China's identity—would be harnessed to the development of coastal/urban industries, perceived by Wang and Chen to be the core of China's *minzu* economy. At stake was not just a shift of priority from agriculture to industry but also the socioeconomic and cultural foundation of the modern Chinese nation. On one side were the newly emerging coastal economy and society characterized by a cosmopolitan understanding of modernity. On the other were the villages in the hinterland, where local elites, with a few exceptions, such as Jiangnan,[1] strove to protect their privileges and to maintain the status quo. Autarky thus required a new relationship between these two Chinas, which, as many observers of the time lamented, had grown increasingly isolated from each other. This new relationship would bring China to a higher level of economic integration, thus helping the country to become the "economic unit" advocated by Wang and Chen. It would also establish the coastal economy (its social groups and its economic culture) as the foundation of the new nation, while demoting the village to a subordinate position.

In the 1930s, the "rural question"—as the role of the rural village in China's modernization was dubbed at the time—had become the focus of unprecedented attention for a variety of reasons. The success of the Communists in the mobilization of the peasant masses posed a challenge to the Nanjing government and to the sociopolitical unity it sought. In addition, most Chinese leaders and intellectuals regarded the economic decline of the rural areas as one of the main reasons for China's failure to modernize and considered rural recovery crucial to the salvation of the nation as a whole. The rural question, therefore, came to be at the center of a heated debate over the causes of the current crisis and how best to solve it. Nationalist and Communist leaders and sympathizers approached the problem from different perspectives. The CCP favored a redistribution approach, focusing primarily on land reform. The GMD, instead, took a productivist approach that sought to end rural poverty and economic decline mainly by increasing production. Generally associated with Fascist notions of nation building, productivism differed in two main ways from the desire to increase national production of most schools of economic thought. Productivism not only was connected with autarky—an autarkic nation must be able to produce all the goods it needs—but also attempted to respond to Communist arguments for the redistribution of wealth. During World War I, for example, Mussolini developed the idea that the solution to Italy's economic and social problems required an expansion of production. This appeared to him to be the best strategy for solving Italy's social problems because it would increase national wealth and improve the economic conditions of the Italians, thus offering an alternative solution to class struggle as proposed by the Communists.[2]

While agreeing on the overall productivist approach, the Nationalist camp was divided on the nature of and solution to the rural crisis. Jiang Jieshi, in keeping with his overall military outlook, saw the military elimination of the CCP as the prerequisite for any form of intervention in the rural economy. Wang and Chen believed the CCP's strength could be curtailed through an immediate effort to increase production, which would have improved peasants' lives and made the CCP's message of land reform and class struggle less appealing. Wang and Chen also disagreed with Nationalist approaches to rural reform constructed around a romantic view of China's rural essence. Some Nationalist intellectuals, such as Fang Xianting, perceived the rural village to be the locus of China's traditional values and intrinsic essence. The treaty ports, as the point of encounter with foreign imperialism, were considered to be polluted by negative Western influences.

Agencies for rural reconstruction sponsored by local governments and private groups began springing up all over the country, articles on the rural question filled the pages of journals and newspapers, and the role of the rural economy in the modernization of the country became one of the most discussed and controversial issues of the time. It was on this issue in particular that Nationalist leaders, intellectuals, and sympathizers came to be divided, generating a heated debate on China's economic identity and the limits of Western modernity. The 1930s debate on rural rehabilitation reflected the wide variety of developmental options that the Chinese leaders and economists were considering at the time. After World War II, the debate came to be limited to the confrontation between Communist land reform and military protection of the status quo as pursued by Jiang Jieshi, but in the prewar period a variety of alternatives emerged, all of which appeared to be equally valid. The 1930s debate on the rural question, therefore, went beyond the discussion on Communism in China and also focused on issues of population, national identity, and anti-imperialism. In this respect, it anticipated issues and problems facing today's Chinese leaders. While the theme of autarky and self-reliance continued to influence the Maoist years—fostered by the isolation dictated by Cold War politics—in China's current private economy and market system, the problems of the growing gap between rural hinterland and industrial urban/coastal China, increasing population pressure, and economic integration at the national level are just as urgent as they were in the 1930s.

Remapping the National Economy

The theme of the divide between rural and coastal China forms the focus of much debate in recent Western historiography on China. Like its predecessor in the 1930s, today's debate concerns the spatial and modernization divide between treaty ports and hinterland after the 1895 Treaty of Shimonoseki, which sealed China's defeat by Japan and marked the beginning of the establishment of foreign factories on Chinese territory. This year is regarded as the beginning of a process of industrialization that was confined to the treaty ports and excluded most rural and hinterland areas. Economic historian Thomas Rawski has challenged this interpretation, arguing that the economy of the treaty ports also stimulated economic activities in rural areas previously barred from long-distance trade.[3] More recently, Lynda Bell has shown that the rural economy in Jiangnan became closely integrated with the development of modern industries as peasant-family manufacturers took advantage of and benefited from the new business opportunities created by the modern industries in the cities.

Discussing silk filatures in Wuxi, Bell argues that before World War II "'two Chinas' emerged as part of the continuum—one populated by sophisticated, urban-based merchants and industrialists, the other by peasant families who remained in the countryside producing raw materials upon which silk filatures depended." Rural production of raw materials was, in fact, quite important for China's bourgeoning modern industry, leading Bell to argue that "what was most distinctive about Chinese development in the early twentieth-century was the fusion of modern factory production with peasant-family production, and the interdependence of the two systems."[4] Bell's, and Rawski's, argument, while accurately describing the Jiangnan area, hardly applies to most of rural China in the 1930s. Historically, Jiangnan had been one of the regions that enjoyed the highest level of agricultural commercialization and regional integration. Its situation can hardly be taken as an example of economic integration in other regions. The work of Kenneth Pomeranz, for example, reveals a very different situation in Shandong, where he discovers a very uneven level of integration. Pomeranz stresses the gap between the economies of the treaty ports and most rural villages, in terms of actual economic conditions and elites' interests.[5]

Regardless of the level of national economic integration that China had enjoyed previously, by the 1930s, years of war had done much to destroy communications and to isolate the hinterland from urban centers. At the same time, the political division of China into spheres of control by warlords added to the disruption of patterns of national integration. Most warlords minted their own money in the areas they dominated and often used transportation taxes to replenish their coffers. Contemporary observers commented that railways and roads were in disarray while taxes and levies hindered the circulation of goods. According to one contemporary study, for example, between Tianjing and Beijing there were "seven tax barriers. . . . A cargo of soy beans sent by the producing district of Fuchin to the manufacturing district of Harbin had to pay . . . no less than twenty-two separate dues." As a result the peasant was "obliged to sell to buyers in his immediate neighbourhood," furthering the separation of city and country.[6]

To Chen, the separation between coastal and hinterland regions appeared to be a major obstacle for China's economic unification and its progress toward autarky. He firmly believed that an autarkic China required coastal factories to stop looking outward to the international market and to turn instead to the rural hinterland for an abundant and steady stream of raw materials. Because of the decline of the international market, coastal manufacturers also needed to rely on the rural hinterland for marketing their finished goods. Increasing rural production was thus essential for integrating the two economies. Not only would it ensure much-needed domestic raw materials, but, according to Chen, it would raise the standard of living of the peasants and transform them into consumers. Chen believed that the development of rural industrial products would naturally create more wealth in the rural areas, increasing the purchasing power of the peasants and turning the countryside into a large domestic market for industrial goods.[7] To Wang this strategy offered the solution to China's development problem. In rather optimistic terms, Wang described the basic logic of his productivist plan: "As a result of agricultural reconstruction, the productive powers of the farming population will be developed and their purchasing power increased. Industry and commerce will flourish and make rapid progress until full development is achieved."[8] Rural decline, instead, would spell disaster for the autarkic goal of China's *minzu* economy, since only a significant increase in rural production accompanied by a higher standard of living could support an autarkic industrial development as well as China's integration into a single economic unit.[9] Rural recovery was, therefore, crucial for Wang's and Chen's vision of modern nationhood with its very specific objectives (autarky and national unity), but it was never, to them, an end in itself. Rural recovery was, rather, just a means used to achieve their final goal of industrialization. Wang and Chen, in fact, never stopped believing that it was industrialization that made modern nations and that modern nationhood was the ultimate source of power China needed to survive its current crisis. In this respect, Wang and Chen subordinated the rural economy to the development of the light industry that had slowly emerged in the coastal areas. Their idea of industrialization and of the role of the rural economy in it differed from that of Jiang (who focused on heavy industry in the hinterland) as well as from that of many rural reformers who perceived the Chinese village as the essence of China's identity. The latter group came to favor a model of industrialization centered on the rural village, the exact opposite of what Wang and Chen advocated. In other words, while most reformers supported industrialization as a crucial aspect of Chinese nation building, the exact kind of industrialization that would best fit China was an issue of debate.

Rural China and Economic Modernization

In the 1930s, Chinese insecurity in an increasingly isolationist and protectionist world encouraged many Chinese political leaders and intellectuals to stop looking beyond China's borders and redirect their gaze toward the rural hinterland. This new attitude was inspired not only by the shrinking of foreign markets for Chinese goods, leading many economists to focus on domestic markets rather then relying on exports, but also by the feeling that, if China did not follow the emerging protectionist trend, it would become even more vulnerable to aggressive imperialist states. The 1930s became marked by a general feeling that the cosmopolitan spirit of free trade that had characterized the years preceding World War I was now over. In this environment, Chinese intellectuals, such as the economist Fang Xianting, returned to the imperial trope of Chinese rural essence to counter the power of urban cosmopolitan industrialization. In this context, rural China came to be perceived as still possessing China's traditional values, values that needed to be protected from the influence of foreign imperialism and the culture of the treaty ports.[10] The issue of the role of China's alleged rural essence versus Western-style urban industrialization created divisions within the Nationalist camp itself, highlighting the complex dimensions of the rural crisis.

In the political imagery of imperial China, agriculture was perceived as the foundational economic activity of China, responsible for ensuring its social stability and national strength.[11] This idea belonged largely to the tropes of social harmony promoted by the Confucian establishment but was not reflected in the practices or hierarchies of power transpiring in everyday life.[12] The rhetoric of *yinong liguo,* "founding the country on agriculture," hurt the state more than it hindered the development of commerce. Even in late imperial China, which was characterized by a rapid growth of trade, the Chinese government considered the land tax to be the fiscal base of the state and eschewed taxation of what Qing officials believed to be economic activities that were not so central to the political and moral establishment of the empire. According to Wang Yejian (Wang Yeh-chien), in 1753 land tax accounted for 73.5 percent of all revenue. The remaining portion was made up of miscellaneous taxes, such as property deed tax, pawnshop and brokerage taxes, and sales taxes.[13] It was only at the end of the dynasty that the government began to tax trade and transportation more earnestly, adopting two new taxes, the *lijin* (*likin;* an internal customs tax) and maritime customs (aimed at taxing import and export trade), which, together with increased revenue from the salt tax, came to form a growing percentage of the total fiscal balance of the state. However, according to Wang Yejian, the land tax, and above all the belief in its value to the fiscal stability of the empire, were still important in the late Qing period. Although merchant culture was actually very well integrated into the late imperial body politic and economic system,[14] the idea of *yinong liguo* constituted a powerful rhetorical image that Chinese officials and intellectuals found difficult to abandon.

It was in the mid–nineteenth century that the debate over China's economic life came to reach beyond the Confucian discourse on domestic stability and to be framed within the discourse of the nation and anti-imperialism, shaking the basis of the idea of *yinong liguo*. Late Qing officials, such as Wei Yuan and Zheng Guanying, struggled to find a balance between China's rural values and the challenges coming from foreign imperialism. In his book *Warning from an Age of Prosperity* (*Shengshi weiyan*), Zheng identified the basic difference between China and Western powers as the fact that China had its foundations in agriculture (*zhongguo yinong liguo*) while foreign countries had theirs in commerce. Zheng considered the profits derived from agriculture to be fundamental (*ben*), while those derived from commerce to be of peripheral importance (*mo*). In this way, Zheng claimed that China had a moral advantage over the scientifically and militarily superior West in a way reminiscent of Nationalist movements in the phase identified by Partha Chatterjee as the "moment of departure." This initial phase of the development of nationalism in the colonial world, Chatterjee argues, was characterized by the leaders' vision of a division of "the world of social institutions and practices into two domains—the material and the spiritual." While the material became open to Western trends, the "spiritual, on the other hand, remained an 'inner' domain bearing the 'essential' marks of cultural identity."[15] In China, this approach was embodied in the Self-Strengthening *tiyong* formula.[16] In this vein, Zheng recognized the strength of the powerful trade system of the Western powers but believed that China's agriculturally based economy was morally superior. Zheng, however, was a pragmatist and conceded that moral superiority was inadequate to stop foreign imperialism. In such a situation, Zheng asked: "If we want to restrain the West by Self-Strengthening, is there anything better than promoting commerce? How can we say that commerce is a peripheral matter [*mowu*]?"[17] Practical considerations of sources of power eroded Zheng's idea of what constituted a "peripheral" or "fundamental" economic activity and brought him to reformulate his economic rhetoric in favor of commerce. Commerce, and not agriculture, Zheng argued, had to become China's fundamental economic activity. Zheng's justification of this change was still clothed in the Confucian rhetoric of social harmony. Commerce, he explained, acted as the harmonizing agent between China's four social groups—peasants (*nong*), workers (*gong*), merchants (*shang*), and literati (*shi*)—by forming a network that connected all their activities. Commerce thus exercised the function of circulation of capital and goods, which he considered more important than production.

At the turn of the twentieth century, however, the idea of developing industrial production began to replace commerce in the rhetoric of

Self-Strengthening. By 1900 the same Zheng Guanying had revised his position. "The richness of Western people," Zheng reasoned, "does not rest on commerce but on industry," because without the technology for producing goods there would be no commerce at all.[18] By the time Sun Yat-sen was formulating his Three People's Principles, this had become a widely held belief. According to Sun, China's most urgent task was to modernize and industrialize as "the key to China's strength" in the modern world.[19] In a parallel development, the positive image of rural China was reversed. In the late 1910s and 1920s, at the height of the New Culture Movement (the iconoclastic intellectual movement that directly attacked China's traditional Confucian society and advocated the adoption of Western science and political institutions), urban-based Chinese intellectuals constructed an image of rural areas as intrinsically "feudal." In their writings the village emerged as the bulwark of the worst and most degrading aspects of Chinese tradition, ultimately responsible for China's inability to modernize and stand up against foreign imperialism.[20]

The 1930s were marked by a renewed focus on the countryside, a result of the international economic depression that was believed to have hobbled China's rural economy and of a neoconservative backlash that followed the New Culture iconoclasm. The 1930s came to be characterized by nativist trends in response to the cosmopolitanism of the 1920s. While most Western countries retrenched behind protectionist barriers, many intellectuals and political leaders in China began to reject foreign cultural and economic influence. For example, they came to reject urbanism "because they associated it with Western progress . . . materialism and decadence."[21] Some intellectuals, such as Liang Shuming, completely opposed industrialization, perceiving it as eroding the very foundation of the nation.[22]

It was in this period that the idea of *yinong liguo* was once again brought to the forefront of the debate on China's modernization, coming to be used to create models of economic modernization intended to preserve what many considered China's "native" identity. These models mostly relied on the use of rural cooperative societies for expanding already existing rural manufactures. The basic notion was that this reorganization along cooperative lines would allow small rural industries to modernize their modes of production and become the core of China's new industrial system. One of the main economic rationales for the notion of rural industrialization rested on the fact that China's population was overwhelmingly rural, and that a model of development leading to the impoverishment of the countryside would have negative consequences for China as a whole.

Moreover, according to its proponents, this model would allow China to take advantage of its strengths, such as abundant manpower, while working around one of its main weaknesses, a lack of capital. Cooperative societies were presented as a way to mobilize manpower in the rural hinterland and had the virtue of requiring small capital investment. This argument was often accompanied by the claim that China's identity was rural and that it was in the rural village that one could find the pristine essence of Chineseness. The coastal areas and the major cities of the country, the argument went, had been polluted by the culture brought in by the foreign imperialist presence. In order to preserve China's identity, it was important to keep Chinese peasants in the village by offering them employment opportunities beyond working the fields. In this way, rural industrializers claimed, the peasants would stop migrating to the city, where they became morally and socially corrupted. At the same time, the peasants' standard of living would improve and China would embark on an original but effective path of development.

The idea of rural industrialization led to experiments with cooperative societies in various "model counties" as well as to a lively debate in specialized journals. Among the most vocal and enthusiastic representatives of this ruralist trend was Fang Xianting. Fang wrote several articles on this topic in widely read newspapers and journals such as *The Impartial* (*Dagongbao*), the *Nankai Social and Economic Quarterly,* and *Research in Chinese Economy* (*Zhongguo jingji yanjiu*).[23] In 1935 under Fang's supervision, the Economic Institute of Nankai University launched an experimental project in Jining County in Shandong Province, a project funded by the Rockefeller Foundation and cosponsored by the North China Council for Rural Reconstruction. The project was short lived since Jining soon fell to the Japanese.[24] But model counties experimenting in rural industrialization prospered in other regions and were generally regarded as successful. The famous Chinese anthropologist Fei Xiaotong popularized one of these experiments in his seminal book *Peasant Life in China* (1939). In a 1936 interview, a Mr. Chen,[25] a local official responsible for initiating the reform of the silk industry in Kaixiangong, Jiangsu—the focus of Fei's study—told Fei that the development of that industry needed to follow two main principles: it "should remain a rural industry" and should be reorganized according to "the principle of co-operation (*hezuo*)."[26] Like Fang, Mr. Chen joined the cohort of those who believed that in China industrialization needed to be mostly rural and that this seeming contradiction could be resolved by the organization of rural manufactures into a system of cooperative societies.

The Wang Group and the Rural Question

Both Wang Jingwei and Chen Gongbo recognized the importance and urgency of the rural crisis and placed its solution at the center of their reform plans. As already mentioned, however, they approached the problem from a different angle than rural industrializers and those who rejected industrialization outright. In 1933, in response to critics who accused him of ignoring the fate of the countryside, Chen asserted that "China's agricultural products make up 90 percent of the total national production, and peasants make up around 70 percent of the total population"; consequently, it was impossible not to recognize the "importance of agricultural development and state intervention in rural areas."[27] In Chen's own words, "reviv[ing] the countryside appeared as the medicine for China's life or death."[28] This view was also shared by Wang, who wrote in 1934 that "to talk about national reconstruction without giving particular attention to the problems of the men and the land would be utterly futile" since 80 percent of the Chinese population was formed by people working in the agricultural sector.[29] Chen, however, attacked those who attempted to revive the idea of *yinong liguo,* which, he argued, placed an exclusive focus on agriculture at the expense of industrialization. He wanted to abandon the idea of China as a rural entity because it was harmful to China's modernization: "Rural rehabilitation is a must today. However, I am afraid that everyone will be dazed and use *yinong liguo* just because they are proud [of China's ancient tradition]. [I am afraid that everyone will] believe that *yinong liguo* is the only way China can go and will start referring to it as an unalterable principle."[30]

According to Chen, there were three main problems with *yinong liguo.* First of all it would place too much stress on agriculture and, in this way, hinder China's current goal of import substitution, the first step toward autarky, without promoting significant growth in exports. Reversing China's unfavorable balance of trade could not be realized by preserving China's rural nature.

> First, with *yinong liguo* we definitely cannot make good [China's] unfavorable balance of trade [*ruchao*]. I basically think that, were we to follow *yinong liguo,* at best we could arrive at making up for one-fourth of annual imports of agricultural products such as rice, wheat, and cotton. After this, it appears that we will meet with natural barriers, which will not let us advance one step further. . . . Apart from this, large exports of products . . . will be impossible, unless we find a different solution other than agriculture. At the minimum we must start focusing on industry.[31]

The second problem, according to Chen, was that the formula of *yinong liguo* did not really have the meaning his contemporaries assigned to it. It was only an expression of China's feudal economy based on the exploitation of all productive forces by a small feudal class. The rhetoric of *yinong liguo,* according to Chen, had been used since the Han dynasty (200 BC–AD 220) for the sole purpose of supplying the noble and gentry classes with goods and food.[32] Emphasizing the purely rhetorical nature of the formula, Chen described it as a weakness of the imperial system that had led to the stifling of economic development. Since Han times, Chen complained, repressing commerce had been strictly a rhetorical device. In reality, repression had been applied to all economic activities, agricultural and commercial.

> During its past history, in spite of its stress on agriculture, China barely succeeded in becoming a "supplier of agricultural products" [*nong gong guo*]. It actually never succeeded in becoming a "country founded on agriculture" [*yinong liguo*]. . . . It is clear that the so-called "stress agriculture and repress commerce" position resulted only in repressing commerce. It is not clear, however, how it ever stressed agriculture.[33]

The third reason for Chen's opposition to preserving China's rural foundation was rooted in his economic determinist and evolutionist understanding of history. Agricultural countries were the victims of the expansionist drive of world powers (industrialized nations). All colonized countries, Chen explained, had agricultural economies, weak systems of industrial production, and low exports and high imports. China, Chen warned, was destined to become a colony unless it abandoned its traditional policy of giving priority to agriculture and started focusing its energies on industry.[34]

> An agricultural country [*yinong liguo*] not only will experience a constant decline of its economy but will also easily turn into a colony. . . . Countries with a peasant population of under 5 percent are all rich and powerful countries. Those with a peasant population of over 55 percent are all poor. Colonies such as Egypt and India all have [a peasant population of] over 60 percent.[35]

Maintaining a large rural population was thus, according to Chen, an invitation to be colonized. In addition, Chen did not believe in small-scale industry, which he considered absolutely incompatible with modernization. Small scale was, in his eyes, irremediably compromised by its connection to feudalism: "Old warlords go and new come. This is because our infant industry cannot set itself free from a small-scale, rural dimension."[36] In Chen's evolutionary scheme, the rural economy was tightly linked to a feudal political structure and small scale was equated with fragmentation, the antithesis of unity and modernity. Preserving the *yinong liguo* policy would not only deepen the rural crisis but also prevent China from moving forward in its evolutionary development. Without breaking the "undeniable feudal nature of the Chinese economy, China will have no chance to become a modern nation."[37] It was thus necessary to "revise this policy . . . in order to follow the development of the human endeavor."[38] The connection between the ideas of industrialization, modernity, and national power was at this point complete in Chen's analysis. "Does China have a way out?" Chen asked. His answer was "We have to transform *yinong liguo* into *yigongnong liguo* [a country founded on industry and agriculture]. This is the way to save China."[39]

In Chen's eyes, however, the development of the rural economy was to be subordinated to the development of the industrial sector and aimed at its support. In spite of its claim to respect the idea of "founding the country on agriculture," the plan lent agriculture foundational status only because of its importance in autarkic industrial development, not only as a supplier of raw materials but also as the privileged market for domestic goods: "China is an agricultural country and the success or decline of agriculture is strongly related to its foundations [*gouben*]. All commercial and industrial development depends on shifts in peasants' purchasing power. In the last few years, agriculture has increasingly declined and so has the livelihood of the peasants."[40] The rationale for rural development favored by Chen, and by the other leaders of the Nanjing government's National Economic Council (NEC), was thus different from that of Fang Xianting and other rural industrialists who wanted to base national economic development on the rural economy. The NEC instead sponsored the growth of agriculture in support of urban industrial development.[41]

One more important tactical difference between Chen and the rural industrializers was their approach to the problem of excessive population pressure on the land. The latter, as mentioned above, hoped to keep peasants in the village and thus focused their efforts on bringing development and new employment opportunities to the rural areas. The creation of nonagricultural jobs in the countryside, they argued, would relieve the current situation. Because he did not believe in small rural industries, Chen saw the migration of peasants toward urban industrial centers as the only solution to the problem.

Land, Population, and Development

One of the main reasons for Chen Gongbo's opposition to all policies inspired by *yinong liguo* was that they allowed an excessive growth of the peasant population. These policies had strained the country's agricultural resources and prevented an increase in agricultural output. This situation had, as Chen saw it, two major negative effects. First it had led to the fragmentation of arable land into small plots. "Too many peasants necessarily means land fragmentation," he lamented. In China, "generally . . . the peasants have very little land. [If we draw] a comparison with the United States, where farmers have an average of more than 70 *mu* [1 *mu* is equal to 0.1647 acres] each, [we can see that] the difference [in size between land plots in the two countries] is too large."[42] The small size of the plots was a reason for the chronic poverty of the peasants because they did "not generally have enough land to ensure self-sufficiency." The smallness of the plot also hindered technological innovation because "[if there are] too many peasants, mechanization of production [*jiqi shengchan*] becomes impossible. . . . In fact, too many peasants means that labor is necessarily cheap. If rural labor is cheap, then machines cannot be used. . . . At the same time, there is no need to use machines because land plots are too small."[43]

According to Chen, the pressure of such a large population on the land and the consequent small size of the agricultural plots were at the heart of a vicious circle that trapped China in economic stagnation. Because the plots were so small, it was impossible to mechanize agricultural production, thus limiting productivity. "If we don't find a way to reduce the number of peasants, China will not have any hope to have a large agricultural production."[44] This low level of productivity, Chen argued, led to a lack of any significant economic return. In this situation the peasants could hardly make enough to survive, let alone save any money, and this in turn led to a failure to accumulate capital to be invested for improving production or for expanding the area of arable land.

> While labor productivity [*laoli de gongneng*] is limited, the productivity of machines is not . . . but because [in China] it is not possible to use machines, production remains too small. There is [a relationship of] mutual causality. . . . Fertilizers are also an important factor in agriculture. Because [Chinese] peasants do not have savings they cannot buy chemical fertilizers. They can only use natural fertilizers. This makes it difficult to supply large-scale plots of land. This is another important reason why in China we cannot open up new land.[45]

Land reclamation, a traditional means of easing population pressure on agricultural resources, was also made impossible by a chronic lack of savings among peasants. Moreover, because the peasants could not afford new investments, they were even forced to give up those fields that had suffered damage from natural disasters.[46] "Arable land is already scarce but wasteland is actually increasing. It is very clear that after natural and manmade disasters, the [peasants have no other choice but] to abandon the land because generally there are no savings or no energy to plow the fields again."[47] Wasteland was thus increasing in a period when an expansion of arable land was most needed.

Chen completed his grim picture of China's agricultural vicious circle by describing the peasant trapped on his small plot, which "couldn't even support the simplest lifestyle," while contemplating the impossibility of ever being able to handle a larger plot. "Theoretically, the appropriate measure of [land] distribution [depends, on the one hand, on] . . . a man's ability [to work it] and the level of productivity of the land. [On the other, it] is [determined by the] relationships between these two variables and the return needed to support a family." In China, these two variables were not balanced, since land productivity and man's energy invested in the land did not yield enough to support a family. "China, at the moment, only employs man and animal power for plowing. This means that even if a man had 70 *mu* [to cultivate], he would not have enough energy to plow and seed them."[48] For Chen the rural economy thus seemed to be caught in a trap created by the mutual relationships between the unfavorable ratio of peasants to arable land and the consequent lack of capital accumulation, which prevented technical innovation and expansion of arable land. In this context, land redistribution, which would have generated even smaller land plots, appeared to him to be dangerous to China's economic development.

Chen's theory of agricultural stagnation immediately brings to mind the theory of the "high level equilibrium trap" presented by Mark Elvin in the early 1970s.[49] According to Elvin, Chinese agriculture had actually achieved its highest productivity level much earlier than Europe. Because of this early fit among productive factors, however, it had ultimately been trapped in stagnation in the modern period. Agricultural stagnation posed the most serious obstacle to development. Only the infusion of new technology, Elvin argued, could help China break free from its predicament. Elvin's theory was challenged in the mid-1980s by such scholars as Victor Lippit and Carl Riskin, who argued that China's primary problem was not the inability of its agriculture to produce a surplus. Surplus was actually generated, but it was wasted by the elite to sustain its extravagant way of life rather than being reinvested in economic activities. Carl Riskin contended that the success of the CCP after 1949 was due to its ability to gain control over that surplus. From this point of view the failure of the GMD was not its inability to stimulate the economy but its inability to mobilize the resources horded by the gentry. Development thus required social changes before production would increase.[50] The North American debate over agricultural problems in Republican China thus reproduced, to some extent, the basic split between the Nationalists' productivist and the Communists' distributionist approaches in the 1930s.

Chen's vision of the problem of land and population is also echoed in Richard Tawney's book *Land and Labor in China,* published in 1932. This should come as no surprise, since Tawney, an English economist and Christian Socialist, carried out the research for his book in close collaboration with Chinese economists. Above all he relied on essays from *Research in Chinese Economy* (*Zhongguo jingji yanjiu*), published by the renowned Economic Institute of Nankai University and its director of research Fang Xianting. Tawney was an official expert sent by the League of Nations to work with the NEC to help its leaders plan rural reform. In this capacity, he worked closely with Chen and the NEC reformers. Because of Tawney's close collaboration with Chinese economists, *Land and Labor in China* exemplifies a process of mutual influence. Tawney's *Land and Labor in China* resounds with themes and arguments that had been at the center of the Chinese discourse on the rural crisis in the late 1920s and early 1930s. At the same time, Tawney's book was accepted by Chinese and Western intellectuals as the first properly "scientific" study of China's rural economy, lending increased legitimacy to those Chinese themes and arguments since it came with the imprimatur of both the League of Nations and the British academic establishment. The Western method was, after all, unanimously considered the model of objective scientific research.

Like most Nationalists, Tawney did not believe that the problem in rural China was one of land tenure or class conflict. Instead, he argued, the most serious problem China faced was its increasing population. "The fundamental fact," he argued in *Land and Labor in China,* "is of a terrible simplicity. It is that the population of China is too large to be supported by existing resources." According to Tawney, contemporary "well-intentioned reforms do not begin to cope" with this overwhelming problem.[51] The only solution he saw was to develop an industrial system that would encourage peasants to migrate to the cities, thus relieving pressure in the rural areas. However, industrialization, he pointed out, was still a long-term goal and China needed to focus on stimulating agriculture as much as it could, mostly through technology transfer and improved marketing.

Tawney and Chen, therefore, shared a basic assumption about China's development. They both believed that in order to solve the rural crisis it was essential to break the pattern of stagnation in the agricultural economy. In spite of the similarities between Tawney and Chen and the mutual influence between foreign advisers and Chinese leaders and economists, Chen's rural policies were firmly rooted in the Nationalist productivist tradition that had begun in the 1920s with Sun Yat-sen and had been adopted by the Nanjing government at the time of its establishment in 1927. The productivist policies initiated by Sun were based on the assumption that rural poverty was a consequence, not of uneven distribution of wealth, but of insufficient production. A successful solution to the rural crisis would, therefore, be reached only by stimulating agriculture and focusing on technological innovation.

The Nationalist Productivist Approach

The first productivist position of the GMD was foreshadowed in Sun Yat-sen's 1924 lectures on the Principle of People's Livelihood (*minsheng zhuyi*). In these lectures Sun discussed the "social problem" of the impoverishment of the working masses that characterized the modern world, reaching the conclusion that it was primarily an economic issue and therefore required a strictly economic solution. The origins of the social problem, Sun explained, were to be found in the mechanization of industrial production, which had led to the replacement of workers with machines and, consequently, to unemployment and poverty. The socialists' attempts to solve the problem had been laudable but had been based on "moral stands and concerns" for equality, not on economic considerations, and therefore had ultimately failed to bring about any significant improvement. This failure demonstrated, Sun continued, that only a purely economic solution could be successful. Sun thus presented the socialist demand for wealth redistribution as a moral or social, rather than economic, measure, and as such, he declared it—together with Marxism and socialism in general—a utopian and unpractical dream that disregarded practical economic issues.[52] The only practical and economic solution that could solve the social question, Sun concluded, was increasing production, expanding the economy and generating enough wealth to comfortably support the entire population of the country. Sun's attempt to go beyond the socialist notion of wealth redistribution, closely tied to that of class struggle, had, once again, led him far away from the original meaning of Marxism, which saw wealth redistribution and the passage of control of the means of production to the workers as an intrinsically economic measure because it would deeply transform the economic structure of a country. Sun was generally reluctant to abandon the socialist rhetoric of social justice, but in an attempt to avoid class struggle and to promote the socioeconomic unity of the nation, he proposed alternative productivist means, which he described as strictly economic, to realize Socialist goals.[53]

Sun's combination of socialist goals and productivist solutions is exemplified most clearly in his policy of "land to the tillers" (*gengzhe you qitian*). The peasants "should own the land they till" and be able to directly enjoy the benefits of their work, free from landlords' exploitation. This goal, however, was to be achieved by adopting a program of "land equalization" (*pingjun tudi*). This program focused on rent reduction and tax reforms aimed, not at expropriation, but at a market-driven readjustment of landed property. As Sun explained, landlords themselves should declare the value of their land. Land tax and rent would then be calculated according to the figure they put forward. This strategy would result in deflating unfairly high rents while leading to a just taxation system. Landlords would be discouraged from submitting figures that exaggerated the real value of their land for fear of ending up paying too much in taxes. At the same time, they could not undervalue their property since they would then receive low rents. Sun believed that this strategy would encourage absentee landlords to sell their land since they could no longer rely on excessively high rents while having to pay only moderate taxes. This would make land available for peasants to buy at fair prices. The government would then assist them by offering credit for land purchase. At the same time rents would become cheaper, allowing the tillers to make a decent living from their hard work.[54]

Sun's productivist approach is further highlighted by the fact that he placed the issue of land reform in the section of his lectures on the Principle of People's Livelihood that was devoted to methods for increasing production, treating it at the same level of importance as technological improvements and land reclamation. According to Sun, if the peasants owned the land they worked and could enjoy the fruits of their labor, they would be more motivated to work the fields. Consequently, the number of peasants would increase, inevitably leading to larger crops. In calling for more labor on the land, Sun was holding on to an approach to agriculture that would soon be displaced by economists' concerns about China's growing population and the consequent increased pressure on the land. Fundamentally, at stake were two different ideas of economic modernity. The socialist (or communist) saw socioeconomic justice as the crucial characteristic of the most advanced economic system, going beyond the historical stage marked by capitalism and bourgeois rule. Sun, on the other hand, embraced newly emerging productivist notions which were to find their most extreme and radical manifestation in the Italian Fascist concept of production *ad oltranza* ("to the bitter end," as Il Duce liked to say) as the epitome of economic modernity.

In spite of his call for "land to the tillers," Sun was at odds with the Chinese Communists and communist theories at large, since he ultimately identified an increase in national production as the central solution to the social problem. In addition, he advocated only a limited amount of readjustment in land ownership and the use of market and tax-based methods (rather than expropriation and class struggle) as the preferred methods of readjustment of land ownership. In other words, for the CCP land redistribution was the most essential factor in solving the rural crisis, while for the GMD a limited readjustment in land ownership was only one among a number of equally important tools for increasing production.

The Principle of People's Livelihood was at the foundation of the productivist approach adopted by the Nanjing government in 1927. In 1928, Song Ziwen, then the minister of finance, stated that the goal of the government was economic development through expansion of national production by application of modern and scientific technology.[55] This productivist stance was reiterated in the 1931 *Provisional Law for the Tutelage Period* (*Zhonghua xunzheng shiqi yuefa*). Kong Xiangxi, minister of industry, explained that this law was based on the idea that China's problem was a problem, not of distribution, but of inadequate production. Increasing production, Kong argued, would naturally lead to an increase in national wealth that would be shared by the entire Chinese population.[56] In 1930 the government issued guidelines for agricultural reform, which, however, turned out to be more of a long-term goal than an immediate call to action. As such, it remained largely unimplemented. These guidelines followed Sun's principles of land equalization and also included the creation of credit facilities in rural areas to help farmers buy land while reducing rents by 25 percent.[57] Their productivist nature was also reflected in the priority they placed on increasing production by technological improvement while assigning the problem of land tenure peripheral importance. Following the promulgation of the 1930s guidelines, the GMD began preparing a land law. An ad hoc committee, the Land Commission, was established to conduct extensive land surveys and come up with a draft, which was then to be approved by the legislative body of the government, the Legislative Yuan. The commission was slow to produce a final report, which as expected remained within the parameters of the general idea of land equalization. The process of approval by the Legislative Yuan also proved slow and controversial. The land law was finally promulgated in 1937, just in time to be overridden by new wartime regulations.[58]

While the land law was held up in the legislature, some form of land reform was included in specifically targeted projects. They too, however, remained largely paper policies. This was the case, for example, with the "bandit extermination campaigns" launched by Jiang Jieshi in the 1930s. In December 1932, while speaking at the Land Affairs Bureau of the Central Political School, Jiang directly addressed the issue of land reform as an important aspect of his anti-Communist campaigns. In his speech, Jiang stressed the importance of resolving the rural question in order to successfully stop the Communists. Jiang argued that mere military force could not achieve the goal of "pacification." For this reason, he announced, the headquarters would adopt a new approach that included changes in land tenure. The bureau was invested with the task of drafting new regulations for land reorganization and determining quotas for land distributions. The goal of land redistribution was, according to Jiang, to transform renters into small landholders. Jiang, however, warned the audience that it was going to be a process of gradual transformation. Further, reforms would be implemented only after extensive research. Land redistribution, in this case also, ended up remaining a vague and theoretical goal for the distant future. Jiang perceived the support of the local elites to be crucial in his fight against the CCP in the rural areas and thus hesitated taking any action that went against their interests. In the areas involved in Jiang's anti-Communist military campaigns, in fact, land became even more concentrated in the hands of the elites, at the expense of the peasants.[59]

The few reforms Jiang adopted in support of his anti-Communist military activities were focused on gaining political and military control of the village, rather than rehabilitating it economically. He promoted the establishment of garrisoned villages (*tutian*), which were to combine two main functions: open up new land and ensure rural security. This project became a channel for the political and military mobilization of the peasants, who were regimented in new state-led economic-military organizations.[60] Even the name used for these villages was drawn from the military colonization of the former imperial system. Jiang, in keeping with his general approach to nation building, had transformed rural reforms into a vehicle for the anti-Communist militarization of the peasants, imitating the strategy he had so much admired in the work of the Qin official Guan Zhong.[61]

Wang and Chen, on the other hand, saw productivism as an alternative to Jiang's military anti-Communism, and in this sense they more closely followed the Nationalist productivist tradition initiated by Sun. For them, only an increase in production could lead the peasants out of poverty and offer a solution to the Communist problem. In 1934 Wang asked, "How can we exterminate Communist banditry?" His answer was that, "on the one hand, we must adopt military measures; on the other, we must employ political and economic means to develop productive enterprises. Only thus can the problem be fundamentally solved."[62] For Wang it was important to offer an alternative to the class-based revolutionary option advanced by the CCP. If the peasants, he argued, saw their standard of living improve, they would no longer be motivated to support the Communists. In short, Wang and Chen were as anti-Communist as Jiang but envisioned different ways to counteract them. They thus perceived productivist reforms in the village as the solution to both the Communist challenge and China's crisis as a whole. Wang's and Chen's productivism also differed from Fang's, who perceived the improvement of the rural economy as a means to preserve China's rural identity, paving the way for industrialization based in rural cooperative societies. The productivist policies of Chen and Wang, on the other hand, represented a way to transfer to the rural areas technologies and modern business practices that had already developed in the urban centers, all the better to support the industries of the urban centers. It was the urban cosmopolitan identity of China that was to lead the country's modernization. The native identity of China preserved in the rural village was perceived by Chen and his collaborators as mostly backward and feudal and consequently an obstacle to development.

Transferring Modernity: From Shanghai to the Rural Village

Chen Gongbo's view of the role of urban and rural areas in China's modernization was shared by those members of the Shanghai economic elite who closely cooperated with him in the realization of economic reform during the years of the Wang-Jiang coalition. As products of the new coastal economy, they perceived the rural areas as a different China from the one they experienced in the treaty ports, a China that was still trapped in medieval times and lacked the basic institutions of modern entrepreneurship. They contrasted grim images of a backward and dormant rural village in opposition to the energetic and "modern" entrepreneurial spirit of Shanghai. On the basis of this modernity, they claimed that the coastal economy should lead the economic development of the entire nation. Especially vocal among the urban industrializers was Chen Guangfu, founder and director of the Shanghai Commercial and Savings Bank (*Shanghai shangye chuxu yinhang*). As a member of the NEC and the chairman of the Cotton Control Commission (CCC), a subcommittee of the NEC discussed at length later, Chen Guangfu played an important role in the realization of Chen Gongbo's economic plan.

Chen Guangfu received his education in the United States, an experience which made a deep and lasting impression on him. Upon his return to China he became committed to transforming China's financial institutions in keeping with Western models. At the same time he continued to cultivate good relationships with prominent businessmen in the United States and Europe while attempting to attract foreign capital investment in China.[63] Chen began his career as inspector for the Jiangsu Provincial Bank, and in 1914 he was appointed adviser to the Bank of China. In 1915 he left the Jiangsu Provincial Bank and founded the Shanghai Commercial and Savings Bank, which he tried to mold into a modern institution of the kind he had observed in the West. His pioneering work in modern banking was not limited to the introduction of Western-style accounting, working style, and personnel training but also involved the scope of his bank's activities. The Shanghai Commercial and Savings Bank was among the first in China to open savings accounts for private customers, even accepting small deposits of a few yuan, and stressed the importance of offering such a service to the community on the model of many American banks. The bank also extended credit to factories, not only to merchant enterprises, as traditional banks generally did. Credit was usually secured on the factory's stock of raw materials, which was left with the factory under the surveillance of a bank representative. Branches were opened along major railroad lines in order to support the marketing of industrial raw material by offering credit facilities away from major urban centers.[64]

In 1933 Chen Guangfu compared the vital economic life of the coastal areas with life in the rural hinterland. He concluded that the future of China lay in the urban economic modernity of the coastal cities and not in the medieval stagnation of the rural village in the interior:

> When one travels abroad, no matter if in England or the United States, [one can hear] everyone asking each other, "How is your business?" But, when one goes to China's hinterland . . . [one hears] people asking each other when meeting, "Has this been a good year?" If it has been a good year, everyone rejoices. If it has been a bad year, everyone is absolutely stricken with grief. This is the so-called "rely on Heaven for food" [*kaotian chifan*] approach. The idea that one must "rely on Heaven for food" is the greatest danger for our future. This "rely on Heaven for food" implies that when one meets with a bad year, one immediately takes refuge in the notion that "fatal calamities are difficult to escape."[65]

Chen Guangfu was thus unconcerned with preserving a presumed Chinese identity. For him modernity resided in the Western industrialized countries, which represented the model that China should follow. The rural areas fell short because they seemed to be living in the equivalent of the European Middle Ages, when superstition and fatalism trapped people in poverty and backwardness. It was the ability to break free from this lethargic attitude, to fight against nature and harness it to serve man's purpose, that, according to Chen, marked the beginning of the modern era in Europe. For this reason, he wrote, "today in Europe this [attitude] belongs to the past and to fairy tales. It is clear that people are resourceful in changing Heaven's will. The hopeless delusion that one must 'rely on Heaven for food' must be destroyed." For Chen, European modernity was marked by the use of science and technology, which determined its superiority and constituted its source of power. "[Foreigners] use scientific means of production, while we cannot avoid suffering nature's whims to the point that men lack the basics of clothing, food, shelter, and means of travel [*yi, shi, zhu, xing*]." Resorting to the trope of clothing, food, shelter, and means of travel, Chen stressed how the decline of the rural village threatened the very life of the peasants and of the nation as a whole. "Today we cannot have lofty talk of economic problems, such as currency, customs duties, unemployment, etc. . . . Our country has not yet solved its problem of basic survival [*bensheng*]." It was therefore the awakening of the people to the power of science, technology, and modern entrepreneurship that became central to Chen's assessment of modernity and the backwardness of the Chinese peasants. "Common people in the interior are in a state of dreamy delusion,"[66] he bemoaned, echoing a view of the village popularized by the urban and cosmopolitan intellectuals of the New Culture Movement.

In contrast to the backward medieval mentality of the rural hinterland, Chen Guangfu presented the modernity and vitality of the urban coastal areas. He argued that the commercial ports of China had reached a more advanced stage of development than the countryside. The gap between the two economies, rural-interior and urban-coastal, and between the mentalities of the people of these areas, he feared, was increasing dramatically. Following the main Nationalist stream of rural rehabilitation thinking, Chen believed that the way to rescue the village from its state of "dreamy delusion" was to import those institutions that made Shanghai modern: banks, credit organizations, and marketing.

> I have often traveled in the interior, but never before have I received such a deep impression. In large coastal commercial ports we generally see banks, exchanges, large factories, as well as credit, production, and marketing organizations. But these are present only in tiny numbers in those

> areas of our country with yellow earth and large masses of population. If we compare the number [of such organizations in the rural areas] with those of our national economy, we can say that they are completely insignificant.[67]

It was thus the duty of the modern, awakened, urban entrepreneur to save China by exporting to the countryside the modern economic institutions of the cities.

The Shanghai entrepreneurs thus shared with agriculturalists, economists, and reformers basic assumptions about the solution to the rural crisis, specifically the need for an infusion of credit into the rural economy and for improved marketing strategies, themes also discussed by Fang Xianting and Chen Gongbo. Differences, however, persisted between rural and urban industrializers in the ultimate vision of development. Chen Guangfu's mobilization of the countryside was to be completely in support of the urban-coastal industry. Like Chen Gongbo, he identified large scale with modernity, listing it as one of the signs of urban progress. For Chen Guangfu the rural and the urban economy needed to be intimately connected, overcoming the current gap in time and evolution. The urban areas, cut off from the international market, could not just discard the hinterland and move by themselves toward progress. Their close relationship with the countryside forced them to slow down and to wait for their poor and unenlightened traveling companion to catch up. According to Chen Guangfu, the rural villages' lagging behind was not only a living symbol of China's backwardness but also an obstacle to the health of the urban-coastal economies. In 1933, at the time of his participation in the CCC, he argued that "the prosperity of the commercial ports relies completely on the economic power [*jingjili*] of the interior."[68]

On the more practical side, the productivist approach of the Wang group was particularly appealing to many Shanghai industrialists, and especially cotton entrepreneurs, who, trapped between the effects of the Great Depression and the loss of international markets due to emerging protectionist and autarkic policies worldwide, found themselves forced to reconfigure their production and marketing strategies. The cost of imported raw materials was becoming increasingly prohibitive as a result of the rise in the price of silver. Forced to rely on low-quality domestic supplies and to produce low-quality goods, Chinese mill owners were unable to compete in foreign markets and at home were easily outsold by Japanese and British cotton imports. The rehabilitation of domestic raw material and an increase in peasants' purchasing power were thus perceived as essential for the survival of Shanghai's cotton mills.

Conclusion

The 1930s debate on the rural question reveals the uncertainty about nation building among China's Nationalist leadership and the diversity of approaches supported by different groups within its camp. The reform plans supported by the Wang group and by Fang Xianting, although they differed on the issue of China's national identity, shared a deep commitment to extensive reforms that would have significantly changed the economic landscape of China. Jiang Jieshi's militarist approach and his attempt to postpone reforms to a moment in the future when the Communists would be eliminated deprived the Nationalists of an opportunity to economically rehabilitate rural China on a large scale. The Nanjing Decade was followed by full war with Japan and then by a violent and disruptive civil war that drove the GMD from the Chinese mainland.

The question thus arises once again of whether a reformist GMD, committed to economic reform and focused on economic recovery, would have ultimately been more successful in its confrontation with the CCP in the interwar years. Productivist policies per se were not enough to undermine the credibility of socialist and communist movements in European countries, because the regimes (like the Italian and the German) that adopted them most often accompanied them with social-conservative measures that kept wealth concentrated in the hands of the higher classes and imposed limits on the prosperity of workers in general, and especially peasants. The reformist spirit of Wang Jingwei's and Chen Gongbo's approach to rural reconstruction, however, could have had better results, since, in China, communism had not yet developed as a mass movement and did not have the socioeconomic roots it had in Europe. In addition, in Europe the prewar socialist movements that marked the resistance against Mussolini and Hitler were politically strong both before and after the war, and both times were on the verge of gaining control of their countries. The European political discourse at large thus precluded the success of productivism in a way that would not necessarily be repeated in China.

Like most economic policies advocated by the Wang group, productivism came to reach beyond its economic dimension to become a basic strategy for nation building. It aimed at bridging the gap between the rural and urban economies and thus potentially could have contributed to the formation of a nationally integrated economic system and, in Chen's words, its transformation into an economic unit (*jingji danwei*). It also supported the development of an autarkic *minzu* industry and, consequently, had the potential for ending dependency on Japan. Solving the rural question thus became crucial in defining national identity, counterposing rural essence and hinterland, on the one side, and coastal industry and cosmopolitanism, on the other. The role of the village in China's modernization and the question of what industrial model would best fit the country were vital elements of the discourse on the nation as reflected in nation-building strategies.

Wang's and Chen's plan for rural recovery and their idea of the role of the village in the nation appears to contain one major contradiction. The autarkic China they were trying to build was to rely on the country's most cosmopolitan groups and on the areas that had based their modernization on contact with the outside world. In other words, although their call for autarky would have led China to insularity, it was an insularity that would have rested on China's most cosmopolitan groups (the coastal business elites) and on full participation with global trends. This contradiction is, however, only superficial. For Wang and Chen, autarky represented a model of economic modernity and as such could not look back to China's traditional economy. It had, instead, to be based on modern industries, advanced technologies, and the modern economic outlook of those who, like Chen Gongbo himself and Chen Guangfu, had been exposed to Western modernity.

Although the rural question, with its anti-Communist goals and productivist strategy, evoked main themes of Italian Fascism, it also departed from it in significant ways. The rhetoric of Italian Fascism was redundantly pro-rural. "We must ruralize Italy," Il Duce declared.[69] Ruralization was supposed to foster the physical and moral health of the race, family values, and the joy of creative work.[70] The Italian regime thus announced that its goals were to give land to peasants (*sbracciantizzazione*, "elimination of rural wage work") and encourage cooperative societies, rural credit, and land reclamation.[71] This rhetorical stand, which came closer to the position of the Chinese rural modernizers than to that of the NEC leaders, did not preclude the Italian government from pursuing policies in favor of the large industrial interests. Fascist land reclamation programs and the Wheat Campaign helped war preparation and industrialization more than the rural economy. In addition, although autarkic policies forced urban and industrial Italy to increase their reliance on the rural areas for supplies of raw materials, Italian leaders did not perceive the integration of rural and urban areas as crucial for national unity and nation building. This was not only because, after unification, Italian concerns for national integration were focused on the north-south divide but also because of mere geographical reasons: villages and cities in small and narrow Italy were more integrated and physically closer than in China. In this respect, China's geographical characteristics, especially its vast and remote hinterland, created a different set of problems for Chinese reformers and influenced their notion of nation building.

The 1930s debate on rural China inevitably leads us to establish a parallel with today's China. It is the coastal cosmopolitan economic elites who are now, once again—after years of Maoist rural rhetoric—called to lead the country toward development and modernization. As in the 1930s, however, doubts and questions arise about the effect of China's participation in the global consumer culture on China's identity and about the corrupting influence that consumer culture exercises on the morals of the nation, as discussed in more detail later.

Building the Corporativist State PART II

叁

CHAPTER 3

The Politics of Reconstruction: Song Ziwen and the National Economic Council

The building of the *minzu* economy and the transformation of China into the autarkic and centralized system envisioned by Wang Jingwei and Chen Gongbo required, as Chen fervently argued, a powerful state capable of exercising economic control at all levels of the economy. The Nanjing government was, however, far from meeting these requirements. Its authority was challenged by provincial leaders who resented its centralization effort, seriously limiting Nanjing's ability to carry out reforms in the provinces. Even more serious, however, were the problems that afflicted the central government itself. Nanjing politics were characterized by deep political divisions that brought its decision-making process to a halt and prevented any sustained reform effort.

This state of affairs in Nanjing was the antithesis of the idea of centralization that informed the Nationalist discourse on modern nationhood. Although most Nationalist leaders, including Wang Jingwei and Jiang Jieshi, believed that centralization was the prerequisite to a modern state, they were unwilling to allow centralizing reforms to be carried out under the aegis of one of their opponents promoting a different vision of nation building from their own. Ironically, it was the very attempt to build a highly centralized state that led to the fragmentation of the Nanjing government. The idea of democratic centralism that had inspired Sun Yat-sen's 1924 reorganization of the party precluded the creation of official channels for political negotiation. Dissent, therefore, could not be expressed at any level of the decision-making process and leaders who supported competing political lines were destined to be marginalized. In this situation, each faction, unable to control the entire government and unwilling to concede to their political rivals, attempted to gain control over one or more administrative bodies and to use them as political strongholds and as channels for the realization of their political agendas. The entire bureaucracy was thus fragmented into administrative blocks responding to competing political leaders, making political coordination impossible.

The instability and fragmentation of the Nanjing government was above all the result of the two competing political lines within the GMD that had developed in Canton: the military line headed by Jiang and the reformist civilian line headed primarily by Wang Jingwei and Hu Hanmin. Because he controlled the military, Jiang was undoubtedly the strongest of the three leaders. However, he had not yet achieved enough political power and legitimacy to be able to completely exclude Wang and Hu from the government. Jiang's view of a militarized Nationalist China was, in fact, not popular among most GMD leaders or among the intellectual and economic elites who had supported the party so far. Jiang was thus forced to enter into coalition governments, first with Hu (1927–31) and then with Wang (1932–35), eventually resorting to unyielding obstructionism against any reform initiative they launched.

Because of the importance of economic modernization in the Nationalist discourse on nation building, the economic administration of the government became a particular object of contention. Each of the three leaders established his own economic planning agency and attempted to gain control over economic reforms and to set the country on what he perceived to be the correct path to nation building. Hu established the National Reconstruction Commission (*jianshe weiyuanhui*) (and assigned his close associate Zhang Renjie to chair it), and the Wang group the NEC. These agencies differed in their reform plans, reflecting the different economic ideas of their leaders, but shared two important traits. They both placed the economy at the very core of nation building and identified the Jiangnan industrial elite as the foundation of the new nation. To further complicate the administrative incongruities of the Nanjing government, Jiang secretly developed a parallel and competing economic planning agency, the Military Planning Commission, which he hoped to elevate to the top of the economic bureaucracy once he had silenced his civilian opposition. Three different visions of China's modern economy and nation thus competed to gain control over the government and to shape it according to their goals.

When the Wang group arrived in Nanjing, it faced the contradiction of planning the economic centralization of the country within a deeply divided central government. The early years of the coalition were, however, marked by the hope that the Wang group could consolidate its control over the government and confine Jiang to the military. The Wang-Jiang coalition began with the Wang group solidly in charge of ministries it considered crucial to carrying out its plan and ensuring government-wide coordination. The Wang group controlled the Ministries of Finance (Song Ziwen), Industry (Chen Gongbo), Communications (Chen Mingshu), Railways (Gu Mengyu), and Foreign Affairs (Luo Wengan).[1] Wang's success seemed especially to be guaranteed by Song Ziwen's support. In 1931 Song had established the NEC, planning to make it the highest economic planning agency of the government. Because it was placed above all the other bodies of the government bureaucracy, Song hoped that the NEC could manage to achieve the much-needed, but elusive, interdepartmental coordination and thus become a vehicle for unified decision making and effective reform implementation. Song's cooperation and the Wang group's unobstructed access to the NEC (a hostile Song could have employed the same obstructionist tactics used by Jiang) were thus particularly important for the Wang group. The NEC became the expression of the Song-Wang alliance and of the civilian reformist vision of economic nation building. As Wang stated in 1934, "'Unification by Reconstruction' is the settled policy of the National Government, and it is proposed to reach that goal to a large extent through the agency of the National Economic Council."[2]

Song Ziwen also brought to the Wang group firsthand knowledge of the dynamics of Nanjing politics, which Wang and Chen had not experienced due to their forced exile. Song had been in charge of Nationalist finances since the time of the party's reorganization in Canton. After the establishment of the Nanjing government in 1927, he had energetically resumed his work of modernizing the government's financial and economic administration. By 1932, Song had become frustrated with Nanjing's decision-making impasse and Jiang's unyielding obstructionism and was ready to support Wang. Song hoped that the political backing of Wang, who was the new chairman of the Executive Yuan, would finally allow him to carry out his reform plan. Similarly, Wang needed Song's political and economic connections, experience, and administrative skills to carry out his. Their cooperation was not just opportunistic but was built on shared goals. Like Wang and Chen, Song strongly believed in economic and financial unification and opposed Jiang's military nation building. The three leaders also shared the goal of reorienting the Chinese economy away from Japan's influence as a way to resist Japan's imperialist ambitions. Song was also a supporter of the Jiangnan entrepreneurial elites and considered them the foundation of the modern Chinese nation. For this reason Song had attempted to include them in the Nationalist nation-building effort since the establishment of the Nanjing government.

In this chapter I will introduce two closely interrelated themes. I will discuss Song Ziwen's ideas of economic modernization and show that Wang's and Chen's ideas of nation building had wide resonance among most of the Nationalist civilian leaders. Wang's ideas embodied the main strands of Sun Yat-sen's reformist heritage laid out in *Fundamentals of National Reconstruction* and in the Three People's Principles, which, as I argued in previous chapters, provided the foundation for Nationalist political and economic thought, in spite of their occasional ambiguities and vagaries.

In addition, I will examine how the political disunity of the Nanjing government and the uncertainty caused by the struggle for its leadership prevented the modernization of the state, as formulated by Song, Wang, and Chen, undermining their reform effort. Faced by Jiang's obstructionism, the three leaders were forced to abandon the idea of centralizing the government. Even the NEC, their last hope for government-wide coordination, gradually lost its centralizing and coordinating powers, while Jiang reasserted his control over large portions of the administration. Ultimately, the NEC was able to extend its reformist intervention to only a few industries, falling short of its proposed national scope.

The Wang group was unable to resolve the contradiction between the idea of centralization as a prerequisite to modern nationhood and the political split in the party. The question thus arises of whether the economic modernity proposed by the Wang group could have been achieved without political and administrative modernization (understood as centralization). In 1936 a bitterly disappointed Chen Gongbo lamented that "for realizing economic control two conditions are needed: unified government and unified *minzu*." Without these, he continued, there was no chance of success. After his experience in the Wang-Jiang cabinet, therefore, Chen himself questioned the policy that he had outlined in 1933 and that aimed at using economic control as the most effective tool for national unification. He had now come to believe that political unification was actually the prerequisite for economic control.[3]

Song Ziwen

Song Ziwen was the son of Charles Jones Song, a prominent businessman who, taking advantage of the opportunities offered by the treaty port economy of Shanghai, built a fortune in the late nineteenth and early twentieth centuries. Song Ziwen completed his education in the United States and was apparently more comfortable speaking English than Chinese, and his Westernized manners made him a favorite within Western financial circles.[4] Because of his strong personality and independent attitude toward political affairs, Song's relationship with the Nanjing government was often stormy. Jiang Jieshi valued Song's financial abilities but disagreed with his ideas on economic and financial reforms and, above all, with his determination to cut military expenditures and to concentrate capital investment in support of the development of the coastal (and especially Jiangnan's) industrial sector.

A major difficulty in understanding Song's political career arises from the contradiction between his disagreements with Jiang in the Nanjing Decade and his participation in the Nationalist government through World War II and the postwar years. This contradiction is even more mystifying because of the ambiguity that surrounds Song's personality and ideas. Unlike many other leaders of his time, Song never wrote his memoirs or left behind theoretical writings that could shed light on his work and behavior (a factor that has influenced the tone of this chapter, since, in order to understand his political goals, I had to rely solely on an analysis of Song's political activities rather than on his writings). Some have argued that his family ties with Jiang, who married his sister, Song Meiling, in spite of Song's early opposition, explains his protracted presence at the apex of the government.[5] If this is this case, Song must have been torn between family loyalty and his faith in financial and economic modernization. Yet this is only a partial explanation of the apparent contradiction of his political career. Other factors to be taken into consideration emerge from an analysis of Song's vision of modern finance and economy, his reform project, and the means he used to realize it. Such an analysis shows that Song placed much emphasis on financial and economic centralization. Although Song was not completely satisfied with Jiang's leadership, his belief that China needed a strong, centralized state led him to be loyal to the central government even if under Jiang's leadership rather than to join one of the many separatist movements that challenged Jiang's authority.

His decision differed from Hu Hanmin's and Wang Jingwei's, who, rather than accept political compromises, preferred to fight Jiang, and the entire Nanjing Government, from outside. Wang participated in the government from 1932 to 1935, believing he could influence its political direction. When he could not, Wang preferred to wage opposition first from Canton, before 1932, and later from Nanjing, when he collaborated with the Japanese (an issue that forms the focus of chapter 7). Song, on the other hand, believed that China needed urgent reforms and that the government should set aside factional struggles in order to proceed immediately to reconstructing the country.[6] For Song, unity often justified compromise. We can speculate that, being a pragmatist, Song knew that no one had a political future outside Nanjing. Leaving the government would lead ultimately only to political oblivion. For this reason, in the prewar years, Song opposed further political fragmentation and preferred to play the role of a skillful political *trasformismo*[7] from within the government itself. He used a variety of strategies to force Jiang to accept his reforms, manipulating different groups in order to realize his agenda.

Centralization of finances and economy under the GMD's authority was Song's foremost goal, inspiring his work from the time he was first appointed as minister of finance to the Nationalist government in Guangdong in 1925.[8] At the time, Sun Yat-sen was preparing for the Northern Expedition and Song's task was to create a solid financial base to support it. To achieve this goal, Song embarked on a reorganization of the central and local tax administrations, ostensibly aimed at eradicating corruption and waste but, in reality, also intending to consolidate Nationalist control at the expense of local authorities and economic elites.[9] Following the establishment of the new national government in Nanjing in 1927, Song was eager to start working on China's financial and economic reconstruction and administrative centralization, expanding to the national level the work he had initiated in Guangdong. Only two weeks after the National Revolutionary Army (NRA) entered Beijing in June 1928, Song sent a telegram to provincial governments in which he called for centralization, warning them that the autonomy they had enjoyed was over: "Now that the Northern Expedition has been completed, finances must be unified, all reconstruction work must be planned, and measures actively taken."[10]

In 1928 centralization and unification of finances were, however, daunting tasks. A variety of currencies circulated inside China until the currency reform of 1935.[11] Provincial governments and local militarists freely minted their own money, flooding the markets with devalued currency. This situation was a major obstacle to any attempt at a planned economy or central control over the money supply. It also hindered the expansion of commerce by limiting the circulation of goods among the various regions and deepening the regional character of the Chinese economy. This regionalist trend was further deepened by the fact that local governments often devised currency policies targeted at promoting the local economy in competition with both neighboring provinces and Nanjing.[12] The taxation system was equally fragmented and harmful to interregional trade, as exemplified by the existence of the *lijin* tax, which Song eliminated in 1931 as part of his plan for financial unification.[13] As had been the case with the Guangdong reforms, Song's drive for national financial centralization was Janus faced. On the one side, it found strong justification as a prerequisite to any effective nationwide reform effort, being crucial for economic development and stability. On the other, it served the goal of consolidating the GMD's power and eliminating pockets of resistance in the provinces.

As was the case with most Nationalist reforms in this period, the main obstacles Song encountered did not come from the provinces, but from within the Nanjing government. Song had to face Jiang's fierce obstructionism, since his reform goals went against Jiang's own plans. Song, like Wang and Chen, wanted to focus nation building on financial and economic reforms. He thus pushed for demobilization and for shifting resources from the military into economic development. In addition, Song saw the emerging Jiangnan industrial economy as the foundation, the very "lifeblood" in his own words, of the modern Chinese nation and eagerly sought to establish what he perceived to be a mutually beneficial relationship between Nanjing and the Jiangnan entrepreneurial elite.

The National Economic Conference: Defining the Chinese Modern Economy

Demobilization and alliance with the Jiangnan elite constituted the main themes of the National Economic Conference (*quanguo jingji huyi,* June 1928) convened by Song soon after the NRA entered Beijing. As Song stated in his official call for the conference, the military phase of the revolution was over and the government was finally turning to reconstruction.[14] This meant, he continued, a shift to civilian leadership, a reduction of the military budget, and the employment of government resources in development-inducing policies. In spite of the fact that the reform program Song presented at the National Economic Conference was similar to the one attempted in Guangdong—strengthening central authority, unifying finances, and creating a solid financial base for the government—its goals widely differed, since it would no longer channel resources to support military action but into demobilization and economic reconstruction.

The reforms that Song presented at the conference reflected his stated purpose of creating a propitious environment for economic development. Song promised that the government would end the unpopular policy of bond floating. As soon as the NRA approached Shanghai in 1927, the GMD had resorted to the sale of government bonds and direct borrowing from Shanghai's major bankers and industrialists, who had, sometimes voluntarily and other times under coercion, contributed to its military effort.[15] Bond floating was considered by most of the civilian political leaders of the GMD and Jiangnan's businessmen to be a short-sighted policy and ultimately harmful to China's finances and economy. Their main criticism was that bonds did not lead to productive employment of already-scarce

Chinese capital but rather turned it into fuel for civil war and factional military struggle. In his opening speech, although Song justified the GMD's issuance of bonds to finance the Northern Expedition, he apologized for that measure and then promised that the government would undertake a fresh start in all economic matters and funnel funds into productive activities.[16] The government would also introduce a policy of open (*gongkai*) finances, in contrast to the existing practice of secret management of government resources, to make sure that, under the scrutiny of the Chinese people, resources were properly employed for developing economic production.

In addition, Song announced a comprehensive currency reform and the establishment of a National Budget Commission, which was to cooperate with the Ministry of Finance to set up a national budget system. The commission was to have the task of deciding on government expenditures as well as controlling their use by various agencies in order to curtail corruption and the expenditure of funds in a manner contrary to the original intent determined by the budget committee.[17] A reliable budget and unified financial system, Song explained, were vital to the modernization of China's financial administration and to the success of any government action on the economy.

Finally, Song advocated the establishment of a close collaborative relationship between Nanjing and the Jiangnan elite. Song explained that governmental finances and private economy were closely connected and highly interdependent. Only a healthy national economy could produce a reliable national tax base and provide the central government with the capital necessary to fund national reconstruction. As he explained in 1928, Song believed that "finances are the lifeblood of the government; financial reorganization must focus on the national economy"; for this reason "an . . . effort [must be made] with the cooperation of the people" and "public opinion must be taken into consideration."[18] This statement not only advocated a relationship of interdependency and collaboration between Nanjing and the private economy but also assigned the Jiangnan elite a privileged place in the new nation by directly identifying them with its basic socioeconomic group—in other words, its "people."

When Song used the term "people," he referred exclusively to the Jiangnan entrepreneurial elite. It was this group that he invited to participate in the conference, while excluding representatives of other socioeconomic interests. Seventy percent of the conference participants were leaders of Zhejiang's major industrial and financial groups and natives of Zhejiang and Jiangsu. Among them were Chen Guangfu; Yu Hede (styled Qiaqing), founder and director of the Ningbo Commercial and Savings Bank (or Simin

Savings Bank), director of the Shanghai Stock and Goods Exchange (*zhengquan wupin jiaoyisuo*), and chairman of many Shanghai-based commercial and industrial associations; Rong Zongjing, owner and manager of the Shenxin cotton mills, the largest industrial group in China; Zhang Jia'ao, a member of the GMD political studies group, a prominent economist and banker, general manager of the Bank of China, and vice-minister of finance under Song Ziwen; Wang Xiaolai, director of the Shanghai Chamber of Commerce; and the omnipresent Xu Xinliu, a member of the committee for tax collection in the international foreign concession and of the board of trustees of Fudan University and whose interests also expanded into banking and the textile industry.[19]

The press did not fail to remark on Song's elitist policies and harshly criticized Song for relying only on the business community. The exclusion of peasants, workers, and student representatives from the conference, critics pointed out, would certainly lead to a one-sided policy similar to that implemented in capitalist countries. This, the criticism continued, contradicted the official GMD doctrine as laid out in Sun Yat-sen's Three People's Principles (referring specifically to the Principle of People's Livelihood, which embodied the Nationalists' most socialistic trend) and raised suspicions that the conference represented only the capitalist class.[20] These criticisms were fully justified by Song's selective invitations. The conference made it clear that Song's first concern was with increasing industrial production as a means to achieve the modernization of the country, revealing the early roots of the full-fledged productivist approach he developed in the 1930s.

The 1928 conference seemed to confirm Song Ziwen's reputation as the strongest supporter of liberal capitalism among the Nationalist leaders of his time. This was, and still is, the prevalent opinion in the United States, where Song had studied and worked for some time and where he enjoyed close relationships with prominent financial magnates such as J. P. Morgan. Song indeed showed a marked probusiness attitude, which can be ascribed in part to the fact that he was a businessman himself. His political involvement with the Nationalist Party was a long-standing family affair, initiated by his father. Charlie Jones Song had been an early supporter of Sun Yat-sen and had generously helped finance Sun's political ambitions. Business and politics were naturally connected in Song's view. Song's probusiness attitude, however, can hardly be identified with mainstream liberal capitalism, since it developed within the general antiliberal trends of Nationalist political and economic thought. Song's formulation of the relationship between Nanjing and the private economy was rather vague. In keeping with the tutelage policies of the Nanjing government,

Song gave businessmen no assurance other than the goodwill of the government with respect to their interests. Following Sun Yat-sen's *Fundamentals of National Reconstruction*, which decreed a three-phase transition to democracy—revolution, tutelage, and democracy—the Nanjing government had decreed that it was now engaged in the political education of the Chinese people, postponing the realization of representative democracy to a future moment, when they would be able to shoulder the responsibility of active political participation. The Nationalist state, in fact, did not allow any channel of official representation of socioeconomic groups within the government and did not hold the government responsible to any kind of constituency. The only power the Jiangnan entrepreneurs held at the time was their ability to pay taxes and to finance the famously bankrupt Nanjing government. The presence at the conference of Xu Xinliu, who on this occasion appeared to represent the tax collection office of the Ministry of Finance, clearly illustrates how much Song appreciated this ability.

Although the National Economic Conference marked an unprecedented overture by the government to the Jiangnan elite, it highlighted how Nationalist political and economic thought precluded a liberal-style relationship between government and private business. Negotiations between Song and the Jiangnan representatives had to take place outside the conference, since active participation of societal groups in politics was not permitted in Nanjing politics. The conference itself was a staged ritual, devised to testify to the unity of intent and interests between state and private economy. The conference was therefore preceded by a series of preparatory meetings organized by Zhang Jia'ao, which produced a series of proposals for Song's consideration. Zhang, who acted as the official spokesman of the entrepreneurs, presented these proposals at the conference.[21] The conference was a carefully staged political ceremony, performing a mostly symbolic function and showing to the public and to the government factions that opposed demobilization that Song was the link to the Jiangnan economy, the main source of capital for the Nanjing government.

The conference, however, cemented an alliance between Song and the Jiangnan elite since Song's proposed reforms appear to have satisfied the entrepreneurs' main concerns. Their official statement at the conference, which was the result of the preparatory meetings and was presented by Zhang, complained about the disruptive effects of prolonged military conflict on Shanghai's economy and welcomed the government's resumption of economic reconstruction. It stressed the importance of restoring social order and private rights in order to ensure proper conditions for private investment while freeing the economy from pressure by reducing military expenses and setting up a healthy financial and banking system. Although this statement recognized the leading role of the state in promoting industrial development, it also expressed the hope that the government would respect the private sector and support its development. The representatives of the economic community also presented proposals for returning properties previously confiscated by the government and for the regulation of labor activism.[22] In fact, entrepreneurs had found in Song a champion for their cause in Nanjing. As Zhang announced, they agreed to rely on him, because he was "one of the people, having close relationships with economic circles."[23]

As the documentation of the conference shows (even if probably manipulated by Song to fit his political agenda), the alliance between Nanjing and the Jiangnan economic elite appeared, in this early stage, to be based on a concrete series of shared interests. The alliance, however, was more specifically between Song and the Jiangnan elite rather than between the state and private economy at large. The conference established their cooperation in as official a manner as the political background allowed and gave Song the strength and legitimacy to pursue his plan. This was a point that the press was also ready to denounce, claiming that Song had worked singlehandedly, excluding the rest of the Nanjing bureaucracy because he wanted to control the government's financial and economic administration, cutting off agencies that represented political opposition to his plan.[24] Song's tactics soon became clear. One hundred representatives of the economic community who had participated in the conference went to Nanjing at the time of the National Financial Conference (July 1928), a government meeting that was to officially approve Song's plan. Yu Hede led the delegation, which represented the Shanghai General Chamber of Commerce, the Nandao and Zhabei Chambers, the Shanghai Bankers Association, and sixty Shanghai guilds. The Shanghai delegation issued an ultimatum threatening to deny any further loans to the government if the decisions reached at the National Economic Conference were not approved. Under such pressure the National Financial Conference and, soon afterward, the party's Fifth Plenum passed Song's plan.[25]

At the Fifth Plenum, however, exactly at the moment when it seemed that Song had scored a major victory, his plan, although accepted, was stripped of its original spirit. In spite of his successful mobilization of the Jiangnan elite, Song's victory proved only nominal and fell victim to Jiang's opposition. Understandably, Jiang and other military leaders opposed Song's plan, since the introduction of a budget system, operating under the control of a civilian Budget Commission, and the opening up of financial records to public scrutiny would have severely limited their access to government resources. Generally speaking, the militarists were in favor of continuing the current style of fiscal administration, which gave them a great deal of flexibility under the very convenient screen of secrecy. Control over the Budget Commission became a much-valued prize in the factional struggle. Major militarists (including Jiang Jieshi, Feng Yuxiang, Yan Xishan, and Li Zongren) managed to be appointed as its members and to stall its activities, thus defeating Song's original goals.[26] As a consequence, the committee changed its name, membership, and regulations many times during the Nanjing Decade, never actually becoming operational.

The centralization of Nanjing's finances proved an elusive goal due to the lack of political unity. Complete defeat came at the Third Party Congress, held on March 15, 1929. This congress followed the end of the Hu-Jiang coalition and marked the temporary consolidation of Jiang's power over the party and government. Largely dominated by Jiang, the congress officially rejected all decisions made at previous economic conferences. As a consequence, Song resigned in protest.[27] The beginning of the central plains campaign (1928–30), however, soon forced Song to return to his post and, making demobilization unthinkable, compelled him to resume the infamous practice of floating bonds.[28]

Despite two years of work, no reform had been approved nor was any change in economic policy seriously considered by the Nanjing government. Jiang had succeeded in blocking institutional and economic reform that would have forced him to share government responsibilities with other political groups, since a civilian financial administration proposed by Song would have fallen under the jurisdiction of Hu Hanmin, at the time the chairman of the Executive Yuan. More important, it would have limited his access to economic resources and awarded the Jiangnan private economy a central place in nation building.

The 1928–29 skirmishes brought up two thorny issues. The first issue was who was going to control the financial and economic resources of the government. Jiang was not going to allow any amount of centralization if it was to happen under the control of other political groups. The second issue concerned the relationship between the state and the private economy and the role the Jiangnan entrepreneurs would play in the new Chinese economy. The cooperation proposed by Song, even if limited by the Nationalist tutelage policies, went against Jiang's military priorities. Differences between the two leaders on this point had come to the surface in 1928–29 and continued to feed the confrontation between them over the next few years.

A Change in Strategy: The Establishment of the National Economic Council

Having lost faith in the possibility of controlling the national budget, Song adopted a new strategy to pursue reform goals and began focusing on the creation of a special economic organization, the NEC, that would be capable of bypassing the regular bureaucracy and operating above Nanjing's factional quagmire. Song introduced his new plan in the *Annual Report* for the 1930 fiscal year (March 1, 1931). The report reviewed the old argument for centralization but also struck a new chord by suggesting "the creation of a really effective planning organization which would guide the productive forces of the country, coordinate the activities of the ministries, and rigidly map out" a development plan.[29] A mere three years after the establishment of the Nanjing government, Song had already lost faith in its ability to pursue a centralized reform effort. He had come to believe that only a new agency, placed above the quagmire of the bureaucracy ridden with factional struggle, could succeed in reforming the economy and finances.

The report listed the goals that Song wanted to achieve through this new agency. Above all he wanted to bypass the Budget Commission and all of its equally ineffectual reincarnations. For this reason he worked with both the League of Nations and the government of the United States to obtain independent funding that would not be subjected to Jiang's control. Song thus negotiated with the League a program of technical cooperation designed to strengthen China's relationship with Western countries and provide a channel for importing Western capital and technology. The project was officially launched in January 1931 in cooperation with Dr. Ludwig Rajchman, the director of the Health Section of the League of Nations. The League had been particularly active in China in the field of public health, dealing mainly with epidemics and quarantine problems. Rajchman himself had worked closely with China for fifteen years and had strongly supported Song and the Chinese case before the League, gaining a reputation for being politically pro-China.[30] The League asked for the establishment of a central reconstruction agency that could serve as a channel for the League's activities in China and as a base for the League's experts, while guaranteeing the proper employment of technical and economic aid granted to China.[31] In addition, Song negotiated with the US government for a loan in silver to be devoted completely to the development of national production related to the program of cooperation with the League and to be placed under the jurisdiction of the NEC.[32]

The second goal Song wanted to achieve through this new agency was similar to those he had pursued at the 1928 National Economic Conference.

Song wanted to mobilize the Jiangnan entrepreneurs in support of his reform plan, as well as of Nanjing's nation-building effort at large. Representatives of this group were to be appointed to positions of leadership within the NEC.[33] The language Song used this time, however, departed even further from liberalism, reflecting his gradual acceptance of ideas of productivism and economic control. The new agency, Song stated, would organize and mobilize China's "productive forces" (a standard productivist refrain), reflecting Song's wish to use the NEC as a tool to intervene in the private economy and regiment its resources in support of nation building. At this time, when Song was not closely cooperating with Wang and Chen, he already envisioned the NEC as a sort of corporativist organization, anticipating the final characteristics of the NEC in the years of the Wang-Jiang coalition. Song's political and economic vision was, in this respect, in keeping with the main guidelines drawn by Sun Yat-sen in his Three People's Principles. Song was, in fact, embracing Sun's idea of productivism and mobilization of productive forces (discussed at length in the next chapter) as the key to China's modern nation building. The goal, Sun argued, was for "everyone to become a producer" so that China could achieve strength and prosperity.[34]

The NEC was established in 1931; however, it fell short of Song's expectations in spite of all his efforts. This time obstacles came not only from Jiang's obstructionism but also from inclement weather. The disastrous 1931 Yangzi River flood imposed new economic priorities on the government, which had to set aside general economic development in favor of urgent relief work. The flood struck sixteen provinces of central China. The damage was particularly severe in the rice-producing areas of Anhui, Jiangxi, Jiangsu, and Hunan, bringing devastation and famine to the peasants. To face this emergency, a Flood Relief Commission was established shortly after the flood, and many of the League experts were transferred to this new organization. The promised US loan was also channeled into the new committee in the form of relief wheat.[35] The 1931 NEC thus fell short of Song's expectations and, as its regulation specified, ultimately came to depend on the National Finance Commission, a new, but equally ineffective, version of the defunct Budget Commission.[36]

The main problem, however, was that Song's political brilliance was actually matched by Jiang's, who was also an expert in political manipulation and *trasformismo*. The June 1931 regulations passed by the government's Political Committee, which was then dominated by Jiang after the split of the Hu-Jiang coalition, placed the NEC directly under the Executive Yuan, now chaired by Jiang, who was also to act as chairman of the NEC.[37] Zhu Jiahua, who was a close associate of Jiang and linked to the Blue Shirts, was appointed as the NEC's secretary, reinforcing Jiang's tight grip on the council.[38] The composition of the 1931 NEC membership did not reflect Song's original intention that the council should be a site for mobilization and cooperation with the private economy. Its membership was, instead, mostly composed of officials. The few members representative of business were confined to marginal and merely consultative positions.[39] The 1931 NEC had been established as a highly centralized state organization with limited powers under the strict control of Jiang.

The NEC remained largely an advisory body devoid of any ability to decide and to implement reforms.[40] The only activities it was able to carry out were linked to the League of Nation's program of technical cooperation and flood rehabilitation work, paid for by US loans. The NEC focused on water conservation, public health, and road building, privileging, due to Jiang's direct influence, roads that were of strategic importance for the military.[41]

The first round of confrontation between Song and Jiang had highlighted the importance of economic reforms in Nanjing politics. It was not just a matter of who had access to crucial resources for furthering personal careers and reform agendas but a confrontation between the two strands of nation building that divided the Nationalist Party. Song's perception of a modern Chinese state and economy relied on a centralized finance system open to public scrutiny and on a healthy taxation system based on a healthy private economy. These goals did not mean much to Jiang, who, at that time, was focused on funding the military unification of the country with whatever means possible. Song thus shared Wang Jingwei's and Chen Gongbo's belief that the military phase of the revolution was over and the consolidation of China's unity could be achieved only through financial and economic centralization. Open and centralized finances would restrain military feuds between Jiang and those militarists who still controlled recalcitrant provinces.

Although his attempt to implement his reform failed in 1931, Song seized the new opportunity presented by the formation of the Wang-Jiang coalition. The new cabinet attempted to politically marginalize Jiang and to make it impossible for him to undermine reforms.

The New National Economic Council

The establishment of the NEC was followed by a politically turbulent period marked by renewed attacks by the Japanese and the fall of two consecutive cabinets (the Jiang cabinet that had followed the Hu-Jiang coalition and the Sun Ke cabinet). The few months from September to December

1931 were marked by political upheaval and changes in the government. The crisis initiated by the Japanese attacks on Shanghai led to a peace conference among all GMD groups that was devoted to achieving a measure of political unity in order to present a united front against Japan. Wang Jingwei left Canton for Shanghai to negotiate with Jiang, who remained in Nanjing, while Song Ziwen shuttled between the two cities and acted as messenger and facilitator between the two leaders. The NEC became one of the most important points around which negotiations revolved, testifying to the importance of economic reforms in the political discourse on national salvation. At the end of the negotiations the Wang-Song line of economic nation building had emerged victorious (it is worth remembering here that the ultimate result of the Shanghai-Nanjing negotiations was the establishment of the Wang-Jiang coalition and the acceptance of the *an'nei rangwai* political platform—pacify the domestic front while resisting on the external front), and the NEC became the agency expressing the civilian reformist view of nation building supported by both Song and Wang.

During the Shanghai negotiations the NEC gradually (the negotiations proved long and full of setbacks) passed from Jiang's control to Wang's. Zhu Jiahua was removed from his position at the head of the NEC, and Qin Fen, who was close to Song Ziwen (since February 1930 he had held the position of director of the Accounting Section of the Ministry of Finance), was nominated to take his place.[42] The new NEC was also removed from the direct control of the Executive Yuan in order to shield it from actions like those that had curtailed its scope in 1931.[43] The NEC was placed under the direction of a Standing Committee, whose members were Song Ziwen, Sun Ke, and Wang Jingwei, thus ensuring its administrative independence from other government bodies and allowing it to act as a government-wide coordinating agency. All ministers whose jobs concerned economic development were included in the NEC membership, along with representatives of the Jiangnan elite.[44]

The Shanghai-Nanjing negotiations made it clear that Wang and Song were working together. Wang was promoting changes in the NEC that followed Song's original ideas, and Song was helping Wang in his quest for leadership over Nanjing by ensuring the support of the Jiangnan business community. To garner its support, Wang, while in Shanghai for the negotiations, convened a National Salvation Conference calling important Shanghai personalities to act as "people's representatives." At this conference Wang stressed the importance of public participation in his reform plan and expressed his commitment to the independence of societal associations. The conference, which carried the signature of Song's longtime political strategy, cemented the alliance between Wang, Song, and the

Jiangnan business community, creating a powerful lobby for Wang during these delicate negotiations. Although the 1928 and 1931 conferences used a similar strategy, that is, mobilization of the Jiangnan elite in support of Song's (and, later, Wang's) political agenda, they were also characterized by fundamental differences. By 1931 Jiang's opposition to economic reform had become well known and economic reforms had become a weapon to be openly used against him. At the same time, the recent Japanese attacks on Shanghai, and the crisis that followed, had further tightened the relationship between economic reforms and national salvation, as the name of the conference testifies. The message of the conference was that national salvation depended, now more than ever, on the realization of reform, and specifically the "correct" nation-building reforms advocated by Wang and actively supported by Song, who, in keeping with his general style, preferred to remain behind the scene.

On April 25, 1932, after Wang became the chairman of the Executive Yuan and Song returned to the Ministry of Finance (he had left that position during the short interval of the Sun Ke cabinet), the NEC was officially reopened.[45] Most of its members were representatives of the Jiangnan elite.[46] In addition to Zhang Jia'ao, Wu Dingchang, Zhou Zuomin, and Yu Hede (who had been members since 1931), bankers Chen Guangfu, Qian Xinzhi, Ye Zhuotang, and Peng Xuepei were appointed in 1933 along with industrialists Liu Hongsheng, Rong Zongjing, Shi Liangcai,[47] and Wang Xiaolai. Xu Xinliu, representing the state's taxation interest, was also a member.[48]

The reorganization of the NEC reflected the division of labor that characterized the early stages of the new Wang-Jiang government. The Wang group attempted to keep Jiang at the head of the military while excluding him from the NEC and many of the higher political bodies of the central government, which were mostly controlled by the Wang group and other members of the anti-Jiang coalition, such as Song Ziwen. The composition of the cabinet had completely changed, reflecting the new political composition of the administration.[49] The economic administration of the government was thus filled with representatives of groups favoring civilian (versus Jiang's military) reconstruction consistent with Wang's interpretations of the *an'nei rangwai* policy. Jiang's position during this early stage of the coalition was thus greatly weakened. He was confined to the military, whose actions were, in turn, limited by the framework determined by the civilian component of the new government. Jiang appeared to be in exactly the position he had most strenuously avoided—under a centralized budget system managed by civilians.

At this point Song began, once again, to search for independent funding for the NEC in order to avoid dependence on the government's still-erratic budget. In April 1933, Song left on a trip to the United States and Europe accompanied by Arthur Young, the American financial adviser to the Nanjing government. The official purpose of the trip was to attend the World Economic Conference in London, but for Song it was mostly an opportunity to seek financial support for the NEC.[50] While in Europe, Song traveled to Geneva and arranged with the League of Nations to expand its program of cooperation and to send a special technical mission, headed by Dr. Ludwig Rajchman, to assist the NEC's development plan.[51] Song also worked to attract private foreign investment to China and to establish an international consortium that was to provide long-term credit for industrial and railway development. The project was to involve American, Italian, English, and French businessmen, but excluded the Japanese.[52] Song hoped to reorient the Chinese economy away from Japan's influence by attempting to integrate it financially with the Western powers. In his pragmatic way, and without the theorizing that characterized Chen Gongbo, Song strove to build what Chen labeled China's *minzu* industrial system. Song focused his energy on the development of Jiangnan industries, which at the time were among the strongest industries of native origin in China. For Song, they represented the foundation of the modern Chinese economy, and keeping them free from Japan's influence was one of his main objectives. The Japanese were very much aware of Song's goals and saw them as a direct threat to their own objectives. Their protests to the Nanjing government over Song's anti-Japanese policies ultimately contributed to Song's political marginalization. In 1934, in fact, under the pressure of an infuriated Japan, Song was forced to resign from the Ministry of Finance.

In May 1933, when Song was still firmly in control of the Ministry of Finance, he traveled to Washington to negotiate a cotton and wheat loan with the US Farm Board, prompting, once again, protests from the Japanese government. The loan granted the Chinese government a credit of fifty million US dollars, four-fifths of which were to be spent on 600,000 bales of American cotton and the remainder on American wheat. The loan was secured on China's customs revenues at 5 percent annual interest and was to be repaid in three years. The Chinese government was to sell the American cotton and wheat on the domestic market and to invest the profit in economic reconstruction.[53] Song was instrumental in obtaining the support of the League of Nations and the US loan. His American education and his personal ties with financial and economic groups abroad served to reassure officials that the effort of Western nations would not be wasted. Accordingly, the NEC was chosen as the selling agent of the American cotton and wheat and was to control the use of the proceeds.[54]

Finally provided with independent funds, the NEC was ready to expand its plans and to begin reconstruction at the national level. As decided at the first meeting of its Standing Committee, the NEC would focus on the development of the lower Yangzi River valley and, within that area, the rehabilitation of those industries that required the least investment. This decision designated the Shanghai cotton and silk industries as the privileged target for NEC assistance.[55] Chen Gongbo had also designated this area as the center of his 1933 four-year industrial plan.[56] Even if, at a first glance, the NEC and the CCC appeared to be primarily working to support agriculture, most of the agricultural activities focused on the production of industrial raw materials.[57] Even most of the public-health budget was allocated to the improvement of agriculture by concentrating on pest control. Funds for water navigation were mostly intended to be used for the development and operation of the China Merchants Steamship Navigation Company, which was brought under the control of the NEC in 1934 to facilitate new strategies for the marketing and transportation of raw materials and domestic goods.[58] The absence of a significant budget specifically devoted to industry cannot obscure the industrial bias of the NEC and its focus on the development of the Jiangnan *minzu* industry.

In addition, at its third meeting, the Standing Committee clearly stated the productivist goals of the NEC and its commitment to urgent economic nation building, echoing the plan of its new leaders—Song, Wang, and Chen (who as the minister of industry was also a member of the NEC and exerted much influence over it). At this meeting, the Standing Committee allocated three-fifths of the American loan for the promotion of agricultural and industrial production, two-fifths for currency reform, and no funds for military purposes.[59] The Standing Committee also created guidelines for the NEC and established the three main principles that were to inform its work.[60] First was the determination to engage in reforms without delay, a statement that revealed the three leaders' frustration with Jiang's prioritization of military affairs and repeated postponements of reforms. The NEC's 1934 Plan thus opened with a double pledge: reforms were to be realized and not remain empty words, and all funds from the US cotton and wheat loan were to be invested to complete large-scale national economic reconstruction. The second principle was the centralization and national integration of the economy. Last was the promotion of industrial production.[61] The new NEC reflected the main ideas on which the alliance between Song and the Wang group rested: productivism, mobilization of and cooperation with the Jiangnan economic elite, centralization, and priority of economic reforms over military action.

Conclusion

During the Nanjing Decade the struggle between two competing Nationalist strands of nation building split the government and the country at large, preventing the realization of a unified nation, which was the heart of the Nationalist political program. Song Ziwen's mobilization of the Jiangnan economic elite, although intended to foster unity between state and private economy, contained a divisive element, since he planned to impose his reform agenda on the government and overcome Jiang's opposition. In these years, economic reform, nation building, and political factional struggle were so closely intertwined that it is impossible to discuss one without the others. The modernization of the state was predicated on the solution of the Nationalist leadership crisis. On the other hand, the launching of nation-building reforms depended on the creation of a modern state capable of taking action in support of economic development.

The need for a strong state was rooted not only in the antiliberal Nationalist approach to politics but also in the fundamental idea that economic development was an integral part of nation building as well as a tool for resisting Japan's growing influence. Song Ziwen saw the development of the Chinese Jiangnan *minzu* economy as a means to create a modern China as well as to resist Japan's imperialism. While Chen was outspoken on this point and discussed it widely (although even Chen did not dare to name Japan directly and limited his discussion to a generic threat of colonization), Song, in keeping with his pragmatic style, did not publicize his overall plan. His intent, however, emerges clearly from an analysis of the reforms he attempted.

During the Nanjing Decade, building a modern government/state seemed impossible, as the government was trapped in practices that had characterized the warlord years and, before that, the imperial government. Militarism and its control over finances were hard to overcome. At the same time, the relationship between state and private economy appeared to be following patterns developed in the late Qing Self-Strengthening period, when reforms had been implemented by informal networks of officials and private entrepreneurs, associations that were never officially recognized by the imperial administration. The administrative centralization of the Nanjing government, combined with a deep political rift at the higher echelons of its leadership, encouraged the formation of similar informal economic-political networks, a topic discussed at length in the next chapter. It is, however, important to remark here that the ambiguity of the role of the private industrial elite in the nation has been a characteristic of modern China from the late Qing. The Nanjing Decade witnessed, arguably, the first significant attempt to clarify and institutionalize it. After being silenced by Jiang Jieshi's militarism and Mao Zedong's radical Communism, the industrial elite has inevitably reemerged with the reintroduction of a free-market economy in the post-Mao years. The determination of today's Communist leadership to maintain a highly centralized government, still inspired by the idea of democratic centralism, raises, as urgently as before, the question of what role it is destined to play in China's new economy and what relationship with the state the economy will ultimately enjoy.

Song's reform attempts in the years before the inauguration of the Wang-Jiang coalition testify to the wide appeal of Wang's and Chen's plan for the development of China's *minzu* economy. Its appeal did not rest solely in its attempt to reverse Jiang's militarization of government and nation but also resided in the fact that it reflected an important political and economic trend within the GMD. Rather than being an isolated and short-lived manifestation of Chinese political thought in the prewar years, the plan proposed by the Wang group represented a well-established Nationalist political trend embraced by other civilian leaders, such as Song.

肆

CHAPTER 4

The Cotton Control Commission and the Corporativist Organization of the Nation

In 1932, a year after its establishment, the NEC finally emerged as the special agency originally envisioned by Song Ziwen. It had also come to represent the Wang-Song alliance and the expression of the civilian reformist faction that challenged Jiang during the Nanjing Decade. Inspired by belief in the importance of the Jiangnan *minzu* economy for China's nation building, the NEC pursued, as one of its most important tasks, the mobilization of this economic group. In this respect, it was a novel kind of organization in the Chinese body politic, since it aimed at institutionalizing the informal state-private networks that had characterized Song's political tactics since 1928, as exemplified by the National Economic Conference. The origins of this type of network can be traced back to the joint state-private (*guanshang*) reform formula initiated in the Self-Strengthening period. At this time private businessmen had become involved in developing China's industries in cooperation with local authorities as a means for achieving nationalist goals. Zhang Zhidong's formula of "saving the country with business" (*shiye jiuguo*) rested on the assumption that a common interest and duty linked state and elites and that both could actually profit from cooperating. The most obvious example of such a strategy was the China Merchants Steamship Navigation Company (Zhaoshangju), established in 1872 by Li Hongzhang in cooperation with private merchants as part of the Self-Strengthening reforms. This company pursued both anti-imperialist and business goals. It competed with foreign steamships, which at the time dominated the business, and was supposed to be profitable for the entrepreneurs who sponsored and managed it.

The NEC can thus be considered a development of Self-Strengthening reforms and business practice. However, its leaders combined this Self-Strengthening heritage with contemporary corporativist trends that were sweeping through Europe at the time. They organized the NEC according to the principle of cooperative economy (*hezuo jingji*), a term that came to denote cooperation between the state and the nation's productive forces as well as among groups in society, while also referring to a network of cooperative societies that was intended to be the channel for the NEC's intervention at all levels of the economy (economic control). The idea of cooperative economy was thus inspired by productivist and corporativist trends in its focus on unity among producers and their mobilization.

Corporativism in China was rooted in Sun Yat-sen's ideas of productivism and mobilization of the country's productive forces. These notions had influenced Song Ziwen's original conception of the NEC and were widespread among Nationalist leaders. Corporativism, however, emerged in its most developed form in Chen Gongbo's plan for the reorganization of Nanjing's economic administration, which was to be organized into "control commissions" (*tongzhi weiyuanhui*), each devoted to the reorganization and mobilization of a specific sector. Chen planned the establishment of six commissions, dealing with agriculture (*nongye tongzhi weiyuanhui*), industry (*gongye tongzhi weiyuanhui*), commerce (*shangye tongzhi weiyuanwei*), transportation (*yunshu tongzhi weiyuanhui*), banking and insurance (*yinhang ji baoxian tongzhi weiyuanhui*), and labor (*laogong tongzhi weiyuanhui*).[1] The commissions were to act as the government's higher economic departments. Each commission would be organized into a centralized hierarchical structure of subcommittees covering different aspects and industries in each sector.

Chen's ambitious plan was never fully realized because of the short duration of the Wang-Jiang coalition and Jiang's increasingly effective political opposition, which forced the Wang group to focus its reforms on the NEC rather than on the reorganization of the entire government administration. The NEC (and the Ministry of Industry to a lesser extent), however, did establish a few corporativist agencies such as the CCC (the main focus of this chapter) and the Silk Improvement Commission (*cangsi gailian weiyuanhui*, hereafter SIC). The CCC and SIC were the only national-level associations in their respective industries, and with the sponsorship of the government, they each aimed at creating a unified body representative of their productive forces, including industrialists, merchants, experts in the rural production of raw materials, bankers, and union leaders.[2] The Standing Committees of these commissions, residing in Shanghai, constituted the decision-making leadership, while a network of cooperative societies organized producers involved in all stages of the industry and ensured the implementation of reforms decided by the Standing Committee. In this way, the CCC and SIC were able to mobilize two of China's *minzu* industries and extend its reforming arm to all stages of their productive process.

The notion that Song Ziwen supported a system of controlled and planned economy might appear perplexing because of his fame as a champion of liberal capitalism in China. As mentioned earlier, however, Song's probusiness attitude was limited by the general antiliberal stance that characterized Nationalist political and economic thought and by his fundamental wish to use the economy to create a modern China and resist Japan. In addition, faced with chaos within the Nationalist political and administrative structure in Nanjing, Song came to increasingly appreciate the potential of economic control as an effective means for centralizing, organizing, and rationalizing economic decision making and implementation. When he traveled to Washington in 1933 to negotiate the cotton and wheat loan, Song found the United States in the midst of the Depression, the bank crisis, and the beginning of New Deal policies. This experience probably influenced him to adopt a policy of economic control in China, a step that he might well have perceived as following the example of Western industrialized nations and not in direct contradiction to capitalism.[3] Upon his return to China, Song met with Chen Gongbo to discuss the establishment of an economic control agency for the cotton industry within the NEC.[4] Soon after this meeting, on October 13, 1933, during a speech in support of national economic reconstruction, Song officially introduced economic control as part of the NEC program.[5] At this time, he also published an essay, "Telling the People about Controlling the Cotton Industry," in which he argued that the NEC had "the task of developing the national economy and the responsibility of planning, as a whole, all aspects of economic enterprises linked to People's Livelihood [*minsheng shiye*]. . . . It is specifically for this reason that we establish control commissions."[6] Song's passage echoes Chen's ideas of how the goal of autarkic productivism justified control over industries considered crucial for national salvation. This nationalist approach led Song to argue in favor of "the concentration of power and the planning of the various aspects [of the cotton industry]" in the hands of the CCC.[7]

Both the CCC and the SIC embodied alliances that had already developed regionally and informally between entrepreneurs and government officials. The CCC, for example, institutionalized the alliance between Song and the Jiangnan elite that had existed since the National Economic Conference of 1928 and had now extended to include Wang. The CCC thus reflected the priority of industrial interests over the interests of other groups such as peasants and workers that had emerged at the time of the conference. At the same time, however, it perpetuated the same ambiguity about the character of the relationship between the state and private entrepreneurs, leaving open the question of whether the CCC, and the NEC at large, was a tool for controlling private entrepreneurs or for opening up new venues for their participation in economic decision making. The outcome depended on how the power relationships among all of the industry's diverse components would develop in the actual process of reforming the industry.

Corporativism

To understand the complexity of corporativist thought in 1930s China, it is important to reexamine the meaning of corporativism as an economic and political system. According to the most general and widely accepted definition, a corporativist system is characterized by the presence, at the national level, of a single representative organization for each industry or for each economic group, such as workers, businessmen, and farmers.[8] These national organizations are recognized and legitimized by the government, with which they are, at least in theory, in a relationship of equal partnership. Corporativist organizations are entrusted by the government with carrying out or facilitating the implementation of state policies. The state, in turn, acts as the supreme arbiter or mediator between groups within the corporation and helps organize the relationships between them, in its capacity as "the guardian of the common good, of a national interest that supersedes the parochial interests of each sector." What all forms of corporativism share is a commitment to the idea that "consensus and cooperation are needed" for achieving a common goal or a national mission, "in contrast with [the] divisive competition and conflict entailed by pluralist interest-group models of organization."[9]

According to Gregory Kasza, most 1930s corporativist organizations can be considered a form of "administrative mass organization" (AMO), a model of mass mobilization that prevailed at that time worldwide, being adopted by such totalitarian states as the Soviet Union, Nazi Germany, the Italian Fascist state, and imperial Japan. According to Kasza, the AMOs found their inspiration in the idea of military conscription, which came to be extended to various groups in society according to gender, age, workplace and industry, and place of residence. These organizations extended from the grass roots to the national level in a pyramidal structure and were used for mass mobilization and nation- or empire-building purposes. Kasza uses, among others, the example of 1930s Japan, which he argues, used AMOs in this manner "not only at home but also throughout their Asian empire." In Taiwan and Korea, for example, the Japanese authorities established women's organizations. They created the Harmony Society (*kyōwaki*) in Manchuria and "the New People's Society (*shinminkai*) in northern China, both intended to mobilize the local population against the Chinese resistance. In China's cities, the conquerors set up neighborhood groups (which the Communists were to reestablish after 1949)."[10] Above all the Japanese used corporativist organizations as part of their effort to gain control over local economic resources during Japan's occupation of Taiwan and mainland China.[11] One striking example of this strategy is the system of "material control" established in Shanghai after 1937, examined in chapter 7.

It is generally believed that Japan was the first Asian country to adopt corporativism in the early twentieth century.[12] The Nationalists, however, also used corporativist organizations in China in the 1930s.[13] The GMD, therefore, began experimenting with corporativism at roughly the same time as Japan did. AMOs, in fact, came to be used not only for empire building but also for anti-imperialist purposes, as was the case with the NEC. Corporativism in this case assumed a defensive stance, aimed at nation building and resistance to foreign imperialism by mobilizing resources and rerouting them in support of autarkic development and away from Japan's control. In its national-defense efforts, China thus applied very similar strategies to those employed by Japan in its empire building.

In the years between the two world wars, although the political dimension of the corporativist state—such as gender- or age-based associations—was crucial for ensuring the fascist or social-nationalist states' control over society, the corporativist organization of the economy constituted the real core of their nation building. Through these economic AMOs they could achieve a sweeping reorganization of the economic structure of the nation because of their unprecedented ability to mobilize wide sections of society. As Kasza has pointed out, corporativism was employed to "alter control over the means of production. Decisions on ownership, investment, product, prices, employment, and profit are the substance of economic power, and many regimes have designed AMOs to change the way these decisions are made." The following are ways in which an AMO can increase state control over production: "(1) By humbling workers' interest groups, the AMO can eliminate organized labor from economic decision making. . . . The AMO can also check the power of landowners and private business. (2) The AMO can redeploy labor between economic sectors. . . . (3) In order to free capital for public investment, the AMOs can depress wages and force savings. (4) Through education, competitions, and coercion, the AMO can raise the productivity and technological level of labor."[14] These were some of the major goals pursued by fascist and social-nationalist regimes in the interwar period. They were also shared by the CCC in China. Technological improvement, higher productivity, repression of workers' interests, and the encouragement of capital investment were basic objectives of the CCC productivist approach.

The fact that Japan, Italy, and Germany all resorted to AMO-style corporativist organizations in their nation-building efforts did not preclude the development of significant differences in their corporativist policies. Within the AMO category Kasza distinguishes three different patterns: "The rightist pattern, in which both officials and big business gained influence; the Leninist pattern, in which officials alone gained influence; and the power-sharing pattern, in which both officials and the AMOs' mass membership gained influence. Fascist Italy's labor syndicates . . . illustrate the rightist pattern, Soviet trade unions the Leninist pattern, and Yugoslavia's work collectives and Egypt's agrarian cooperatives the power-sharing pattern."[15] Kasza thus emphasizes that AMOs can develop in different ways as a result of different power relations among the groups that they represent. An increase of state control does not necessarily imply diminished power of nonstate groups involved in the AMO. Various combinations of power relations can occur, generating the three variations listed above. Kasza's model thus elaborates Philippe Schmitter's classic discussion of corporativism, which distinguished between "authoritarian" and "societal" corporativism.[16]

An analysis of corporativist thought in the 1930s reveals that different trends of corporativism coexisted in a single country. If we look at Italy during the Fascist years, for example, we find that different forms of corporativism competed within the Fascist camp. Alfredo Rocco advocated a form of *corporativismo dirigista* (dirigistic corporativism). Rocco valued national interests more than those of the individual citizen, thus establishing the power and welfare of the nation-state as the ultimate goal of the Italian corporativist organization. He also argued, however, that "the carrying out of the economic functions can, generally, be left to private individuals. . . . Nationalism requires the private organization of production, not because it is weak vis-à-vis the interests of private entrepreneurs, but because that system allows better results in economic production. Nationalism wants private property of capital not for the interests of the owners, but because it is only private property that allows accumulation of capital. We consider entrepreneurs and capitalists crucial for national interests."[17]

Rocco's model eventually prevailed over more radical models, including the one supported by Ugo Spirito. Spirito advocated a *corporazione proprietaria* (ownership corporativism) that stressed state control over all economic forces, including capital, leading to the creation of a bureaucratic-totalitarian economic apparatus that can be identified with Kasza's Leninist AMOs.[18] Spirito not only opposed workers' unions but also private property, which he proposed to organize into property cooperatives. Spirito's final goal was to overcome the dualism between economy and politics, guaranteeing the supremacy of a technical leadership aimed at realizing a "programmed economy, which is the only means for overcoming the chaotic nature of traditional liberalism." Advocating industrialization *ad oltranza* (to the bitter end)—a popular expression in Italian Fascist rhetoric—Spirito saw the real obstacle to Italian industrialization in the fragmentation of the *strutture imprenditoriali* (entrepreneurial structures) and in "an individualist and anarchic habit."[19] The main task of the corporativist state, Spirito continued, was "the disciplining of all productive forces of the Nation into a unitarian organization."[20] Spirito's corporativism thus possessed a revolutionary and Leninist nature that distinguished it from Rocco's rightist model.

Spirito's vision of corporativism was not realized in Italy. The Vidoni Palace agreement of October 2, 1925, in which representatives of the state met with those of the General Federation of Italian Industry (Confederazione generale dell'industria italiana, hereafter GFII), marked the beginning of new power relations in the Italian economy. As a result of this agreement, labor organizations were deprived of any significant power, industrial management strengthened its power within the factory, and the GFII strengthened its authority over individual firms.[21] In this way the most powerful among the industrialists in Italy—organized in the GFII under the leadership of such magnates as Agnelli, Olivetti, and Pirelli—gained the upper hand not only over the workers but also over weaker industrialists. The GFII was also guaranteed a position of more or less equal power vis-à-vis the government. Mussolini favored Rocco's approach to corporativism over Spirito's more radical plan and, on a more practical note, was not in a position to challenge the powerful industrial interests represented by the GFII. Thus, Italian Fascist corporativism largely followed the rightist AMO pattern.

Appreciating the flexibility and diversity of corporativist trends around the world is crucial to understanding the 1930s Chinese debate on "cooperative economy" and the many interpretations that it generated. Although corporativism was embraced by most GMD leaders, it assumed different meanings when pursued by different factions. In the 1930s we can distinguish two main corporativist trends within the Nanjing government. The one that has been the focus of some previous research is that championed by Jiang Jieshi. This model, described accurately by historians Joseph

Fewsmith and Parks Coble, favored heavy state control over and regimentation of the private sector and can be characterized as belonging to the Leninist model.[22] The other trend, promoted by the Wang group, supported a more equal partnership between state and private entrepreneurs and more closely resembled Kasza's rightist model and the form of corporativism realized by the Italian Fascist regime.

A Nation of Producers

At the base of corporativist thought is the imagining of the nation as founded on its economy and formed by producers, rather than citizens or soldiers, for example. The idea of a nation of producers implied a criticism of the Communist perception that the nation was organized into economic classes and attempted to go beyond this divisive view in order to promote social and political unity. In 1924, Sun Yat-sen had already moved in this direction. In his Principle of People's Livelihood, he had attempted to widen the notion of proletariat as the main force supporting the industrial economy by arguing that various groups in society contributed to economic production, not only "workers." He included in the productive forces peasants, technical personnel, people involved in running transportation, inventors, merchants, and consumers. In this view, they all participated in industrial production in different ways by supplying raw materials, conveying it to the factory, improving productivity, and creating a market for Chinese goods.[23] In this way, Sun tried to break down the opposition between industrial workers and bourgeoisie and to encourage wide social alliances under the aegis of the GMD.

The notion of a nation of producers (*shengchanzhe*) became widely accepted with the increasing popularity of productivism and was embraced by diverse political circles in 1930s China. The leaders of the Fujian federalist movement advocated the establishment of a federal system kept together by only one common principle, "political power for the producing masses." Having formed a Producer Party (*shengchandang*), they promoted as one of their slogans "Establish a Government of the Producing People!"[24] This idea was also part of the Blue Shirts program, the goal of which was to make everyone a producer in society, under their slogan "Nationalize, Militarize, Productivize."[25] Borrowing the idea of nation as an "imagined community" from Benedict Anderson, one can argue that for these leaders it was not a common language or ethnicity that constituted the glue of the national community but its productive structure.[26]

Wang Jingwei and Chen Gongbo shared this vision. Their notion of *minzu* economy and their productivist approach led them to conceive the nation as a community of producers working together for the greater good of the country and overcoming group conflicts. "It is essential [for the salvation of the Chinese nation] that different factors in production should learn to understand one another," Wang argued, advocating national alliance and condemning social conflict.[27] To cooperate was the duty of both the government and the people. "The Government . . . in economic matters not only should not seek to work alone, but should go out of its way to secure the understanding and co-operation of the people. . . . The Government must co-operate fully with the people and their organisations."[28] On another occasion, Wang stated: "The entire populace, from the highest to the lowest level, must co-operate in attempting to realize the national economic policy."[29]

In the minds of many Nationalist leaders, therefore, the producers came to represent the Chinese masses that needed to be mobilized, economically and politically, and be directed toward their revolutionary, or just reformist, goals. As was often the case with Nationalist China, agreement on political issues was, at best, partial, reflecting the general political split of the GMD leadership. A controversy also emerged over who was going to lead the masses of producers and in what direction. Everyone was ready to evoke Sun Yat-sen's idea of "partyfying the masses," claiming that the party was the only political formation in China that truly represented the interests of the nation and thus the only legitimate claimant to the leadership of the Chinese population. Unfortunately, the nature of the party was not yet settled and its political platform remained a point of conflict. As to be expected, Jiang's model of corporativism and mass mobilization differed widely from that of the Wang group.

Cooperation or Economic Control? The Ambiguity of "Cooperative Economy"

Harking back to Sun's idea of partyfying the masses, Chen Gongbo expressed particular concern for mass mobilization. It was important, he argued, that the Chinese masses be mobilized for the correct nation-building goals rather than harnessed for destructive purposes. For this reason Chen believed that the GMD should hurry to place itself at the head of mass organizations, a policy that, he complained, the party had abandoned to the Communists after the Northern Expedition. Even more dangerous, he argued, was the GMD's failure to mobilize the people in those areas where the Communists were not present. In these areas, local petty criminals, militarists, and bullies controlled trade unions and all sorts of mass movements. Chen was thus concerned that mobilization was being channeled in the wrong direction, not only toward the divisive goals of class struggle advocated by the Communists but also toward the equally divisive support of warlords and other shady local-interest groups, among which Chen most probably included more legitimate federalist and regionalist trends that resisted the GMD's centralizing drive. The most negative developments of all were the cases in which merchants working for foreign firms—whom Chen called "compradors"—headed merchants' associations. This was particularly harmful since these merchants were often cooperating with imperialist economic forces and thus mobilized the Chinese producers to achieve the exact opposite of the goals of the GMD as they increased dependence on foreign imperialism instead of promoting self-reliance. This phenomenon, Chen complained, undermined the revolutionary goals of mass mobilization, which—following the spirit of the national revolution promoted by the GMD since 1911—should be aimed at unifying and strengthening the country against foreign imperialism.[30]

Wang Jingwei also stressed the revolutionary nature of mass mobilization, which, he claimed, should bring the party and producing masses together and allow them to keep bureaucracy, imperialist forces, and capital in check. "To prevent reconstruction from transforming itself into a tool of imperialism or bureaucratic capitalism we must (1) train the masses to rise and really participate in the government and (2) unify the party so that it can really lead the masses and check on the government."[31] According to Wang, then, the mobilization of producers should aim not only at resisting imperialism but also at making sure that the government followed the party line closely and did not betray its revolutionary goals.[32] In his scheme for mobilizing the masses, however, Wang assigned the *minzu* economy a special position, as a privileged group deserving of special rights because of their contribution to nation building. The goal of the tutelage period, Wang argued, was after all to train the people to exercise political power.

> Therefore, in the tutelage period, although the power to organize the government rests with the GMD, it is not possible to avoid [establishing] institutions representative of the people. In the last few years, many comrades, relying on *Fundamentals of National Reconstruction* of the president [Sun Yat-sen] . . . have advocated the legal protection of private rights [*renmin siquan*] and the gradual increase of their political rights in order to realize democratic politics [*zhuyi zhengzhi*].[33]

Although highly rhetorical, this statement reinforced Chen's argument that the *minzu* producers should be allowed to form their own organizations and to maintain a high degree of independence because they could play an important role in developing China's economy and helping the government achieve autarky. They were thus to be treated differently from those who supported foreign imperialism, such as compradors or industrialists working with the Japanese. Although in reality many industrialists, including those of the Jiangnan area, had had dealings with the Japanese in the early stages of their career, Chen Gongbo was now determined to draw a clear line of demarcation between *minzu* entrepreneurs and compradors. The latter would not be granted any autonomy and would remain under the strict control of the government.

Like Song, Chen assigned a special place in the nation to the *minzu* producers for a variety of reasons, ranging from a belief in their foundational role in economic nation building to the desire to supplement the scarce resources of Nanjing's notoriously bankrupt government with private capital. Chen identified four sources of capital to mobilize in support of economic nation building: capital raised by the state, special foreign funds (such as those obtained through the American cotton and wheat loan), funds jointly managed by government and private entrepreneurs (*guanshang heban*), and private-sector (*renmin siying*) capital, especially that of China's light industry. A few months later, in December 1933, in his article "Telling the Chinese People about the Industrial Plan" ("Wei shiye jihua gao guoren"), Chen argued that private banks should expand their investments in support of his plan, since, he believed, they had the cash to do so. Private capital was also to play an important role in Chen's plan for the development of urban and rural areas. In urban areas private firms would own all public utilities for twenty or thirty years, at which time they would finally be nationalized. In rural areas private firms would help establish cooperative producer societies at the village level. In addition, chartered private companies would be formed to promote new agricultural techniques to boost agricultural production.[34]

Such reliance on private business appeared as a highly exploitative strategy on the part of the NEC. Anticipating criticism, Chen specified that he was motivated not only by the government need to mobilize capital but also by a desire to keep China's vital *minzu* forces alive. As Chen wrote in 1933, all productive forces, including both capital and labor, ought to be the target of government mobilization but, at the same time, should be allowed to develop and be encouraged with proper legislation. "Productive forces (*shengchanzhe*) still are productive forces and [policies which do not respect them] will not only harm [their function as] production tools (*shengchan gongju*) but also obstruct their vitality." Wang echoed this idea in 1934, reasoning that, "in such circumstances, with the consolidation of the people's strength, the national strength will automatically become consolidated."[35] Chen and Wang thus argued that the GMD, although placing itself at the head of the corporativist organization of the economy, should grant private *minzu* entrepreneurs considerable autonomy, since their participation as active members of China's corporativist organization was essential to the expansion of its national economy and its struggle against imperialism.

How much Chen Gongbo's statements in support of *minzu* entrepreneurs reflected a genuinely held belief is hard to gauge. Chen was aware that the policies of economic control and corporativism harbored a latent conflict with business interests and he acknowledged the "people's reluctance." Chen, however, believed that such diffidence was unjustified, because the Wang-Jiang administration and Chinese businessmen ultimately shared the same nationalist goals. Saving the nation and resisting Japan's economic penetration were important objectives of both groups. Chen hoped that a sense of urgency about the fate of the nation (as well as of their businesses) would finally cement cooperation between state and business. "I hope the Chinese common man will consider the future of China as well as his own and will rush to invest in domestic production. The government, for its part, will offer not only plenty of guidance but also protection and help."[36] In reality, Chen continued, the businessmen themselves realized that the current economic crisis was driving them out of business and therefore they were the first to call for a strong central government and its intervention in the economy.[37] "Since the effects of the economic depression began to be felt in China, they all, regardless of their trade, have been looking for help from the state [*guojia*]. . . . Chinese industrialists have also asked for state protection in such various matters as the raising of customs duties on imports and reducing domestic taxation. [In short, the development] of industry relies on political [reform]."[38] Chen struck the usual balance between high rhetoric and practical business concerns, highlighting how the state and business relied on each other.

In spite of his efforts to reconcile the business elite with his policies, Chen's view of corporativism was potentially threatening to the autonomy of private entrepreneurs. Although industrialists had long been asking for state support, they did not expect it to extend to the reorganization of their businesses. They hoped, rather, that it would be limited to the implementation of favorable legislation, taxation, and customs duties. Chen's idea of state support for private industry was more comprehensive. He believed that entrepreneurs were unable to take the initiative for reform. Above all, he believed them to be fragmented and unable to come together to provide leadership for economic development.[39] In such a situation only vigorous action by the state could "save" them.

Chen complained that "Chinese merchant organizations are inherently unsound" and generally mismanaged their factories.[40] Chinese businessmen were still steeped in "familism" (*jiazu zhuyi*), that is, an excessive reliance on the family structure for the management of business, which created a major obstacle to modernization. Appointments in the factories were based, not on qualifications or skills, but family relations. As a result managers rarely visited the factories and remained distant from the workers. Familism and the consequent employment of unskilled managerial personnel were also responsible, according to Chen, for inadequate accounting systems. Since factory managers were not appointed on the basis of expertise, many knew little about accounting. These managers often failed to calculate depreciation of machinery and at the end of the year divided up all profits without allowing for depreciation or the accumulation of reserve funds. For this reason debts piled up and factories quickly went out of business.[41] Such mismanagement, Chen commented, was ultimately responsible for retarding modernization.

Chen also lamented that industrial production in China still appeared to be an extension of commercial operations rather than a specialized economic activity. For example, because most merchants did not own the silk factories but only commissioned their work, they did not care about the state of machinery. Most of them regarded the silk industry as an investment opportunity and not an enterprise to be undertaken independently. If the price of silk went up, they commissioned silk production at existing factories. If it went down, they simply stopped production and tried their hand at another product. Government bonds could save silk merchants but definitely could not save the silk industry, whose future ultimately depended on its thorough reorganization.[42]

Chen's writing on the nature of cooperation between state and private business reveals a certain amount of ambiguity in regard to the extent of state control. This ambiguity was, however, matched by that of the NEC entrepreneurs, who, in the 1930s, were struggling to define their role in the nation amid a global crisis of liberal capitalism, escalating Japanese aggression (military and economic), and a Self-Strengthening heritage of responsibility for modernization and nationalism.

The Cotton Control Commission's Entrepreneurs

The entrepreneurs who participated in the CCC belonged to an economic and financial group generally identified as the Zhejiang-Jiangsu group.[43] Most of the members were involved in the cotton and silk industries in Zhejiang and Jiangsu Provinces, which had developed through heavy reliance on Shanghai's international market network.[44] These industrialists began their careers in the provinces in the late nineteenth and early twentieth centuries. Several ended up cooperating with provincial and county officials and with new Western-trained scientists in reform projects aimed at improving industrial production, introducing new technologies, and expanding the marketing of industrial goods within the framework of Self-Strengthening, whose spirit and goals continued to influence reforms through the early years of the Republic. Their involvement in industrial modernization extended through the first half of the 1930s.[45] As the silk and cotton industries developed, a trend toward vertical integration emerged. By the late 1920s the number of families controlling the Zhejiang and Jiangsu silk and cotton industries had sharply decreased.[46] The management of these powerful new industrial groups came to be characterized by a blend of new and traditional patterns of economic and political behavior. Traditional reliance on family members survived side by side with various capitalistic innovations: new technologies, new forms of managerial organization, and new regulations aimed at raising the quality of raw material and finished goods.[47]

In her study of silk filatures in Wuxi, Lynda Bell traces the origins of the 1930s cooperation between the government and prominent silk factories, embodied in the SIC, back to Self-Strengthening state-private reform networks. In this way Bell places the SIC in a tradition of economic modernization begun in the late nineteenth century.[48] In a similar fashion, the CCC brought together, in a national organization, a group of mill owners, bankers, and agriculturalists who had long been engaged in reforming the cotton industry in collaboration with local authorities.

Bell clearly traces back to the Self-Strengthening movement the basic network that came to constitute the SIC, showing that participation of private business in this government-sponsored agency was restricted to selected groups who had a long history of involvement in reforms carried out in cooperation with local authorities. A key figure in the trend for reform of silk filatures in the Wuxi area was Xue Shouxuan. In addition to creating modern silk filatures, Xue established the Sericulture Affairs Office (*canshibu*) in 1903, built egg hatcheries, organized cooperative societies "promoting extension work and sale of eggs,"[49] and carried out a series of reforms very similar to those later implemented by the SIC. Not surprisingly, Xue became a member of the SIC as soon as it was established in 1934.

The CCC followed the same pattern and privileged the Zhejiang-Jiangsu financial and industrial group over others. This group of businessmen had led local reforms, as noted in the previous chapter, and been allied with

Song Ziwen since 1928, identifying him as the protector of its interests in Nanjing. This privileged alliance was based not only on a shared interest in economic modernization but also on the prospect of a mutually beneficial long-term political relationship. While the businessmen expected participation in national reconstruction, state protection, and new business opportunities, Song tried to mobilize them for political support, cajoling them into supporting government bonds and paying higher and higher taxes. Song was crucial in ensuring the participation of Chen Guangfu and other private entrepreneurs in the CCC. Because Chen Gongbo did not enjoy an equally productive relationship with the Zhejiang-Jiangsu economic elite, he had been unable to gain their support through the Ministry of Industry, as he complained in 1936.[50] It had only been through the NEC, officially Song's agency, that he had been able to obtain their participation in his reform plan.

By 1928 most of the industrialists of the Zhejiang-Jiangsu region had moved their headquarters to Shanghai's foreign concessions, the heart of China's business life, where they would be protected, to some extent, from political and military turmoil. Foreign police stationed there even offered effective protection against social unrest and the activities of labor movements. In Shanghai they adapted to the new political environment marked by the establishment of the Nanjing government and the emergence of national, rather than provincial, politics. Industrialists and bankers brought with them patterns of managerial and economic behavior developed during the early stages of their economic success in the provinces.[51] As Bell has argued in her studies of Wuxi, the Jiangnan elite transferred their practices of cooperation with political authority and patronage to the new national arena, expecting support and recognition for the role they played in China's economic development and modernization.[52] Having been politically active at the local level before 1927, the Jiangnan industrialists were now willing to participate in the political and economic reconstruction of the country and were seeking representation. Particularly active were the Rong brothers, Rong Zongjing (later a member of the CCC) and Rong Desheng, owners of the Shenxin cotton mills and the Fuxin wheat mills and among the most prominent cotton mill owners of the Wuxi and Shanghai area. The Rong brothers had been involved in industrial reform since the early years of the Republic and continued their involvement after the establishment of the Nanjing government. They "were favored participants in the constellation of Guomindang commission, committee, and model districts that singled out certain key industrialists in the Yangzi river delta region for more direct involvement in government policy-making with respect to industrial development."[53] Similarly, industrialist and agriculturalist Mu Ouchu (styled Xiangyue; a future member of the CCC) had a history of collaboration with local officials in cotton improvement programs. Upon his return to China from the United States, where he studied agriculture, Mu became involved in early experiments in cotton growing and quality improvement while at the same time opening up cotton yarn factories. His fame was such that he was called the "giant of cotton yarn."[54]

Conscious of being the major source of financial support for Nanjing, the Zhejiang-Jiangsu entrepreneurs hoped the government would fulfill their expectations regarding China's political consolidation, implementation of reforms in support of industrial development, protection of Chinese economic interests against foreign penetration, control of the growing Communist-led Chinese labor movement, and recognition of the rights of private capital. This group had thus rallied around Song Ziwen at the time of the National Economic Conference (1928) and lobbied the Nanjing government in support of his reform plan. In 1932 they were even more motivated to seek government support due to the growing effects of the Great Depression. In addition, the general crisis of liberal capitalism and the widespread feeling of distrust of capital, together with mounting pressure from Japanese economic imperialism, further encouraged private businesses to seek connections and cooperate with the government. Cooperation in government reconstruction programs and privileged connections with GMD leaders in Nanjing, in fact, could offer excellent business opportunities.

The development of the Jiangsu-Zhejiang economy had not only produced cotton and silk industrialists with a modernizing and capitalist mentality but also a group of enterprising new-style bankers. Chen Guangfu was among the first bankers to turn to industry for investment and to participate in the rehabilitation of production of agricultural raw materials for manufacturing. The Shanghai Commercial and Savings Bank's involvement in Chinese industry had started as early as 1916 when it first extended credit to a cotton mill in Wuxi. Soon it specialized in the cotton and wheat industries and, in 1919–20, built close business relationships with Rong Zongjing and Rong Desheng. Cooperation with the Rong brothers in purchasing foreign raw cotton and wheat with letters of credit allowed Chen to expand the bank's activities into the area of foreign currency exchange and international marketing.[55] As the volume of the bank's business expanded so did its involvement with the textile industry. Chen, however, did not limit himself to this sector and, pursuing the opportunities created by the Yangzi River flood of 1931, expanded his business in rural credit, thus starting his partnership with Song Ziwen.

In 1925, having risen to a position of prominence in Shanghai, Chen Guangfu was elected to membership in the city's provisional government. In 1927, when Jiang Jieshi arrived in Shanghai, Chen and the Shanghai merchant Yu Hede organized the Jiangsu and Shanghai Financial Committee—chaired by Chen—which offered Jiang three million yuan in exchange for Jiang's protection against the Communist-led labor unions.[56] Chen's loyalty, however, seems to have shifted to Song Ziwen soon after the Nanjing government was established, reflecting the general disappointment of Shanghai businessmen with Jiang.[57] With Song, Chen shared a feeling of urgency for reforms, as well as a similar view of the nature of China's modern economy. Like Song, Chen had tried to use his international ties to attract foreign capital to China in order to reorient it away from Japan. In 1931 he thus established a joint Sino-British venture, the Baofeng Insurance Firm.[58]

Chen Guangfu, the Rong brothers, and Mu Ouchu exemplified the "modern" reform-minded Jiangnan entrepreneurs. Along with other urban industrialists, they believed it was necessary to promote "modern" business and eliminate "feudal" business practices that were holding China back. Chen Guangfu, for example, distinguished between two kinds of businessmen: those who were eager to carry out much-needed innovations and were involved in production and those who continued along traditional lines and insisted on limiting their activities to speculative and commercial business.[59] Chen's view on this issue reflected his productivist bias, a trait that he shared with Song and the leaders of the Wang group. Chen prided himself on being an innovator, a pioneer of modern banking in China and Western-style efficiency, and a promoter of Chinese industry.[60] Reforms were thus accepted in this nationalist and modernizing spirit even though they might require the intervention of the state. In June 1933, four months before the establishment of the CCC, Chen published an article denouncing the evils of liberal capitalism and advocating the government's "jurisdiction over production, consumption, and transportation" in order to achieve the rationalization of the Chinese economy.

> Under the capitalist system there are all kinds of conflicts because everyone goes after his own good. . . . Under the capitalist system, for example, we permit A to open a shop. Then we cannot deny the same permit to B and C (all three open barber shops) although this has a bad influence not only on A's business but also on the business of B and C—because supply exceeds demand. If we go on like this, business will keep declining, going bankrupt. Opening all those competing shops is a suicidal policy.[61]

Chen was strongly in favor of economic control as a means for planning national production and demand.

> On the one hand, [economic control can] balance gains and losses. On the other hand, it can] totally eliminate any form of irrational economic activity and also completely abandon contradicting and conflicting economic organization inspired by the pursuit of personal profit. Thus, as the core of the social system, we can substitute the entire society—that is, the entire country—for the individual. This is a first step in realizing economic control.[62]

Based on these observations, Chen questioned the role of capitalism in the world economy after World War I. As did many other economists in China, Chen believed that all countries would eventually abandon liberalism and adopt some form of controlled economy. While Chen Gongbo and Fang Xianting regarded Roosevelt's policies as exemplary of new trends in government intervention, Chen Guangfu preferred to refer to a banker and businessman like himself to illustrate his idea: "Economic control and democracy are the most fashionable slogans of the last few months. In reality in Europe during the Great War, economic control was already advocated by Walter Rathenau and it has already yielded adequate results."[63] Walter Rathenau, the progeny of a rich and powerful German Jewish family, attempted to answer the criticism of Socialist activists by expanding on his view of the role of industry and capital in society and on the relationship between industry and the state. Rathenau devised his own version of productivism in which the expansion of production was integrated with the education and moral improvement of the masses.

Rathenau's vision was not just a personal eccentricity; it reflected an international trend most notably represented in the United States by John D. Rockefeller Jr. The American millionaire was dedicated to the edification of the masses, and his sense of social responsibility led him to embrace philanthropy on a large scale.[64] After World War I, Rathenau became the minister of reconstruction and foreign affairs for the Weimar Republic. In this capacity he drafted a plan for an industrial society that combined some aspects of socialist state control while preserving freedom for private enterprise. Rathenau was murdered in June 1922 by a political fanatic close to the army and was never able to realize his plan.[65] The problem was not only the fact that Rathenau was Jewish and thus represented an entrepreneurial group that could not survive in Germany after the ascent to power of the Nazis but also, under the new regime established by Hitler, German industrialists came to be increasingly under the control of the militarized state, precluding any leadership role for industrial magnates. In the late 1920s and early 1930s Germany also witnessed a heated debate on corporativism, the autonomy of business, and the limits of state intervention. Conflicting trends competed within the Nazi Party, much as they did within the Italian Fascist regime and the GMD. The groups linked to the theorist Othmar Spann favored a form of societal (or, following Kasza's categorization, rightist) corporativism. By 1934, however, Hitler and his supporters had succeeded in depriving the state corporatist organization of actual power, transferring it to a new economic administration based on a structure of controlled economy, which firmly established the state authority at all levels of the economy. The new economic structure of the Nazi state—which came closer to Jiang Jieshi's notion of corporativism—although corporativist in nature (comparable to authoritarian or Leninist corporativism), avoided the term "corporativism," which had come to be associated with the notion of shared authority between the state and large businesses in all economic matters.[66]

It is clear that Chen Guangfu identified with Rathenau and shared his concern for the future of capitalism and its role in modern society. Chen believed that capitalism needed to develop new forms in order to adapt to new world developments and to survive the current crisis. Extensively quoting from the book *Capitalism to Survive Must Have New Ideas*, by Malcolm Forbes Sr., American millionaire and founder of the magazine *Forbes* (1917), Chen argued that the new mission of industrialists and financiers was "to serve society" (*fuwu shehui*). Such an "adjust[ment] to the new trends of the period" was society's only hope for survival.[67] This should thus constitute, according to Chen, the new model for China's industry.

Chen Guangfu anticipated the concerns of the other businessmen who participated in the CCC. In his address at the first meeting of the CCC, he denied that supervision of industry by the CCC would amount to nationalization. The CCC would intervene to stabilize prices, coordinate finances, and reduce speculation, and on specific occasions, the government would use its power to force changes when individuals refused to make them voluntarily. Ultimately, however, the CCC would allow private capital to thrive.[68]

Chen Guangfu gave voice to the hopes of many in the Shanghai business community. In 1934 the prominent banker Lin Kanghou, secretary general of the Chinese Bankers Association and chairman of the National Merchants Association, was concerned with economic cooperation and economic control. Harking back to China's long tradition of rural mutual-aid societies, Lin contended that foreign imperialism had destroyed the original character of the Chinese economy and imposed its own version of a utilitarian economy upon it. Because of this, China needed to develop a system of cooperation between state and private business based on economic control and cooperative societies and in this way return to the original spirit of the Chinese economy. Lamenting the state of contemporary business, he wrote:

> Today's economic system is not for the people but for the sake of money. . . . Seeing this, various countries are trying to solve the crisis through economic control, regulating production and consumption. Economic control means planning the economy, producing for consumer needs. An improvement of the economic system cannot be undertaken by the government alone but must be carried out with the experience and assistance of the people. Therefore, progressive countries have organized cooperative societies in order to make the people responsible and to realize a mutual-aid system.[69]

Although Lin was not a member of the CCC or of the Zhejiang-Jiangsu group, he held a prominent position within the Shanghai business community. His statements on economic control reflect the depth of the crisis of liberalism in China's most prosperous treaty ports, revealing that the views of the members of the CCC entrepreneurs were not unique in the Shanghai business environment. They were, however, distinct in a few fundamental ways: their industrial outlook, modernizing drive, and involvement with government-sponsored reform.

From this point of view, the Zhejiang-Jiangsu entrepreneurs represented the first "national" industrialists because they went beyond local or sector associationism to promote the importance of industrial development in modern nation building. The worldwide crisis of liberal capitalism certainly played a major role in making Chen Gongbo's plan attractive to the private entrepreneurs. His plan, however, addressed the problems experienced by the industrial modernizing elite themselves.

The CCC thus mobilized all parts involved in the cotton industry who appear to possess *minzu* and productivist qualities. Merchants who dealt with foreign economic firms, generally labeled with the negative appellation of "compradors" (*maiban*), were excluded because their economic activities were antithetic to the CCC's anti-imperialist goals. Merchants in general were excluded because they were identified with speculative activities rather than production, and the CCC planned to replace them, in the long run, with cooperative marketing societies, which were supposed to more closely follow productivist goals. In the productivist atmosphere of

1930s China, merchants were, in fact, perceived as parasitic middlemen, hindering the modernization of the industry, as discussed in the next chapter. For this reason they were not considered part of the *minzu* economy.

Private business in the CCC was thus represented by modern industrialists, bankers, and scientists who shared many of the same ideas advocated by the NEC's leaders. The CCC was a site for real cooperation between state and private economy, or at least the urban industrial sector. Still, much ambiguity remained on the issue of state control and how far the entrepreneurs were willing to go along with the reforming vision of the NEC's leaders, a topic that is taken up in chapter 6.

The Cotton Control Commission and the Rightist Pattern of Corporativism

The membership of the Standing Committee of the CCC—its real center of power—drew together the various elements of the broad productivist community that had gradually developed in Jiangnan. The Standing Committee was composed of representatives of three main interest groups. Private business was represented by cotton mill owners Li Shengbo (owner of the Dazhonghua, Dawan, and Dashachan cotton mills) and Tang Xinghai, who was closely linked to Chen Gongbo (having sponsored Chen's studies at Columbia University), and by banker Chen Guangfu, the chairman of the CCC.[70] The state was represented by the director of the Consolidated Tax Division of the Ministry of Finance, Xie Qi (styled Xie Zuokai), who would ensure that the state share the benefits resulting from the development of the cotton industry. His presence reflected Song Ziwen's idea that the new industrial sector was to be the base of China's finances, namely, its tax base. Song had been one of the most active promoters of the new tax, called the Consolidated Tax, that was specifically designed as a unified national tax to replace the local *lijin* tax and to tax China's emerging industrial sector.[71] Official interests were also represented by Ye Zhuotang, a banker and member of the board of directors of the China Merchants Steamship Navigation Company.[72] From 1911 to 1927 the China Merchants Steamship Navigation Company was under the exclusive control of Shanghai commercial authorities and ended up opposing the GMD during the Northern Expedition, preferring to side with local warlords.[73] Ultimately, the company was brought under the control of the NEC in 1934. The presence of Ye Zhuotang on the Standing Committee was thus emblematic of both the potentially intrusive reach of state intervention in the private economy and the impossibility of drawing a clear line of demarcation between state and private interests. The CCC Standing Committee also included the agriculturalist Zou Bingwen, who represented the third group: experts focused on ensuring technological innovation. A member of the Science Society and founder of the magazine *Science,* Zou was a pioneer in agricultural extension reforms and was also director of the Agricultural Bureau of Chen Guangfu's Shanghai Commercial and Savings Bank.[74]

The CCC regular membership reflected similar interests and was composed of mill owners Rong Zongjing,[75] Guo Xun, and Nie Lusheng; the general manager of the Bank of China, Zhang Jia'ao (styled Gongquan); and the director of the Foreign Exchange Office of the Bank of China, Bei Songsun (styled Zuyi).[76] The regular membership also included prominent cotton industrialists and cotton cultivation experts Mu Ouchu and Sun Enlin (styled Yushu), who also served as the director of the CCC's Central Bureau for the Improvement of Cotton Production (*zhongyang mianchan gaijingsuo*).[77] Representatives of governmental and party agencies were also included in the CCC's regular membership: He Bingxian, director of the International Trade Office of the Ministry of Industry; Wu Xingya, a member of the Shanghai branch of the GMD and director of the CC clique (the GMD group headed by the brothers Chen Lifu and Chen Guofu, who worked closely with Jiang Jieshi) in Shanghai;[78] Chen Bozhuang, a member of the Legislative Yuan; and Liu Yinfu.[79]

The only link with labor unions was the presence of Du Yuesheng in the general membership. Du was the main leader of the Green Gang (*qingbang*), which was the most powerful secret society and organized-crime group in Shanghai. The Green Gang had been developing ties with the Nationalist government since 1927. Du had started as a small-time thief but had evolved into a successful businessman and prominent personality in the local economic and political community. His illegal activities, mostly opium dealings, were carried out under the guise of his new respectability. When Wu Xingya, who was believed to be a member of the Green Gang, arrived in Shanghai as the head of the local organization of the CC clique, Du and Wu became very close.[80] The two successfully cooperated in the resolution of labor unrest, such as the 1932 anti-Japanese strike wave and the May 1932 postal workers' strike.[81] Du's new respectability took on an official aura during the Japanese attack on Shanghai in 1932. On that occasion, Du served side by side with some of Shanghai's most prominent personalities in many of the local organizations created to fill the vacuum left by the disintegration of the local GMD administration.[82]

Although Du was also a cotton mill owner and banker, his presence in the CCC reflected, above all, the CCC industrialists' need to control labor. In the 1930s, Shanghai workers were particularly active and, under the leadership of the Communists, launched a series of strikes. Even if the strikes did not produce noticeable improvements in the conditions of the workers—due to repressive measures adopted by industrialists and political authorities—they created considerable trouble for industrial management and raised the specter of future uprisings. In the 1930s, having displaced the Communist union leaders, the Green Gang came to exercise unchallenged control over unskilled labor in the Shanghai area. In the process Du gained fame as an efficient labor representative and mediator of labor disputes. Du's actions were not always at the expense of the workers. On certain occasions, Du found himself defending the rights of workers against both management and political authorities. Green Gang labor activities were sometimes in opposition to those of the GMD unions, and the labor disputes of the 1930s were generally complicated by the interplay of several actors, including the Green Gang, the CCP, the GMD unions, and the industrialists. Du became an indispensable mediator, earning money and respectability in the process.[83] The presence of Du Yuesheng and Zhang Xiaolin—the other important leader of the Green Gang and the man who had supported Du and supervised his rapid rise through the Gang's ranks—in the CCC suggests the importance that the CCC placed in disciplining the cotton labor force.

The CCC attitude toward labor was not just a result of political conservatism but also of the fear that production would be disrupted by frequent strikes, thus hindering the CCC's productivist goals. Peasant and rural interests in general were also completely ignored by the CCC. Its only members working in the rural areas were agriculturalists, such Mu Ouchu and Zou Bingwen, who came from urban industrial backgrounds and approached rural reforms from the point of view of improving supplies of raw material for industrial production. In comparison with peasants and workers, and even rural landlords, the modern economic elite held a privileged position within the corporativist organization of the CCC. In general, the CCC was poised to realize the model of corporativism that Kasza labels "rightist" and associates with the Italian Fascist regime.

The Cotton Control Commission and the Debate on Civil Society

The corporativist nature of the CCC and the intricate network of interests described above reveal the inadequacy of Western-centered theories of the relationship between state and society in an attempt to explain the CCC. These theories are generally based on the idea that state and society have intrinsically conflicting interests. As a consequence, societal groups are thought of as generally engaged in a struggle with the state in an attempt to defend their autonomy. Inspired by this dichotomist view, Western historians, most prominently Parks Coble and Marie-Claire Bergère, portrayed 1920s and 1930s Chinese "capitalists"—their term for describing the elite linked to the emerging industrial economy—as united by the common interest of resisting the Nanjing government's interventionist aspirations.[84] At the same time, they represented the Nationalist government as largely in agreement in its desire to control, even to outright nationalize, private business. In their influential books on politics and business in Shanghai, Coble and Joseph Fewsmith identified economic networks that connected groups in the government with groups in the private economy, but they viewed them primarily as marks of factional struggle fueled by personal economic and political motivations and as channels for corrupt practices of "bureaucratic capitalism"—that is, officials' use of governmental positions to help the private business to which they were directly or indirectly connected.[85] The Republican period on the mainland has come to be particularly infamous for this corrupt practice. Although these networks seemed to run across the dividing line between state and society and to fragment the government, as well as private business, into competing groups, the main interpretive approach throughout the 1980s remained the paradigm of conflict between state and private economy.

This perspective was encouraged by the work of the German philosopher Jürgen Habermas on the emergence and transformation of civil society in Europe.[86] Habermas identified the development of a public sphere in eighteenth-century Europe as a sign of modernization and democratization of the body politic. Motivated by the desire to prove that Chinese society had not been dozing before Western imperialism came to awaken it—an argument supported by much pre-1980s scholarship—China historians such as William Rowe, Mary Rankin, and David Strand focused their work on the rise of merchants or other interest-group organizations in the late imperial period. Following Habermas's paradigm, they argued that these organizations brought about a separation between state and society, generating a genuine, although embryonic, public sphere. They could thus argue that Chinese society had experienced the same changes, although to a lesser degree, that had marked the modernization of Western Europe.[87] These studies generated a heated debate on the existence of a public sphere in China and the applicability of Habermas's model to the study of Chinese history. Among the most vocal critics were historians Frederic Wakeman and Philip Huang.

Wakeman denied that a public sphere had ever had the opportunity to develop due to the totalitarian nature of the Chinese state.[88] Huang, instead, confined his criticism to the use of Habermas's model in Chinese history, pointing out that Habermas himself had stressed that his study was limited to the European experience in the eighteenth century. Huang thus proposed a new interpretive framework based on the idea of the existence in China of a "third realm" between state and society. According to Huang, it was especially in the Republican period that this third realm expanded, creating an arena for joint elite-state action. He identified "water control, road maintenance, philanthropy, academies, dispute mediation," as well as "new activities of gentry and merchant elites, and especially the reform-minded among them," as an emerging intermediate space between state and private spheres. Huang further stated that "with these changes the third realm became more institutionalized. The activities of gentry and merchant elites found expression in new institutions that ranged from the semiofficial bureaus of public works to 'self-government bureaus.'" In spite of the uneven and volatile nature of the development of a third realm in China (Huang himself conceded that some of the new third-realm institutions represented a mere process of bureaucratization while others revealed new trends of privatization), Huang identified the growth of joint state-private institutions in Republican China as "a part of the process of modern societal integration" and "the continued working together of state and society in the third space between them."[89]

An analysis of the CCC further complicates the debate over the relationship between state and society in the Republican years. On the one hand, it confirms Huang's argument of the development of a "third realm" in the Republican years. The corporativist trends that marked these years indeed had the ideological goal of creating a new space between state and society on the basis of common interests. On the other hand, we cannot place the CCC squarely within the third realm. Cooperation among CCC groups shifted on specific issues and alliances remained flexible, materializing and dematerializing case by case. The same institution constituted a place of cooperation but could also turn into a site of conflict according to circumstances, as testified by the CCC's difficulty in reforming factories' managerial practices, discussed in chapter 6. The CCC's experience also reveals the unevenness and limitations of the trend toward the development and gradual institutionalization of a third realm in 1930s China. It, in fact, shows how its uncertain future depended both on a clarification of the idea of the state's functions and on the success of the Nationalist civilian reformist strand against the more totalitarian and statist nation-building model pursued by Jiang. The Wang group's corporativist organizations would have allowed the development of organizations such as the CCC that had the potential to become the expression of Huang's third realm. Jiang's idea of corporativism—inspired by the one realized in Germany after 1934—on the other hand, would have led to its suppression because it would have led to the more totalitarian form of corporativism.

In this uncertain background, Coble's and Bergère's assessments of the conflicting nature of the relationship between private economy and state were a result of their focus on the economic reforms led by Jiang in late 1935, following the defeat of the Wang-NEC group. Historian Richard Bush, however, writing on the Jiangnan cotton industry before 1935, concludes that the cotton industrialists had a strong hold on Nanjing and were able to manipulate the government to their advantage.[90] The divergence in the conclusions of these historians reveals the inconsistency in attitudes toward private business among groups in the government rather than a problem with these historians' research. Their assessments are, in fact, all accurate and only need to be integrated into the wider picture of political division that characterized the prewar Nationalist regime.

Conclusion

The popularity of the ideas of corporativism and of a "nation of producers" underscores the importance of economic thought in the construction of national identity in prewar China. The nation was, in fact, envisioned as being composed of economic actors, united by their common goal of increasing production and saving the nation. In addition, the economic function of Chinese citizens defined their positions in the nation. Contributors to national production were allowed to participate in the national enterprise on the basis, at least theoretically, of equality and freedom. The idea of *minzu* economy was not just a rhetorical device but found concrete expression in the way the Nationalist government shaped its relations with socioeconomic groups—which economic actors it privileged and which it marginalized. "Nonproducer" citizens, such as merchants and compradors, and industrialists whose commitment to modernization and nation building did not match the objectives of the NEC's leaders were confined to the margins of the *minzu* economy and subjected to state control.

The idea of a nation of producers assumed a distinctive meaning in China, where it became associated not only with productivism, as it was in most Western countries, but also with anti-imperialism. Corporativist trends in China were influenced by the country's distinctive situation. Because of the presence of foreign enterprises on Chinese territory, national borders did not define the boundaries of the national economy. Corporativism could not follow geographic logic but needed a powerful criterion of exclusion from citizenship based on each individual's position with respect to the *minzu* economy.

Although anti-imperialist, and specifically anti-Japan, the *minzu* corporativist organization of the CCC took inspiration from trends that had developed in Europe and Japan. It was, in a sense, the case of using imperialist modernity to resist that same imperialism. It thus combined an inward-looking autarkic logic of nativism (*minzu*) with a cosmopolitan approach to modernization. In other words, the Chinese leaders considered modernity to be essentially cosmopolitan, although it was used as a weapon for achieving autarkic isolation. This tension between China's participation in worldwide trends and its domestic goals characterized Nationalist thought and policies, which were, in fact, generally the result of the encounter of domestic late Qing trends with theories that reached China from the West (at times through Japan itself, the very target of China's anti-imperialism). The origins of the idea of the state's cooperation with the private economy can be traced back to the Self-Strengthening period. At this time joint state-private (*guanshang*) interests became involved in economic reform aimed at the modernization of the country, motivated by the same combination of nationalism and economic interests that would characterize the CCC in the 1930s. From this perspective the CCC and the NEC were a continuation of the pattern of reform originating in the late nineteenth century, although with some significant differences. Similar to the CCC's reform strategy, the Self-Strengthening *guanshang* reforms were a response to the state's lack of capital and the desire of reform-minded government officials to tap private funds. In both periods the government created incentives to encourage private investments in modern industry. The *guanshang* partnership, however, had allowed much more independence to private entrepreneurs than did the CCC's, since, although supported by the state, the *guanshang* partnership was not subjected to a highly centralized system of controlled economy. By the 1930s the idea of the state and its functions had undergone dramatic changes. The Nanjing government pursued political and economic centralization to an unprecedented degree. In their encounter, *guanshang* and corporativist trends modified each other, leading to the CCC's attempt to institutionalize the unstructured relationship between business and government to create a modern political system—corporativism.

The CCC's corporativist organization inherited much of the confusion of state and private resources dating back to the late imperial period and its potential for bureaucratic capitalism, an issue addressed at length in chapter 6. It is important to emphasize here that, although a certain number of corrupt practices linked to bureaucratic capitalism can be found in the CCC, and the NEC at large, the CCC must be placed within the wider context of changes in state-society relationships and the efforts by groups within the GMD to institutionalize them. From late Qing to 1935, networks of bureaucratic capitalism were an integral part of emerging economic and political strategies. These networks provided channels for cooperation between the government and private economic circles in the absence of other means for political participation.

The problem of defining or institutionalizing the relationship between state and private economy remains relevant for today's China, where professional or sector associations can be considered a form of AMO. While in the Mao years these associations were prevalently an expression of the state economy and a vehicle for political control, in the new market economy they are undergoing a significant transformation. To a certain extent they have become a site of negotiations between socioeconomic groups and the state. They have, for example, served as an instrument for workers to organize and present demands to the state.[91] At the same time, the dismantling of the state economy and the development of the private economic sector have, in fact, created a communications gap between the two and required the establishment of new kinds of associations. Therefore, the Chinese government has established new trading and planning commissions that often include some of the current leaders of private industry, a development reminiscent of the NEC.[92] Whether these new associations can be considered corporativist organizations or a sign of the development of a civil society is a controversial issue. Disagreement among scholars on this topic reveals the ambiguous nature of the associations and the uncertainty about how today's centralized Chinese state is going to resolve the problem of keeping a measure of control over the private economy while fostering its development. In other words, Chinese leaders today are still in the process of defining the relationship between the Chinese nation as a whole (including its political identity) and the booming Chinese economy. Although issues of anti-imperialism have been replaced by a milder form of nationalism that does not influence the perception of the Chinese economy in the way that the notion of *minzu* economy did in the prewar years, notions of resistance to new forms of imperialism and of negative aspects of capitalism still influence the state's attitude toward the private industrial economy and create tension between the two.

From Theory to Practice PART III

伍

CHAPTER 5

Implementing Rural Reforms

The construction of an autarkic *minzu* economy, the primary goal of the NEC, required a remapping of the socioeconomic structure that had characterized the Chinese village in the late imperial and early Republican periods. Abandoning the idea that agriculture was the foundation of the nation and identifying the urban industrial elite as the basis of China's modern nationhood implied that the interests of the village elite were no longer protected by the state and that they would be sacrificed for the sake of industrialization. The NEC leaders, in fact, perceived the rural elite as "feudal" and an obstacle to modernity and national salvation. In their view, village landlords, moneylenders, and merchants—called "middlemen" by the Nationalists and always cast in an unfavorable light—were not a vital part of China's *minzu* economy because they were not actively engaged in production and were mostly involved in speculative activities. Their interests thus needed to be subordinated to those of the industrial elite, the most important among the *minzu* "producers." In the new economic geography of the nation, the village elite were thus destined to be marginalized while the industrial producers assumed a central position.

As reports from the field reveal, the village elite fiercely resisted this marginalization in the country's economic system. Their resistance was not necessarily ideological but was motivated by very real economic interests. Even if some of the rural elite agreed in theory with the idea of industrialization and believed in the need to strengthen China, they were dismayed at the usurpation of their economic and social power base by new urban bankers and entrepreneurs. As Pomeranz contends, only those who were able to take advantage of the new economic networks created by the Nationalist nation-building efforts were willing to cooperate with state reforms. Others had too much to lose.[1]

The rural elite's reaction to the CCC was also influenced by the indisputable fact that the CCC was colonizing the village to support the growth of urban centers. Although Chen Gongbo's original plan also aimed at benefiting the rural economy in order to increase the peasants' purchasing power, during its short life the CCC appeared intent on ensuring cheap raw material for the cotton mills, losing sight of wider reform goals. This was probably the result of the ambiguous corporativist nature of the CCC. While some of its most reformist members remained focused on the CCC's nation-building agenda, some of its mill-owner members saw the CCC as an opportunity for cutting production costs by acquiring cheap domestic raw material.

The innovative aspect of the CCC's plan did not rest in the kind of reforms and technological improvements it promoted, since similar techniques for the improvement of cotton quality and the expansion of its production had been tried with a good measure of success since the late Qing period by a myriad of local cotton improvement agencies. The goal of the CCC was to bring these agencies under its control and coordinate them within a wider national and autarkic framework, reversing their regional and mercantilist character. The CCC also aimed at extending cotton improvement programs beyond the areas where they had already spontaneously been implemented. The preexisting cotton improvement programs developed around industrial centers and especially in Jiangnan and Hebei, catering to, respectively, Shanghai and Tianjin factories. The CCC planned to expand cotton cultivation in more remote areas, especially in the northwest, relying on its interregional marketing network to bring cotton from these more distant provinces to the Shanghai market. In these areas, which lacked local cotton improvement initiatives and were not yet integrated into the new industrial economy, the CCC intervened more directly in agricultural production and marketing. As discussed in more detail later in this chapter, the CCC was especially active in Shaanxi because of the particular political and economic circumstances of this province.

This chapter assesses the impact of the work of the CCC in rural areas at two levels. It evaluates the CCC's success in establishing the foundation for a nationwide network of state intervention in the cotton industry, especially its ability to reach into the village and alter local long-established patterns of credit and marketing. By 1937, its final year,[2] the CCC appeared to have failed to develop into a highly centralized and full-fledged control committee as envisioned by Chen Gongbo. In fact, it had developed into an alternative credit and marketing network competing with the village's moneylenders, merchants, and brokers rather than controlling the village economy. Its attempt to use marketing mechanisms to free the peasants from indebtedness, bring them better returns on the sales of their crops, and reduce the cost of marketing had the potential to deeply change the village and to stimulate agricultural growth. Because the CCC existed for only four years, however, the CCC credit and marketing cooperative societies did not have enough time to become established vis-à-vis local competitors and gain the trust of the peasants. In 1937, therefore, the CCC was still struggling to overcome fierce competition by local economic interests.

In addition, this chapter examines the CCC's impact on the expansion and improvement of the agricultural production of raw cotton. At this level, the CCC contributed significantly, although not crucially, to helping the Chinese cotton industry weather the 1930s economic crisis. Against the background of the general decline of rural production, supplies of raw cotton remained steady and its quality improved. This achievement was mostly the product of a joint effort of the CCC and the myriad of reform agencies that had been active since the turn of the century and that the CCC had gradually brought under its control.

One of the main questions about the impact of the CCC's work in the rural economy is whether, in the long run, it would have benefited the village economy or simply have exploited it to support urban industrial development. In this respect, the CCC's plan was quite problematic. Its full realization would have transformed the village into a mere supplier of agricultural products while industrial production would be concentrated in the urban areas. This strategy would have eventually led to the decline of the rural handicraft industry, which had traditionally played an important role in the economy of the village.[3] At the same time, marketing societies would have worked as cotton-collecting agencies channeling rural products to urban markets, with the potential of triggering the decline of rural markets, which had also traditionally played an important role in the rural economy. The CCC leaders, in general, tended to underestimate local market forces and the cultural trends that supported them, both because they regarded them as feudal and harmful to economic modernization and because (as discussed later) they held misconceptions about the nature of China's market that were common at the time.

The main obstacle to the successful realization of the CCC's plan was, however, Jiang's opposition and obstructionism. The main sources of disagreement between the NEC leaders and Jiang were the same ones that fueled the overall political confrontation: the role of the private Jiangnan economy in China's nation-building efforts, Jiang's military approach to the "pacification" of the countryside (i.e., to defeat the Communists), and the productivist reforming approach of the Wang group. The rural village thus became one more site of confrontation between the two competing views of China's modern nation building that was splitting party, government, and country at the time.

Cotton and Nationhood

The choice of the cotton industry as the first target for the NEC's intervention derived from three main considerations. The first was that Song Ziwen had just contracted the cotton and wheat loan with the United States and urgently needed a specialized agency to deal with it from within the NEC. Second, the cotton industry possessed all the requisites laid down by the NEC at the first meeting of its Standing Committee: China was a natural cotton-producing area, and thus the industry could rely on domestic resources.[4] It was one of China's strongest industries and enjoyed the highest concentration of capital. The general expectation was that this industry did not require a large injection of state funding, since it was already the richest in the country, but just needed a thorough reorganization and rationalization of the various phases of the production process.

One more consideration made the cotton industry an ideal target of reform for the NEC. The cotton industry made a particularly good case in support of Wang's and Chen's autarkic policies since, by 1933, it had grown increasingly dependent on Japanese business. According to historian Peter Duus, Japanese cotton yarn and manufactures poured into the Chinese market, while Japanese mills in China, which could rely on large capitalization and strong organization back home, waged unfair competition against the products of Chinese-owned mills.[5] By 1936, almost 40 percent of China's machine-spun yarn and 75 percent of its machine-woven cloth were produced by Japanese cotton mills in China. Duus describes the situation as follows:

> On the eve of the China War, Japanese-owned cotton mills also accounted for a substantial portion of private Japanese investment in China. According to one contemporary estimate, Japanese investment in China, including loans to Chinese enterprises and loans to the Chinese government, amounted to 1.583 billion yen in 1936. Slightly more than half of this amount (about 840 million yen) consisted of direct investment in Japanese-owned business enterprises. . . . Of these firms, the most important were engaged in foreign trade and cotton manufacturing, each industry representing an investment of about 300 million yen. While Japanese

> trading firms were active in the rest of the world, the Japanese cotton industry sought overseas investment outside of the formal empire only in China.[6]

This passage illustrates well the extent of Japanese penetration into the Chinese cotton industry, not only in terms of amount of capital invested but also as a conscious choice to use China as the privileged site for development of the Japanese cotton industry. Unable to face such fierce competition, the Chinese mills were, one by one, driven out of business and fell under the control of Japanese capital. The cotton industry thus constituted a perfect example of an economic victim of Japanese imperialism.

The case was even more glaring since, in the eyes of many Chinese, this industry was traditionally the oldest and strongest in China, possessing nationalist qualities that particularly fitted Chen's autarkic rhetoric. In the years between the two world wars, not just in China but in different geographical regions, cotton goods and the cotton industry emerged as closely linked with ideas of national identity and anti-imperialism. Mahatma Gandhi, for example, came to identify Indian cotton as an essential characteristic of Indian national identity. Although he did not insert the production of domestic cotton into the framework of industrialization and nation building, he promoted the idea of homespun cotton as a symbol of living in tune with India's cultural and economic essence and as a symbol of resistance to British imperialism and its attempt to invade India with British cotton goods.[7] In an example that more closely resembles the Chinese discourse on cotton and nation, the Italian Fascist regime placed great importance on the production of *il cotone nazionale* (national cotton) and placed it at the heart of its colonial and autarkic aspirations.[8] In the same vein, Chen Gongbo placed the *minzu* cotton industry at the core of his autarkic plan, declaring that cotton was crucial to China's survival. In times of peace, he explained, cotton fulfilled the clothing (*yi*) function, which, as argued earlier, had been elevated by Sun Yat-sen's Three People's Principles to one of the Four Great Necessities of the People—clothing, food, shelter, and transportation (*yi, shi, zhu, xing*)—that constituted the foundation of the People's Livelihood. Chen thus invested the NEC's intervention in the cotton industry with a special aura of political legitimacy. In times of war, Chen continued, the cotton industry provided military uniforms and bandages, assuming an important defensive function.[9] The idea of the foundational nature of the cotton industry emerged in the writings and speeches of many industrialists and economists, who used Sun's metaphors to frame their concerns for China's current situation. This was also the case with Song Ziwen, who, at the time of the establishment of the CCC, argued that "the cotton industry had an especially strong relationship with People's Livelihood." "From today on," he added, "the cotton industry must begin to shoulder responsibilities related to national power."[10]

Even Fang Xianting, whose opinions differed from Chen's on many issues, argued that the cotton industry supplied "one of the prime necessities of life."[11] According to Fang, since the Ming dynasty cotton had become the most popular textile material among the Chinese people, and he claimed that, at the time he was writing, it made up "more than nine-tenths of the fabric worn in China."[12] His appeal to revive the rural economy was also focused on the rehabilitation of the cotton industry because it was important for improving the standard of living of the peasants and was directly linked to national survival. For this reason most of Fang's writings were concerned with the cotton industry in his region, the Tianjin area and Hebei. Mu Ouchu also believed in the importance of developing the cotton industry for the sake of China's salvation: "Reviving the cotton industry is not just closely related to the people's livelihood. It also has a great influence on the national economy. Therefore, by reviving the cotton industry we can not only solve the poverty problem but also save the nation." This was not only because most peasants relied on the production of cotton for their survival but also because cotton provided for one of life's basic needs: "Clothing is the great foundation of human life. The need for wearing clothes is significant. Not inferior to that for food." Mu then lamented that China's imports were rising, particularly those from Japan. "Japanese goods fill our markets and are so many that we cannot even start counting them. This is the prevalent situation for daily-need goods. But among all imports those of cotton yarn and cloth are the most numerous." Because the Chinese production of cotton textiles had decreased, "foreign daily-need goods used by the people constituted one-third of all imports. . . . [I]f we continue like this and do not try to remedy [this situation] . . . the single matter of cotton imports will be sufficient to drain our fat and blood and sever our lifeline."[13] This statement was carefully phrased, stressing that "the people" were the first to be affected by China's economic dependency. This image of the depth of the threat to China's population was further reinforced by the particular metaphors (blood, lifeline) used.

The CCC 1934 Annual Plan reflected this widespread support for autarky and the perception of the foundational nature of the cotton industry. Opening with a statement denouncing the current lack of self-sufficiency, it bemoaned China's dependency on foreign imports, which gnawed at the foundation of the nation: "Our country has a large territory and is rich in resources. The area fit for growing cotton is vast. However, domestic production of raw cotton does not meet demand. Its quality is not fit to be used. Consequently, the annual value of imports of foreign cotton—raw, yarn, and cloth—is huge. This seriously damages the foundations of the country." The basic reason for these problems was that the Chinese mills were unable to compete with foreign products, and unless a solution was found, the industry would reach the point of no return.

> As for cotton mills and cotton cloth factories, those managed by foreign merchants are all equipped with modern machinery and enjoy low production costs. Those established by the Chinese, on the contrary, mostly use old machinery, while their management lacks technical expertise. As a consequence, they pile up debts and cannot even survive a single day. If we do not find a way to save them as soon as possible, the Chinese cotton and textile industries will enter into a crisis from which it will be impossible to rescue them.[14]

Following the blueprint laid out by Chen Gongbo in the 1933 industrial plan, the CCC proposed to save the Chinese cotton industry in two ways. It would intervene in improving the domestic production of raw cotton while acting directly to modernize industrial production and management (the latter field of intervention is discussed in the next chapter). Chen and the CCC leaders believed that the improvement of rural raw materials was essential for the modernization of the industry and vital for achieving autarky. According to Chen, Chinese cotton was outsold by foreign imports because it was of poor quality. In addition, the cost of its transportation from the region of cultivation in the interior to the factories in the cities, on average, tripled its price, making it much less competitive in both the domestic and the international markets.[15] Chen's assessment pinpointed two of the main obstacles facing the cotton industry. Cotton manufacturers complained that domestic yarn could not be used with modern textile machines because it was well below the required twenty-four counts. In addition, its supply was often unreliable due to the unstable military situation in the interior and disruptions in the transportation system. Cotton mills were thus trapped in a vicious circle. They could not afford to buy foreign raw material because it was too expensive, especially after the rise in the price of silver following the 1934 American Silver-Purchase Act. Forced to rely on low-quality domestic supplies and to produce low-quality goods, Chinese mills were unable to compete in foreign markets and at home. They were thus easily outsold by Japanese and British cotton imports. Upgrading the Chinese mills' equipment was difficult because new machines had to be imported at extremely high prices and, in any case, they could not be used because domestic yarn count was too low and the foreign variety was too expensive.

When Chen Gongbo first arrived at the Ministry of Industry he attempted to solve these problems by promoting the improvement of cotton growing in order to provide Chinese mills with reliable and high-quality raw cotton. Under his leadership, the ministry sponsored research and experimentation in collaboration with experts at various universities and in various experimental fields around the country. It also organized a cotton transportation company in cooperation with the Ministry of Railways, which was at the time headed by Gu Mengyu, a member of the 1927 Reorganization Group and a close associate of Wang Jingwei. This company was to offer low prices to Chinese mills in order to encourage them to rely on domestic raw materials.[16] Upon its establishment, the CCC took over the work initiated by the Ministry of Industry. The 1934 Plan of the CCC mapped out its work, stressing its autarkic and modernizing goals: "(1) Increase production of raw cotton in order to balance supply and demand and make up for the current shortfall in production; (2) improve the quality of raw cotton in order to supply raw material of twenty-four or more counts and meet the needs of the cotton textile industry."[17] Consistent with the productivist approach favored by the Nationalists, the CCC focused on two main areas of intervention: bringing capital and technology to rural areas. The implementation of this basic plan required first of all bridging the gap between hinterland/rural and coastal/industrial economies. In other words, before capital and technology could be expected to pour into agricultural production, the CCC needed to create connections between the two Chinas.

It was through its centralized structure of cooperative societies that the CCC attempted to create these connections and develop a circular flow of technology, capital, and goods between the hinterland and the coastal industrial centers. This model was laid out, in rather optimistic terms, in the 1934 Plan:

> [By building cooperative societies] raw-cotton productivity can increase and its quality improve. At the same time, through cooperative societies, banks will be able to invest money with the peasants. The peasants, therefore, will be able to have access to sufficient cash flow for their work while [selling their cotton] at an excellent price. On the other hand, cotton mills can obtain supplies of raw material fit to use [for industrial processing]. Because the peasants' income will increase, their purchasing power will also increase. This will have an extremely important influence on the agriculture, commerce, and industry of our country. For these reasons, organizing production and marketing cooperative societies throughout China is one of the most important tasks of this commission.[18]

Cooperative societies would create a new relationship between agriculture and industry, allowing urban capital to support the growth of the rural economy. The capital invested in the rural economy through credit societies was then supposed to return to feed the coastal economy in the form of interest paid by peasants and profits from the sale of industrial goods on the rural markets. The cooperative societies would thus make it possible for capital to find its way to the rural village, raw cotton to coastal mills, and finished goods back to the village, creating a circular flow that would make China a self-sufficient economic unit.

The CCC's five-year implementation schedule included in the 1934 Plan reflected the ambitious nature of the CCC's projected work and the overall optimism of the plan. CCC leaders estimated that in three to five years its intervention would bring about a considerable improvement in the quality of domestic cotton and an increase in the volume of production. The conclusion of the Plan read:

> If we can really implement this plan we can in three to five years already have good seeds and good cultivation techniques that we can distribute to various areas, according to terrain and weather conditions. . . . [We can also] enlarge arable land surface. . . . In this way we hope to save domestic cotton production, improve varieties, and increase productivity. . . . If indeed we can continue our efforts, then the cultivation of new varieties of cotton will constantly increase, techniques of cotton growing will everyday improve, and the organization [of cooperative societies and improvement bureaus] will be everyday tighter . . . developing greater efficacy. . . . [It] is not difficult in the near future to become self-sufficient and improve cotton quality to meet the needs of cotton mills.[19]

Success and self-sufficiency seemed at hand. National data on cotton cultivation seem to confirm this optimism, as supplies of raw cotton expanded and its quality improved. As already mentioned, it is difficult to understand how much credit should be assigned to the CCC for these achievements, as cotton improvement reforms had already begun at the turn of the century. According to extensive research on cotton cultivation carried out by economic historian Richard Kraus, long-trend values for cotton yields and supplies remained steady during the 1918–36 period, although short-trend values show a slight decline in 1931–33 and a recovery in 1934–36. Kraus also argues that imports of cotton supplies (raw cotton for industrial production) reached their peak in 1931–33, falling sharply by approximately two-thirds in 1933–36.[20] These data seem to speak of a crisis in cotton cultivation in the early 1930s and of an impressive recovery in the following three years, as well as a measure of success in import substitution. This recovery can be credited to various factors, ranging from a natural recovery from the disastrous 1931 Yangzi River flood to the CCC's decisive boost to cotton improvement efforts, which contributed to the recovery of cotton cultivation beyond preflood levels. An evaluation of the work of the CCC has, however, to be carried out at two levels. First, we need to understand the CCC's direct impact on cotton cultivation. Second, the most important goal of the CCC cannot be measured in numerical data, since its main objective was a deep transformation of the socioeconomic and political structure of the cotton industry, including the breaking down of networks of economic interests in the village and changes in the marketing pattern of raw cotton and rural-credit practices. After all, nation building (making China an autarkic economic unit) was for the CCC leader as important as the development of the cotton industry.

Determining the contribution of the CCC at both levels is, however, difficult for several reasons. A permanent shift in the general trends of cotton cultivation in China could not be accomplished in four years. Improved access to credit, for example, was intended to lead to the replacement of traditional village moneylenders. These new sources of credit would have ensured lower interest rates for peasants, thus freeing capital to be reinvested in improving production (allowing peasants to purchase fertilizers, better tools, improved seeds varieties, and so on). This process, however, would necessarily have been slow and gradual, taking a few years to be completed and be reflected in statistics and reports. On a more practical note, statistics and data from this period, although already more consistent and reliable than those from earlier decades, are still sporadic and inconsistent. Most often, CCC reports appear overpositive and read as bureaucratic documents, in which only positive results are presented. These reports also lack basic information on the difficulties encountered in the implementation of policies at the local level. They do not offer comments on which initiatives proved successful and which failed. It is ironic that much of the useful information available today on the CCC's intervention in the rural village was compiled by foreign experts who often could not speak Chinese and were not familiar with the local situation. Especially illuminating are the reports of one of the experts of the League of Nations, W. K. H. Campbell, and they figure prominently in the discussion of the performance of the CCC in this chapter.

Rural Credit

The idea that rural China suffered from a shortage of modern credit facilities and that this shortage trapped peasants and agriculture in stagnation inspired the work of many organizations concerned with rural reconstruction, from James Yan's Mass Education Movement to the China International Famine Relief Commission (*Zhongguo huayang yizhen jiuzai zonghui,* hereafter CIFRC).[21] These organizations were the first to adopt credit cooperative societies as a tool for economic rehabilitation. The systematic expansion of rural cooperative credit can be attributed mostly to the CIFRC.[22] J. B. Tayler, the chairman of the CIFRC Committee on Rural Cooperation, sponsored one of the first extensive studies on cooperative credit in China. This study, published in 1926, made an early case for using cooperative societies as a channel for investing urban capital in the village. The reports stated that the "present credit organization makes impossible the application of the surplus of wealth of . . . some districts to those which need it."[23] City banks, the publication continued, were unable to do business with individual farmers because the small amount involved in such loans could not justify the cost of investigating each case. Peasants thus ended up contracting loans from local moneylenders at usurious rates, falling into a vicious cycle of indebtedness.[24] Cooperative societies were supposed to overcome this difficulty by allowing city banks to extend loans, not to individual farmers, but to a larger agency.

When the Nationalist government adopted cooperative societies as an important aspect of its nation-building plan, societies soared to unprecedented numbers. In 1927 there were 384 societies in China, a significant increase from the 19 in 1923. By 1931 the number of societies had soared to 3,487, beginning a sharp rise that was to reach 37,318 societies in 1936. A diversification of societies also occurred as they became more involved in production and marketing. In 1931, credit societies constituted the 87.5 percent of all societies. As the number of societies grew, however, they came to form only 55.3 percent.[25] As for most of the data related to rural credit in the 1930s, the numbers can be misleading because societies were often multipurpose, extending credit while also getting involved in production and marketing. This was the case with most of the societies sponsored by the CCC.[26]

As with other aspects of its work, the NEC aimed at expanding preexisting trends in rural credit, transforming them into national policies. More specifically, the NEC wanted to mobilize through its corporativist structures Shanghai entrepreneurs who had already been active in rural credit, thus transforming projects that were mostly local in scope into a nationwide policy. In 1931 Song Ziwen and Chen Guangfu (who was appointed chairman of the CCC in 1933) had already successfully experimented with the infusion of Shanghai capital into the rural areas through the Flood Relief Commission (FRC; *shuizai jiuji weiyuanhui*). The FRC was largely composed of the same group later involved in the CCC, including, in addition to Chen Guangfu, prominent industrialist Rong Zongjing and agriculturalist Zou Bingwen. Chen's experience with the FRC cemented his collaboration with Song and proved very profitable, presenting an unparalleled opportunity to expand his business into rural credit. The government soon organized other agencies which used cooperative societies for relief in areas afflicted by floods or other problems. Established in 1932, the North China War District Relief Commission, for example, was designed to extend relief to regions that had been affected by Sino-Japanese military clashes. These agencies, often sponsored in collaboration with the CIFRC, were crucial for the dramatic growth of the cooperative movement in the early 1930s. Rong Zongjing and Chen Guangfu were among the first to participate in these projects. In Hebei Province alone, Chen's bank, the Shanghai Commercial and Savings Bank, contributed $20,000 to support the FRC rural-credit activities, increasing its offer to $50,000 in the following year. Other banks soon joined. The Jincheng Banking Corporation offered $50,000 for the creation of marketing cooperatives.[27] The FRC, the North China War District Relief Commission, and other similar government agencies of the early 1930s were the first attempts of the government to tap into a trend that had started some years earlier. As described in chapter 4, urban industrialists and bankers had gradually become involved in the rural production of raw material for their factories and, in this context, began extending credit to peasants.

At the time the CCC was established, in 1933, it appeared that rural cooperation had tremendous potential, relying on an unlimited supply of private capital attracted not only by new business opportunities and the industrialists' need to control the flow of supplies to their factories but also by the new security offered by government sponsorship and support. Traditionally bankers had not invested in either industry or agriculture, generally preferring to extend high-interest, short-term, low-risk loans to commercial enterprises. Financing agricultural or industrial activities presented a higher level of risk and required long-term loans, which had limited the expansion of rural credit. Both Song Ziwen and Chen Gongbo tried to reverse this situation by offering the security of government sponsorship. More important, they spread the risk of such investments by pooling the resources of several banks under the auspices of government agencies. The investment of urban capital in the government rural-credit program also benefited from the Shanghai real estate crisis of 1931, which left bankers seeking new channels for investment.[28] When the CCC was established, therefore, it appeared to offer much-needed new investment opportunities, opening up a market traditionally controlled by local landlords or moneylenders.[29]

According to a 1937 report, the banks most involved in extending credit through the CCC's network were, in addition to Chen Guangfu's Shanghai Commercial and Savings Bank, the Jincheng Bank (which had already invested in the FRC), the Bank of Communications (*jiaotong yinhang*), China Farmers Bank (*Zhongguo nongmin yinhang*), and the Zhejiang Bank for the Promotion of Business (*Xingye yinhang*). These banks came together to form the China Agricultural Cooperative Credit Banking Group (*Zhonghua nongye hezuo huokuan yintuan*) and were later joined by other banks. In three years, this group extended a total of five million yuan in credit, focusing mostly on production, marketing, and consumption.[30] Within this group, the main investor remained the Shanghai Commercial and Savings Bank, followed by the Bank of China and the China Farmers Bank.[31] In 1934 in Shaanxi, where the CCC was most active, the Shanghai Commercial and Savings Bank invested 232,830 yuan. The Bank of China invested 572,000 yuan in this region. However, a League of Nations expert in rural cooperative societies, Max Brauer, when surveying Shaanxi, found out that the Shanghai Commercial and Savings Bank had actually made available only between 120,000 and 150,000 yuan. Puzzled by the discrepancy, Brauer speculated that 572,000 yuan was probably the amount promised by the bank but not yet invested.[32] Brauer's experience should serve as a warning on the limited reliability of the available data from this period, since official budgets made no distinction between capital actually invested and capital only promised.

By 1937 the total amount of credit extended through the CCC's network was around five million yuan.[33] When compared to the overall investment of rural credit, this amount appears rather insignificant. According to one survey, in 1934 only 2.6 percent of total farm credit was supplied by cooperative societies (followed by the 2.4 percent of credit extended to peasants by modern banks directly or through other channels), with landlords and merchants supplying, respectively, 24.2 and 25.0 percent.[34] The CCC, however, focused on a highly specialized sector of the rural economy: quality improvement and expansion of cultivation of cotton destined to supply the coastal textile factories, which was a small portion of national agricultural cultivation. It thus was a significant economic effort to develop the cotton industry, if not the agricultural sector at large. The main problem with CCC-sponsored credit societies was not the total sum it was able to mobilize but its ability to effectively reach the peasants by circumventing the resilient socioeconomic structure in the village.

In the Rural Village

As mentioned above, some of the reports that most reveal the difficulty encountered by the CCC in its work in the village are those written by W. K. H. Campbell. Invited by the NEC to help organize its system of cooperative societies, Campbell arrived in China in late 1935. In the following months he traveled extensively in several provinces with the task of assessing the work of cooperative societies in general, not just those directly managed by the NEC or its agencies. Campbell was chosen because of his extensive experience in establishing cooperative societies in Pakistan and India, but he had no experience in China. After a few weeks in the country, he candidly remarked: "At least now I know what a Chinese farmer looks like."[35] In spite of his lack of familiarity with China's situation, his reports are more enlightening than those of the NEC members. In reading Campbell's reports, his different approach to economic cooperation becomes immediately apparent. Diametrically opposed positions are evident, for example, on the speed of the movement's development. Chinese reports based their claims of efficiency and success on the rapid increase in the number of societies. Campbell, on the contrary, commented that China was afflicted by "an attempt to set up cooperative institutions at a pace which [it] is impossible to attain without sacrifice of quality."[36] Cooperative societies were, in fact, established with tremendous speed all over the country, according to Campbell's data growing from 5,335 (with a total of 184,587 members) in 1933 to 14,649 (with a total of 557,521 members) at the end of 1934.[37] Campbell's report on Hunan, which he visited in early 1936, states that there were 886 societies registered in that province alone. Such speed, Campbell noted, was possible because of the inaccurate and rushed process with which societies were registered with the proper authorities. It generally took only about a month to organize a society, too short a time to ensure the proper training of its members. Such "precipitation," as Campbell put it, was dangerous, he concluded, because it left no time for peasants to learn about cooperation, resulting in "a mass of overdue loans [and] people avoiding meetings to evade embarrassing questions."[38]

This difference in views was not just a product of an alleged naivety about cooperative matters on the part of the Chinese. Rather, it was because the goals of the CCC leaders differed from Campbell's. For the CCC leaders, cooperative societies were a vehicle for economic control. They were not designed to foster the initiative of the peasants. The CCC was eager to organize as many societies as possible because each one allowed the CCC to extend its reach into the agricultural community. Campbell, instead, held a more liberal view of economic cooperation and envisioned wider peasant participation in the formation and management of societies. He believed that in China, as in other "backward" countries, the government had a duty to aid in the society's initial development to compensate for the peasants' ignorance about the principles of economic cooperation; however, he drew the line against state intervention at a much earlier stage than did the Chinese.

In spite of Campbell's lack of understanding of the political goals of the NEC and CCC, his reports shed light on the difficulties encountered in the implementation of their system of rural credit. As he pointed out, most of the loans granted were never repaid. One reason was that loans were to be repaid after the harvest, using profits from the sale of crops. In extending these loans the societies assumed considerable risk due to the high frequency of natural disasters in the hinterland. As Campbell pointed out, it was a wonder how loans were ever to be repaid since "the lands of the debtors seem to be permanently submerged."[39] Campbell's observation highlights the state of disrepair of the water conservation and irrigation systems in the rural areas. While natural disasters were unavoidable, the poor conditions of dikes, ditches, and riverbanks led to more frequent flooding of fields than necessary.

A report published in 1937 in the journal *Mianye yuekan* also pointed to long-standing problems in loan repayment. The author, Xu Zhongdi, reported that, in Shaanxi, banks and local authorities involved in rural credit had decided to extend deadlines for repayment. Originally, locally two kinds of loans were extended to peasants: wheat loans and cotton loans. Wheat loans were extended in winter and were to be repaid at the end of July. Cotton loans were extended in June and July; the amounts varied according to the acreage cultivated in cotton (each peasant would receive one yuan for each acre). The cotton loans were to be repaid at the end of October. A problem, however, soon arose. Most peasants did not repay their wheat loans in July because after the sale of their crop they had scarcely enough wheat left to feed their families through winter. For this reason, in 1935, lending banks and local authorities decided that repayments of both loans should be scheduled at the same time in late October. This report highlights both the influence of crop cycles on loan repayment and the peasants' extreme poverty, which constituted one of the main obstacles, as Campbell remarked, to the smooth administration of rural credit. Finally, in 1936, the Shaanxi authorities decided to offer a unified "production loan" (*shengchan daikuan*), which was to be extended in April and repaid in December.[40] It is impossible to know whether the new system had encouraged steadier repayments of loans because the Japanese invasion and the demise of the CCC soon posed an end to the program.

Campbell also reported that many peasants, unable to repay their loans, would resort to the practice of "fictitious repayment." That is, they would take out loans from a cooperative society to repay previous loans contracted with local moneylenders.[41] Reliance on this repayment method was encouraged by the fact that the societies offered greatly reduced rates of interest. Peasants thus tended to borrow from them to repay more expensive loans. This practice frustrated the goal of the rural-credit program, since the peasants remained trapped in the old cycle of indebtedness while urban capital ended up in the coffers of moneylenders rather than being applied to improving agricultural production.[42]

According to Campbell, the problem was worsened by the fact that the peasants were unable to manage their new financial responsibilities properly. Loans could not be completely repaid at the time of the sale of the first crop but needed to be extended over several years. Unable to "draw up [their] own private balance sheet"[43] and calculate a schedule for repaying the society, they ended up spending all their capital and being forced to turn, once again, to village moneylenders. In addition, Campbell reported that the finances of the societies were generally unsound due to a general tendency toward mismanagement and improper use of funds.[44] According to the regulations imposed by the sponsoring agencies, the societies required a Western-style accounting system, which was virtually unknown in the countryside.[45] Although the CCC created a Cooperative Accounting Commission (*hezuo huiji zhidu weiyuanhui*) to train personnel and members of its societies, the process of training all individuals involved in rural credit was necessarily slow.[46] Even when corruption was not a factor, the personnel of most societies were too inexperienced to keep proper accounts and to manage their capital. Most societies failed even to maintain a reserve fund to cover unforeseen expenses.[47] To make things worse, most Chinese societies were multipurpose organizations that required sophisticated management skills. It is not surprising that, faced with numerous responsibilities, managers often transferred funds among departments and did not keep separate accounts for each department. This led to financial confusion. At times the returns from one department were distributed among all members even when not all the members were connected with that department. To add to the general financial unsoundness, most societies covered up losses with fresh loans from banks.

Given the situation described by Campbell, it is unlikely that the CCC would have been able to achieve significant results in the four years of its life. Obviously, time was needed for peasants to learn about the workings of cooperative societies, for society managers to learn accounting, and for old debts to be settled and a fresh start attempted. As the problems described above already suggest, the traditional village-based credit structure and ingrained patterns of production and marketing were, however, the two main obstacles encountered by the CCC. The successful implementation of the CCC's system of cooperative societies would have taken away from the village elite control over local wealth and resources and channeled them into the state's and coastal industrialists' coffers. The CCC thus found a competitor in the village where the old socioeconomic structure survived parallel to the new cooperative institutions. One of the main problems created by this competition was that cooperative loans were always the last to be repaid. This delay happened not only because they were cheaper than the ones offered locally but also because local moneylenders were a well-known presence in the village and more coercive in pressuring for the repayment of debts.[48] The CCC's cooperative societies, and those of the NEC at large, could not exercise the same amount of social pressure. In general, peasants ended up continuing to borrow from both the cooperatives and the moneylenders, juggling loan after loan to keep their heads above water. It appears that peasants perceived the arrival of CCC credit societies in their locality as one more pawn to play in the day-to-day struggle for making ends meet rather than as an agent for revolutionizing socioeconomic life in the village. The divergence between the goals of the CCC and the activities of both peasants and local power holders illustrates the resilience of village life and its ability to absorb into its logic attempts at reform imposed from above.

The CCC, for its part, was trapped in its productivist rhetoric and often ignored the long-established social practices embedded in rural society. CCC societies, for example, did not extend loans for personal use, but only for production or marketing. This had not been the practice of early cooperative credit societies. For example, the original 1923 model constitution of the CIFRC included loans for necessary social obligations, but this stipulation did not survive the formation of the production-driven NEC.[49] Because the CCC credit societies, like all the societies of the NEC, would offer loans only for production-related items, the peasants ended up borrowing from traditional moneylenders to pay for funerals, weddings, and other family or religious ceremonies.[50] By not adequately addressing the needs of the peasants, both productive and social, the CCC's original intention to displace the local moneylenders fell by the wayside.

The tendency to re-create the status quo in the rural village by assimilating the NEC's organization into local socioeconomic patterns is confirmed by a NEC-sponsored study of reform in the tobacco industry in Fengyang, a tobacco-growing region in Anhui Province. According to the prominent Chinese economist Chen Hansheng, the local gentry had created an Association for Tobacco Peasants. Through the local office of the Consolidated Tax Division, they secured loans from banks and then used this money to extend loans to peasants. They thus functioned as middlemen between the banks and the peasants. By 1934, however, the banks began to organize independent cooperative credit societies and to extend loans directly to the peasants. This was, according to Chen Hansheng, a strategy pursued vigorously by Chen Guangfu's Shanghai Commercial and Savings Bank, which, he remarked, was particularly active in attempting to directly reach the peasants engaged in the production of industrial raw material. The local gentry were thus forced to reduce their lending activities, although their associations continued to operate and to generate considerable profit. According to Chen Hansheng, the local gentry mounted a fierce resistance to the new reforms sponsored by the NEC and the Shanghai Commercial and Savings Bank and succeeded in gradually gaining control over the lending process at the expense of the NEC. As one peasant complained, the cooperative became a means for the "rich [to] have government relief grain to eat and the bank loan for the cooperative to spend." Chen's own observation confirmed that the elite

> through the co-operative . . . pay the bank a monthly interest of one-and-a-half per cent, but they also keep a differential interest of 1.8 per cent per month. In re-distributing the loan they are sometimes very lenient toward their relatives and friends who may be charged at the same interest rate that the bank demands, but more often they exact an interest as high as the prevailing usury rates of the locality. A middle peasant by the name of Zhuan Hongsheng, in the nearby village of Si-chien [Sijien], borrowed ten Chinese dollars from a member of the co-operative and, three months later, had to pay back eleven Chinese dollars.[51]

According to Chen Hansheng, the tobacco cooperative societies thus acted "exactly like the Chinese compradors of the British-American Tobacco Company (B.A.T.)."[52] He was thus very skeptical of the achievements of the reforms and of their beneficial impact on China's industrialization. Chen, one of the most active editors and contributors of the *Chinese Village* (*Zhongguo nongcun*), an economic journal closely linked to the CCP, was often overly critical of all reforms initiated by the GMD. His remarks on the work of the NEC in Fengyang, however, revealed the NEC's tendency to neglect the interests of the peasants, an obvious object of concern for a Marxist economist like Chen. More important for the present work, his comments also highlight the fierce struggle over local resources between the local elite and the urban-based reformers rallied around the NEC and illustrate the elite's complex and diverse strategies, which ranged from direct opposition to assimilation of new elements into the preexisting order.

Marketing societies sponsored by the CCC also suffered from fierce local competition because local merchants invariably attempted to sabotage their work. Campbell reported that generally after a society was formed, the members invested money in hulling or ginning machines, warehouses, offices, vehicles, salaried staff, and so on. At this point, local merchants began to feel threatened. When peasants sold their crops to the society, they received only an advance on the total sum because the society would pay them in full only after a sale on the final market had taken place. Merchants, taking advantage of the peasants' need for cash, offered to buy their product for more money than the society could advance, but for less than the value of the crop. They also started rumors that the societies were a sham and the final bonus would never materialize. In this way they were generally able to win over the peasants, and the societies inevitably incurred heavy losses.[53] When the societies tried to neutralize the competition by increasing their first payment, they often encountered other problems, especially when their initial payment exceeded the final market price for the cotton. As discussed in detail later, the inability to control the marketing of improved cotton became a major obstacle in the achievement of the CCC's ultimate goal of boosting the Chinese cotton industry.[54]

Opposition and sabotage from moneylenders and merchants testify to the revolutionary potential of the cooperative movement. The NEC clearly stated its goal of replacing local moneylenders and commercial middlemen with modern credit and marketing institutions.[55] The elimination of the local elite, implied in the CCC and NEC reform program, would have brought about deep social changes in the rural village, as revolutionary as the CCP's attacks on "local bullies and evil gentry."[56] The GMD, however, was trapped between two contradictory desires. On the one hand, it strove to create political and social stability. On the other, it aimed to restructure the economy, which would inevitably lead to a restructuring of social hierarchies and networks in the rural areas. These changes were sure to create hostility and reaction from the groups in power in the rural areas, thus undermining political support for the GMD and stability in the village. The political ambiguity created by these contradictory goals made it difficult to overcome this problem. Short of an open social revolution and the adoption of more extreme forms of economic control, such as those adopted by the CCP after 1949, the process of elite replacement was naturally slow.

The CCP, on the other hand, was armed with a revolutionary rhetoric of class struggle and felt justified in accomplishing the task with violent means. The Communists were thus able to resolve the problem mainly through land reform, which, often by the use of force, swept away landowners, moneylenders, and "local bullies and evil gentry" in general, opening the door for a new leadership and economic reform in the village. The contradiction between its political conservatism and its centralizing drive became a major issue in the Nationalist state-building effort, since centralization and a successful implementation of nationwide reforms could not be achieved without either the collaboration or the elimination of the local elite. As Prasenjit Duara and Kenneth Pomeranz have demonstrated, the village became the site of a struggle for power between the new national state and the social, cultural, and political system that had thrived during the late Qing period. Reforms sponsored by either the Nanjing government or regional authorities were often frustrated by the resistance of the village elite, who saw their power eroded by increased state penetration.[57] As Pomeranz has argued in his study of Shandong Province, those areas where the local elite were strong and still enjoyed significant economic advantages staged a powerful opposition to centralizing reforms. Only the elite groups who had experienced economic and political decline were eager to be co-opted by the provincial government and to take advantage of the new opportunities created by its reform.[58] Pomeranz's study thus highlights the complexity of circumstances in the hinterland. While in commercialized Jiangnan the rural economy came to be spontaneously (or, at least, not as a consequence of the state's economic control) integrated with the emerging industrial economy as reformist elites sought participation in national reconstruction, as discussed by Bell, in more insular areas (less commercialized and less linked to the international market or major industrial centers), the dynamics of interaction between local hierarchies and new forces (central state and urban industrial elites) followed a different logic.

Technology Transfer

In addition to the development of credit and marketing facilities in the rural areas, technology transfer constituted an important aspect of the CCC's plan for the improvement of the agricultural production of cotton.[59] Most of the CCC's work in this field focused on increasing the acreage of land cultivated in cotton and the yield per *mu* (one *mu* is roughly equivalent to one-sixth of an acre) by introducing new high-quality varieties of seeds, fertilizers, and anti-pest products and new cultivation techniques such as crop rotation.[60] In its technological extension effort, the CCC also reproduced the centralized structure that characterized all aspects of its organization. At its vertex was the CCC's Central Cotton Production Improvement Bureau (*zhongyang mianchan gaijin suo*). This bureau was connected to local branches established in cooperation with the reconstruction office of local governments in provinces that were considered particularly fit for cotton cultivation (Shaanxi, Jiangsu, Hebei, Henan, Hunan, Gansu, and Shandong). These branches established experimental fields and cotton improvement guiding bureaus (*zhidasuo*) to help new and already-existing provincial agencies improve cotton production. Skilled personnel were trained in collaboration with Central University and Jinling University, which developed specialized courses on cotton improvement and economic cooperation (*jingji hezuo*).[61] The newly trained specialized personnel were then stationed at village-level cooperative societies to assist farmers in the application of new techniques and the cultivation of new cotton varieties.[62]

New technologies were also employed for boosting land reclamation, focusing especially on Jiangsu, Gansu, and Shaanxi. In Jiangsu, for example, the CCC began the recovery of submerged wasteland along the seacoast. In Shaanxi, land reclamation—placed under the jurisdiction of the NEC Northwest Office, which worked closely with the CCC—focused on the irrigation of dryland destined for cotton growing. Central to this project was the construction of the Jinghui dike, which was, optimistically, supposed to raise productivity in the region to 60–120 *jin* (1 *jin* is half a kilogram) of raw cotton per *mu*. Other land reclamation strategies focused on creating terraced fields on mound areas and on introducing crop rotation in weed land.[63]

When attempting a general evaluation of the CCC's work in technological improvement we meet with the same difficulties discussed earlier. The short life span of the CCC meant that its work was often curtailed before it could move out of the experimental fields and could begin to influence the peasants at large. In addition, the CCC's main task was coordinating at the national level already-existing efforts in cotton improvement. Isolating the results obtained by direct CCC intervention from a general trend of improvements is thus often impossible. Data on quality improvement and cultivation expansion, for example, often include the results of efforts of agencies only loosely affiliated with the CCC. Even Campbell's and other NEC reports did not differentiate between societies directly managed by the CCC and NEC and others more or less loosely associated with them. The latter problem reminds us that, especially in the case of technology transfer, the CCC was above all a planning agency, intended to coordinate the work of the many preexisting cotton improvement programs and transform them from local experiments into nation-building policies.

The CCC engaged in direct implementation mostly in specific areas where local efforts had not been initiated or circumstances offered special opportunities. Most of the CCC's direct involvement, in fact, focused on Shaanxi. This province, especially the area of the Wei River (crossing the province from west to east and passing near the provincial capital of Xi'an), as well as pockets in the northeast and southwest, was considered one of China's cotton belts (the others being Hebei Province and the Jiangnan area). Cotton cultivation in this province, however, had sharply declined. By the time League of Nations experts visited it in the 1930s, opium cultivation had expanded at the expenses of cotton.[64] No significant industrial center had developed in the province to emulate Tianjin and Shanghai.[65] For this reason cotton cultivation in the province had not witnessed the same kind of lively intervention by local authorities and industrialists for the improvement of raw cotton that characterized Hebei and Jiangnan, thus inviting more direct leadership by the CCC than in other regions.[66] In 1926, a study of the conditions of cotton cultivation in Shaanxi concluded that "several factors" had contributed to prevent the development of the local cotton weaving and spinning industry, the "chief being the unsettled conditions of the province."[67] This province, in fact, had seen many conflicts among local warlords. It had finally been brought under tighter control of the Nanjing government in 1930, when the local warlords, Yan Xishan and Feng Yuxiang, were finally defeated. In spite of the fact that the defeated militarists managed to retain a certain measure of power locally, the Nationalists were able to increase their political control over this region and to intervene directly in the local economy. In this context the NEC established a new agency, the Northwest Office (*xibei banshichu*, established March 1, 1934), which was to supervise Shaanxi and other provinces that had recently fallen more firmly under Nanjing's authority (Gansu, Ningxia, and Qinghai). Song Ziwen personally appointed Liu Jingshan, who was close to him, to direct this office. Liu's task was to use the thirty million yuan made available by the League of Nations Technical Mission to China to promote production in these four regions. The activities of the Northwest Office clearly illustrate the economic nation-building goals of the NEC and its attempt to create tight economic links between Nanjing and the provinces, especially those provinces that had been under the leadership of warlords who had resisted Nanjing's leadership.

Armed with an independent budget and encouraged by the new political situation in the region, Liu started to work with enthusiasm, focusing especially on cotton cultivation.[68] According to Liu, this crop was particularly appropriate to the climate of Shaanxi and Gansu, since cotton could thrive in these predominantly dry regions. Liu reported that he worked closely with the CCC in this field.[69] In his memoirs he proudly states that this collaboration greatly contributed to laying the foundation for the development of the national textile industry. Liu did indeed work closely with the CCC's chairman, Chen Guangfu. Together they visited the poorest rural areas of Shaanxi in order to decide whether they were suitable for cotton cultivation. Having decided that indeed they were, Liu and Chen started actively promoting cotton cultivation there. Other factors made Shaanxi an optimal target for CCC intervention. Shaanxi's climatic conditions and terrain proved to fit particularly well two of the best varieties of American high-quality cotton (Stoneville no. 4 and Delfos no. 531) that the CCC was attempting to adopt in China.[70] Finally, by focusing on this area, the CCC leaders also aimed at isolating newly imported varieties of cotton from the fields of low-quality domestic varieties, which were mostly concentrated in Jiangnan. In this way the CCC hoped to prevent cross-pollination, a problem that had frustrated many previous, locally based experiments. It was in Jiangnan especially where it had proved very difficult to maintain the high quality of imported seeds due to the proximity of experimental fields to the already-existing low-quality plants cultivated by peasants in that area.[71]

In Shaanxi, the CCC divided its work into two main activities. It first promoted the cultivation of already-tested cotton varieties, mostly the American Million Dollars and Caret, bringing the acreage of land cultivated in these varieties from 191,000 *mu* in 1934 to 1,026,973 *mu* in 1936. The CCC also tested the Stoneville no. 4 and Delfos no. 531 varieties for three years in the province's experimental fields. In 1936, when the experimentation period was over, it began promoting these new varieties among the peasants. In that year the CCC bought 101,351 *jin* of Stoneville seeds, which were used in 1937 to bring the acreage planted with Stoneville in Shaanxi from 1,119 *mu* (1936 acreage) to 11,346 *mu* (1937 acreage).[72]

In the late 1930s, Shaanxi experienced a steady increase in the production of all varieties of cotton. In 1936, for example, cotton production had grown to an estimated 614,063 piculs (for an acreage of 2,905,630 *mu;* 1 picul is 133.33 pounds) from the 464,946 piculs (2,592,065 *mu*) of 1935. Productivity had also increased. In 1935 the yield was estimated at 17.94 *jin/mu*. In 1936 it had risen to 21.13 *jin/mu*. These general province-wide data also include results obtained by agencies other than the CCC. The CCC, however, appears to have been the leader of most of the cotton improvement activities in the region and was largely responsible for the increase in acreage and productivity.[73]

The CCC's second-largest effort in cotton improvement was in Jiangsu. Here the CCC worked mostly in cooperation with local agencies—although it had also established its own experimental field and guiding bureau—bringing the acreage of land cultivated in high-quality cotton from 330,204 *mu* in 1934 to 608,760 *mu* in 1936.[74] In this area the CCC focused especially on the cultivation of Caret cotton, which responded better to the local environment.

According to Richard Kraus's extensive research on cotton cultivation, nationally the acreage of land in cotton increased from 58.8 million *mu* in 1928–30 to 61.6 million in 1931–33 and to 69.9 million in 1934–36. In 1936, of these 69.9 million *mu* of land in cotton, only 3 million were cultivated with fresh seeds (i.e., newly imported seeds, rather than obtained from a local crop, and therefore free from any cross-pollination).[75] According to data collected by the Chinese historian Wang Shuhuai in his study of the CCC, in 1936 the CCC was responsible for 2,676,025 *mu* of land in fresh seeds (of which 1,026,973 were in Shaanxi).[76] This figure would give the CCC credit for most of the acreage in fresh seeds. This result appears credible only in consideration of the fact that by 1936 the CCC had centralized control over various cotton improvement agencies and, for this reason, the numbers it reported came close to the national average. Even if the CCC national data were inflated, the results it obtained in Shaanxi (1,026,973 *mu*) would constitute one-third of the entire national expansion of cultivation in fresh seeds, a very significant contribution. When looking at the numbers related to land in fresh seeds, it is important to keep in mind that fields of high-quality cotton were threatened by cross-pollination, which could in the long run compromise the quality of the final product.[77] According to Kraus, however, China was well on its way to keeping cross-pollination under control, having already gone through decades of seed selection.[78]

According to Wang Shuhuai, in Shaanxi the CCC's intervention was responsible, not just for expanding the acreage of land cultivated in cotton, but also for an increase in yield per *mu* from the 1931–36 average of 0.26 piculs to 0.32 in 1938, an increase of almost 10 percent.[79] Kraus's figures confirm this increase in yield per *mu*, although with an important qualification. From a peak of 25.4 catties per *mu* (1 catty is equal to 0.5 kilogram, or 1.10 pound) in 1924–25, cotton yields fell to 23.6 catties in 1928–30 and 22.1 in 1931–33. In 1934–36 they jumped back to 24.6 catties per *mu*. The long-term average remained steady, leading Kraus to argue that China experienced no significant long-term trend in yield per *mu* in the years 1918–36.[80] The comeback of the 1934–36 years from a period of decline is, however, quite significant because it shows that cotton production was able to weather the 1930s agricultural crisis. In addition, we need to keep in mind that Kraus's national data on cotton production also include low-quality cotton, intended for a variety of uses ranging from hand weaving and for padding of clothing and furniture, both enjoying lively markets at the local level in 1930s China.[81] As mentioned earlier, the CCC focused its intervention specifically on cotton destined to supply the modern cotton mills in Shanghai, a very specialized portion of the national product. For this reason the effects of the CCC's intervention are more accurately reflected by numbers focused on the expansion of new high-quality varieties rather than general measurements of national production.

In evaluating the impact of the work of the CCC, however, the question arises of whether the CCC was on its way to achieving its much touted goal of self-sufficiency in cotton supplies for the cotton industry. According to Kraus, domestic "factory yarn supply and cotton consumed in the spinning of factory yarn clearly kept increasing throughout the period [1918–36] and China both rapidly approached and achieved self-sufficiency in the Twenties."[82] Kraus's long-term analysis, therefore, points to a steady trend in the 1918–36 period that minimizes the impact of the CCC, since self-sufficiency was achieved in the 1920s, well before the CCC was established. In this instance as well, however, short-term fluctuations, for both raw cotton and cotton yarn, show increased imports in the late 1920s and early 1930s.[83] In 1933 imports of raw cotton constituted 7.29 percent of China's total imports, second only to rice (11.17 percent).[84] The late 1930s, however, marked a return to low imports.[85] These data were influenced by a variety of factors, including the loss of Manchuria in 1931, since Manchurian imports suddenly ceased to be included in national statistics. The main cause of this sharp decline in the 1930s, however, has mostly to be found in the increase in domestic production of high-quality cotton.[86] When comparing short-term trends in production and imports, in fact, we find a clear correspondence between the two. This short-term analysis, therefore, shows that when production fell, imports of cotton supplies increased. Although the long-term trend remained steady, the short-term analysis shows a crisis in the late 1920s and early 1930s that was overcome with the important (if not sole) contribution of the CCC. The intervention of the CCC and other agencies in response to the crisis contributed to the return to the level of production and imports that characterized the early years of Kraus's long-term trend. Advances toward self-sufficiency were also made in cotton textiles. China's output of machine-made cloth increased dramatically in the 1930s (while production of handmade cloth experienced a decisive decline), recovering from a slump in the late 1920s.[87] Imports of cotton goods also declined following the expansion of the domestic product.[88]

Going beyond the issue of whether the CCC deserves credit for the national increase in cotton production and decrease in imports, a question that is not easily answered, we may ask whether the CCC was able to ensure that improved domestic raw cotton was channeled to support Chinese *minzu* industry and did not end up benefiting foreign factories on Chinese soil. The CCC, while seeking autarky as its ultimate goal, was immediately concerned with stimulating the growth of Chinese cotton mills, making them competitive with their Japanese counterparts. An article in the *Chinese Village*—always critical of Nationalist reforms—actually criticized the CCC, claiming that its work, rather than strengthening the *minzu* economy, resulted in improving supplies for imperialist factories in China.[89] Chen Hansheng also supported this critical view of the Nationalist effort to improve supplies of agricultural raw material. In his work on the Chinese tobacco industry and the role of the British-American Tobacco Company, Chen wrote: "It seems quite clear that the increase of raw material in a semi-colony had not helped to promote national industry, but has materially extended the influence of foreign industrial capital instead."[90] According to Chen, the British-American Tobacco Company controlled not only the new credit organizations—in cooperation with the local gentry it had co-opted—but also the marketing of tobacco, ensuring that the newly improved raw material went directly to supply its factories. In this work, therefore, Chen clearly presented the very important question of whether the means devised by the CCC, and the NEC at large, were effective in fighting imperialism and freeing China from its semicolonial status or whether they instead deepened the hold of foreign imperialism on the Chinese economy. The autarkic goals of the CCC and its effort to develop a *minzu* Chinese economy were thus very much predicated on making sure that Chinese factories were the first to take advantage of new, improved supplies of domestic cotton and could thus compete effectively with Japanese mills.

Marketing and Markets

The issue of who benefited from China's improved cotton rested ultimately on the CCC's ability to establish effective control of the marketing process. On this point, however, the CCC's plan reveals three major problems. First, although its goal was to exercise economic control, it relied on market mechanisms, which often curbed its ability to effectively control the circular flow of cotton (raw cotton from the village to coastal factories and industrial cotton goods back to the village) that was to ensure the autarkic development of the *minzu* cotton industry as well as the transformation of China into an economic unit. The second, and related, problem was that the CCC leaders relied on an abstract, modernist narrative of the market that betrayed little understanding of current patterns of marketing and consumption and led them to underestimate rural market forces and trends. Finally, the CCC leaders did not take into account China's semicolonial status (using Chen Hansheng's terminology), which prevented the Nationalist leaders from freely adopting protectionist measures in support of the *minzu* industry.

In 1934 the CCC established in Shanghai the National General Marketing Office for Cotton Production and Marketing Societies (*quanguo mianhua chanxiao hezuoshe yunxiao zongbanshi chu*). This office was supposed to help cooperative societies market their products directly on the Shanghai market under the best possible conditions and by supplying local societies with up-to-date information on the Shanghai market.[91] Each society, assisted by local cotton improvement bureaus, would handle the ginning, packaging, grading, and transporting of cotton to the market. The idea was that through these societies peasants could sell their cotton directly to the market and obtain higher prices while avoiding merchants' speculations. The logic of the CCC's marketing strategy was therefore similar to the one for rural credit. The state would establish new infrastructures devised to help peasants avoid middlemen (in this case, merchants and brokers) and maximize their returns. The peasants would then be economically motivated to abandon traditional marketing structures and take advantage of the new CCC marketing networks.

This system, however, did not work as well as expected. The lure of higher returns was not enough to make the peasants break old habits. Above all, the risks and the delayed payments involved in cooperative marketing discouraged the peasants' full participation in the CCC's scheme. For peasants, selling through cooperative societies meant not just delayed payment for their crops, since the society would pay only a fraction of the crop price at the time of collection and delivered the rest of the money only after the sale had been completed. In addition, it also meant assuming significant risks. Society managers did not fully understand the commercial quotations provided by the general office and found it difficult to navigate the market in the way the CCC leaders had hoped.[92] The local elite were ready to exploit this problem and compete against the societies in order to maintain control over the village crops, as Campbell's reports discussed earlier have already revealed. Aware of the peasants' chronic need for cash, local landlords and merchants—often the same groups involved in moneylending—offered to buy their crops for cash. The peasants found it very difficult not to accept their offers, although it always meant selling at a lower price.

Some cooperative societies also experienced serious problems resulting from China's inadequate transportation system. When societies attempted to sell their products directly on the larger provincial or urban markets in order to obtain better prices and to avoid middlemen, they often found that their cotton could not reach the market in a timely fashion because of train delays and the general disarray of China's transportation system. They would thus incur losses. Because of transportation problems, the flow of supplies to the urban markets was very uneven at times, creating severe shortages one day and an overabundance of the same product the next. A market could be suddenly flooded with a surfeit of cotton, which would cause its market value to fall, and the society would be forced to undersell its cotton. Even a single day of delay could affect prices dramatically. In addition, storage expenses skyrocketed when cotton was forced to sit for days in an intermediary station before being shipped to its final destination. Some societies decided to limit their losses by selling on the local markets, which, although offering lower prices than the Shanghai or Tianjin markets, did not present the risks involved in long-distance transportation.[93] As a result of these problems, in 1934, not all the cotton produced by the societies was marketed through the CCC system.[94] According to a CCC report, only 25,540 piculs of cotton were marketed through cooperative societies, a small fraction of the total crop of improved cotton.

In response to the problems encountered in 1934, the CCC changed its marketing organization. In 1935, the Central Cotton Production Improvement Bureau established marketing branches in the provinces. Peasants would now sell their product directly to cooperative societies, which paid them cash immediately upon receiving their cotton. The societies purchased and marketed cotton on behalf of the provincial branches of the central bureau, which ultimately shouldered all financial risks and responsibilities.[95] This change eliminated uncertainties and delays and encouraged peasants' participation. As a consequence, the quantity of cotton marketed through the CCC's organization rose to 52,271 piculs in 1935—not including cotton produced in Hebei that was sold on the Tianjin market and was not included in the figures calculated by the CCC office in Shanghai. Of these 52,271 piculs, however, only 2,228 piculs were marketed directly to factory representatives.[96] The rest ended up on local markets or, even when it reached Shanghai or Tianjing, became available to both Chinese and foreign buyers.

This system, although more successful then the previous one in bringing higher returns for peasants and improved cotton to *minzu* cotton mills, transformed the CCC's societies into one additional broker for the marketing of rural cotton. In his report on cooperation in Shaanxi, Campbell described the CCC's marketing work in the province, commenting on both its success and its speculative (noncooperative) nature.

> A marketing branch of the Cotton Industry Commission [CCC] was established in Sian [Xi'an]. This branch borrowed extensively from the banks

> and also $50,000 from the Provincial Government and the Cotton Industry Commission. It then published to every society a maximum price at which it could buy its members' cotton. This price was based on the price ruling in Shanghai, but conservatively fixed with a substantial safety margin. It undertook to buy all cotton offered at this rate plus $1.00 per picul, of which $0.50 went to the societies to cover their expenses and the other $0.50 into a special fund constituted to pay off . . . overdue loans. These terms were generally accepted. The marketing branch sold the cotton in Cheng-chow [Zhengzhou], Shanghai and Tsingdao [Qingdao], and, with the help of good luck in the matter of prices, made substantial profits, which also went into the special fund. . . . Of course the 1935 operations were not co-operative at all, but mere speculative trading cotton.[97]

As we have seen earlier, Campbell's liberal idea of cooperative societies contrasted with the Nationalists' use of economic cooperation as a channel for economic control, leading him to complain that the CCC societies did not really function as marketing societies "but rather [as] local collecting stations for a marketing union to which they are affiliated."[98] This view was also shared by Sun Enlin, the director of the CCC's Central Cotton Production Improvement Bureau. Discussing the new marketing methods, he lamented that the new practices went against the purpose of rural cooperation, since societies had now become "merchants in disguise."[99] Sun commented that mill owners were especially satisfied with the 1935 marketing regulations, which allowed them to send representatives to the cotton production and marketing societies in the rural areas and directly purchase raw cotton. While this practice ensured the elimination of middlemen (the traditional merchants and brokers), who often adulterated raw cotton to increase its weight and improve their profits, it disregarded the original idea that peasants were to benefit from the new system of cooperative marketing.[100] Sun's remarks reveal the tension among the CCC's different components and his dissatisfaction with the mill owners' focus on acquiring cheap and high-quality raw cotton for their mills at the expense of the CCC's wider reform goals. From the CCC mill owners' point of view, however, collecting improved cotton was exactly the function the societies should perform. The problem rested instead in their inability to collect more cotton more efficiently.

Campbell's and Sun's remarks highlight the logical incongruity of the CCC's cooperative network. The CCC originally planned to achieve control over the rural economy by triggering new marketing trends. As this strategy proved slow and complicated, it resorted to more direct and less cooperative marketing strategies. Like Campbell, Sun blamed this failure to adhere to cooperative principles on the haste in which cooperatives were established and on their members' and managers' consequent lack of proper education in cooperative and marketing matters. This lack of education, Sun argued, made it impossible for societies to deal properly with the marketing of cotton and led to a more decisive intervention from the CCC.[101] The problem, however, appeared to rest primarily on the fact that, by 1937, one of the most crucial issues of the CCC—that is, the boundaries of state intervention in the economy and the extent of economic control—was still largely undecided, and the CCC's various components still held different ideas about it.

In spite of their ambiguous position between controlled and market economies, CCC societies, when able to function, succeeded in lowering marketing costs, as pointed out by Campbell's report on Shaanxi. This success was also reported by Fang Xianting in his study of Hebei. Fang's study showed that the cost of marketing through commercial channels averaged around 21.6 percent of the selling price at the terminal market, while the cost of cooperative marketing averaged only 4 or 6 percent. At the same time, Fang argued, the fact that the grower participated in the cooperative society's program for cotton improvement ensured a higher price for his crop and a better profit from its sale.[102] It is true that Fang was an enthusiastic supporter of cooperation and probably was overly optimistic in his assessment. In general, however, cooperative marketing, even if performance varied regionally, had the potential to significantly decrease marketing costs and ensure higher returns for the peasants at the expense of merchants and brokers. Cooperative marketing, therefore, had the potential to slowly erode the power of the local elite in the village as peasants' trust in societies improved and their debts decreased. The CCC did not survive long enough, however, for its cooperative network to become established and bring about the desired results.

The reduced costs of cooperative marketing also had the potential to ensure cheaper supplies for Chinese *minzu* mills, especially after 1935, when cotton mills were allowed to purchase raw cotton directly from the producers through the CCC cooperative organization. Most of the cotton produced by societies, however, ended up available for everyone on the market and was not channeled directly to *minzu* mills. Even in this case, however, cotton mills could now rely on expanded supplies of affordable, high-quality cotton, which previously was mostly imported at high prices. Whether this development supported the growth of the Chinese *minzu* industry vis-à-vis the Japanese, as intended by the CCC leaders, is difficult to tell. Comparative data on cotton production in Chinese and foreign mills show the Chinese factories gaining vis-à-vis foreign competitors, although it is impossible to determine to what extent this was the result of increased availability of cheap domestic raw cotton.[103]

The development of the *minzu* industry at the expense of its foreign counterpart, however, did not depend solely on the availability of cheaper supplies. The application of wider "control" policies, such as the adoption of protectionist regulation, was also necessary. The Chinese government, however, was unable to manipulate import and export tariffs or adopt new taxes favorable to Chinese-owned mills. When, for example, in 1933 China finally gained the freedom to set its own tariffs, pressure from Japan blocked any effective action. On May 22, 1933, Song Ziwen, at the time the minister of finance, issued new tariffs aimed at protecting China's industries. Song also attempted to launch regulations for clearly labeling goods according to the country of origin.[104] Heated pressure from Japan, however, resulted in the elimination of the regulation on import labeling and the new tariffs and their replacement with new ones, highly favorable to Japan.[105] Nationalist leaders attempted to use boycotts as a tool to compensate for their inability to regulate import duties. In spite of the popularity of the National Product Movement (*guohuo yundong*) and its attempt to get consumers to buy Chinese goods, boycotts proved only sporadically successful and did not have a significant economic impact.[106] Chen Gongbo's productivist approach led him to argue that boycotts would always have a limited effect if domestic goods could not be produced in sufficient quantities to meet the demand. For this reason he hoped that, as quoted earlier, "the Chinese common man will consider the future of China as well as his own and will rush to invest in domestic production."[107] Chen's statement illustrates the CCC leaders' attempt to circumvent their inability to adopt protectionist measures (which were, in reality, crucial for achieving autarky) with alternative ways to influence the market, mostly by promoting nationalist behavior among Chinese consumers and stimulating the production of domestic goods.

The circular flow of raw material and finished goods between village and urban industrial center that was at the very core of the CCC plan, however, was a more complicated matter than the CCC leaders envisioned. In general, they tended to underestimate and misunderstand local market forces in their attempt to impose new long-distance and centralized marketing trends. They mostly worked on the assumption that the rural consumer would rush to buy Chinese industrial cotton goods and would eventually be able to absorb an unlimited amount of them, allowing the Shanghai cotton industry unbounded growth. The CCC's narrative of development of the rural market and national integration, however, offered a greatly simplified representation of the complex and diversified demand for cotton goods. The CCC leaders devised their plan based on the view, well established at the time and still very fashionable today, that, in the words of Kraus, "China was the scene of a pitched battle between a superior machine-made cloth and an inferior hand-woven cloth, and that inevitable defeat of the latter awaited only proper transportation facilities so that it could be ferreted out of its isolated, hard-to-get- to strongholds."[108]

Demand for cotton goods, however, followed a different logic than just availability of machine-made cloth. While factory cloth was generally preferred by the urban middle class, it was not popular in the rural areas.[109] Even if handwoven cotton was coarser and often more expensive than the machine-made variety, it was warmer and more durable. For this reason it enjoyed a solid market in the rural areas, where peasants preferred it to cheaper industrial goods. The CCC's plan to bring prosperity to the villages, in order to increase their purchasing power, would not necessarily have translated into increased sales of industrial cotton goods from the coastal areas. Only a high level of prosperity could have supported the CCC leaders' plan: in this case, the peasants would stop worrying about durability and, knowing that they could afford to buy cloth more often, would begin to prefer the smoother and softer machine-made goods.[110] In general, demand for cotton goods depended not just on prices and supplies but on cultural factors and the social composition of a specific market. In this respect, the CCC leaders appear to have glossed over the complex characteristics of the rural market, favoring instead a modernist and productivist approach that disregarded the peasants' needs and habits.

Two Nations, One Village

The work of the CCC in the rural areas was also affected by the different nation-building visions of Jiang Jieshi and the Wang group. This political split played itself out not only in Nanjing, but also in the provinces. The rural village also became a site of confrontation between Jiang and Wang for control over local economic and political resources. Even in Shaanxi, where the CCC was particularly active and successful, the CCC met with political opposition. In his memoirs, Liu Jingshan, the chairman of the Northwest Office, complains of a lack of support from the local authorities, who, in fact, turned out to be quite hostile to the reforms sponsored by the NEC. In Shaanxi the Nanjing government had appointed its own personnel to replace officials who had been loyal to the previous warlords. In 1933 Shao Lizi, secretary of the Huangpu Military Academy under the directorship of Jiang Jieshi in the mid-1920s,[111] was appointed chairman of the Shaanxi provincial government. Yang Hucheng, a native of Shaanxi and a GMD military strongman who had participated in the Northern Expedition under Jiang Jieshi, was appointed chairman of the Xi'an Pacification Office (*Xi'an Suijing shu*).[112] Thus, Jiang's followers were charged with keeping political order in the region while the NEC took care of economic reconstruction.

Liu tells us that both Shao and Yang "expressed their willingness to collaborate with the representatives of the central government and were willing to cooperate in any possible way. But then in the most important issues, because they disagreed with me, they made sure that my plans came to naught."[113] While in Shaanxi, Liu attempted to persuade private banks from the region and from Shanghai to invest in water conservation. The banks would offer low-interest loans to the provincial government, which would run the water irrigation system. The peasants would pay a fee of about three yuan per *mu* to use the new irrigation system. These fees would then be used to return capital and interest to the banks. According to Liu, the plan would be beneficial to the banks, which were offered a fairly low-risk opportunity for investment since the loans were guaranteed by the state. In exchange for this safety, they would express their commitment by accepting a low margin of return on their invested capital. The plan would also benefit the peasants, who desperately needed irrigation and would find the water-use fees reasonable.[114]

This plan, however, met with the opposition of Shao Lizi, who told Liu that "the peasants suffer much because of droughts and famines. I cannot bear to take money from them."[115] For this reason he wanted the government to shoulder the entire financial burden. Liu argued that the government could not afford to finance the irrigation project. Moreover the project was meant to circumvent the effects of drought and famine and to increase production per *mu,* thus eliminating the very problem that was the basis of Shao's opposition, poverty. Although Liu repeatedly tried to convince him, Shao Lizi did not change his mind. The local government thus refused to guarantee the loans, and therefore no banks were willing to invest in Shaanxi, since they could not have any assurance of repayment. Ultimately, government funds never materialized and the project was abandoned.

The confrontation between Shao and Liu was symptomatic not just of a general difference of opinion—Shao representing the antibusiness view common to the Jiang group, in opposition to the NEC leaders' model of joint state-private nation building—but also of diverging reform priorities that fuelled the struggle over political and economic control over resources between the group rallied around the NEC and the militarists linked to Jiang. Jiang was interested in carrying out public-works construction but gave priority to projects that served immediate military purposes. This was the case with road construction. Two of the major road construction projects carried out by the NEC, with the full political support of Jiang, were the Three Provinces Road (Jiangsu, Zhejiang, and Anhui) and the Seven Provinces Road (Henan, Hubei, Anhui, Jiangxi, Jiangsu, Zhejiang, and Hunan). They were both originally planned by either the Military Commission (*junshi weiyanhui*) or the Henan, Hubei, and Anhui Bandit Suppression General Headquarters and only later assigned to the NEC for execution.[116]

Jiangxi Province also fell under the direct control of Jiang, jeopardizing the NEC's work in this region. Prompted by the launching of Jiang's fifth anti-Communist campaign in this region on January 27, 1934, the NEC established the Jiangxi Office (*Jiangxi banshichu*), which was dedicated to the military defeat of the Communists and therefore was placed under the control of Jiang.[117] The launching of these military campaigns marked the end of Jiang's exclusion from the NEC. In January 1934, he succeeded in being appointed to the Standing Committee of the NEC, which was now composed of five members: Wang Jingwei, Song Ziwen, Sun Ke, Jiang Jieshi, and Jiang's close associate Kong Xiangxi, in his new capacity as minister of finance.[118] At the same time Jiang began to promote his military interpretation of the *an'nei rangwai* platform. At the five-province bandit suppression meeting, held in Lushan on June 9, 1932, in preparation for the Fourth Anti-Communist Campaign, he delivered a speech entitled "To Resist Foreign Aggression We Must First Pacify the Domestic Front" ("Rangwai bixian an'nei"). This speech shifted the priorities originally established in the *an'nei rangwai* agreement that had cemented the Wang-Jiang coalition government. While the elimination of the Communists constituted an important element of *an'nei* (pacify the domestic front)—even for the Wang group, who, however, subordinated it to economic reconstruction—Jiang's speech gave it absolute priority and placed military action above economic reform.[119] This reinterpretation of *an'nei* became a common refrain of Jiang's up until the end of the Wang-Jiang coalition government. "The only way to resist Japan," Jiang insisted, "was to defeat the Communists."[120]

The Jiangxi Office opened in Nanchang on June 22, 1934, directed by Xiao Chunjin and staffed with personnel chosen by Jiang and Kong.[121] In spite of the fact that its regulations were identical to those of the Northwest Office,[122] the Jiangxi Office functioned in a very different way, reflecting Jiang's concern for counteracting Communist influence in the rural areas around the CCP's Jiangxi base.[123] After the failure of campaigns previously launched by Jiang to wipe out the Communists, Jiang had decided on a "three parts military, seven parts political" action, reflecting his interpretation of the *an'nei rangwai* platform of the Wang-Jiang coalition. This formula signaled that the new campaign was to pay more attention to political organization and less to the military. The Jiangxi Soviets, as the Communist base was called, were to be placed under a close blockade. Jiang organized the surrounding rural areas into fortified villages while the Nationalist army controlled public roads, limiting access to the area under siege.[124] The Jiangxi Office became engaged in both economic and political activities through a series of Rural Services Centers (*nongcun fuwuchu*).[125] These centers, ostensibly part of the NEC network of cooperative societies, officially focused on agriculture, education, public health, and economic cooperation, but they also hosted special public-order bureaus and New Life Movement divisions.[126] The movement for economic rehabilitation and public health in Jiangxi was thus accompanied by major political reorganization and propaganda efforts. The new political network seized upon Jiangxi with such a firm grip that the centers came to substitute officially for the regular provincial administration, thus defying the national Cooperation Law, which decreed that cooperative societies be subordinated to the provincial government and not vice versa.[127]

The Jiangxi Office was thus mostly concerned with political control. It was in the area under its jurisdiction, more than in other areas, that the NEC's cooperative network showed its authoritarian face. A League of Nations expert, Max Brauer, reported in 1934 that half of the local population in Jiangxi belonged to "so-called utility societies" (the Rural Services Centers), which, he remarked, significantly departed from the work usually carried out by cooperative societies. They, in fact, focused mostly on political work, disregarding much needed help in agricultural production.[128] The Jiangxi Office took the province by storm with its intensive propaganda and regimentation of the local rural population into associations of all kinds, from youth groups to Baojia (village-based organization of households for mutual security) training, from village beautification to personal-improvement teams. Ceremonies in ancestral halls, public lectures, and "wholesome" forms of entertainment were provided to reeducate the villagers and counteract the CCP's call for land redistribution. Finally, new organizations devoted to the solution of disputes were supposed to ease the tension between peasants and landlords, which had led many peasants to join the growing ranks of the Communists.[129] The work of the NEC in Jiangxi, therefore, came to closely reflect Jiang's idea of garrisoned villages (*tutian*), discuss in chapter 2.

In an attempt to accomplish economic reforms in Jiangxi, in keeping with the original reform spirit of the NEC, Song Ziwen asked the League of

Nations to send an expert in economic rehabilitation. However, the reform plan suggested by this expert, Carlo Dragoni, was never seriously considered by Jiang and was promptly rejected, confirming the Jiangxi Office's general disregard for economic reforms and preferential focus on military and political control.

The Jiangxi Office, therefore, split the NEC into two different directions. The original NEC, including its original commissions such as the CCC and SIC, pursued economic nation building. The Jiangxi Office focused on the military nation building promoted by Jiang, even if it found its legitimization as an expression of the domestic consolidation (*an'nei*) and general anti-Communist policy that was at the base of the Wang-Jiang coalition. In addition, departing from the NEC's original goal, the Jiangxi Office avoided cooperation with private entrepreneurs and remained a strictly governmental agency. Rather than relying on private capital, as the CCC did, the Jiangxi Office established a Farmers Bank, which operated a system of rural credit in a manner that differed greatly from the CCC model.[130] Led by Chen Lifu, a close associate of Jiang, the Farmers Bank was based in rural areas and relied on local capital. The bank, for example, did not employ the strategy attempted by the CCC and the Shanghai Commercial and Savings Bank of mobilizing industrial coastal capital to help finance cooperative societies; rather, it actually aimed at using the societies for creating the capital of the bank. The Farmers Bank required its societies to deposit the entire amount of their share capital with the bank itself. It justified this new rule by presenting it as a strategy for increasing the overall capital of the bank. This regulation, however, worked as a disincentive for the societies to do business with the bank. The societies were, in fact, unwilling to invest any of their funds and in most cases expected to be totally financed by the bank itself. Most peasants did not have any savings and were unable to join societies under the terms imposed by the Farmers Bank.[131] Considering that it was the peasants' lack of savings that had prompted reformers to establish rural-credit organizations in the first place, one can argue that the attempt of the Farmers Bank to raise funds among the peasants reversed the approach that had characterized rural credit from the early 1910s to the late 1930s and reversed one of the NEC's main strategies by excluding the participation of private business.

After 1935, when Jiang took control of the economic administration of the government, the Farmers Bank became the major player in rural credit nationwide, and by 1936 and 1937, the participation of private banks linked to the NEC group had sharply dropped. In Hunan in 1936, for example, the Shanghai Commercial and Savings Bank officially sponsored only one cooperative society, although it had previously been the largest investor in rural credit, having extended loans totaling $175,789 to cooperative societies.[132] Overall, between July 1934 and June 1935, the Shanghai Commercial and Savings Bank loaned over $2 million to 125 cooperative societies in seven provinces where the CCC was most active. Meanwhile, the Bank of China—at the time under the leadership of Jiang Jia'ao, who had strongly supported Song Ziwen at the National Economic Conference and was currently a member of the NEC—nearly quadrupled its loans to agriculture in two years (1933–35).[133] However, by 1937, private business had gradually been cut off from rural-credit institutions under the direct control of Jiang Jieshi. Chen Lifu, the head of the Farmers Bank, clearly expressed his view on the matter. During a conversation with Chen Guangfu, he repeatedly complained that the management of cooperative societies was no concern of bankers because it fell under the scope of government intervention, arguing, "You cannot do this; this is our job."[134] Chen Guangfu ultimately lost control of his bank in 1935 with the ousting of the Wang group from the government.

The confrontation between NEC-style and Jiang-style rural credit was, therefore, not limited to the Jiangxi region, further contributing to the general confusion and lack of coordination that characterized most reform projects launched by the Nationalists. Despite the centralizing efforts of the NEC, rural credit was never really unified and continued to be characterized by competition among different agencies. In certain areas one agency would prove stronger than others. In addition to banks from the NEC group and Jiang's Farmers Bank, provincial reconstruction and cooperation bureaus sponsored their own credit agencies and maintained their own cooperative field staff to take care of their local investments.[135]

It is clear, however, that nationwide the most active banks were the Farmers Bank, the Shanghai Commercial and Savings Bank, and the Bank of China, thus identifying Jiang's and Wang's groups as the two main competitors.[136] In 1936 in Hunan, for example, the administration of cooperatives was divided between the Provincial Bureau of Reconstruction, the CIFRC, the Farmers Bank, the Shanghai Commercial and Savings Bank, and Nanjing University.[137] All agencies except the Farmers Bank and the Provincial Bureau of Reconstruction worked in cooperation with the NEC, which indirectly controlled most of the societies in the region.[138]

Campbell noted that at least two different sets of model constitutions for cooperative societies were in use in Hunan. The CIFRC, the Shanghai Commercial and Savings Bank, and Nanjing University followed the Cooperation Law, which had been drafted by the NEC. The Farmers Bank and the Provincial Bureau of Reconstruction followed special "regulations of the Military Headquarters of the Generalissimo."[139] Campbell reported that in 1936, in Anhui and Hebei, where the NEC Cooperative Commission (established in 1935 to bring order to rural cooperation and take cooperative societies nationwide, tasks it was never able to achieve) was particularly strong, cooperatives were unified under the national law, which he deemed effective and well suited to the local situation. Provinces where the NEC was weak appeared to be moving in a different direction. Sichuan, for example, appeared to be in the process of unifying under the "wrong law" (i.e., the Military Headquarters regulations), as Campbell put it. Oblivious to the factional struggles under way at the time, Campbell could only wonder at the peculiarity of this situation: "It is not obvious what advantage there can be in this [situation]. . . . This is possibly merely a case of instructions having failed to reach those concerned. . . . Every-one at least pays lip service to the idea that administration and control ought to be unified, but there seems in many places to be a lack of real enthusiasm for giving effect to this badly-needed reform."[140]

The political conflict between the Wang and Jiang groups over the role of private capital in rural development echoed a wider discourse on the role of private capital in China's economic reconstruction. Although modern banks had been involved in rural credit since 1931, their participation was highly controversial. Critics argued that private banks were representative of unscrupulous speculation by private capital, and therefore, the government needed to control them. They also claimed that only the banks benefited from their activities in the rural areas, substituting themselves for traditional middlemen while the farmers just passed from one creditor to the next.[141] A common view was that private banks had turned to rural credit only because of lack of investment opportunities in the cities. It followed, therefore, that they were interested, not in rural reconstruction, but in exploiting the peasants.

Campbell also joined in criticizing the work of the banks. His view of cooperative society as an expression of grassroots associationism, rather than a tool for top-down nation builders, led him to argue that "societies ought to come into being because members have realized that by means of them they can overcome economic difficulties from which they suffered, and not because anyone else wishes to find a field for the investment of idle money."[142] Max Brauer was also critical of the use of private banks in the Shaanxi cooperative movement. He especially complained that banks, focused on making profits and avoiding investment risks, tended to invest only in the villages that needed investments less, because they already enjoyed good irrigation and favorable general conditions for cotton cultivation. Private banks tended to avoid the poorest villages in the province, which suffered from poor irrigation and needed an influx of outside capital the most. Brauer recognized that "not much would be done" without investment of private capital and argued that the NEC should find more effective means to encourage investment in less fortunate districts.[143]

These criticisms pinpointed some of the main characteristics of the credit network created by the NEC, although they did not place them in their wider reform context. The NEC and its banks indeed aimed at replacing the traditional middlemen as well as solving the banks' investment crisis. In addition, their main concern was not in helping the peasants but in supporting the Jiangnan modern *minzu* economy. The NEC's nation-building and economic modernization policies were based on making it beneficial for private urban banks to invest in the rural areas as a way to attract capital to the village. Although this business-oriented strategy indeed presented some limitations, it had the potential for mobilizing much-needed capital.

Conclusion

The problems encountered by the CCC in the rural areas exemplify the difficulties encountered by the Nationalists in their effort to build a centralized nation-state. Breaking the village's strong socioeconomic network dominated by local elites was a tremendous challenge that required a slow and uncertain process of change. These changes proved more easily realized during the early years of the PRC, when land reform and the political campaign against "local bullies" swept away, often violently, the local elite and created the economic and social vacuum in which a new state-led village organization could emerge. Class struggle and land reform were not in the Nationalist agenda, although most of the reformist Nationalist leaders and intellectuals perceived the elimination of the rural elite as the first step toward economic modernization and nation building. On this point, Nationalists and Communists shared a similar goal, but they differed on how to achieve it. A major difference between the CCC leaders and the Communists, however, is that the CCC leaders were interested in bypassing only the members of the rural elite they could not co-opt, while they had no problem with those who participated in their reform effort. That the local elite tended to take over the state's cooperative networks was not a problem for them, as it had been for Chen Hansheng, if it did not hinder their reform program. After all, their goal was not class struggle or socioeconomic justice but improving and expanding supplies of raw cotton and establishing strong economic ties between rural hinterland and industrial Shanghai (transforming China into an autarkic economic unit).

Chen Gongbo's discussion of controlled economy and the corporativist organization of the state described a level of centralized economic planning and control that the NEC and CCC never achieved. This discrepancy was the result of the business interests represented in the CCC, which led to a weakening of the control policies envisioned by Chen. It was also a result of the CCC's strategy of relying on market mechanisms for stimulating agricultural production and channeling raw cotton to the Shanghai market. Even if adopting a less forceful form of controlled economy, the CCC still had the potential to change the economic life of the village. Changing the traditional pattern of credit and marketing could have helped overcome the economic stagnation that most Chinese and foreign experts perceived to be one of the main causes of China's rural crisis. On the other hand, the CCC's intervention in the rural economy, aimed mostly at supporting the development of urban industrialization, had also the potential to trigger the decline of local commercial opportunities. Lively local markets would be gradually overpassed by the interregional networks of the CCC's marketing societies. Interest on loans would go to enrich urban banks rather than local moneylenders, draining away rural capital. In addition, the local handicraft industry, which was an integral part of village economic life, would have suffered from the competition from coastal industrial goods.[144]

In the final analysis, however, the CCC deserves credit for instituting a national network for reforming the cotton industry and, as a consequence, ensuring the good performance of the cotton industry in the Nanjing Decade. Although it built on a trend that had begun as early as the late nineteenth century, it was particularly successful in developing these earlier experiments and setting up an effective nationwide system of quality standards, cotton grading, and controls. The national reach of the CCC was also crucial for its success in improving the quality of cotton, a task that had proved a challenge for previous, locally based reform projects. The national-level structure created by the CCC survived beyond 1949. Although the higher echelons of the CCC were politically compromised by their association with the GMD, most of the CCC experts represented a new group of technocrat government officials who acted outside the GMD factional struggle. Most of the CCC's experimental bureaus, field offices, directing offices, and personnel continued their work undisturbed under the Communist regime. The Central Experimental Bureau of the NEC, for example, became the leading office of the early PRC's efforts in industrial development.[145]

The CCC was also successful in its corporativist goals, at least when it came to its rural work. The CCC, in fact, decided on and implemented rural reforms with a significant unity of intent among its various constituencies. The main reason for this success, however, mostly rests in the common interest of CCC members, who could, with no exception, only benefit from channeling rural resources into the Jiangnan industrial economy. While the CCC's rural reforms went against the interests of the rural elite, they directly served those of the urban entrepreneurs. The corporativist and reformist unity of the CCC was threatened, however, when it came to reforming the industrial production of cotton. As discussed in the next chapter, this reform effort raised sensitive questions about the autonomy of the private entrepreneurs and the limit of economic control and jeopardized the socioeconomic alliance that was supposed to sustain the CCC's nation-building effort.

Ultimately, however, the most significant challenge to the CCC's work came from the lack of sustained support from the central government. The difficult task of bringing the rural village under Nationalist control was severely hindered by the political split in Nanjing, which affected China's political life from the capital to the village. As mentioned in the beginning of this chapter, the issues at stake were the persisting differences over the role of the private economy in nation building and over the solution to the rural crisis (productivism versus military pacification).

陸

CHAPTER 6

Officials, Industrial Magnates, and Bureaucratic Capitalism

The communality of interests between the NEC leaders and the Jiangnan entrepreneurs that had sustained the CCC's work in the rural areas did not extend to all aspects of its reform plan. In general, the various components of the CCC tended to agree on rural reforms, as they did not infringe upon their economic turf but only opened up new business opportunities at the expense of the rural elite. Such harmony between state and business representatives, however, tended to disintegrate when the CCC's intervention reached into factories and ran up against the immediate economic interests of the industrialists, triggering resistance. The CCC's attempt to "rationalize" (*zhengli*) industrial production and factory management illustrates the difficulties that the Wang group faced in striking a balance between state intervention and the idea of fostering the private *minzu* industrial economy, an idea that was at the center of the CCC's corporativist project.

The *minzu* definition adopted by the leaders of the NEC and the CCC involved more than the geographical distinction between the coastal industrial areas and the hinterland. It, in fact, required the exclusion of those industrialists within the Jiangnan industrial elite who placed immediate economic interests before the goals of modernization of the industry as a whole and national salvation or, at least, did not share in the CCC leaders' notion of modernization. The very membership of the CCC came to be split along this line. Cotton mill owner Rong Zongjing, who had been a pioneer in the modernization of the cotton industry, became an unexpected target of the interventionist arm of the CCC. While Rong appeared to have shared the CCC's concern for cheaper and improved raw materials, he proved reluctant to implement some of the reforms promoted by the CCC for the modernization of industrial management. These same reforms, however, were wholeheartedly supported by cotton mill manager Li Shengbo and cotton mill owner Mu Ouchu, whose vision of the development of the cotton industry more closely matched that of the CCC leaders.

The CCC leaders expected *minzu* cotton industrialists to be willing to embrace change and abandon existing business practices in order to benefit the entire industry and save the nation. If a Chinese industrialist was not willing to do so, the economic-control apparatus of the CCC would intervene to impose change. Private industrialists, although respected as producers, were to be circumvented if they followed their own interests and not those of the industry and nation. In that case they would lose their right to cooperate with the state and would become part of the economy that needed to be controlled. In other words, the private sector was fostered only if it played the right *minzu* role in the CCC's nation-building program. The relationship of the CCC entrepreneurs with the political leaders of the CCC, such as Wang Jingwei, Chen Gongbo, and Song Ziwen, was thus complicated and can be understood only if we understand the modernizing agenda of the CCC alliance.

Different attitudes among the CCC's industrialists demonstrate that ideas of economic modernity neither were subordinated to economic interests nor constituted a mere rhetorical cloak for self-serving economic operations. Instead, they were an integral component of the reform-minded industrialists' perception of what was beneficial to their business. The reform-minded industrialists perceived themselves as the new modern economic elite of China and believed they were saving the cotton industry and, with it, the nation. Li Shengbo (member of the CCC Standing Committee) and Mu Ouchu (regular member of the CCC), like Chen Guangfu, had organized their businesses along what they considered modern principles and expected other factory owners to do the same. The attention to reform of these industrialists, therefore, did not contradict their business interests. The American oil magnate John D. Rockefeller, for example, built his fortune on a combination of reform and unscrupulous business practices at the expense of the competition. He believed that the American oil industry needed to be centralized and restructured into a large-scale organization. This would allow the industry to adopt technological innovation more efficiently while overcoming competition from British and Russian oil companies. The American oil industry did indeed become stronger, but so also did Rockefeller's Standard Oil at the expense of weaker and smaller American oil firms.[1] The example of Rockefeller testifies to the difficulty of separating reform rhetoric from business interests and how businessmen can genuinely believe in reform while trying to maximize their benefits from it. This combination of idealism and self-interest undoubtedly characterized Li and Mu. These two cotton magnates believed that the reform of industrial management was crucial both for the development of the cotton industry as a whole and for the ability of factories to make a profit.[2]

Differences between Li and Mu, on the one hand, and Rong, on the other, were also rooted in their different backgrounds. Mu had begun his career as an agriculturalist and reformer and later had managed important cotton mills in the Zhejiang-Jiangsu area. He became a mill owner on the strength of the knowledge of advanced technologies that he had acquired during his studies in China and the United States. Mu had translated the work of Frederick Taylor, especially *The Principles of Scientific Management,* into Chinese and, following Taylor's theories, was a strong supporter of reforms aimed at the rationalization of industrial production.[3] Li shared a similar background with Mu. He had begun his career, not as a merchant or mill owner, but first as an expert in the silk industry and later in cotton weaving. Unlike Mu, he had not acquired his own factories but continued to work as a professional cotton mill manager, becoming the director of some of the most important cotton mills in Shanghai, such as the Dawang and the Hengda.[4] Rong, however, was a product of traditional-style business. The family fortune was made in old-style Chinese banks. Rong had moved into cotton textiles and food processing (flour mills). Although he embraced modernization, he still believed that the right way to manage his enterprises was with a combination of newly imported Western technologies and old Chinese practices.[5] Thus, although all the CCC industrialists belonged to the Jiangnan industrial elite, they differed in background, vision, and interests.

Eventually, Jiang Jieshi assumed complete control over the government and was able to pursue his own vision of nation building. He therefore eliminated the administrative agencies that had been the expression of competing visions, such as the NEC. The ideas that had inspired the NEC, however, did not disappear. In the case of Wang Jingwei and Chen Gongbo, these ideas contributed to their decision to collaborate with the Japanese during Japan's occupation of China, as discussed in chapter 7. In the case of Song Ziwen, they reemerged in a form of bureaucratic capitalism, as a new channel for continuing cooperation with Shanghai entrepreneurs. In keeping with his *trasformismo* approach, Song continued to pursue his reform goals within the limits of the new situation of the Nanjing government. He thus resized his reform plan—which had already shifted its focus from the reform of the entire economic administration of the government to the more limited scope of the NEC—and attempted reforms very similar to those implemented by the CCC through the China Development Finance Corporation (*Zhongguo jiansheying gongsi,* hereafter CDFC) and the China Cotton Company (*Zhongguo mianye gongsi*).[6] The informal state-private network that had developed during the Self-Strengthening period and that the Wang group had tried to institutionalize at the national level with the NEC were marginalized by Jiang and deteriorated into bureaucratic-capitalist organizations that lost sight of the wider reform and nation-building goals and more narrowly focused on mere survival in the new hostile environment.

The Cotton Control Commission and Industrial Reforms

The most important goal of the CCC's intervention in the urban coastal areas remained the autarkic development of the cotton industry by reorienting it away from Japan and integrating it with the rural hinterland economy. This goal was a direct continuation of the work carried out in the rural village and aimed at completing the process of modernization of the whole cotton industry that had been initiated at the village level. The improvement of production of domestic raw cotton would fail to bring about self-sufficiency if industrial production lagged behind rural output. According to the leaders of the CCC, the self-preservation of the cotton industry, and of the nation as a whole, ultimately rested on the ability of factories to take full advantage of improved supplies of domestic raw material, to increase their production to meet the needs of the nation, and to improve the quality of their goods to overcome competition waged by Japanese imports on the domestic market. Without good performance in the industrial sector, the remapping of the economy of the cotton industry would be incomplete. The flow of raw cotton from the village to the coastal industries and then back to the village markets in the form of goods would be broken, preventing the autarkic development of the industry and leaving the country open to increasing dependence on foreign products.

The CCC's 1934 plan directly addressed these issues. It focused on technological innovation and rationalization of the industrial process of cotton spinning, weaving, and dyeing by promoting modern industrial management,[7] introducing manufacturing standards aimed at raising the quality of cotton yarn and cloth, introducing modern textile equipment such as spinning and weaving machinery,[8] training skilled labor, compiling surveys and statistics, and facilitating the marketing of cotton goods.[9] The CCC also established textile research centers, which focused on experimenting with new machinery and industrial processing techniques. These centers also trained personnel and had specialized departments that were assigned the task of spreading technological innovations to cotton mills.[10] These departments were to research specific problems faced by factories in their area and send experienced advisers to help solve their problems.[11] The CCC also assumed responsibility for circulating information that it deemed crucial for a "rational" approach to industrial management. For example, the CCC began to compile statistics on the agricultural production of cotton to help cotton mill owners estimate the quantity of raw cotton entering the market and, consequently, its likely price fluctuations. This information would help mill owners decide on production and marketing strategies.[12] In addition, data on domestic cotton were compared with those on cotton conditions in other countries and with international price trends to aid in developing international business strategies.[13]

As was the case with the CCC's intervention in agriculture, the CCC built its work for the improvement of industrial production on initiatives that had already developed at the local level. The CCC aimed at coordinating them on a national scale and so put an end to the current fragmentation of economic reform of which Chen Gongbo had so bitterly complained. The NEC wanted to coordinate local reform programs within a wider scheme of development rather than allowing them to remain anchored to county or provincial interests. For example, to help regulate prices and stabilize the market, the NEC employed the strategy of moving goods from one market to the other, which had already been attempted by the Qing government but had been impossible to carry out because of the regionally fragmented economy of warlord China. According to a 1934 report, in September and October 1933 the Shanghai market was overflowing with cotton, which drove the price down. The CCC purchased 30,000 bales of yarn and marketed it to other ports.[14] This report does not specify the provenance of the surplus cotton. However, considering that the first shipment of American cotton from the cotton and wheat loan would have arrived at around that time, the entire operation appears to have been more of an attempt to deal with a problem created by the excessive amount of cotton suddenly available on the Shanghai market as a result of the loan (for the unexpected negative results of the loan, see later in this chapter) than a success in managing the market. Nevertheless, it highlights the potential of the state for national regulation and for stimulating new interregional-market dynamics. In this spirit, the CCC attempted to organize and develop the domestic market in finished goods, although its work in this area remained limited to research and compilation of statistics on domestic production, foreign imports, consumption patterns, and marketing strategies, as well as costs related to transportation, taxes, and insurance.[15]

The CCC's nationwide reach also allowed it to successfully introduce a standardized system of cotton grading and control against adulteration by coordinating existing inspection bureaus, establishing new ones, and passing and enforcing a national law against adulteration. The goal was to improve the quality of domestic cotton, helping cotton marketing by unifying standards, and finally promoting the employment of these standards in industrial cotton spinning. According to the CCC's leaders, cotton adulteration was a result of the greediness of peasants, merchants, and middlemen who perpetrated the old practice of mixing water and debris with cotton to make it heavier and gain more profit from its sale. Cotton adulteration, however, had the effect of making the cotton ferment, rot, and change color, spoiling its quality and making the industrial spinning process difficult. The merchants and middlemen thus were portrayed as particularly negative figures in the CCC's 1934 plan because they were undermining national interests for the pursuit of selfish profit. The CCC's leaders believed that quality grading and control was essential for improving the quality of domestic cotton manufactures and thus enhancing its marketability vis-à-vis foreign imports. In addition, quality control would help commercial transactions of cotton by offering nationwide regulations to be used for arbitrating trade disputes. On the other hand, a rise in cotton quality, the CCC's 1934 plan argued, benefited the peasants by ensuring higher prices for their products. As a result, according to the CCC's leaders, they would feel encouraged to further expand cotton production. In this way the peasants would have incentives to move toward the productivist goals of the CCC. The CCC's leaders believed that similar market-driven incentives would also encourage industrialists to move in the direction the CCC desired. In fact, although factories would be forced to pay higher prices for improved domestic raw materials (still cheaper than the foreign imported products), they ultimately would be able to compensate for these costs by producing higher-quality, higher-priced goods.[16]

While industrialists like Rong were ready to accept the adoption of controlled economy in rural reform, they were reluctant to do so when it interfered with what they perceived to be their immediate interests. Difficulties arose especially when the CCC tried to regulate labor and to improve factory management. These two areas proved to be especially controversial, being two sites in which state intervention and the interests of the Jiangnan elite often collided.

Controlled Economy: Labor and Industrial Management

In 1930s Nationalist China, the political debate on labor issues had many similarities to the debate on land reform discussed in chapter 2. The already-ambiguous socialist rhetoric (mitigated by the denial of class struggle in favor of national unity) of the Principle of People's Livelihood was overshadowed by the socially and politically conservative goals of the GMD. In this context, although the CCC considered the improvement of labor conditions an essential part of industrial modernization, its ability to regulate labor remained limited. Some of its most powerful members were, in fact, industrialists who wanted to preserve unlimited autonomy in dealings with their workers. At the same time, the governmental component of the CCC was reluctant to take a marked pro-labor stance in order to maintain a safe distance from the CCP, at the time the champion of labor rights. Productivism remained the main concern of the CCC's leaders, leading them to view labor problems from the perspective of production cost and efficiency. Strikes and other interruptions of production were not tolerated because they disrupted production and thus worked against both the economic interests of the industrialists and the CCC's general autarkic goals. In this context, labor conditions in the cotton textile factories, although taken into consideration, remained a subordinate issue.[17] As pointed out earlier, the presence of Du Yuesheng among the CCC's members foreshadowed its repressive approach to labor policy.

The CCC's 1934 plan paid homage to the idea of protecting the workers' standard of living with a few initial rhetorical statements. However, it was mostly focused on carrying out surveys in cotton mills and textile factories to investigate working conditions, wages, health and retirement benefits, food and dormitory situations, and recreational activities. These surveys were supposed to be used by the CCC's members to draft labor regulations that were to be transformed into national law.[18] CCC personnel, however, met with heavy obstructionism every time they attempted to inspect a factory. In addition, when in April 1935 the CCC finally came up with a set of regulations for industrial labor, it was unable to transform them into national law as planned, due to fierce resistance from the business community and groups within the government. The CCC ended up notifying factories of the new regulations and merely suggesting their adoption. A 1935 report claimed that some mills enforced them with good results, although its celebratory but very vague language exposes it as an overly optimistic piece of self-promotion. The fact that the regulations were never able to assume the force of law curtailed much of their effectiveness.[19]

In 1936, acknowledging the CCC's failure to mediate between labor and capital, Chen Gongbo complained that both parties were unable to see beyond immediate gains and take into consideration long-term benefits for the nation. In 1936 Chen mused on the impossibility of mobilizing the nation as he had originally hoped: "China's labor force and capital are not easily brought together. [In such circumstances,] the idea of mobilizing the entire country is just an idle dream."[20] Although Chen believed that workers focused too much on wage increases without considering the difficulties incurred by management, he also blamed the industrialists for capital-labor disputes: "Talking about the cotton spinning industry we all heard about the difficulties [created by] the workers' complaints against management. Honestly, the workers sometimes have excessive requests. . . . For what I know, however, the responsibilities of capital are not few."[21] All that the industrialists wanted, Chen contended, was to eliminate labor unions in order to better control the workers. He also blamed them for attempting to shift the blame for inefficiency in industrial production onto the workers rather than addressing the real problems of industrial modernization. For example, industrialists complained that Japanese mills used three times fewer workers per spindle than their Chinese counterparts and attributed these differences to the inefficiency of workers. They did not see, Chen explained, that it was instead a matter of lack of modern machinery in the Chinese plants. The industrialists, in fact, were unwilling to invest in new machines and tended to rely on cheap manpower for cost-efficient productive solutions.[22] This attitude hindered the modernization of the Chinese industry and allowed foreign mills to maintain their advantage. Chen concluded that the Chinese cotton industry "was not failing in technology but in management."[23]

Chen's attitude toward industrial management was reflected in the 1934 plan of the CCC, which identified the Chinese industrialists' lack of expertise as the main reason for the "backward" status of Chinese cotton mills and factories. The plan specifically pointed to the ignorance of modern accounting and capital management as the cause of the industry's general financial unsoundness. Industrialists misused their resources, the plan asserted, incurred high production costs, and racked up debts.[24] To solve this situation the CCC published a book, *Managerial Standards for Textile Industries* (*Mianfangzhichan jingying biazhun*), which it distributed to all cotton mills. This book offered detailed information on technical and managerial improvement. If followed, Li Shengbo argued, the factories would achieve significant results in two years. The CCC, however, did not have the power to impose the changes outlined in the book, and in the end only sixteen mills appeared to have embarked on serious transformations, inviting the CCC to send technical personnel to assist in the reform process.[25] In general, the response to the CCC reform initiative varied and depended on the goodwill of mill owners. Since the plan had been approved by the CCC's Standing Committee, we can infer that the CCC industrialists were sufficiently committed to the modernization of industrial management to undertake substantial changes in their factories and to impose reforms on more conservative industrialists. In this respect, CCC industrialists like Mu Ouchu resembled the silk magnate Xue Shouxuan, who shared with them a similar background and a similar path to collaboration with the NEC. Xue was very active in the SIC and believed the agency should "more directly supervise and manage cocoon production and marketing." According to Bell's study of the silk industry, Xue, like other industrialist reformers of the period, probably "saw certain future advantages for the silk industry as a whole to forcing out the smallest, least modernized cocoon firms through a combination of higher taxes and implementation of new model district policies on other aspects of cocoon-firm 'control.'" Bell points out that the SIC required cocoon firms to install new equipment and closed down those that could not operate at this high technological level.[26] As was the case with the cotton industry, the most reform minded and strongest among the silk industrialists were more inclined and better able than smaller firms to carry out changes within the management of their factories. The modernizing reforms they promoted would arguably—if the CCC and SIC had had more time to carry out their plans—have consolidated their power at the expense of smaller factories unable to meet the standard imposed by the CCC, in a process similar to that experienced by the Italian GFII.[27]

When the CCC attempted to reform production and management in cotton milling, however, tension developed not only with industrialists outside the CCC but also with some belonging to its general membership. As Chen Gongbo noted, it appeared that some CCC industrialists refused to even discuss problems related to production in the factories.[28] The most famous incident arising from this tension was the crisis at the Shenxin cotton mills owned by Rong Zongjing. The Shenxin mills had incurred severe debts and were heavily mortgaged.[29] As early as 1932, when the first signs of crisis appeared, Zhang Jia'ao and Chen Guangfu arranged for a large loan to two of the Shenxin mills through the banks they controlled, the Bank of China and the Shanghai Commercial and Savings Bank, respectively. Thanks to their intervention, the financial problems of the Shenxin mills were temporarily solved. The two banks sent personnel to the mills to assist with accounting matters, but Rong actively hindered their work, frustrating Zhang's and Chen's hope of using the loans as a means to reorganize the Shenxin mills. The two bank envoys, Yao Songlin (Bank of China) and Shen Weijing (Shanghai Commercial and Savings Bank), concluded that the problem of the Shenxin mills was mostly managerial. They especially criticized the higher managerial echelons, led by Rong himself, while remarking on the high quality of middle managers and engineers.[30] As a consequence, Zhang pushed for Rong's resignation, insisting that his subordinate Wang Yuqing take over as general manager. On July 1, 1934, in the wake of a renewed crisis, Rong finally resigned in favor of Wang, while Li Shengbo agreed to manage the Shenxin mills. In exchange, Rong asked the government for a new loan to once again rescue the Shenxin mills. It was, after all, Rong argued, the excessive tax burden imposed by the government that constituted one of the main causes of the crisis. Over the past three years, Rong complained, his taxes had risen to ten million dollars.[31]

Wang Jingwei and Chen Gongbo decided that this time the crisis was to be handled by the CCC, which would investigate the Shenxin situation but allow its factories to continue production. Their productivist bias led them to avoid as much as possible the closing of factories, which would have meant both a decline in production and a reduction of the tax base for the state. The CCC created a task force composed of Lin Yinfu (director of the Industry Department of the Ministry of Industry and longtime reformer of the cotton industry) and CCC members Zou Bingwen and Li Shengbo. During a meeting with Chen Guangfu, Zhang Jia'ao, and Li Shengbo, Chen Gongbo, addressing the Shenxin crisis, argued that the only way to save the mills was for the CCC to arrange for a loan and assume the management of the firm for at least six months, until a thorough reorganization was completed. The report explained that creditors, namely the Bank of China and the Shanghai Commercial and Savings Bank, were unwilling to continue to support the Shenxin mills unless drastic changes were made. Rong, the report continued, had lost his credibility and could not be trusted with new loans. The report went on with a long list of complaints about the mills. They were managed in the most casual way. They were too small. Their managers did not attempt to keep a budget, plan production, or take market trends into consideration. In addition, their operation was highly speculative in nature. For example, Rong was given to buying as much raw material as possible, irrespective of the production needs of his mills. At times, the report continued, Rong would sell some of the raw material on the market at a slightly lower price than that prevailing on that day.[32] In this way Rong attempted to realize some easy cash, of which he was always short. Rong's tendency for speculation must have been particularly alarming to most members of the CCC Standing Committee in view of their productivist and antispeculation orientation. To them, Rong appeared to betray the duty that came with the privilege of being a *minzu* industrialist because his behavior jeopardized the CCC's nation-building goals.

Rong's business philosophy appeared to confirm the doubts of the CCC leaders. Rong had been very active in the boycotts in protest of the May Thirtieth Incident,[33] generally showing strong nationalistic feelings. He often complained about the excessive amount of foreign goods on the Chinese market in comparison to those manufactured in China and identified this imbalance as a threat to national survival. "Chinese industries are not many. Foreign wheat flour and cotton yarn, on the other hand, are sold in large amounts in our country. Clothes and food are basic needs of man's life. To solve the problem in these two areas we need to develop more flour mills and cotton textile factories." The nationalistic inclinations of Rong were, at least at the level of rhetoric, matched by his desire to modernize and expand his business. In the early twentieth century, Rong had been among the first industrialists to use electric-powered machinery and to strive to improve the quality of the goods he produced. He remarked that his factories all had "fast production times, new equipment, good workers . . . not a month passes by without acquiring new machines." He also used to proudly discuss his plans for increasing the number of spindles under his control: "At fifty I have five million spindles. At sixty I want to reach six million; at seventy, seven million; and at eighty, eight million." This catchy but somewhat simplistic strategy of expansion of the Shenxin mills, however, did not mean development toward large-scale production. In practice, it translated into the acquisition of old factories. Rong preferred this strategy because "(1) it was cheaper; (2) the workers can remain in their positions and Shenxin does not need to hire more people. It only needs to transfer people from one factory to the other and the burden [of paying too many workers] can actually be reduced; (3) from the point of view of the head office, it only needed to add an account book, without having to establish a special new managerial organization; (4) by [acquiring a factory] we actually diminish competition." Rong believed that taking over an existing factory allowed the Shenxin mills to expand with minimal effort while, at the same time, subsuming the competition into the Rong empire. This strategy inevitably left Shenxin with small factories, generally out of date and not fit, in the eyes of the CCC inspection team, for modern indus trial production.[34]

A second business practice of Rong's also conflicted with the CCC Standing Committee's idea of modernity. Rong ran his mills mostly on credit. He borrowed heavily from banks, relying on loans to carry out daily production activities. For this reason he was always deeply in dept and mired in financial crisis. This strategy was seen by the CCC reformers as a speculative strategy, more appropriate for a merchant than for a modern industrial magnate, who should not speculate on capital but focus on creating a sound financial base for his industry. Their belief that Rong was not fully adopting modern industrial practices was reinforced by the industrialist's own statements. Rong believed in a combination of Western-style technological improvements and old Chinese business practices. Paraphrasing Zhang Zhidong's famous Self-Strengthening slogan, he claimed: "Traditional knowledge as essence, and new knowledge for practical use, according to what is appropriate for the occasion."[35] Although he recognized that the old Chinese accounting system was not suitable for modern industry, he argued that it should not be abandoned. The new system should be used for external business transactions and the old for strictly internal matters, with the two systems integrated with each other. Rong's contradictory business outlook was a constant source of disagreement with bankers Chen Guangfu and Zhang Jia'ao, on whom his business almost completely relied, as well as with other NEC and CCC leaders.

In addition, Rong's relationship with Song Ziwen and the CCC had been ambiguous since the establishment of the commission because Rong attempted to exploit his connection with Song to further his business interests. As Richard Bush's extensive research has demonstrated, Rong outmaneuvered Song in the latter's negotiations with the US Farm Board on the cotton and wheat loan. While in Washington, Song had relied on Rong's assessment of China's need for raw cotton. To obtain abundant and cheap raw material, Rong greatly exaggerated this need, leading Song to acquire more raw cotton and wheat than China could absorb.[36]

In 1932 Rong had already tried to substitute the US government for Japanese firms as a supplier of financing for cotton purchases. In June he had submitted a proposal to Song for a purchase of 400,000 bales of American cotton, to be guaranteed by the Chinese government. Song had accepted the proposal, which was presented to the US Farm Board only to be rejected. In October, Rong failed to get a loan from the American Reconstruction Finance Corporation for the purchase, over three years, of one hundred million bales of cotton and one million bushels of wheat, secured by his own note and a mortgage on his cotton and flour mills. When Song Ziwen and Arthur Young arrived in Washington in 1933, however, the American Reconstruction Finance Corporation was now willing to grant the Chinese government fifty million dollars in credit to buy American wheat and 600,000 bales of cotton. During the transaction, Song received a cable from officials in the Ministry of Finance stating that Rong had urged an early agreement to the loan since stocks of cotton back in China were sufficient only for one month of mill operation. Rong also stated that he alone could use 50,000 bales over the next twelve months. Cables from Kong Xiangxi and the vice-minister of finance, Zuo Lin, followed, all relying on Rong's statement. Song concluded the agreement on May 29, 1933, and officially announced the loan on June 4, 1933. Before Song returned to China, however, it was already clear that Chinese cotton mills could not absorb such a large quantity of raw material. Mill owners, preoccupied with the negative effects of such a large quantity of foreign cotton on the Chinese market, began protesting to the government. The situation was made worse by the fact that China's cotton harvest in 1933 turned out to be exceptionally good, nearly 20 percent above normal. As a consequence, the American cotton was at least 10 yuan per bale more expensive than the local product. The Nanjing government found itself unable to sell the American cotton and began a protracted bargaining process with mill owners over its price.[37] For Rong, however, the cotton and wheat loan turned out to be a success by lowering the price that he, as a mill owner, had to pay for raw materials. In February 1934, Kong Xiangxi, a longtime associate of Rong's and at that time the minister of finance, reached an agreement with Rong, who purchased most of the loan cotton at extremely low prices.[38]

Given these circumstances, it is not surprising that the CCC saw the 1934 crisis of the Shenxin mills as one more proof of Rong's questionable business practices and as an opportunity to modernize them. This was considered crucial for the future of the entire cotton industry because the Shenxin group was the largest cotton enterprise in China, operating the most mills and employing the most workers. Rong was the largest producer of cotton and wheat products, two products considered crucial for the NEC's autarkic goals. As the crisis deepened, disagreement between Rong and Li Shengbo also surfaced, resulting in Li's abandonment of his position as the manager of the cotton textile operations of Rong's firm and his siding completely with the CCC reform team.[39]

It was at this point that rumors began to spread that Song Ziwen and the NEC were planning to take over Rong's mills and nationalize them.[40] This rumor reflected both the ambiguity of the CCC's policy of economic control (in this case, the extent of its intervention into private factories) and the difficulty of clearly explaining the policy to the general public, leaving ample room for speculation. At the same time, the rumor reflected disagreement within the government on how to address the Shenxin crisis. In his plea to the government, Rong had tried to bypass the CCC and had written a letter to Jiang Jieshi. In the end, Kong Xiangxi supported Rong's request for help. Going against the recommendation of the CCC, Kong decided that a loan should be given to the Shenxin group and that Rong should be kept as general manager. Further, he allowed the Shenxin group to delay payments of the Consolidated Tax and created a committee led by Rong's brothers, Rong Desheng and Rong Weiren, to oversee the modernization of the mills. Kong thus saved Rong, as Rong acknowledged several times later on.[41]

The Shenxin affair brought to light divisions among state groups, as well as among private interests, represented in the CCC. Mill owners were naturally threatened by the specter of nationalization and were willing to accept reforms only to the extent that they did not interfere with personal profits and entrenched patterns of management. Bankers and agriculturalists, such as Zuo Bingwen, and professional cotton mill managers, such as Li Shengbo, were instead eager to deepen reforms. On the government side, Jiang's and Kong's opinions on how to solve the crisis differed from those of the leaders of the CCC. Although at first the CCC was the main agency involved in the Shenxin crisis, its power was not sufficient to keep other groups from intervening. In the end, it was Kong who decided to reverse the CCC's verdict and support Rong's requests.

Richard Bush, who has written extensively on the Shenxin crisis, has argued that Jiang and Kong favored supporting industry while Song and the CCC favored nationalization. It was, however, Jiang who used the term "nationalization" in discussing the Shenxin affair. Bergère argues that the Shenxin crisis was an additional manifestation of Jiang's desire to nationalize, or bring under direct control of the state, the private economy, and therefore, it must be understood in the context of the 1935 "banking coup" (discussed later in this chapter).[42] Jiang's position in the Shenxin affair, therefore, arguably foreshadowed his general economic outlook and the extensive nationalization of industrial plants that he carried out after 1935. The CCC, on the other hand, did not challenge private ownership, although it often pushed for reforms that were not welcomed by the industrialists. Finally, although Kong might have aimed at saving a personal friend (rather than reforming the cotton industry), he might also have been concerned, in the context of the Nationalist factional struggle, with curtailing the CCC's influence over the cotton industry by denying it control over the Shenxin mills.

The Shenxin affair thus shows that the cotton industry had become, along with agriculture, a site of struggle between different groups in the government. The 1935 solution to the Shenxin crisis that prevented the CCC from exercising its reformist influence on one of the largest cotton mill enterprises reflected the changes in political fortunes in Nanjing and the growing political marginalization of the Wang group by Jiang, a marginalization that had effected the demise of the CCC's strategy of mobilizing private banks for rural credit. It was this marginalization that increasingly eroded the CCC's capacity to pursue reforms.

The Political Marginalization of the National Economic Council

Disagreements between Jiang and the Wang and NEC group emerged only a few months after the establishment of the Wang-Jiang coalition (January 1932). Jiang, determined to press his interpretation of *an'nei* as the military extermination of the Communists and to channel national resources into the military, announced an anti-Communist campaign. At that time, Jiang asked Song to finance the campaign by floating another bond, ignoring all agreements reached before the formation of the Wang-Jiang coalition.[43] Song denied his request and, on June 4, 1932, resigned.[44] Venting his frustrations about dealing with Jiang and his financing methods, Song stated that in the last four months the national government had succeeded for the first time in balancing the budget without floating a single bond. For him, this was the "fulfillment of a dream" toward the creation of "a permanent foundation for constructive efforts."[45] He also declared that the Ministry of Finance should not supply funds for the anti-Communist campaign and should refuse to resort to further borrowing, which would mean the "ultimate disaster" and the continuation of the "vicious circle of meeting deficits with short-term loans."[46] Shanghai banking and finance circles had endured much hardship during the period of the Japanese attack. If now they had to provide the government with a huge amount of money, Song reasoned, it would mean the end of trust in the market and disaster for national finances.

Following Song's lead, two members of the Wang group, Minister of Foreign Affairs Luo Wengan and Minister of Communications Chen Mingshu, also resigned. Jiang, while launching his anti-Communist campaign, not only had requested that the finance minister resume the bond policy but also had transferred the Nineteenth Route Army from Shanghai to Fujian. This army, commanded by Chen Mingshu, had become the symbol of Chinese resistance to Japan after it had successfully defended Shanghai in 1932. Its removal enraged not only Chen but also those who felt that China should concentrate on fighting Japan. Jiang's act, instead, showed his determination to assume a conciliatory stance toward the external enemy while making the Communists the main target of his military efforts.

The June 1932 crisis was finally resolved through elaborate negotiations. Song, again relying on lobbying by the Jiangnan entrepreneurs,[47] was able to negotiate the terms of his return to the Ministry of Finance.[48] On the one hand, he gave in to Jiang's request for funding and agreed to issue a new bond. On the other, he succeeded in reviving the defunct National Finance Commission (NFC), a new reincarnation of the Budget Commission, which remained as inactive as its predecessor.[49] In October 1933, Jiang announced a new military campaign against the Communists—the previous one having failed to eradicate the CCP base in Jianxi—and renewed his request for more government bonds. Song resorted once again to the tactic that had proved successful in the past. He resigned from the Ministry of Finance and mobilized the Jiangnan business lobby in his support. This time, however, because of increasing pressure from the Japanese government—which had been clamoring against Song's anti-Japanese stand—he was promptly replaced by Kong Xiangxi.[50] Kong was also a prominent member of the GMD and a powerful politician. His position in Nanjing was assured, in a similar fashion as Song's, not only by his long involvement with the party but also by his marriage to Song Ailin, one of Song's three sisters.

Kong appeared to have been more closely aligned with Jiang, and the change of guard at the head of the Ministry of Finance marked the beginning of a drastic reversal in its policies. Appeasing Japan and supporting Jiang's anti-Communist campaigns became the main goals of the Ministry of Finance. Kong declared his full support for Jiang's military initiative and floated new bonds. He also replaced Song's anti-Japanese tariffs with new ones, highly favorable to Japan.[51]

Song Ziwen's loss of the Ministry of Finance was not the first blow to the Wang and NEC group. In October 1932, Chen Mingshu had been replaced at the Ministry of Communications by Zhu Jiahua, the previous secretary of the 1931 NEC and a close associate of Jiang's. These changes in the higher echelons of the administration frustrated the NEC leaders' hope of coordination with the rest of the administration. Against the increasingly pro-Jiang composition of the government, the NEC and the Ministry of Industry remained, for a while, the stronghold of the Wang-Song alliance.[52]

The final demise of the NEC came with Wang Jingwei's resignation in December 1935. Jiang assumed full leadership of the government and established a new cabinet, called the Cabinet of Action or the Cabinet of the Political Studies Clique because most of its members belonged to the Political Studies Clique. Weng Wenhao was appointed secretary general; Zhang Jia'ao, minister of railways; and Zhang Jun, the leader of the clique and a sworn brother of Jiang Jieshi, minister of foreign affairs.[53] The cabinet was also called the Peace Cabinet because most of its members had studied in Japan and favored a Sino-Japanese rapprochement. Wu Dingchang, who had recently led an economic mission to Japan, replaced Chen Gongbo at the head of the Ministry of Industry.[54]

This cabinet also marked the emergence within the Nationalist administration of, using Bergère's terminology, the "technical intelligentsia," a new group of Nationalists, such as Wu Dingchang and Zhang Jia'ao, who by the late 1930s rose to the higher echelons of the central government in Nanjing. This view is shared by Kirby, who argues that the leaders of the Natural Resource Commission—which replaced the NEC after the demise of the Wang-Jiang coalition and the establishment of the Cabinet of Action—represented a new "technocratic elite."[55] Most of them had studied abroad and had extensive experience in technical or university careers before entering the government.[56] According to Bergère, "these experts tended to form a group relatively independent from the central power, a 'techno-structure' which collaborated with the political system but did not identify with it."[57] This attitude allowed some of these technocrats to be active during different administrations, regardless of their political orientation, and explains why we find Zhang Jia'ao working closely with Song Ziwen and the NEC and then participating in Jiang's Cabinet of Action.

At the first meeting of the new cabinet, Jiang Tingfu, also a member of the Political Studies Clique and new director of political affairs of the Executive Yuan, made a series of proposals that included a plan for coordinating the building of transportation infrastructure (roads, railways, and water transportation) which, he argued, was in disarray because of the lack of cooperation between the Ministry of Communication, the Ministry of Railways, and the NEC. He also recommended the "abolition of the National Economic Council and the National Reconstruction Commission, [because] these two bodies duplicate each other and at the same time duplicate the work of other existing bodies."[58] Jiang Tingfu's proposal reflected Jiang Jieshi's ultimate victory over his opposition and the elimination of the two administrative bodies that were their expression.[59] Once in control of the government Jiang Jieshi proceeded to carry out those centralizing reforms he had previously opposed because they would have brought the administration and its resources under the control of his opponents. In fact, centralization had been the original goal of both the National Reconstruction Commission and the NEC and both had failed mostly because of Jiang's political opposition. The members of the new cabinet accepted Jiang Tingfu's proposal. Road and water conservation activities, of relatively low political significance, were the last to be taken away from the NEC. The first to go were those activities connected with agriculture and cooperatives, which constituted channels for political control over the countryside and access to economic resources. In May 1936, at the fourteenth meeting of the NEC Standing Committee, Jiang Jieshi proposed the transfer of all the NEC's responsibilities having to do with agriculture and cooperatives to the Ministry of Industry, which, since December 1935, had been under the direction of Wu Dingchang.[60] The proposal was approved and in May 1936 the government issued an order for the elimination of the

NEC Rural Reconstruction Commission, Agricultural Division, and Cooperation Commission, transferring all of their affairs to the Ministry of Industry.[61]

The end of the Wang-Jiang coalition thus marked the end of the NEC and the ascent of the Military Planning Commission, which was promptly transformed into the Natural Resource Commission (*ziyuan weiyuanhui*). Jiang had created the Military Planning Commission as early as November 1932 but had kept its existence secret. Headed by the geologist Weng Wenhao, this agency was, in William Kirby's words, "Chiang Kai-shek's [Jiang Jieshi] private . . . development agency. Set up to plan China's industrialization in cooperation with Germany, it would come to control all of China's state-run industry."[62] This agency operated on very different premises than the NEC. Rather than giving precedence to the rehabilitation and development of China's consumer industry, it pursued an industrialization model inspired by the German, and Prussian before it, experience. The Natural Resource Commission encouraged the growth of heavy industry in support of the military. It did not allow the participation of private capital or ownership and moved the industrial center from the coast to the interior.

As argued throughout this book, these differences between the Natural Resource Commission and the NEC were a result of different visions of nation building. Jiang's military approach was probably more realistic considering the escalation of Japanese aggression. In late 1935 it appeared that appeasement policies could not solve China's crisis and that China did indeed need to focus all its resources on military resistance to Japan. Going beyond this immediate consideration, however, the two approaches also reveal different ideas of a modern China. For Jiang, political control was more important than economic reform and growth. The establishment of the new cabinet was soon followed by what has become known as the bank coup, in which several private banks, including Chen Guangfu's Shanghai Commercial and Savings Bank, were brought under government control. Chambers of Commerce suffered the same fate.[63] The establishment of the Cabinet of Action thus marked the end of what historian Marie-Claire Bergère has called "the golden age of the Chinese bourgeoisie."[64]

The political defeat of the Wang group was the main factor leading to the demise of the NEC. Problems that had plagued the NEC since its early days could have been solved if addressed in an environment of sustained political support from a central government committed to a prolonged reform effort. The rural elite's opposition to NEC attempts to organize the peasants, for example, might have been overcome if the CCC had been able to persist in its reforms, which would have changed the economic structure of cotton growing and marketing. In the same way, problems created by disappointing developments in relation to the US cotton and wheat loan, which left the NEC with a budget much reduced than originally expected, might had been overcome if the NEC had been able to rely on a centralized budget and had been allowed to pursue its mobilization of private urban capital. The loan was supposed to help the Chinese cotton industry weather the current crisis and jump-start its modernization, but only a long-term system of consistent financial investment could have ultimately stabilized the industry.

After the demise of the Wang group and the NEC, Song continued to hold important positions in the Nanjing government. Together with some members of his group who had participated in the NEC, he continued to try to modernize the cotton industry, even if on a smaller scale. Song's vision of economic reforms and state-private collaboration as a means of nation building had to undergo a gradual resizing. In 1928 he had hoped to be able to implement his reform plan at the national level in his capacity as the minister of finance. He had later realized the tenacity of Jiang Jieshi's opposition and his own inability to control the entire government administration, and for this reason Song had used the NEC as the instrument for reform. With the demise of the NEC, Song retreated further to the even more narrow scope of bureaucratic capitalism, as exemplified by the CDFC and the China Cotton Company.

Although the CDFC has been viewed primarily as a vehicle for the corrupt practices of bureaucratic capitalism, the next section argues that it should also be understood as Song's and his associates' last attempt to carry out the modernization of the cotton industry already attempted with the CCC. Deprived of any direct channel of representation within the government after the NEC's failure to institutionalize cooperation between state and economic elites, they resorted to the more informal practices originating in the Self-Strengthening period.

From Self-Strengthening, to Corporativism, to Bureaucratic Capitalism

As argued earlier, more than any other subcommittees of the NEC, the CCC and the SIC reflected the NEC leaders' idea of state cooperation with China's modern industrial elite. Through both subcommittees, the NEC attempted to institutionalize, at the national level, patterns of cooperation between local economic elites and authorities developed since the Self-Strengthening period. These networks survived the collapse of the NEC and continued to pursue their economic and reform agenda in semiprivate structures, such as the CDFC and the China Cotton Company. In the new centralized environment of the late 1930s, however, national reconstruction was the exclusive prerogative of the state. The CDFC became a bureaucratic-capitalist structure mostly devoted to the economic survival of its members in the increasingly deteriorating economic conditions of China.

The SIC and the CCC followed a similar devolution from official government agencies to bureaucratic-capitalist enterprises. In her research Bell finds that in 1936, when the SIC was on the verge of being dismantled and private business had been pushed aside by the new Jiang cabinet, most of the members of the SIC, and most prominently Xue Shouxuan, established the Xingye Silk Company (*Xingye zhisi gufen youxian gongsi*). This company was created to raise capital, but it was also intended, Bell argued, "to end the chronic problems in filature investments and management once for all. Further, the Xingye Silk Company was now to provide the framework within which competition for raw materials and external markets would be made more manageable." The Xingye Silk Company thus shared the basic goals of the SIC and is considered by Bell as a reform agency rather than a corrupt business based on cliental relationships between business and authorities.[65]

The CCC's development mirrored that of the SIC. In 1934, when the political fortunes of Wang began to dwindle, the NEC Standing Committee established the CDFC. According to its mission statement, the CDFC was to operate strictly as a business organization aimed "at directing the flow of Chinese and foreign capital into new enterprises. Its formation is a sign of the increasing confidence in banking, as such, and of the recognition that there is little hope of securing the capital for industrial or other enterprises from the National Treasury."[66] A 1935 report of the CDFC declared that its goal was to address the international economic crisis and capital shortage afflicting China. To accomplish this goal, the CDFC vowed to cooperate with the government as well as with domestic and foreign financial and industrial groups.[67] The CDFC also worked to support the development of light industry. Stating its concerns "for the weakness in the structure of many industrial and commercial" enterprises, it extended long-term loans to industrial enterprises in an attempt to facilitate their reorganization. A 1936 report shows that the CDFC also became involved in railway construction, the development of communications and energy, and the issuance of public and private bonds.[68]

The stated goals of the CDFC thus overlapped to a large extent with those of the NEC. They both attempted to improve transportation and communications to help marketing, rescue light industry, and solve the capital problem. Both the NEC and the CDFC were determined to create a channel through which private capital and entrepreneurs could participate in national reconstruction. The close connection between the NEC and the

CDFC is exemplified by the latter's work in support of the NEC's Northwest and Jiangxi Offices.[69] The CDFC was especially active in Shaanxi, a region where the CCC had been active and successful and private investment more welcome. The CDFC established a branch in Xian, headed by Xie Zuokai, previously director of the Consolidated Tax office, and worked to develop electricity supplies and coal mining.[70]

Most of the businessmen involved with the CDFC came from the Jiangnan group linked to Song Ziwen and involved in the NEC, including the NEC secretary Qin Fen.[71] As Parks Coble argues in his seminal work *The Shanghai Capitalists and the Nationalist Government*, the CDFC was conceived to continue Song's strategy to reorient China's economy away from Japanese influence by collaborating with Western powers. In 1934 Song had met with Jean Monnet to discuss the creation of the CDFC and in May of the same year had invited Shanghai-based bankers to join in his plan. As Coble explains, "the company was to be a private firm which would serve principally as a conduit for the funds provided by other institutions."[72] Coble also points out that the CDFC claimed to be a private enterprise but relied heavily on government connections. The ambiguous position of the CDFC was obvious and drew heavy criticism. The journal *Shehui xinwen* (Mercury Society), which was influenced by the Blue Shirts, accused the CDFC of being a semiofficial or unofficial agency of the NEC.[73] The mixed membership of the CDFC, therefore, came under fire from supporters of Jiang Jieshi, who opposed the participation of private business in economic reforms.

Bureaucratic capitalism has been viewed as a product of the corruption that characterized the Nanjing government. Without denying the presence of extended corruption within the Nanjing government and the NEC and its subcommittees, I would rather stress the ambiguity of the role played by networks of bureaucratic capitalism in China's economic reforms from the late nineteenth century to 1935. The CCC, and the NEC as a whole, represented the Wang-Song group's effort to create an official channel for private business to participate in national reform. It would be wrong to assume that this participation was inspired by liberal ideas: it was to be developed within the political framework of the tutelage period, which denied direct political representation of private interests. Bureaucratic-capitalist networks were the only means for elite participation in government. This had been the case for economic reforms at the local level during the late Qing and early Republican years, and it remained so when the reform effort expanded to the national level. In addition, participation of private business in national reconstruction was based on the idea that the interests of the modern economic elite coincided with those of the state, or at least the state as envisioned by the Wang-Song group, and that the modern industrial sector was crucial for national survival. The state's interest in fostering private industry was mostly motivated by nationalism, not democratic spirit. With all its limitations, however, the CCC, as a channel of cooperation between state and business, represented the culmination of a grassroots trend that emerged during China's most liberal period (from the late Qing to the establishment of the Nanjing government in 1927). Although thwarted by the prevalence of statist ideas in the 1930s and channeled into a corporativist organization, communications between state and business would have been kept open with the survival of the CCC. At the same time, in the years that concern us, although cooperation developed along bureaucratic-capitalist networks, it still allowed the modern elite to share in decision making and economic profit. After 1935, with the demise of the NEC, the corporativist organization of the state became a one-way channel for a few powerful officials of the state to exploit economic resources.

The confusion between private and state economies was encouraged by the fact that the state did not have the funds to support its reforms and was thus forced to rely on private capital. This problem was not lost on Chen Gongbo, who was open about his reliance on private business to finance his reform plan. He not only channeled private capital through the NEC but, having met with enormous difficulties in financing his four-year plan for the Ministry of Industry, also turned to what he called a "less costly" method. The Ministry of Industry granted monopoly rights to private enterprises, such as the Chinese Alcohol Distillery Company, while maintaining its financial interests in such operations. Chen Gongbo explained that "single control [was] necessary to avoid the common cycle of industrial development, speculative boom, over-competition, and decline." For this reason he was applying "the principles of controlled economy through private management."[74]

The practice of joint state-private reforms had never before been met with open criticism. It had actually characterized all major reform agencies established by the Nanjing government. The National Reconstruction Commission constitutes yet another example of the difficulty of keeping the legitimate participation of economic elites in government reforms free from bureaucratic-capitalist practices. Zhang Renjie, the chairman of the commission, had helped to found it with 4,000 yuan of his own capital.[75] He also used his personal connections with Shanghai banks to raise additional funds. The commission mostly operated in Jiangsu, where Zhang was extremely influential. The leadership of the commission as well as its financing and operation developed along the lines of the Hu Hanmin–Zhang Renjie cliental network. At the time this confusion between private and public interest appeared normal and legitimate. We can thus speculate that the criticisms leveled against the CDFC represented an idea of a division between state and private economies that had not existed before.

Conclusion

The abolition of the NEC led to the disintegration of the alliance that had supported it. Wang Jingwei left the country, and although Chen Gongbo remained in the Nanjing government, he never again held a prominent position. Song Ziwen continued to "ride the tiger" of factionalism in Nanjing and managed to continue to secure important government positions. The Jiangnan entrepreneurs continued to rely on Song's patronage, but their moment of direct and legitimate participation in national reconstruction had passed, and their role in the building of the national economy was greatly diminished.

As Bell argues in her discussion of the SIC, we will never know "the full range of potential economic outcomes of collaborative efforts between China's first truly 'big business' . . . and the Guomindang."[76] The short lives of the CCC and the SIC prevent us from fully understanding the economic and political potential of their rightist corporativism. In the case of Fascist Italy, the development of the industrial corporativist organization into a rightist pattern allowed the industrial leadership to mitigate government intervention and to postpone, to some extent, the implementation of stricter policies of autarky and dirigisme. Even during the years of crisis in the 1930s, when the relative laissez-faire of the 1920s came to an end due to the international economic crisis and the sanctions imposed by the League of Nations on Italy for its attack on Ethiopia, the industrialists in the GFII received generous support from the government aimed at helping them survive the crisis. In addition, during these years, the corporativist organization of the GFII allowed the industrial interests it represented to find opportunities to expand at the expense of other businesses, thus eliminating most of the competition. In short, according to historian Roland Sarti, "the partnership with fascism was a profitable business venture for the industrialists."[77]

The same conclusion can be reached for the CCC, which obviously enjoyed many of the same benefits. Differences are, however, important. While the Italian GFII industrialists looked with suspicion at Mussolini's nationalist and autarkic rhetoric, those in the CCC had every reason to share in the nation-building and anti-imperialist goals of the Wang group. The Chinese national crisis was very real for the Chinese entrepreneurs, while the Italian national crisis was created by Mussolini, first abstractly by his revanchist rhetoric and, later, concretely by his attack on Ethiopia and increased military ambitions. Most important, most reforms carried out by the CCC had already been initiated by the entrepreneurs in their efforts to modernize and expand their industry and thus embodied long-term reform trends in the private economy. Although they might not have agreed with all aspects of the CCC's plan, the CCC's industrialists supported its economic goals.

The CCC, like the GFII, however, operated at the expense of other groups and sectors, whose interests were not so successfully represented by the state. This was not just the case with workers—industrial workers saw their pay cut several times in response to economic crises—but also with the agrarian sector, which was never able to negotiate effectively with the government. The land reclamation projects so much touted by Mussolini, for example, never achieved their intended results, and the Italian agricultural sector was not able to reap the expected benefits. During the Depression, in order not to burden the urban industrial economy, laws were passed restricting the mobility of farm labor, leading to wide rural unemployment.[78] In short, the rightist nature of the GFII organization, by cementing the alliance between industrial elites and the government, created the conditions for the suppression of the interests of other groups. In the same vein, the policies of the CCC were devised to support the modern cotton industry of Shanghai and would not necessarily have benefited the rural village but rather exploited it. In addition, the consolidation of the cotton industry would have deeply changed the Shanghai economy. Small workshops carrying out diversified and flexible activities, from trade to weaving, were an integral part of the Chinese economy.[79] The CCC leaders, however, perceived them as a hindrance to economic development, the centralization and rationalization of industrial production, and, ultimately, nation building. The CCC reforms would, in the long run, lead to their gradual disappearance, with effects hard to gauge on the Chinese economy as a whole.

The Cabinet of Action followed a different strategy of economic development from the Wang-Song group. The next few years saw an increasing tendency toward outright nationalization of major industries and financial institutions as well as the transformation of the state corporativist structure into the form identified by Gregory Kasza as Leninist-style corporativism. As William Kirby has argued in his groundbreaking work *Germany and Republican China,* the Natural Resource Commission sponsored economic reforms that were focused on the hinterland, not on the coastal urban modern economy.[80] It thus marginalized the *minzu* "sprouts of capitalism" (the private entrepreneurs of the treaty ports) in favor of a state-owned heavy-industry economy oriented toward the military.

In this new economic and political environment, bureaucratic capitalism remained the only channel for relationships between the Nanjing government and the Jiangnan entrepreneurs. Especially in the postwar period, bureaucratic capitalism allowed only a few well-connected individuals informal access to government officials and favors and hardly constituted a tool for nation building and reform. Postwar bureaucratic capitalism fragmented the government and the private sector, not along ideological lines, but along those of short-term economic interests.

Defending Which Nation? PART IV

柒

CHAPTER 7

From Nationalism to Collaboration

The confrontation between Jiang Jieshi and Wang Jingwei played out its final act during the years of Japanese occupation. The Marco Polo Bridge Incident (July 7, 1937), which initiated full-fledged military hostilities, did not bring an end to the Nationalist factional struggle but actually deepened Jiang's and Wang's disagreements on nation building, national defense, and the political legitimacy of Jiang's leadership. Wang's and Chen Gongbo's idea that the *minzu* economy would be the heart of a modern and independent Chinese nation came once again to oppose Jiang's notion that the state (including its upper leadership, its heavy industry, and its political ideology) formed the foundation of the nation, fracturing the Nationalists' response to Japan's occupation and ultimately leading Wang Jingwei to collaborate with Japan.

Disagreeing with Jiang's response to the Japanese invasion of China, Wang Jingwei launched the Peace Movement (*heping yundong,* 1938–40) in October 1938, and two years later he established a competing Nationalist government in Nanjing in collaboration with the Japanese (Jiang had abandoned the capital and retreated to the interior at the end of 1937), the Reorganized National Government, or RNG (*gaizu guomin zhengfu,* 1940–45). After a long period of indecision, Chen Gongbo joined him in 1940, in time for the official inauguration of the new political formation.[1] When Wang Jingwei died in 1944, Chen found himself at the helm of a government he had joined very reluctantly. With the defeat of Japan in 1945, Chen, along with other former leaders of the RNG, was brought to trial for collaboration (*hanjian*) and was finally executed in 1946. Wang's timely death had spared him the humiliation of trial and execution, and so Chen became the main target of anti-*hanjian* sentiments.

To explain Wang's and Chen's decision to collaborate with the Japanese, PRC historians have especially stressed their anticommunism, which the historians date back to their 1927 acceptance of Jiang's split with the Communists. They cite as evidence the pledge to defeat the Communists in China and throughout East Asia included in the agreement reached by Wang with the Japanese. PRC historians have also published extensively on the RNG's infamous secret service and the "clear the countryside" (*qingxiang*) campaign, which was aimed at purging the rural areas of Communist elements while facilitating the acquisition of food and goods at the expense of the welfare of the population. Chinese and Western historians alike have also favored narratives that describe Wang and Chen as political opportunists devoid of any political goals in their collaboration. These narratives are in many respects incorrect. The RNG was indeed a brutal regime, and a quest for personal power and a certain amount of vanity seem to have been weaknesses of Wang in particular and certainly played a role in his determination to assume supreme leadership over the GMD and to collaborate. Isolating this aspect of Wang's personality and considering it the main motivation of his actions is, however, a very limited view of the complex combination of factors that inspired Wang's career (political ideas, personal aspirations, and recognition that power was essential for the realization of his nation-building program).

These narratives have in general oversimplified Wang's and Chen's motivations and the history of the RNG as a whole. First of all, they do not recognize that Wang's and Chen's gradual move from leftist mass organization in the 1920s to anticommunism and fascist ideology in the 1930s and 1940s was not simply opportunistic but followed a pattern of political development similar to those of many leaders in Europe, as discussed in chapter 1. Thus, their participation in anti-Communist activities (Jiang's first and the Japanese later) was not necessarily a sign of their willingness to "sell out" or lack of political beliefs but the result of a political transformation common to many political leaders in the years between the two world wars. In addition, these narratives fail to recognize that Wang's and Chen's willingness to compromise with Japan was rooted in their longstanding vision of nation building and national defense as well as in their effort to oppose Jiang's leadership over the Nationalist government. Although the motivations that inspired Wang and Chen are complex and diverse (the two leaders were divided on some important aspects of collaboration), their participation in the RNG cannot be simplistically explained as the result of political opportunism or a lack of nationalism.

Instead, it must be placed in the context of the 1930s discourse on the Chinese nation and the struggle over competing nation-building visions within the GMD.

The RNG deserves a much more extensive and comprehensive study than the one attempted in this chapter, which is intended to be only an epilogue to the nation-building efforts of the 1930s. This chapter explores only how Wang's and Chen's understanding of China's crisis and its solution influenced their decision to collaborate and the goals they pursued in their years in Nanjing. It especially focuses on the intellectual journey that led them to "return the capital to Nanjing" (*haidu*)[2]—the expression they used to refer to the establishment of the collaborationist government—their motivations, and their goals and how they planned to achieve them. In other words, this chapter attempts to shed light on the ultimate fate of Wang's and Chen's vision of nation building rather than to study their collaboration per se. This is indeed a limitation, since it artificially isolates Wang's and Chen's aspirations from the actual experience of collaboration, which is mired with difficult moral questions on nationalism and disregard of basic human rights. I leave, however, these important issues to be addressed by other scholars, as they go beyond the scope of this book. The current growing interest in collaboration in China has produced—and continues to produce—abundant and high-quality works that clarify the nature of this phenomenon while emphasizing its complexity and diversity.[3]

Wartime collaboration is still, to this day, a sensitive issue, intertwined with painful memories that have haunted humanity since World War II. As a consequence, until recently, narratives on collaboration were characterized by a sharp distinction between evil and good. In postwar European imagery, the "collaborator" is generally a villain who revels in an orgy of cruelty or is simply motivated by greed for power or wealth. Any intermediate position was inconceivable because of the highly emotional and political content of the issue and its protracted effects on postwar politics.[4] Scholars still find it difficult to overcome the highly rhetorical and polarized dichotomy between "resisters/nationalists" and "collaborators." Only recently have works on Vichy and Salò brought to light the ambiguity that often characterizes this issue, adding grays to the black-and-white narratives that we inherited from the postwar years.[5]

New works have aimed at the outright redemption and justification of the Fascist collaboration years in Salò; especially notable in this area is the work of the late Italian historian Renzo De Felice.[6] Others, instead, have tried to understand the intellectual foundations of high-level political collaboration or the small betrayals that punctuated the daily practice of coexistence with invaders.[7] The latter trend attempts, not to invest collaboration with positive value, but only to attain a more nuanced understanding of its complexity and its different faces. This chapter belongs to the latter trend, since it does not want to be an apology for the RNG but only to improve our understanding of the complexity of Chinese collaboration.

A Lost War?

One of the main ideas that influenced Wang's and Chen's decision to cooperate with the Japanese was their conviction that, if the two countries ever engaged in a military conflict, China would suffer a humiliating defeat. This had been the basic notion of the *an'nei rangwai* political platform supported by Wang during the years of the Wang-Jiang coalition. By 1938, when Wang launched his Peace Movement, his perception of China's military weakness had not changed. According to Chen's 1945 defense document (*zibaishu*) in which he answered the accusations brought against him at the *hanjian* trials, after the 1933 Gubeikou[8] incident Wang had became increasingly convinced that China was unable to fight Japan. At that time repeated communications from the front stressed the military inferiority of China, describing how the Chinese troops' fire power was so inferior to that of the Japanese that, to shoot the enemy, Chinese soldiers had to get very close and, as a result, would be shot down by the powerful precision weapons of the Japanese. The Chinese soldiers could not muster any meaningful resistance to Japan's invading forces; they were killed even before they could sight the enemy. At the time, both military leaders and officials emphasized the fact that, although soldiers and generals were willing to fight, the army was simply not equipped to do so. According to Chen, it was those reports and the conclusions drawn by the very military leaders at the front that reinforced Wang's belief in the futility of military resistance.[9] The feeling that war with Japan would have disastrous consequences was further strengthened by the speed of the Chinese retreat in the face of Japan's aggression in 1937–38, reinforcing Wang's view that the war was lost even before it had begun.

Like Wang, Chen also became even more convinced than before that China would inevitably lose the war. Chen, however, continued to stress China's economic, rather than military, weaknesses. In 1945, he again bemoaned the fact that, in 1937–41, the country had not been ready for war because "[it] did not even have a military industry worth talking of." Even more debilitating was, in his eyes, the fact that China had not reached autarky: "each year China is even short 16,000,000 piculs of rice . . . 20,000,000 piculs of wheat flour [to meet its needs]. . . . In 1932 China's production of cotton only reached 7,000,000 piculs. What to do? If China goes to war, food and cloth will not be sufficient, and there is really no way we could survive." Chen's belief that China's lack of self-sufficiency would have a negative effect on the nation's ability to sustain the war effort was thus unchanged from his years at the Ministry of Industry. As he repeatedly emphasized, his belief had been strengthened by that experience: "It was part of my job at the Ministry of Industry to study and decide on these problems."[10] These years of study had strengthened his perception of China's problems.

That Chen made these statements during his trial in 1945 could cast serious doubt on their veracity. Chen had every reason to cast his decision to collaborate in the best possible light. His statements, however, are consistent with his prewar understanding of China's crisis, lending them a measure of credibility. At the same time, these statements reveal how, in 1945, Chen still perceived China's situation within the interpretive framework that had influenced his decisions in the 1930s. Chen argued that he and Wang had collaborated because they had believed that the war was lost. Military resistance to Japan did not seem a viable option. Chen thus represented the logic of the *an'nei rangwai* as justification for their unwillingness to fight Japan. In 1946, however, this logic did not sound convincing to the Chinese public (and the judge presiding at the trial) in the wake of Japan's total defeat.

In 1932 that logic, however, had been embraced also by Jiang Jieshi, who now was hailed as the defender of the nation. The Wang-Jiang cabinet had been formed on the assumption that China could not stop Japan militarily, incurring the considerable wrath of those who instead supported outright military resistance. As seen earlier, in 1932 both Wang and Jiang had favored a strategy of attempting to strengthen the nation while delaying as long as possible a clash with the Japanese army, although they greatly diverged on the meaning and means of such strengthening. It is hard to say on what side Jiang would have been if it had not been for the Xi'an Incident—when the Communists kidnapped him and forced him to declare war on Japan and begin a new period of collaboration with them. Even as the leader of China's military opposition to Japan during the war, however, Jiang's strategy of how to deal with Japan was also based on a feeling that China could not beat the Japanese army, a feeling reinforced in 1937 by the loss of Shanghai, where Jiang had committed much of his force.

Since 1932 Jiang had believed that a second world war would erupt as early as 1936 and China would be rescued by the intervention of Western powers.[11] Jiang's approach to war was in general marked by waiting either for a foreign *deus ex machina* or for Japan to collapse on its own. His war strategy rested on two main ideas: exchanging territory to gain time and engaging Japan in a war of attrition. As Jiang argued in a 1932 essay, he was not afraid of losing territory as much as losing Chinese culture. Jiang used the examples of the "barbarian" Wei, Yuan, and Qing dynasties to make the case that, even if invaded, the Chinese would inevitably triumph in the long run. The Chinese people tended to assimilate (*tonghua*) the invaders and defeat them over time with their culture. Consequently, Jiang declared, he was primarily concerned with educating the Chinese—about his interpretation of Chinese culture, that is—rather than preventing the Japanese from invading China.[12] Jiang's essay reveals how Jiang conflated education and culture with political control and indoctrination, as the New Life Movement, a crucial aspect of his idea of cultural education, testified. In addition, by exchanging territory for time, Jiang argued, China would ultimately force Japan to spread itself too thin and be worn down, until it would eventually collapse.[13] Jiang, therefore, never took seriously the possibility of China winning the war on its own strength and never believed in directly engaging Japan militarily.

In this respect, the main difference between Jiang and Wang was Jiang's belief that a Western power, most likely the United States, would come to the rescue. Wang, instead, was convinced that no Western power would intervene in the Sino-Japanese conflict. Because Japan's imperialism was anti-Comintern in nature, he reasoned, its aggression would not provoke the intervention of the United States and Great Britain.[14] Wang's belief was strengthened after Chen's visit to Europe in early 1938. Upon his return, Chen reported that England, France, and the United States would not expand their war to the Pacific in support of China. In addition, Italy, which until then had been a close ally of China, had just signed the Anti-Comintern Pact with Germany and Japan. In spite of its pledges to maintain a "strict neutrality" in the current Sino-Japanese conflict, Italy was in reality gradually increasing its support of Japan. During Chen's visit to Rome, both Mussolini and Galeazzo Ciano—at that time minister of foreign affairs—repeatedly urged him to accept peace with Japan and offered to act as mediators. As Chen wrote in his report of his visit to Italy, regardless of the encouraging words of Mussolini and Ciano, it was already clear that Italy had abandoned its friendly attitude toward China and "if there [are] people who still say that Italy on the surface shelters Japan, but in reality supports China, they cannot be trusted."[15] The perception of China's unavoidable defeat changed dramatically in 1941, after the Japanese attacked Pearl Harbor and the United States entered the Pacific theater of war. It was at that point that Wang's and Chen's predictions proved wrong. China, as part of the Allied forces, now had more than a good chance of ending up on the winning side, fulfilling Jiang's prophecy.[16]

Before Pearl Harbor, believing that defeat was inevitable, Wang saw no alternative but to reach a peace agreement with the Japanese and establish a collaborationist Chinese government in the occupied areas. Achieving a peace as favorable as possible was the only way, he believed, to save what was still possible to save. In 1938 Wang argued that the moment had arrived to exploit the current favorable circumstances and Japan's new attitude toward China to negotiate, if not an ideal peace, at least a peace that would leave hope for the survival of the nation.[17]

The Dream of a Favorable Peace

When talking about the current favorable situation for China, Wang referred to new developments on the Japanese side. In his 1938 program for a New Order for Asia, Japan's prime minister, Konoe Fumimaro, acknowledged that Japan had underestimated Chinese nationalism. Only now, Konoe claimed, had he come to the realization that Japan could never triumph over China since Chinese nationalism "can be found everywhere. You can find it in the Guomindang-Communist collaboration. . . . You can find it in the leaders of the puppet regimes. . . . Nationalism is what enabled China to keep fighting with all her weakness. It is to be found not just at the state level but at the individual level."[18] For this reason, Konoe concluded, Japan had come to understand that it needed to concede something to Chinese nationalism and was now ready to compromise with the GMD on the condition that Jiang step down.

The New Order for Asia also marked a new attitude of the Japanese government toward the Chinese economy. Parks Coble divides Japan's occupation of China into three periods. The first period, from 1937 to November 1938, is characterized by "destruction and chaotic attempts to control the economy." The second period, from November 1938 to the beginning of the Pacific War, begins with Japan's realization of the negative effects on the Chinese economy of a year of unrestrained plundering, which hindered Japan's policy of using China's resources to support the war—"using the war to feed the war" (*yizhan yangzhan*). The conquest of central China had begun to strain Japan's resources rather than help sustain the war effort. For this reason the Japanese government decided to attempt to organize the Chinese economy and bring back production to prewar levels. The third phase, from early 1943 to 1945, Coble argues, witnessed "the collapse of this policy."[19]

Wang started negotiations with the Japanese at the moment when the Japanese wanted to revitalize the Chinese economy and were seeking Chinese cooperation. Konoe's statement gave Wang new hope. Wang was ready to take Konoe's statement at face value because he was convinced that ultimately the Japanese had no intention of completely destroying the Chinese nation but only wanted to defend their interests in the region.[20] This perception was not completely unfounded. The Japanese government had been reluctant to launch a military occupation of central China. On this issue, the views of the civilian leadership in Tokyo differed from those of the military, especially the Guangdong (Kwantung) army in China, which had pushed for military conquest of the lower Yangzi Valley and generally opposed Chinese participation in the political and economic administration of the area. Japan's China policy was thus often chaotic and inconsistent, allowing ample room for speculation.[21] In the negotiations for the establishment of the RNG, Wang dealt mostly with the civilian leadership in Tokyo. The moderate attitude of the Konoe cabinet, together with Wang's hope for a constructive collaboration with Japan, led him to believe that an acceptable compromise was possible. He thus stated that the time had come to exploit Japan's new attitude in order to return to the situation of the 1933 Tanggu Truce, remove Jiang from the government, and gain more time for national reconstruction,[22] which he believed was the only lasting defense against Japan's aggression.

The arguments presented by Wang in the context of the Peace Movement were not new. They had already been used by a previous Chinese collaborationist political formation, the Reformed Government (*weixin zhengfu*, 1938–40). Its two most prominent leaders, Liang Hongzhi and Wen Zongyao, had assumed a similar position, basing their claims for legitimacy on two issues. First, they argued that the war was already lost. Second, they claimed that Japan was not aiming at the destruction of the Chinese nation. The basic difference in the rhetoric of the Reformed and the Reorganized governments can be found in the former's rejection of the GMD political leadership over the country. Liang and Wen felt that the GMD, from Sun Yat-sen to Jiang Jieshi, had led the country astray and advocated a return to a more traditional political system. The leaders of the RNG, on the other hand, challenged only Jiang's leadership and not the Nationalist legacy. They actually aimed at revitalizing the GMD by placing it once again under their leadership and bringing it back to its original political path indicated by Sun Yat-sen. In spite of this difference, both governments regarded collaboration with the Japanese as a temporary solution for attaining long-range political and nationalist goals. In this sense the term "collaborationist nationalism" chosen by Timothy Brook in his study of the Reformed Government appears to also be extremely appropriate for the RNG.[23]

The Reformed Government proved highly ineffective in restraining the Japanese, and its experience could hardly offer inspiration to Wang Jingwei. Nevertheless, Wang was convinced that he would succeed where the Reformed Government had failed. He believed that his government differed from its predecessor in two ways. First, Japan had finally recognized the power of Chinese nationalism and was now more willing to compromise than before. Second, because he enjoyed much more political prestige than Liang and Wen had, he was in a better position to exploit the needs of the Japanese for a strong and legitimate Chinese government and thus would be able to negotiate a more favorable peace. Since the beginning of the war Japan had based its occupation strategy on the development of a strong Chinese administrative structure that would enjoy a high level of legitimacy in the eyes of the Chinese population and, at the same time, protect Japanese interests.[24]

Preserving the Vitality of the Nation

Although Wang had hoped to bargain with the Japanese from a position of relative power, negotiations proved slow and disappointing. When Wang finally signed the Basic Treaty (*jiben tiaoyue*) with the Japanese on November 30, 1940, it was clear that he had had to compromise more than he had expected. Anticommunism, not the survival of the Chinese nation, had become the central issue of the peace agreement, opening the door to Japanese policing activities on Chinese territory. In addition, the treaty virtually consigned China's national integrity to the vague formula of "friendly-neighbor relations," without offering any further assurance of Japan's good intentions. No real agreement had been reached on the timing of the retreat of the Japanese army or on the line beyond which the Japanese would retreat. The future status of Manchuria was also left uncertain, since the treaty assigned to this region an unspecified "special status."[25]

In spite of Wang's repeated invitations to join him, Chen Gongbo initially remained aloof from the Peace Movement. At the time of his trial, in 1945, Chen stated that he had disagreed with Wang's peace treaty because it had failed to deal satisfactorily with China's three most urgent problems: Japan's military retreat, the recovery of Manchuria, and "preserving the 'people's vitality' [*renmin de yuanqi*]." The idea of the people's "vitality" (*yuanqi*), a formula often used in these years to indicate the preservation of the nation, was closely connected to the notion of modern nationhood that had inspired Wang's and Chen's work in the years of the Wang-Jiang coalition. It thus referred specifically to the preservation of China's *minzu* economy. In this context, preserving China's vitality became synonymous with maintaining control over economic resources in order to permit future nation-building efforts. As Wang stated in a conversation with Chen, he believed that "if China wants to reconstruct it needs at least twenty years. . . . Today it is possible to preserve a little vitality [*yuanqi*] for the nation, as the stepping stone for future reconstruction." Since nation building, the prerequisite for resisting Japan, had not been achieved and no time was now left to accomplish it, the only hope for China was to preserve the basic elements with which to develop a *minzu* economy in the long term. This goal was to be achieved through collaboration with the Japanese. The process was not going to be easy, as Wang himself recognized. It was going to be a matter of proceeding "one step at a time."[26]

Preserving China's vitality became Chen's main focus when he finally joined Wang Jingwei in Nanjing shortly after the inauguration of the RNG. Chen continued to see Japan's escalating aggression as a result of the close relationship between a country's control over economic resources and its national power. In the 1940s Chen took this idea, which in the 1930s had been at the core of his understanding of colonization, a step further. "Japan used war to feed war" (*Rijun shi yizhang yangzhan*), he argued. For this reason, "it need[ed] a good producing area" and was attempting to reduce China to this role.[27] The more the Pacific War intensified, the more Japan would tighten its control over the Chinese economy.

By 1939, after two years of Japanese occupation of central China, Chen believed that his worst fears had been fully realized. The Japanese had taken over the core of the Chinese economy. In the early months of 1938 the Japanese army confiscated Chinese industrial plants in Shanghai and other industrial centers and placed Chinese businesses under the control of the Japanese "national-policy companies." In the lower Yangzi Valley, Japan had established a system of "material control" (*wuzi tongzhi*) aimed at ensuring supplies of raw materials and food for their military effort. Japan's "material control" was exercised through control commissions (*tongzhi weiyuanhui*) that organized and mobilized the agricultural production and industrial processing of crucial raw materials, such as grains and cotton.[28] This system very much resembled the one attempted by Chen with his 1930s NEC reforms. The corporativist structure for the mobilization of China's resources and producers that Chen had envisioned as the key for the development of autarkic *minzu* industrialization was now, in the hands of the Japanese, a tool to support their war effort against China. Chen believed that China's economy had been wrested from its people and incorporated into Japan's industrial war machine.

In effect, the Japanese stripped the Chinese economy of its autonomy. As a foreign observer described, Japanese "occupying forces took over all Chinese government property and all means of large-scale production, and monopolized the distributive services. They imposed manufactured goods on the Chinese market in return for Chinese Nationalist government banknotes for foreign exchange. Treating China as an internal market, the Japanese brought in and took out vast quantities of commodities and capital goods without passing through customs at all."[29] The Japanese were particularly interested in the "two whites" (cotton and salt) and the "two blacks" (iron and coal), and to gain easy access to them they kept their prices down and controlled their marketing and transportation. In this way they blockaded unoccupied China and paid nominal prices to the Chinese producers, who were left with no choice but to sell to the Japanese. Japan thus attempted to extract as much from China as possible while placing a stranglehold on Chongqing.[30] In addition, by April 1938, the Japanese government had reached an agreement with the British ambassador in Tokyo that allowed the Reformed Government to deposit all Chinese customs revenue in the Yokohama Specie Bank. This was a tremendous loss for China, since customs revenues from Shanghai alone constituted between 40 and 50 percent of the total revenues of the Nationalist government.[31] In essence, China's resources were used to conquer China and to expand the Japanese empire, just as Chen had feared since 1932.

According to Yuan Yuquan, director of the trade section of the Ministry of Industry of the RNG, Japanese purchasing operations in central China were carried out with no consideration for the peasants and prioritized the feeding of the Japanese troops.[32] As the US consulate general reported in late 1939, the Japanese were buying large quantities of rice from peasants at "practically confiscatory prices" in order to meet military needs, thus creating food shortages and hardship for the population.[33] Japanese acquisition techniques amounted to "ruthless plunder."[34] Food shortages soon became a major problem in Shanghai, making it clear that the Japanese army had no interest in ensuring that the Chinese population had enough to eat. As a consequence, the level of starvation in Shanghai was such that the local authorities began a repatriation program, encouraging people to move to the rural areas. Between December 1941 and January 1942, an estimated 300,000 people left the city.[35]

According to Chen Gongbo, the recovery of control over domestic resources was necessary to save China. It was the only effective way to undermine Japan's war effort while preserving the people's vitality, which is to say, to feed the Chinese and salvage the economic foundations for national reconstruction. However, Japanese behavior in central China had proven beyond a doubt that control over Chinese resources was crucial for Japan's war effort.[36] Japan, therefore, had no motivation to surrender this control, especially since China did not pose a serious military threat.

One factor, however, worked in China's favor. Wang and Chen became aware that the Japanese were having trouble exercising control over the

Chinese population and the economy. Whether it was a matter of nationalism or a desperate attempt to survive, both peasants and urban dwellers found ways to escape Japanese control. The Japanese authorities faced severe difficulties in enforcing the material control system. In central China in 1941, the quantity of husked rice on the market had decreased by 50 percent from before the war. The quantity of wheat on the market also decreased yearly. In central China the percentage of flour mills able to operate dropped from 45.5 percent in 1939 to 33.2 percent in 1942. In 1942 Japan seized 378,000 tons of wheat and 466,000 piculs of cotton, which were only 58.2 percent and 36.7 percent, respectively, of the originally planned quantities.[37] In short, the Japanese were unable to acquire the resources they needed or to control the transportation of staples and goods. Peasants reduced their production of grain and other basic products such as cotton because they were no longer profitable due to Japanese procurements. What was produced tended to find its way to the black market in Shanghai and other cities in central China as well as to the areas under Jiang Jieshi's control, making the blockade against Chongqing less effective.[38] It was in this context that the Japanese became willing to share the burden of acquisitions with a sympathetic Chinese government.

The preservation of the Chinese economy became the underlying theme during Chen's trial in 1945. He was accused of, among other things, "having ransacked goods and supplied the enemy" at the expense of the civilian population, depriving them of basic goods for subsistence, such as rice, flour, and cotton. These accusations directly opposed his claim that the main goal of the RNG was to "preserve the people's vitality." Chen insisted that the RNG had fought tirelessly to preserve goods from the enemy and oppose Japan's plans.

Although the transfer of control over resources to the RNG was one of the very first issues tackled by the new administration and was planned and approved by the Japanese at the earliest stages of collaboration, it proved slow and difficult. Wang had not been wrong in describing the task of regaining control over the "people's vitality" as a "step-by-step" process.[39] The Chinese and the Japanese began a tug-of-war over local resources, and RNG leaders found themselves in the position of working to fill Japanese procurement quotas.

From Theory to Practice: The Struggle over Control of Resources

In 1939, during negotiations with the Japanese in Shanghai, Zhou Fohai—a longtime associate of Wang Jingwei and Chen Gongbo who was to become the third most important personality in the RNG—reached an agreement on the release of part of the customs revenues deposited with the Yokohama Specie Bank.[40] This was a big victory since it returned some financial resources to the Chinese authorities. Encouraged by this early success, as soon as the new Nanjing government was established, its leaders began to plan for the recovery of China's "postwar" (*zhanghou*) economy, the expression they used to indicate the economy of the occupied territory after the establishment of the RNG. The recovery of the Chinese industry became, once again, a priority.

A 1941 document, "Circumstances of the Cotton Textile Industry and Preliminary Plan for Its Recovery," exemplifies the spirit that characterized Nanjing government's economic ideas in this first year of collaboration. The document opens with an assessment of the cotton industry in the prewar years, highlighting the recovery and development that China's textile industry had experienced in the few years before full war with Japan. The document continues with a section devoted to the "postwar period" (*zhanghou*). This second section laments the destruction that the war brought to Chinese textile factories as well as the fact that those factories that were still able to operate had been placed under the management of the Japanese military authorities. The Japanese authorities, the document continues, had however agreed to return Chinese factories to the Ministry of Trade and Industry (*gongshangbu*) of the Wang government, and the stage was now set for restoring the cotton industry to its prewar conditions. The recovery plan presented by this document opens with a pledge to follow as its basic principle what it describes as "Sun Yat-sen's principle of self-sufficiency in the production and marketing of cotton." Recognizing that present conditions were far from allowing self-sufficiency, the plan focuses on a recovery program to be completed in four years. The goals of the program were mostly to return agricultural and industrial production to the levels achieved in the prewar years and to push for further expansion, closely echoing the objective of the prewar CCC. The plan optimistically concludes that, because the Chinese people tend to privilege cotton over other fibers due to cultural and economic factors (echoing the prewar idea of an unlimited rural market for Chinese industrial cotton goods), prospects for the development of the Chinese cotton industry appeared particularly hopeful. The government thus pledged to work for the recovery of the cotton industry and to eliminate the obstacles to its development: insufficient supplies of raw cotton, poor quality, lack of capital, poor technology and management. This plan, the document concludes, would focus on the preliminary recovery of the industry but was to be followed by a second one devoted to the achievement of self-sufficiency.[41]

This document, with its discussion of the *minzu* (a term used in the document) Chinese cotton industry and its goals of a future autarky, exemplifies the initial economic goals of the RNG as well as the RNG leaders' lack of understanding of the nature of their collaboration with the Japanese. The idea that the Japanese would allow the Wang government to continue its work toward Chinese self-sufficiency at the expense of Japan's own economic interests in China—and especially against Japan's intentions of "using the war to feed the war" (*yizhan yangzhan*)—was obviously unrealistic. Most economic plans for 1941 drafted by the Wang government, however, shared this same unrealistic assumption that the Chinese authorities could now resume their work for economic reconstruction interrupted by the war. This was the case with the plans for the recovery of the silk industry and for establishing a Chinese Industrial Bank, which was to invest exclusively in Chinese industries and mobilize private capital through its joint state-private organization.[42] Equally optimistic were the Wang government's statements that economic control of goods of daily necessity was an internal Chinese matter and therefore it was to be exercised by Chinese authorities. Japan, an internal document of the Wang government stated, needed to understand this principle and respect China's independence.[43]

It soon became clear that the Wang government would meet with overwhelming difficulties in achieving its goals and regaining control over the Chinese economy. Negotiations to return Chinese industries to their original Chinese owners proceeded slowly, and only by 1943 had most of these factories, if not all, been restored to the Chinese. This led to the reopening of the merchants guilds and the Shanghai Stock Exchange, bringing back some level of business life to the city and gaining for the RNG the support of local entrepreneurs.[44] Once again, following the strategy already attempted during the Wang-Jiang coalition, the Wang government established a new National Economic Council (RNG NEC) headed by Zhou Fohai, at the time the minister of finance and the chairman of the Central Reserve Bank of the RNG.

The 1940s RNG NEC was supposed to create the same structure of economic control established by its predecessor in the 1930s. Like the 1930s NEC, the new one aimed at bringing the Chinese economy under the control of the Chinese government and away from the Japanese. The RNG wanted the new NEC to be the only control agency in central China. For this reason it requested the abolition of the Central China Development Company (*naka Shina shinko kabushiki kaisha*)—the Japanese organization that oversaw the Japanese system of material control—and the transfer of its functions to the RNG NEC. This request, not surprisingly, met with Japanese opposition. The Japanese were reluctant to dismantle the company because it controlled central China's infrastructures, which they wanted to keep under their direct authority. It was only in 1944 that the Japanese passed over to the RNG titles to a few public utilities in Shanghai—a meaningless move that did not challenge Japanese control over the company.[45]

The transfer of the management of the system of material control over goods, however, was more successful, although it fell short of Wang's and Chen's expectations. In July 1940 the Japanese allowed the establishment of a Grain Management Committee (*liangshi guanli weiyuanhui*), which would be responsible for overseeing the procurements of rice for the Chinese military and civilians. The committee was supposed to guarantee Chinese autonomy in the acquisitions of resources, thus ensuring that a portion of the Jiangnan grain would be made available to the Chinese population. The Japanese were supposed to acquire grain from fifteen rice-producing counties in Jiangnan, while the RNG was limited to the Wuhu area, Nanjing area, and, starting in 1942, five areas of southern Anhui.[46] Chen had high expectations for this new system. When he became the mayor of Shanghai in October 1940, he declared that he "would try to get 14,000 piculs of rice per month to feed Shanghai's starving people."[47] There was a propagandistic ring to Chen's statements, since, as historian Christian Henriot has pointed out in his study of rice regulation in wartime Shanghai, the amount of grain promised by Chen, even if obtained, would have been enough to feed Shanghai's people only for a short time. The new Grain Management Committee, however, marked the first step in taking over from the Japanese the administration of food and other goods in central China.

Reality proved less rosy than Chen had hoped, however. Although the acquisition areas assigned to the Japanese were the best grain-producing regions in central China, they found it difficult to keep within the limits imposed by the new agreement and repeatedly ignored them. Japanese troops continued to buy grain in the areas controlled by the Chinese. They also prohibited transportation of Chinese rice through the areas under Japanese control, often resorting to such measures as seizing the grain just purchased by Chinese merchants. In short, according to Yuan Yuquan, "the Japanese employed all kinds of tricks and the Chinese met with one difficulty after another in their attempt to purchase grain for the people."[48]

Control over grain became a matter of daily confrontation between Chinese and Japanese authorities. The situation was exacerbated by the fact that production in the occupied areas was declining dramatically. According to Yuan Yuquan, the economic situation in Jiangnan became increasingly desperate because the areas were already depleted of resources due to the Japanese policy of "killing the hen to get the egg."[49] As revealed by a survey carried out by Yuan Fudeng, the president of the Chinese Chamber of

Commerce, their methods of procurement had the effect of discouraging production. According to Yuan, one of the major reasons for the decline of rice production in the lower Yangzi Valley was the fact that the peasants were forced to sell their rice at minimal prices, a problem exacerbated by rapid inflation and the inability of the procurement system to keep up with adjustments in grain prices. As a result, many peasants had given up rice growing altogether, thus adding to the already-serious shortage.[50] To make things worse, in 1941, the United States imposed an economic blockade against the Japanese, which included the Chinese occupied areas. As a consequence, neither the RNG nor the Japanese could rely on imports of grain and other basic staples from the British colonies or Southeast Asia.[51]

A new wave of transfers of control over resources from the Japanese to the RNG came in mid-1942 because of Japan's increasing difficulties in coping with its widening war front. The Japanese administration discovered that it was indeed spread too thin. Due to increasing difficulties in managing central China, the Japanese government changed its approach: "In the past we, and one branch of the military especially, have adopted the erroneous attitude of disregarding the Chinese standpoint and discouraging their initiative in such fields as administration and the economy."[52] This statement reveals the frustration Japanese authorities were experiencing in controlling China, but also the discrepancies in occupation tactics between the Guangdong army and the Japanese government in Tokyo. The Japanese army was less willing than the government in Tokyo to make concessions to the Wang administration. The Japanese government blamed the army for the unsatisfactory situation in China.

At the end of 1942 Japan inaugurated the New China Policy (*duihua xinzhengce*), which granted more autonomy to both Japanese and Chinese civilian authorities in the regions while reducing the military role in local administration. Under the new system, finalized in early 1943 and called the "take-charge system" (*danshang guanzhi*), the Japanese were to choose a few individuals among its advising, consular, and military personnel in China and assign them the task of coordinating economic policies with the Wang government. The New China Policy also provided for the complete transfer of responsibility for material resources over to the RNG. This plan, however, was opposed by the Japanese military administration in China, who argued that material control should not be transferred directly to the Wang government but should be handled by an organization composed of both Chinese and Japanese merchants.[53] The Japanese military believed that the RNG lacked the strength to carry out its policies and enforce legislation at all levels of society and thus would be ineffective in handling acquisitions. It was only by co-opting the powerful merchant associations that it would be possible to mobilize local economic resources.[54]

After more than two months of negotiations, finally Japan and the RNG reached an agreement. The current Central Material Control Committee (*zhongyang wuzi tongzhi weiyuanhui*) would be abolished. Japan would transfer power over resources to the RNG, at least in theory, since the highest decision-making committee of the new system, the Economic Control Deliberative Committee (*wuzi tongzhi shenyi weiyuanhui*), was to be composed of both Chinese and Japanese members.[55] Zhou Fohai was appointed as its director and the Japanese ambassador in Nanjing served as assistant director.

Thus, 1943 witnessed a complete overhaul of the material control system in central China, with the Economic Control Deliberative Committee ending up as its highest authority.[56] Its highest agency for policy implementation was the National Merchant Control Association (*quangguo shangye tongzhi zonghu,* generally abbreviated to *shangtonghui*), established on March 15, 1943. Tang Shoumin, the former general manager of the Bank of Communications and a close associate of Zhou Fohai, was appointed chairman of its board of directors, which was composed of thirteen Chinese members.[57] The assistant director of the association was the Japanese ambassador in Shanghai, and the Chinese membership was balanced by an equivalent group of Japanese members. The new economic structure became a site of fierce struggle between Chinese and Japanese authorities for control over China's resources.

By 1943 most of the documents produced by the economic administration of the Wang government focus on the recovery of control over the system of material control. The optimistic productivist tone of the 1941 plan for the "postwar" recovery of the Chinese industry was now replaced by concern for increasing the production of grains, aimed at overcoming the food crisis that characterized the last years of the Japanese occupation.[58] The ubiquitous references in these documents to the importance of grain, and food in general, for the livelihood of the people appears to serve three different purposes. While they expressed a nationalist concern for the welfare of the Chinese people, these references, echoing Sun Yat-sen Principle of People's Livelihood, were also aimed at building political legitimacy for the regime. They also expressed a growing frustration over the loss of control over staples that were crucial for the realization of China's economic autarky.

By 1944, one year before Japan's defeat, the results of the RNG's effort to regain control over China's economy had fallen short of expectations. The work of the National Merchant Control Association had been plagued with problems. The local Japanese authorities were determined to use it as their own long arm, leaving little autonomy to their Chinese counterparts. Meanwhile, the RNG's struggle to maintain some control over local economic resources was mostly in vain. The Japanese proved too formidable an adversary. Concessions to the RNG increased with the deepening of Japan's military crisis and its inability to muster the necessary administrative and military resources to keep central China under its direct control. Historians generally agree that the RNG found itself mostly powerless vis-à-vis the Japanese authorities and that its successes were few. According to Zhang Genfu, "real power remained completely in the hands of the Japanese." Even when the Chinese succeeded in keeping procurements within the limitations agreed upon at the time of the establishment of the National Merchant Control Association, the distribution of resources remained uneven. Zhang found that the RNG Cotton Control Committee, the agency that constitutes the focus of his study, acquired 87 percent of Chinese-owned cotton yarn in 1943 for one-fourth of the black-market price. Sixty percent of the raw cotton was destined for the Japanese military and 40 percent went to Chinese mills, calculated according to the number of spindles rather than the number of mills. However, because Japanese industries had illegally gained control of Chinese cotton mills, they owned, unofficially, one-fourth of their total spindles. So Japanese mills ended up getting 90 percent of the raw cotton destined for China's cotton mills. In May 1944, the difficulty in keeping Japanese procurements within reasonable limits pushed Tang Shoumin to resign from the position of director of the National Merchant Control Association. Tang argued that he had found that he did not have the power to cope with both Japanese interference and the political contradictions within the Wang government. Japan, he complained, controlled every control commission, in spite of their mixed memberships. Ultimately, control of goods was in the hands of the Japanese merchants; the Chinese merchants were at their mercy.[59]

In 1945 Chen Gongbo himself conceded that the Japanese had not allowed Nanjing to directly administer the material control system and had pushed for the creation of a nongovernmental (*minjian*) leadership, which, in actuality, was under the influence of Japanese merchants. As Chen stated, "at the end, Japan isolated Nanjing and turned to the new policy of oppressing the people directly. The so-called Merchant Control Association and the grain and cotton and the other control committees were an ingenious way to isolate Nanjing [that is, the RNG]."[60] Thus, according to Chen, the RNG had encountered insurmountable obstacles in attempting to regain control over China's economic resources and had been highly ineffective.[61]

Chen, however, maintained that the RNG had made a valiant effort to protect local resources and not to serve merely as a procurement agency for the Japanese army. In the five and a half years he spent in Nanjing, Chen argued, not a day went by without conflict between the Chinese and the Japanese authorities. In addition to arguing over the terms of peace, conflict arose over issues such as administrative freedom and unification, military independence and Japan's military retreat, and—in the economic field—the preservation of material goods and of the people's vitality. According to Chen, from 1940 to 1945, Japan had regarded the RNG as an enemy: "Chongqing uses the military to wage war against us; Nanjing uses peace to wage war."[62]

Although Chen's statements cannot be taken at face value (they were written as part of his defense in his treason trial in 1945), they still reveal Chen's continued concerns with preserving the nation's vitality—specifically, economic resources. This line of defense was also taken up by Zhou Fohai. At the time of the Japanese defeat, Zhou chose to remain in Nanjing to deal with Chongqing and preside over what he described as the transfer to Jiang's government of the national resources the RNG had protected from the Japanese at a dear price. As Zhou declared at his trial, he did not expect to be lauded as a hero once the war was over, but he did not expect to be tried as a traitor.[63]

Saving What Kind of China?

At the trials the Wang group directly addressed the issue of what constituted a nation and whether their strategy or Jiang's had been the best way to protect it. Members of the Wang government accused Jiang of being the real *hanjian* because, to save his own political skin, he had sacrificed most of the Chinese land and population to the Japanese. Chen Biqun, who was Wang's wife and was tried with Chen and Zhou, asked: "When large chunks of the Chinese territory were abandoned by the Nationalist government to the Japanese, where was the nation that Mr. Wang could have sold to the Japanese?"[64] According to Chen Biqun, Jiang had abandoned the nation and retreated to Chongqing to preserve his position of power, while Wang had attempted to save the nation by standing his ground in Nanjing. Chen Biqun's viewpoint was shared by Zhou, who believed that Wang's effort to preserve the resources of the lower Yangzi Valley would be recognized as a contribution to the Chinese effort in the war of resistance against Japan.

The discourse on the economic nature of modern nationhood and the importance of *minzu* control over its resources dominated the defense of the surviving RNG leaders, echoing a discussion that had been initiated as soon as Wang had launched his Peace Movement in 1938. At that time Wang had claimed that his main goal was to shield the Chinese people from the brutality of Japanese occupying forces, whereas Jiang had abandoned them during his speedy and chaotic retreat to the interior. In addition, Wang complained, Jiang's alliance with the CCP represented a serious threat to China's sovereignty. The CCP constituted an anti-Nationalist force that denied the nation while supporting an international alliance of the proletariat and that fought Japan for the sole purpose of handing their country over to the Soviet Union.[65] By allying with the Communist transnational forces, Jiang had thus compromised China's sovereignty. Wang's argument echoed those of most leaders of the French Vichy government, who perceived the Resistance as the long arm of Moscow.[66] Wang thus concluded that it was his own alleged betrayal of the nation that constituted the only genuine effort to preserve it.[67] Once again, Wang and Jiang held different views of what constituted a nation and their differences greatly affected their views of the path China should take to survive its crisis. Jiang identified the nation with the state and its ideology/culture and not with its territory and the Chinese people who populated it, as his statements on exchanging territory for time cited above reveal.

For Wang, instead, it was important not to abandon the territories that were the location of China's *minzu* economy. Wang, therefore, perceived losing the Jiangnan area as forfeiting the entire nation, leaving in Chongqing only a simulacrum of the nation and the emblem of Jiang's spurious leadership. The Peace Movement had started in 1938 as an alternative defense strategy to that chosen by Jiang, a strategy that Wang had hoped would carry the same political legitimacy as Jiang's. At the trials at the close of the war, however, Wang's strategy had become equated with betrayal of the nation. The war had, in fact, dramatically changed the discourse on the nation and political legitimacy. The postwar narrative of collaboration—developed during the war and grown to maturity at the *hanjian* trials—presumed a dichotomy between defenders of the nation (resisters) and its betrayers (collaborators) that ignored the uncertainty surrounding the legitimacy of Jiang's leadership over the Nationalist government in the years before the war. Chen Gongbo presented his collaborationist government as a final attempt to oppose what he perceived to be Jiang's spurious leadership over the party. Chen thus acted according to a political discourse whose conceptual categories were more complex than the postwar clear-cut distinction between resisters and collaborators. At the end of the war, however, US support and recognition of Jiang as the supreme leader of China served to fully recognize his rule. Doubts about his legitimacy were forgotten.

Factions, Warlord Politics, and the Emergence of One Nation

The war years witnessed the demise of another element of the prewar political discourse. With the consolidation of Jiang's national government and the elimination of pockets of resistance at the borders of the areas controlled by the GMD (with the exception of the Communist base in Yan'an), the war put to an end warlord-style politics. Warlord political culture and practices had played an important role in China in the years before the war and had also helped shape the response of many Chinese to Japanese occupation, as vividly illustrated by Rana Mitter's study of Manchuria in 1931–33. In his book, Mitter describes how the relationships among local groups and their interactions with Nanjing influenced the choice between resistance to and collaboration with the advancing Japanese army. Mitter identifies three main groups competing for power on the eve of the Japanese takeover. One of the local actors was the strongest warlord of the region, Zhang Xueliang, who had reached an agreement with the GMD and used the backing of Nanjing to establish his control in the region at the expense of minor warlords like Ma Zhanshan, who eventually became the leader of the anti-Japanese resistance movement. The local elite, on the other hand, had lost much of their authority due to the state-building policies of Zhang, who acted in this instance as the long arm of Nanjing and pushed for political and administrative centralization at the expense of local patronage networks. Mitter also identifies smaller warlords, like Ma Zhanshan, whose power base was shrinking due to the competition between Zhang and the local elite.

In this context, Ma appears to have chosen resistance out of his desire to oppose the powerful local elite and the hegemony of Zhang, who abandoned the area before the Japanese occupation. Nationalist feelings and romantic ideas of saving the Chinese nation did not play a crucial role among the Manchurian resisters, who, being far from Nanjing and having grown accustomed to their autonomy, were not especially interested in supporting the growth of a centralized national state. Their motivation in resisting Japan was to protect their power bases. The Manchurian civilian elite, instead, found that the Japanese promised more local autonomy than did Nanjing or Zhang and were easily persuaded to establish local administrative institutions in cooperation with the Japanese. From Ma's point of view the elite were now doing what Zhang had attempted before the Japanese invasion, namely, centralizing political power at the regional level at the expense of marginal warlords like himself. As Mitter demonstrates, in his survival strategies, Ma relied on the logic of local power while playing up nationalist propaganda with an eye to gaining the support of

Nanjing and Western powers. Ma's nationalism was primarily adopted for strategic reasons, but not really embraced, since Ma's perspective was geographically and politically at the margins of the Nationalist discourse of the nation. Ma juggled not only between nation and invaders but also between the new national political environment and Manchurian warlord politics.[68]

The logic of warlord politics also helps us to better understand Wang Jingwei's choice to collaborate with the Japanese. During the Nanjing Decade, alliances with strong military men had been a common strategy used by GMD civilian leaders in their attempts to oust Jiang from his position of power. As much as they wanted to return the leadership of the party and the government to its civilian component, they discovered that mere political means were not as effective as hoped. The GMD civilian leaders thus repeatedly arranged temporary alliances with various warlords in order to use their military power, challenge Jiang, and resolve the leadership struggle. Wang had himself attempted this dangerous tactic twice, with mixed results. He had first allied himself with Feng Yuxiang and Yan Xishan in 1930, only to suffer military defeat at the hands of Jiang. Later, in 1931, he had started a difficult cooperation with Chen Jitang in Canton. This time he succeeded in posing a significant challenge to Jiang in Nanjing and in finally returning to the central government in 1932.

This strategy had an illustrious precedent set by the very father of the Chinese republic himself, as Wang reminded the nation in the early stages of the Peace Movement. Sun Yat-sen had succeeded in strengthening the political, financial, and military forces of the GMD by compromising with the warlord of Canton, at that time Chen Jiongming. It was in those years of compromise, Wang argued, that the foundations of the successful Northern Expedition and the final unification of China under the GMD were laid. Wang ignored the fact that the Northern Expedition, although successful in restoring the GMD's rule over the country, had also brought the military to power in the person of Jiang, who was now stubbornly holding on to his position and slowly driving the old civilian leadership to the margins of the party and the government. Ignoring this ominous sign, the leaders of the Peace Movement repeatedly brought up the Sun Yat-sen precedent.

During the Peace Movement, Wang attempted to present collaboration as a return to this old and accepted tactic, placing the alliance with the Japanese in the context of warlord politics. The collaborationist government, Wang argued, could use the Japanese to put pressure on Jiang to resign. Wang could regain control over the party and the government and set China on the right political path for national salvation.[69] The riskiness of this strategy, foreshadowed by the inability of the civilian leaders to remove

Jiang from his position once they had concluded the Northern Expedition, became tragically apparent in occupied Nanjing when Wang and the other GMD leaders found their ability to negotiate with the Japanese greatly diminished by the overwhelming military superiority of the Japanese. In Republican China, before and during the Japanese occupation, civilian political leaders were not able to manipulate military strongmen of any kind, much less the relentless Japanese army.

The nature of Wang Jingwei's and Chen Gongbo's collaboration differs significantly from the Manchurian case. They do share, however, one basic feature. They both show the configuration of power to be one of multiple centers rather than a clear-cut dichotomy based on nationalism versus collaboration. The local elite in Manchuria attempted to use the Japanese to reestablish their autonomy from the centralizing nation—represented by both Nanjing and Zhang Xueliang. The Reformed Government had attempted the same strategy with the goal of creating a nation outside the Nationalist political legacy. Wang and Chen planned to use the Japanese to defeat Jiang and regain leadership over the Nationalist Party and the nation. The three collaborationist groups used the same tools for different goals: the local elite to defy the "nation," regardless of its leaders, the Reformed leaders to defy the Nationalist nation, and the RNG to strengthen the "correct" Nationalist nation against what they denounced as Jiang's spurious leadership. In spite of differences and similarities, however, most relevant here are the far-reaching effects of warlord-style political practices and how they were used by those who opposed Jiang's leadership and, in the case of Ma Zhanshan, the establishment of a centralized nation.

Conclusion

The eruption of full-blown war with Japan in 1937 put Wang Jingwei's and Chen Gongbo's theory of economic nation building and national defense to its ultimate test. While economic reforms would have indeed strengthened China, it is highly unlikely that their successful completion would have prevented the Japanese invasion. It seems more likely that the more the Chinese resisted Japan's access to its resources, the more Japan would have been motivated to use military force to obtain them. In these circumstances, Jiang's plan to strengthen the military appears more realistic. However, Jiang did not really intend to use his military apparatus to resist Japan—a task he was leaving to the United States—but mostly aimed it at consolidating his political control domestically by defeating the Communists, even though he agreed to a truce during the war years. This strategy did not ultimately save Jiang's regime, since he was defeated by the CCP in the civil war (1945–49) that followed the Sino-Japanese conflict. We can only speculate as to whether the reform path attempted by the Wang-Song group in 1932–35 would have been more successful in the domestic struggle against the CCP.

The state of unpreparedness in which China found itself in 1937, in spite of years of growing Japanese menace, was in part the consequence of the unresolved crisis of leadership that absorbed most of the energy of the political elite. It is also arguable that Japan's reluctance to transform China into a colony kept alive hopes that Japan would stop before erasing China from the world map, giving the Chinese leaders a feeling that there was still time for "strengthening the nation." In this context, Wang's impression that it was possible to salvage an acceptable compromise was justified by Japan's mixed signals. Wang's decision to collaborate, however, revealed his failure to understand the changes that were gradually transforming the Chinese political scene. Wang continued to frame his political strategies within the context of the early Republican years, not seeing that much had changed. Japanese imperialism had reached a point where there was no room for compromise. Japan was not a warlord but a powerful military machine in the process of expanding its empire. At the same time, warlord politics was in decline and being replaced by the growing prominence of the idea of nation, a response to Japan's deepening aggression.

The intervention of the United States in the Pacific War completely changed the Chinese discourse on the nation in two major ways. It first made the idea of China's inevitable defeat obsolete. After 1941 the possibility of an ultimate victory by the Allied forces made Jiang's strategy of trading territory for time the winning alternative. In addition, by supporting the Jiang regime, the United States bestowed on it a level of political legitimacy it had never enjoyed before. Wang Jingwei's and Chen Gongbo's ideas of nation and nationalism became completely discredited in the postwar years, becoming exclusively identified with collaboration and divorced from any memory of their wider prewar political framework. The Wang group, the last GMD opposition to Jiang's leadership, was now synonymous with collaborationism, antinationalism, and war crimes, obscuring its past political history. The postwar discourse on the nation focused on nationalism versus collaboration, replacing the 1930s multilevel struggle among competing images of nationhood.

The memory of Wang's political alternative was erased from the national historical narrative in a process similar to that promoted by de Gaulle soon after the end of World War II in France. As Caroline Wiedmer has argued in her work on postwar Germany and France, de Gaulle demanded the "absolute negation" of Vichy, the French collaborationist government.

While de Gaulle had waged war on Germany from North Africa—where he had joined the Allied forces and established a Provisory Government—the Vichy leaders had remained in France to deal with the German occupying forces. At the trial for treason and collaboration of its main leader, Philippe Pétain, the defense had presented the argument that Vichy had attempted to shield the French population from the Germans and protect them as much as possible while waiting for de Gaulle and the Allies to liberate France.[70] After the defeat of the Nazi regime, de Gaulle promoted a narrative of the war that completely omitted the Vichy regime, redrawing historical continuity as running from pre-Vichy directly to his postwar government. As Wiedmer reports, de Gaulle stated that "Vichy was always and remains null and void."[71] Becoming void was also the ultimate destiny of the RNG and, together with it, the strategy of nation building pursued by Wang Jingwei and Chen Gongbo and their criticism of Jiang's military nation building.

CONCLUSION

George Taylor's comments, quoted in the introduction, that China was "alive with the discussion of her problems" and enthusiastically engaged in the "building of a new society" convey very aptly the atmosphere of the Nanjing Decade.[1] This was a period of high hopes for nation building and intense ideological ferment, marked by a plurality of visions of nationhood and modernity that found their expression in a myriad of reconstruction projects. Although most of these projects were ultimately unsuccessful or only scratched the surface of the problems China was experiencing at the time, they testify to the variety of alternatives that inspired Chinese political leaders and reformers in this decade and to the importance Chinese reformers assigned to economic modernization. The assumption that Chinese leaders only had to choose between communism and a vaguely defined anticommunism represented by Jiang Jieshi (the paradigm generally presented by Cold War historiography) greatly limits our understanding of the Chinese discourse on nation building and of the importance of the Nanjing Decade in modern Chinese history. The Nanjing Decade was profoundly different from postwar Nationalist China because of the richness and diversity of ideas of political and economic modernity and because of the freedom enjoyed by intellectuals and political leaders to creatively combine elements from different trends without being afraid of going against the political line imposed by their parties. Both the Communist and the Nationalist Parties, in fact, were still works in progress, not yet crystallized in the orthodoxy imposed by Mao Zedong and Jiang Jieshi.

As a result of this greater political and intellectual flexibility, the boundaries between the GMD and the CCP were often blurred in the prewar period. Their leaders, for example, shared a view of the modern state as highly centralized, interventionist, and able to mobilize the Chinese people in pursuit of its goals (be they nationalist or socialist).[2] Because GMD and CCP leaders also shared concerns that reflected China's own experiences—going beyond the framework of imported political and economic doctrines—both parties came to assign much importance to rural issues, to perceive the rural elite as an obstacle to China's modernization, and to develop similar tropes on the role of the *minzu* socioeconomic elite in semicolonial China. The Nanjing Decade, therefore, witnessed not only the confrontation between Communists and Nationalists—which involved crucial political issues of class struggle, wealth redistribution, and the eventual, if not immediate, elimination of private property and the free market—but also engagement with such fundamental themes as anti-imperialism and the relationships between rural hinterland and industrial coastal China.

Balancing state control with market forces constitutes one more problem shared by the Nationalist and Communist regimes. As mentioned above, the CCC experiment in this field remains ambiguous because of its short life and because the politically unstable environment of Nanjing never allowed the full realization of Chen Gongbo's original plan for economic control. It is, therefore, difficult to understand how much control the CCC would have had over the market and to what extent the CCC's system of cooperative marketing would have replaced private market networks. The CCC's failure to expand its control over the marketing of raw cotton, discussed in chapter 5, weakened its ability to develop the circular flow of raw materials and goods between village and Shanghai *minzu* mills, an essential strategy for national unification and autarky. Even if the CCC had just developed, as in 1936 it appeared poised to do, into a marketing alternative for peasants and farmers (when not infiltrated by the local elite as in the cases presented by W. K. H. Campbell and Chen Hansheng), it could have played an important role in stimulating rural production through market mechanisms. Freeing the peasants from high-interest loans and the cutthroat marketing practices of the local merchants and brokers and reducing transportation costs of raw cotton to the Shanghai market certainly could have had positive effects on both local and national economies.

The CCC's intervention in the rural economy, however, had some problematic aspects, since, as also discussed in chapter 5, it relied on important misconceptions of the socioeconomic reality of the village. CCC policies could have created problems similar to those generated by the Communist suppression of the market in the mid-1950s, when the Chinese state began to rely on central planning (rather than using market mechanisms) for inducing economic growth and distributing goods.[3] In this period, concentration of industrial production within state factories eliminated rural "sideline" industries, which, in conjunction with the loss of commercial opportunities, caused the decline of the village economy.[4]

The CCC leaders never planned the complete elimination of the market as realized by the Communists. Their corporativist view dictated respect for the private economy, although it was a respect attenuated by the government's intervention and regulation. The CCC leaders, however, shared with the Maoist leadership the desire to reduce the rural village into a mere supplier of agricultural products: food and industrial raw materials. The successful realization of the CCC's plan, with its goal of concentrating spinning and weaving in urban areas, would have taken place at the expense of the rural handicraft cotton industry, thus depriving the village of this important sideline industry. In addition, rather than reforming local credit and marketing structures, the CCC leaders tried to replace them with urban private banks and state-sponsored marketing societies. Although these changes were supposed to channel urban capital into the rural economy, they would have taken away business and commercial opportunities from the village, leaving the rural community to rely exclusively on agriculture. These policies were inspired by the CCC leaders' disregard of rural culture, society, and economy, which they labeled as petty and feudal, vis-à-vis the modern, large-scale economy they were attempting to develop.[5] Even though the NEC leaders were fierce anti-Communists, when it came to understanding the village, they used the same rhetoric of local bullies and middlemen's exploitation of local resources, stressing the damage done not so much to the peasants but to the modernization of the nation as a whole.

Although both the GMD and the CCP were inspired by a statist view of China's body politic, they also experienced a common tension between two different approaches to nation building. The developmental approach, which aimed at co-opting socioeconomic groups perceived as crucial for achieving development, can be identified with the *minzu* nation-building strategies of the NEC and of Mao Zedong's *New Democracy*. The more authoritarian utopian approach, instead, tended to disregard trends and groups in the social and economic fabric of the nation and to redraw the future of China on completely new lines. This vision is more closely embodied by Jiang Jieshi—his military authoritarianism combined with a notion of China's identity based on his interpretation of traditional culture, his vision of a state economy detached from societal modernizing forces, and his New Life social engineering. The authoritarian utopian approach reemerged in the mid-1950s when Mao abandoned the political platform laid out in *New Democracy* in favor of a socialist vision based on highly rhetorical and abstract notions of the peasantry. In these years the Communist government attempted to achieve its objectives through mass mobilization and class struggle orchestrated from above. In the post-Mao period, the Communists have shifted priority back to development, attempting reconciliation with groups in society.[6]

The tension between utopian/authoritarian and developmental approaches underscores the importance for both the GMD and the CCP of successfully determining the overall political identity of the nation and its socioeconomic foundations. This proved to be a crucial issue for the Nationalists, but not because they could actually mold China to their will. China was never the blank sheet of paper that Mao Zedong, and most Nationalist leaders of that period, believed it to be, and the most utopian attempts generally met with disaster. Determining the political identity of nation and party was important, above all, because the political legitimacy of the Nanjing government depended on this definition. In her seminal work on the Chinese civil war, Suzanne Pepper argues that the loss of support experienced by the GMD during the postwar period was responsible for its loss of legitimacy in the eyes of most of the Chinese population, including the modern economic elite, and ultimately led to its final defeat. This view is also presented by historians such as Lloyd Eastman, who argues that the GMD failed on the mainland because of its inability to carry out the program of national reconstruction that had formed its original political platform.[7] Both authors blame incompetence and corruption for this outcome. While corruption was indeed a serious problem for the Nationalists (and it would have been even if the Wang group had remained in power), the main problem was Jiang's inability to fulfill the expectations of the groups that had originally supported the party, to engage any social group in his nation-building project, or to give the impression that the GMD, under his leadership, would be able to guide the country through a socioeconomic transformation that had the potential to build China into a strong and modern nation.

When Jiang Jieshi silenced the Wang group and imposed his vision of military nation building on the Nanjing government and the nation at large, he deprived the GMD of a political platform that had the potential to steal some thunder from Mao's *New Democracy*, the policy that was largely responsible for the CCP's success against the GMD and for the "honeymoon" period of Communist rule.[8] Jiang's move cost the GMD the support of China's reformist elite. Jiang's model of the modern nation based on military authoritarianism (which, however, was not strong enough to ensure domestic stability and effective protection of the nation from foreign aggression) and his attempt to mobilize the Chinese through the New Life Movement never resonated with any social trends. While in Europe fascism was rooted in society (European fascism was a genuine social movement and had, especially in its early stages, widespread popular support), Jiang's military fascism became a self-contained system. The NEC leaders, instead, attempted to co-opt socioeconomic trends and the elite who led them. Even though the outcome of their nation-building program fell short of expectations, it resonated with the discourse on economic modernization and the strengthening of China initiated in the Self-Strengthening period and was bound to have been more appealing to Chinese intellectual and economic elites than one based on military power (especially in view of public opinion's increasing criticism of militarism and warlordism).

Although different from Jiang's more authoritarian idea of corporativism, the NEC's policies were hardly liberal. After all, national economic reconstruction, rather than liberalism, was the Wang-Song group's claim to political legitimacy. The international political atmosphere in the years between the two world wars discouraged a liberal approach to nation building. At the same time Japan's mounting military aggression and the escalation of the confrontation with the CCP strengthened the perception that the national crisis required a strong state, one that could exercise political and economic control. In this context, the participation of members of the Jiangnan economic elite in the NEC corporativist organization did not prevent it from being an authoritarian agency, adopting coercive measures toward China's weakest interest groups, such as workers and peasants, as well as other elite members who did not share its goals of economic reconstruction (rural elites and "non-*minzu*" industrialists). In addition, the rightist corporativist activities of the NEC and the CCC were characterized by a bias toward urban modernity and can be accused of attempting to build up Shanghai's modern industry rather than the nation as a whole. The CCC's rural reforms, for example, were not necessarily going to benefit the village (as already mentioned), and industrial workers were certainly experiencing the strain of the state pro-industrialist approach to labor. In other words, identifying nation building with the growth of the Shanghai modern manufacturing industry was quite reductive. The NEC, however, was still a reformist and developmental agency, and it attempted to realize the political goal of national economic reconstruction that was at the core of Sun Yat-sen's heritage and of the party's political legitimacy.

With the defeat of its leaders and the final consolidation of Jiang's power, the GMD became locked in a conservative stand that resisted significant change. In addition, Jiang's idea of economic development focused on state-owned heavy industry, glossing over commodity industry and agriculture. As a consequence, Jiang's GMD did not advance an economic solution to the rural question, perceived as one of China's most pressing problems at the time, but favored political and military control of the village. In the postwar period there was no longer space within the GMD for any group who wanted to attempt the displacement/replacement of the rural elite and the socioeconomic reform of the village. Cooperative societies, with their potential for revolutionary changes, were also abandoned under Jiang because they were suspected of Communist tendencies.[9]

What ultimately and irremediably discredited the Wang group's model of economic nation building was not its domestic political platform but its policies toward Japan. The policy of relying on the League of Nations to keep Japan at bay while gaining time for national reconstruction appears unrealistic after the League's failure to check Japan's expansion in Manchuria. Attempting to link China to Western economic interests was a more realistic strategy, although it underestimated Japan's determination to control China's resources and markets. The impact of Japan's aggression on China extended beyond the violence and destruction of the Japanese invasion. It also diverted attention and resources from the GMD reform agenda to military buildup, strengthening Jiang's position vis-à-vis the civilian reformist leadership; it exacerbated the differences between the GMD's leaders, splitting the government in half before and during the war; and finally it left Jiang's militarism with no opposition in the postwar period. Although Chen Gongbo and other RNG survivors could hardly have expected to be welcomed by the Chinese public, the actual result was that Jiang had no opposition within the GMD to temper his militarism and political conservatism. The record of his leadership from 1945 to 1949 shows that this was not necessarily a positive development.

The societal reformist trends the NEC attempted to institutionalize, having been frozen in the utopian authoritarian years of Jiang's and Mao's leadership, have once again emerged as crucial in the post-Mao period. The "big business" mentioned by Bell in her work on the Wuxi silk industry is now returning to the forefront, leading China's economic development, as the Communist state shifts its objectives from the construction of a utopian socialist state back to development (not without major controversy within the party).[10] This redefinition of the legitimacy of the state in terms of development has in turn led to a redefinition of the state's relationship to China's economic forces. It is not by chance that Deng Xiaoping reinstated Mao's *New Democracy* in the canon of Chinese Communist orthodoxy—from which it had been marginalized from the mid-1950s to the late 1970s. The ideas of *New Democracy* are now presented not just as a stage on the way to socialism but as a fundamental policy of the Maoist legacy.[11]

In their attempt to redefine the CCP's political legitimacy and its relationship to socioeconomic forces in the country, the Chinese leaders are faced with many of the problems addressed by the Nationalists in the Nanjing Decade. Like the leaders of the NEC, they are caught between a statist view of political modernity—which denies any form of direct political representation of societal groups—and their wish to co-opt the entrepreneurial elite in support of their developmental goals. In this context, corporativism and clientelism are reemerging today as, respectively, a useful institutional model and an unofficial way to merge state and private interests.[12] China cannot be described as a full-scale corporativist state (corporativism does not constitute the overall inspiration for the organization of the state), and the CCP never explicitly uses the term "corporativism." The law that regulates links between the state and society (the 1997–98 "Regulations on the Registration and Management of Social Organizations"), however, has crucial corporativist characteristics. Social organizations are registered with the state and sponsored by state units, which are responsible for their administration. In addition the social organizations have "representational monopoly," since they are the sole representative of their group or sector within their jurisdiction.[13] The existence of these organizations is also consistent with corporativist principles, since they allow the state to establish relationships with the economic elite within a framework of social and political unity and without a significant loss of control. In other words, as was the case with the 1930s NEC, today's corporativist trends represent an attempt to promote industrial development and to co-opt China's economic elite without completely embracing political liberalism. The Communist corporativist organizations, therefore, embody the idea that relationships between state and private entrepreneurs are characterized by unity of intent and interests rather than conflict. For this reason they can pursue simultaneously the two seemingly contradictory goals of, in the words of political scientist Bruce Dickson, "state control over organized interests in society, and also to represent their members' interest."[14]

In his study of the relationships between the CCP and the "red capitalists" (the private entrepreneurs who have been co-opted by the state), Dickson argues that indeed both pursue the common goal of stability and find their relationship mutually beneficial. The CCP wishes to co-opt China's capitalists in order to stave off protest and to garner support for its leadership. On the other hand, the red capitalists tend to constitute a "noncritical realm" in China's emerging civil society and, again in the words of Dickson, are "primarily concerned with the management and regulation of collective goods and services but less interested in changing the political system itself." Because they have found corporativist and clientelist channels to be quite effective in furthering their interests, they have not turned to political action.[15] Through its alliance with the red capitalists, therefore, the state develops a supportive social base at the expense of the "critical realms" (such as political activists). The red capitalists, in return, obtain stability and support for their businesses.[16]

As was the case with 1930s NEC corporativism, in the post-Mao period corporativist organizations can hardly be regarded as a tool for liberal democratization, although they both represented attempts to institutionalize cooperative, rather than coercive, relations between the state and economic elites. Today's corporativist organizations have the potential to develop into a form of rightist (or societal) corporativism. Although Chinese corporativist organizations, today and in the 1930s, exclude and suppress the interests of other socioeconomic groups for the sake of achieving the common goal of development, they have the potential to expand the contractual power of selected socioeconomic groups, enabling them to assert their interests and to successfully mediate with the state.[17] As mentioned in chapter 4, the NEC did not live long enough for the various forces in play to reach a clear balance of power, although both the CCC and the SIC were clearly developing along rightist-corporativist lines. So far, today's corporativist organizations also remain ambiguous, causing scholars and observers to reach different conclusions on their political meaning and potential.

In the case of the NEC, nationalism played an important role in cementing the unity of state and society in the corporativist organization of the state. China's situation today appears dramatically different: no threat of colonization looms over China; the Chinese government is firmly in control of its economic and fiscal administration (including the ability to set tariffs and taxes); and the international economy is marked by intense globalization rather than autarkic and protectionist trends. Still Chinese leaders, entrepreneurs, and people at large tend to perceive China's quest for development as self-strengthening vis-à-vis a perceived wish of the Western powers, especially the United States, to "contain" China.[18] They especially feel threatened by such things as the US military presence in Asia, opposition to China's entrance to the World Trade Organization (China eventually joined in 2001), pressure for domestic changes before granting China the status of most-favored nation (now called permanent normal trade relations), pro-Tibet and pro-Taiwan positions, and, in general, a perceived attempt to impose Western cultural, economic, and political values on China.[19] Building on these elements, the Communist nationalist rhetoric develops around a narrative that connects China's contemporary "containment" directly to early-twentieth-century imperialism.[20]

In this context, Chinese leaders and entrepreneurs, and the Chinese public at large, live one more contradiction: the aspiration to modernize according to global standards and to emerge as a powerful international player is tempered by nationalist feelings fueled by fear of losing state control and national identity. China's entrance to the World Trade Organization, although energetically pursued, raises fears that international action will limit the power of the Chinese state.[21] It, in fact, allows domestic social groups to rely on transnational forces, further eroding the "organized dependence" on the state that had been created during the Maoist years.[22] It also limits the state's ability to adopt protectionist measures aimed at fostering China's economy. These limitations appear to go against the self-strengthening goals of development and to contribute to anxiety that Western powers are attempting to contain China. These fears lead the Communist government to favor neomercantilist policies and to regulate heavily the way Chinese businesses participate in the international market.[23]

While in the 1980s many Chinese entrepreneurs perceived Westernization and globalization favorably and a crucial prerequisite to development, in the 1990s they directly experienced the limits to Chinese economic interests posed by international action. They have thus come to adopt the nationalist rhetoric of the state. Chinese intellectuals have also joined in lamenting China's loss of power and threats of decentralization. For this reason they have come to support the view that China, as a latecomer to modernization, should adopt neomercantilist policies to protect its industries and to create a relatively independent and self-sufficient economic system.[24] Intellectuals have also come to perceive internationalization as responsible for a loss of national identity. Nationalist trends that emerged in the 1990s are well represented by the New Left, which does not oppose internationalization per se, since China has become increasingly strong in the international arena. It instead opposes Westernization of China's domestic life (including the adoption of economic liberalism) in favor of a new Chinese way to development based on the Chinese experience.[25] Today's corporativist organizations are, therefore, cemented by shared development goals as well as a nationalist self-strengthening narrative, in a way similar to the 1930s NEC. The balance between internationalization, on the one side, and the preservation of state control and protection of national interests (from preserving identity to protecting China's industries), on the other, has proved difficult to achieve, however. As economic historian David Zweig argues in his work on China's economic internationalization, "maintaining sovereignty in a global economy . . . even for a state with relatively thick institutions is difficult once a certain level of internationalization had been attained."[26]

Continuities and similarities between 1930s and post-Mao political and economic trends should not overshadow important differences between the two periods and between the Nationalist and Communist regimes. Above all, today's China is not experiencing the urgency of the 1930s national crisis, and the Communist state is far more powerful and established than the Nationalist one ever was. Even if the CCP is now experiencing a loss of control in comparison to the Mao years, its ability to regulate, to enforce, and to implement is still dramatically stronger than that of the Nationalists in the Nanjing Decade. The important themes discussed here, however, run throughout the twentieth century, crossing from the Nationalist into the Communist period. They reflect difficulties and tensions in solving such issues as the relationship between state and private economy, globalization and nationalism, the definition of the socioeconomic foundation of the new modern China, and the geopolitical hierarchy of the nation (hinterland/rural versus coastal/urban China)—issues that have been at the very core of China's historical development throughout the twentieth century. The NEC leaders' attempt to solve these problems and to reconcile these tensions, therefore, constituted an important stage in the long-term process of defining China's national and economic identity and its significance, with effects reaching beyond the Nanjing Decade.

GLOSSARY

People

Chen Gongbo	陳公博
Chen Guangfu	陳光復
Chen Mingshu	陳銘樞
Chen Youren (Eugene Chen)	陳友仁
Fang Xianting (H. D. Fong)	方顯廷
Fei Xiaotong	費孝通
Feng Yuxiang	馮玉祥
Gu Mengyu	顧孟餘
He Lian (Franklin Ho)	何廉
Hu Hanmin	胡漢民
Jiang Jieshi (Chiang Kai-shek)	蔣介石
Jiang Tingfu	蔣廷黻
Kang Youwei	康有為
Kong Xiangxi	孔祥熙
Li Hongzhang	李鴻章
Li Shengbo	李昇伯, styled Shenbo 申伯
Liang Qichao	梁啟超
Liu Jingshan	劉景山
Luo Wengan	羅文榦
Mu Ouchu	穆藕初, styled Xiangyue 湘玥, called the "giant of cotton yarn" 棉紗巨子 *miansha juzi*
Qin Fen	秦汾
Rong Desheng	榮德生
Rong Zongjing	榮宗敬
Shao Lizi	邵力子
Song Qinglin	宋慶齡
Song Ziwen (T. V. Soong)	宋子文
Sun Enlin	孫恩麐, styled Yushu 玉書
Sun Ke	孫科
Sun Yat-sen (Sun Yixian)	孫逸仙 or Sun Zhongshan 孫中山, styled Sun Wen 孫文

Tang Shoumin 唐壽民
Tang Xinghai 唐星海
Wang Jingwei 汪精衛, styled Zhaoming 兆銘
Wang Xiaolai 王曉籟
Wang Yuqing 王禹卿
Xiao Chunjin 蕭純錦, styled Shutong 叔絅
Xu Xinliu 徐新六
Xue Shouxuan 薛壽萱
Yan Fu 嚴復
Yan Xishan 閻錫山
Yang Hucheng 楊虎城
Yu Hede 虞和德, styled Qiaqing 洽卿
Yuan Yuquan 袁愈佺
Zeng Guofan 曾國藩
Zhang Jia'ao 張嘉傲, styled Gongquan 公權
Zhang Zhidong 張之洞
Zheng Guanying 鄭觀應
Zhou Fohai 周佛海
Zou Bingwen 鄒秉文
Zhu Jiahua 朱家驊

Miscellaneous

Agriculture Control Commission 農業統制委員會 *nongye tongzhi weiyuanhui*
assimilate 同化 *tonghua*
autarky (self-sufficiency) 自足 *zizu or* 自給自足 *ziji zizu*
Bank for the Promotion of Business 興業銀行 *xingye yinhang*
Bank of China 中國銀行 *zhongguo yinhang*
Bank of Communications 交通銀行 *jiaotong yinhang*
Banking and Insurance Control Commission 銀行及保險統制委員會 *yinhang ji baoxian tongzhi weiyuanhui*
Baojia 保甲
basic survival 本生 *bensheng*
Basic Treaty (1940, between China and Japan) 基本條約 *jiben tiaoyue*
"building the state through the party" 以當建國 *yi dang jian guo*
Central Bureau for the Improvement of Cotton Production 中央棉產改進所 *zhongyang mianchan gaijingsuo*
Central Material Control Committee 中央物資統制委員會 *zhongyang wuzi tongzhi weiyuanhui*
China Agricultural Cooperative Credit Banking Group 中華農業合作貨款銀團 *Zhonghua nongye hezuo huokuan yintuan*
China Development Finance Corporation (CDFC) 中國建設銀公司 *Zhongguo jiansheying gongsi*
China Farmers Bank 中國農民銀行 *Zhongguo nongmin yinhang*
China International Famine Relief Commission (CIFRC) 中國華洋義賑救災總會 *Zhongguo hua-*

yang yizhen jiuzai zonghui*, generally shortened to 華洋義賑會 *huayang yizhen hui*

China Merchants Steamship Navigation Company 輪船招商局 *lunchuan zhaoshangju*
Chinese Communist Party (CCP) 共產黨 *gongchandang*
"Chinese learning as essence, Western learning for practical use" 中學為西學為用 *Zhongxue wei ti, Xixue wei yong*, shortened to 體用 *tiyong*
The Chinese Village 中國農村 *Zhongguo nongcun*
"clear the countryside" 清鄉 *qingxiang*
collaborator 漢奸 *hanjian*
collective security 集體安全 *jiti anquan*
Commerce Control Commission 商業統制委員會 *shangye tongzhi weiyuanwei*
comprador 買辦 *maiban*
consumption 用 *yong*
control commission 統制委員會 *tongzhi weiyuanhui*
controlled economy 統制經濟 *tongzhi jingji*
Cooperative Accounting Commission 合作社會計制度委員會 *hezuo huiji zhidu weiyanhui*
cooperative economy, economic cooperation 合作經濟 *hezuo jingji*
Cotton Control Commission 棉業統制委員會 *mianye tongzhi weiyuanhui*
cotton varieties:
 Baoji 寶鷄
 Caret 脫字棉 *tuozimian*
 Delfos no. 531 德字棉五三一號 *dezimian wusanyi hao*
 Gold 金字棉 *jinzimian*
 Million Dollars 百萬 *baiwan*
 Stoneville no. 4 斯字棉四號 *sizimian si hao*
curing the roots of the problem 治本 *zhiben* (rather than curing superficial symptoms, 治標 *zhibiao*)
defense document 自白書 *zibaishu*
democratic politics 民主政治 *zhuyi zhengzhi*
development of the human endeavor 人類事業的開展 *renlei shiyede kaizhan*
Economic Control Deliberative Committee 物資統制審議委員會 *wuzi tongzhi shenyi weiyuanhui*
economic cooperation 經濟合作 *jingji hezuo*
economic enterprises linked to people's livelihood 民生事業 *minsheng shiye*
economic power 經濟力 *jingjili*
economic unit 經濟單位 *jingji danwei*
evolution 演進 *yanjin*
familism 家族主義 *jiazu zhuyi*
Flood Relief Commission (FRC) 水災救濟委員會 *shuizai jiuji weiyuanhui*
foundation of the nation 國本 *guoben*
"founding the country on agriculture" 以農立國 *yinong liguo*
Four Great Necessities of the People 民生四大需要 *minsheng sida xuyao* (food, clothing, shelter, and means of travel) (食衣住行 *shi, yi, zhu, xing*)

four social groups (according to Zheng Guanying):
- peasants — 農 *nong*
- workers — 工 *gong*
- merchants — 商 *shang*
- literati — 士 *shi*

fundamental — 本 *ben* (as opposed to peripheral, 末 *mo*)
garrisoned village — 屯田 *tutian*
"governing the state through the party" — 以黨治國 *yi dang zhi guo*
Grain Management Committee — 糧食管理委員會 *liangshi guanli weiyuanhui*
great nationalism — 大民族主義 *daminzu zhuyi*
Green Gang — 青幫 *qingbang*
"Guangdong people rule Guangdong" — 粵人治粵 *yue ren zhi yue*
Guomindang Reorganization Comrades Association — 中國國民黨改組同志會 *Zhongguo Guomindang gaizu tongzhihui*, shortened to Reorganization Group, 改組派 *gaizupai*
Gubeikou — 古北口
guiding bureau — 指導所 *zhidasuo*
Huangpu (Whampoa) Military Academy — 黃埔軍校 *Huangpu junxiao*
The Impartial — 大公報 *Dagongbao*
"industrialize Japan and agriculturalize China" — 工業日本農業中國 *gongye Riben nongye Zhongguo*
Industry Control Commission — 工業統制委員會 *gongye tongzhi weiyuanhui*
Jiangxi Office — 江西辦事處 *Jiangxi banshichu*
jin (equivalent to 0.5 kg) — 斤
Jincheng Bank — 金城銀行 *Jincheng yinhang*
joint state-private management — 官商合辦 *guanshang heban*
Labor Control Commission — 勞工統制委員會 *laogong tongzhi weiyuanhui*
labor productivity — 勞力的功能 *laoli de gongneng*
"land equalization" — 平均地權 *pingjun tudi*
"land to the tillers" — 耕者有其田 *gengzhe you qitian*
lijin (*likin*) tax — 厘金
material control — 物資統制 *wuzi tongzhi*
Military Commission — 軍事委員會 *junshi weiyanhui*
minzu — 民族
minzu (national and Nationalist) economy — 民族經濟 *minzu jingji*
modern nation — 近代式的國家 *jindaishi de guojia, jindai guojua*
mu (roughly equivalent to one-sixth of an acre) — 畝
nation, state — 國家 *guojia*
nation building — 建國 *jianguo*, 立國 *liguo*
National Economic Conference — 全國經濟會議 *quanguo jingji huyi*
National Economic Council — 全國經濟委員會 *quanguo jingji weiyuanhui*

National General Marketing Office for Cotton Production and Marketing Societies 全國棉花產銷合作設運銷總辦事處 *quanguo mianhua chanxiao hezuoshe yunxiao zongbanshi chu*

National Merchant Control Association 全國商業統制總會 *quangguo shangye tongzhi zonghui*, generally shortened to 商統會 *shangtonghui*

National Product Movement 國貨運動 *guohuo yundong*

national production 全國產生 *quanguo chansheng*

National Reconstruction Commission 建設委員會 *jianshe weiyuanhui*

national vitality 國力 *guoli*

Nationalist Party 國民黨 *guomindang*

nationality, ethnic group, national, nationalist 民族 *minzu*

Natural Resource Commission 資源委員會 *ziyuan weiyuanhui*

New China Policy 對華新政策 *duihua sinzhengce*

New Democracy 新民主主義 *Xin minzhu zhuyi*

Northwest Office 西北辦事處 *xibei banshichu*

"pacify the domestic front while resisting on the external front" 安內攘外 *an'nei rangwai*

Peace Movement 和平運動 *heping yudong*

People's Livelihood (classical formulation) 國計民生 *guoji minsheng*

petty nationalism 俠義民族主義 *xiayi minzu zhuyi; xiaominzhu zhuyi*

petty nationalist economies 俠義的國家主義經濟 *xiayi de guojia zhuyi jingji*

"the people's vitality" 人民的元氣 *renmin de yuanqi*

Principle of People's Livelihood 民生主義 *minsheng zhuyi*

private rights 人民私權 *renmin siquan*

private sector 人民私營 *renmin siying*

Producer Party 生產黨 *shengchandang*

producers, productive forces 生產者 *shengchanzhe*

production tools 生產工具 *shengchan gongju*

progress 進步 *jinbu*

Provisional Law for the Tutelage Period 中華訓政時期約法 *Zhonghua xunzheng shiqi yuefa*

random class struggle 社會階級的混爭 *shehui jieji de hunzheng*

raw cotton 棉花 *mianhua*

reconstruction 建設 *jianshe*

Reformed Government 維新政府 *weixin zhengfu*

"rely on Heaven for food" 考天吃飯 *kaotian chifan*

Reorganized Nationalist Government (RNG) 改組國民政府 *gaizu guomin zhengfu*

Research in Chinese Economy 中國經濟研究 *zhongguo jingji yanjiu*

"return the capital to Nanjing" 還度 *haidu*

Revolutionary Alliance 同盟會 *tongmenghui*

Rural Services Centers 農村服務處 *nongcun fuwuchu*

saving the nation 救國 *jiuguo*

"saving the country with business" 事業救國 *shiye jiuguo*

scientific class struggle 科學主義的階級鬥爭 *kexue zhuyi de jieji douzheng*

Shaanxi Province (in the 1930s also spelled Shensi, following the Wade-Giles system) 陝西
Shanghai Commercial and Savings Bank 上海商儲蓄銀行 *Shanghai shangye chuxu yinhang*
Shanghai Overseas Relief Commission 上海華洋義賑會 *Shanghai huayang yizhen hui*
Shanghai Stock and Goods Exchange 上海證券物品交易所 *zhengquan wupin jiaoyisuo*
Shenxin (Rong Zongjing's cotton mills group) 申新
Silk Improvement Commission (SIC) 蠶絲改良委員會 *cangsi gailian weiyuan-hui*
supplier of agricultural products 農共國 *nonggongguo*
take-charge system 擔當官制 *danshang guanzhi*
Three People's Principles 三民主義 *sanmin zhuyi*
"to resist foreign aggression we must first pacify the domestic front" 攘外必先安內 *rangwai bixian an'nei*
trade war 商戰 *shangzhan*
Transportation Control Commission 運輸統制委員會 *yunshu tongzhi wei-yuanhui*
unfavorable balance of trade 入超, *ruchao*
"use war to feed war" 以戰養戰 *yizhan yangzhan*
Xi'an Pacification Office 西安綏靖署 *Xi'an suijing shu*
Xingye Silk Company 興業製絲股份有限公司 *Xingye zhisi gufen yousian gongsi*

NOTES

Introduction

1. For a discussion of different models of industrialization, see the seminal work by German historian Alexander Gerschenkron, who argues that the economic forces that had shaped development in England (the first country to industrialize and, at the time Gerschenkron wrote, generally considered the model for modern nationhood) did not play an important role in the development effort of countries that industrialized in later historical periods. The later the nation-building process occurred, the larger the role assumed by the state in an attempt to make up for the absence of the economic forces that had been operative in England. See Alexander Gerschenkron, "Economic Development in Russian Intellectual History of the 19th Century," in *Economic Backwardness in Historical Perspective,* by Alexander Gerschenkron (Cambridge, MA: Belknap Press of Harvard University Press, 1962).

2. The idea that the concept of nation precedes nation building became established with the work of Benedict Anderson. Anderson convincingly argues that nationhood is a form of identity consciousness developed by members of a society who share similar cultural and sociopolitical experiences. This new common consciousness transforms these individuals into a tight community (although only through their imagining of their shared circumstances) and leads them to pursue nation building. See Benedict R. O. G. Anderson, *Imagined Communities: Reflections on the Origin and Spread of Nationalism* (London: Verso, 1983). See also Liah Greenfeld, *The Spirit of Capitalism: Nationalism and Economic Growth* (Cambridge, MA: Harvard University Press, 2001). Greenfeld argues that nationalism is responsible for the development of capitalism, and not vice versa. Greenfeld begins her inquiry with the examination of European nations in the sixteenth and seventeenth centuries and then examines other countries, including Japan and the United States, as she moves toward the present. Industrialization occurred in these countries, she argues, only after economic activities came to be invested with nationalist meaning. Only then did resources and economic assets—which might have been mature for growth but were not

yet exploited for this goal—come to be channeled by government and business into economic development. The transformation of these economies, Greenfeld continues, was originally motivated by the desire to transform these countries into powerful nations by establishing their economic superiority.

3. No one would question the importance of market forces in the economics of a nation or of the contribution to the development of modern economics of Smith's pioneering work on the market and national development. Today, however, only a few would accept the absolute self-regulating nature of the market envisioned by Smith or deny the necessity of policies devised to protect, regulate, or stimulate the market. The term "modern" can be used to refer to a historically bound movement with certain economic, cultural, and sociopolitical characteristics. On the other hand, this word is constantly used to describe what is generally considered the latest technological or cultural trend. In this sense the modern computer of the 1960s appears as definitively nonmodern when compared with the latest laptop.

4. Chen Gongbo's writings are discussed in detail later. See especially chapters 1 and 2.

5. Xu Youchun, ed., *Minguo renwu dacidian* (Shijiazhuang: Hebei renmin chubanshe, 1991), 439.

6. Other groups such as anarchists and third parties have rightly attracted the attention of historians, although, because of these groups' inability to effectively contend with the GMD and CCP for political power, they were generally confined to the margins of the political landscape. For works on anarchist and third parties, see Peter Gue Zarrow, *Anarchism and Chinese Political Culture* (New York: Columbia University Press, 1990); Arif Dirlik, *Anarchism in the Chinese Revolution* (Berkeley and Los Angeles: University of California Press, 1991); Roger B. Jeans, "In Search of the Middle Way: Chang Chun-mai and the Debate over Democracy and Dictatorship in the 1930s," *Republican China* 10, no. 3 (June 1985): 27–43; Roger B. Jeans, ed., *Roads Not Taken: The Struggle of Opposition Parties in Twentieth-Century China* (Boulder, CO: Westview Press, 1992).

7. See, e.g., Tian Hongmao [Tien Hung-mao], *Government and Politics in Kuomintang China, 1927–1937* (Stanford, CA: Stanford University Press, 1972).

8. On the idea of a one-party system and economic centralization, see John Fitzgerald, *Awakening China: Politics, Culture, and Class in the Nationalist Revolution* (Stanford, CA: Stanford University Press, 1996); Parks M. Coble, *The Shanghai Capitalists and the Nationalist Government, 1927–1937* (Cambridge, MA: Council on East Asian Studies, Harvard University, 1980); William C. Kirby, *Germany and Republican China* (Stanford, CA: Stanford University Press, 1984).

9. Marie-Claire Bergère and Janet Lloyd, *Sun Yat-sen* (Stanford, CA: Stanford University Press, 1998), especially 134, 143ff.

10. Zhi Xisheng [Chi Hsi-sheng], *Warlord Politics in China, 1916–1928* (Stanford, CA: Stanford University Press, 1976), 40; Zhi Xisheng, *The Chinese Warlord System, 1916–1928* (Washington, DC: American University Center for Research in Social Systems, 1969), 55ff.

11. See, among other recent works on China's national identity and nation building, Rebecca Karl, *Staging the World: Chinese Nationalism at the Turn of the Twentieth Century* (Durham, NC: Duke University Press, 2002); Rana Mitter, *The Manchurian Myth: Nationalism, Resistance, and Collaboration in Modern China* (Berkeley and Los Angeles: University of California Press, 2000); Michael Tsin, *Nation, Governance, and Modernity in China: Canton, 1900–1927* (Stanford, CA: Stanford University Press, 1999).

12. Prasenjit Duara, *Rescuing History from the Nation* (Chicago: University of Chicago Press, 1995), chapter 2.

13. Ibid., especially 177–204. On the federalist alternative, see also Fitzgerald, *Awakening China,* 150–53, 160–67. See also the work of Leslie Chen on Chen Jiongming and federalism: Leslie H. Dingyan Chen, *Chen Jiongming and the Federalist Movement* (Ann Arbor: Center for Chinese Studies, University of Michigan, 1999). In his work on collaboration in Manchuria, Rana Mitter also addresses the lack of participation in the narrative of nation building on the part of provincial elites and warlords: Mitter, *Manchurian Myth.*

14. Fitzgerald, *Awakening China.*

15. For a detailed analysis of the economic reforms sponsored by Jiang Jieshi, see Kirby, *Germany and Republican China.*

16. Tsin, *Nation, Governance, and Modernity in China,* 4.

17. The First United Front between the GMD and the CCP (1923–27) was sponsored by the Soviet Union and found inspiration in Lenin's "Preliminary Draft Theses on the National and Colonial Question" (July 1920), in *Collected Works,* vol. 31 (Moscow: Progress Publisher, 1966), 144–51. In this essay Lenin called on the Communist parties in the colonized regions of the world to seek a temporary alliance with bourgeois nationalist forces.

18. Mao Zedong, *New Democracy* (Beijing: Renmin chubanshe, 1953).

19. Lloyd E. Eastman, *The Abortive Revolution: China under Nationalist Rule, 1927–1937* (Cambridge, MA: Harvard University Press, 1974), see especially 1–9; Suzanne Pepper, *Civil War in China: The Political Struggle, 1945–1949* (Berkeley and Los Angeles: University of California Press, 1978), 423–26.

20. Among works on corporativism translated into Chinese were those of the Austrian sociologist Othmar Spann. See Alberto Sorgi, "La programmazione e la politica economica nel pensiero economico cinese degli anni venti e trenta" (Ph.D. diss., Università degli studi di Roma "La Sapienza," Rome, 2002), 54.

21. Roland Sarti, *Fascism and the Industrial Leadership in Italy, 1919–1940* (Berkeley and Los Angeles: University of California Press, 1971), 136. Although assessments of the Italian economy during the years of fascism remain controversial because of continued political sensitivity, it is generally recognized that during the 1920s and early 1930s Fascist influence over the economy was marginal, while more markedly visible in the social and political realms. Fascist economic policies became more decisive after the 1930s, after the impact of the international depression began to be felt in Italy. See Maurizio Vaudagna, "Structural Change in Fascist Italy," *Journal of Economic History* 38, no. 1 (1978): 181–201.

22. Telegramma in arrivo, N. 188 P.H. and N. 2301 P.H. Anno 1933, Telegrammi in Arrivo, Cina, Archivio storico del Ministero degli Easteri, Rome. For an overview of Sino-Italian relations in the mid-1930s, see M. R. Godley, "Fascismo e nazionalismo cinese, 1931–1938: Note preliminari allo studio dei rapporti italo-cinesi durante il periodo fascista," *Storia contemporanea,* Anno IV, no. 4 (Dec. 1973): 754.

23. Chen Kan, interview by author, Oct. 2000.

24. Godley, "Fascismo e nazionalismo cinese"; Chen Kan, interview with author, Oct. 2000.

25. Zhang Li, *Guoji hezuo zai zhonggho* (Taibei: Zhongyang yanjiuyuan jindaishi yanjiusuo, 1999).

26. Frederic Wakeman Jr., "A Revisionist View of the Nanjing Decade: Confucian Fascism," *China Quarterly* 150 (1997): 395–432; Lloyd E. Eastman, "Fascism in Kuomintang China: The Blue Shirts," *China Quarterly* 49 (1972): 1–31.

27. Kirby, *Germany and Republican China*, 172–75, 259, 264–65.

28. A. James Gregor, *A Place in the Sun: Marxism and Fascism in China's Long Revolution* (Boulder, CO: Westview Press, 2000), chapter 4.

29. Tim Mason, "Italy and Modernization: A Montage," *History Workshop* 25 (1988): 129. For an overview of the most popular interpretation of fascism, see Kirby, *Germany and Republican China*, 173–75.

30. Zeev Sternhell, *Neither Right nor Left: Fascist Ideology in France*, translated by David Maisel (Berkeley and Los Angeles: University of California Press, 1986), 3, 28.

31. Ibid., 27.

32. For the turn-of-the-century world political and economic crisis, see Karl Polanyi, *The Great Transformation* (Boston: Beacon Press, 1957), especially chapters 1 and 2.

33. Parks M. Coble, *Facing Japan: Chinese Politics and Japanese Imperialism, 1931–1937*, Harvard East Asian Monographs 135 (Cambridge, MA: Council on East Asian Studies, Harvard University, distributed by Harvard University Press, 1991).

34. Sternhell, *Neither Right nor Left*, 1, 2.

35. See discussion of fascism as state policy versus fascism as mass movement in Kirby, *Germany and Republican China*, 264–65.

36. Doug Thompson, *State Control in Fascist Italy: Culture and Conformity, 1925–43* (Manchester, UK: Manchester University Press, 1991); Sarti, *Fascism and the Industrial Leadership in Italy;* Piero Melograni, *Gli industriali e Mussolini* (Milan: Longanesi and Co., 1971).

37. Ernest Young, *The Presidency of Yuan Shi-kai* (Ann Arbor: University of Michigan Press, 1977), 192ff.

38. Ibid.; Peter Gue Zarrow, "Political Ritual in the Early Republic of China," in *Constructing Nationhood in Modern East Asia*, edited by Kai-wing Chow, Kevin M. Doak, and Poshek Fu (Ann Arbor: University of Michigan Press, 2001), 162–75.

39. George E. Taylor, "The Reconstruction Movement in China," in *Problems of the Pacific, 1936*, edited by W. L. Holland and Kate Mitchell (Chicago: University of Chicago Press, 1936), 381, 384.

40. Guy Alitto, *The Last Confucian: Liang Shu-ming and the Chinese Dilemma of Modernity* (Berkeley and Los Angeles: University of California Press, 1979); Charles Wishart Hayford, *To the People: James Yen and Village China*, The United States and Pacific Asia Studies in Social, Economic, and Political Interactions (New York: Columbia University Press, 1990).

41. For the impact of Japanese aggression on Chinese politics, see Coble, *Facing Japan;* Donald A. Jordan, *China's Trial by Fire: The Shanghai War of 1932* (Ann Arbor: University of Michigan Press, 2001).

42. For a detailed discussion of the crisis of 1931–32, see Coble, *Facing Japan*, 39–69.

43. For a detailed description of the complex series of events that led to the establishment and fall of the Sun Ke government, see ibid.; Lloyd E. Eastman et al., *The Nationalist Era in China, 1927–1949* (Cambridge: Cambridge University Press, 1991); Jiang Yongjing, "Guomindang sanjutou Hu Wang Jiang de fenhe," *Zhuanji wenxue* 62, no. 3 (Mar. 15, 1993): 15–24.

44. So Wai-chor, *The Kuomintang Left in the National Revolution, 1924–1931*, East Asian Historical Monographs (Hong Kong: Oxford University Press, 1991).

45. Wang himself differentiated between those members of the GMD who wanted to continue the revolutionary tradition initiated by Sun Yat-sen, whom he identified with the Left of the party, and those who supported antirevolutionary policies, whom he identified with the party's right wing and who rallied around Jiang in Nanjing. See ibid., 41.

46. See ibid.

47. See ibid. Chen was nominally acting for Wang Jingwei, who was abroad at that time. However, it has recently been argued that the Reorganization Group was mostly Chen's idea, with which Wang disagreed. For Chen's initiative in the formation of the Reorganization Group, see ibid., 62–63, 143. For ideological differences between Chen Gongbo and Wang Jingwei, see ibid., 104–5, 146, 152–53.

48. See ibid., 41.

49. See ibid.

Chapter One

1. Interview with Wang Jingwei, in *Shenbao*, Oct. 22, 1931, 13. All translations are my own unless otherwise indicated.

2. Wang Jingwei, *China's Problems and Their Solution*, China To-day series, no. 2 (Shanghai: United Press, 1934), 13.

3. Ibid., 14–15.

4. Wang Jingwei, "Women yao jianshe zenmeyang de guojia" (July 1927), in *Wang Jingwei wencun* (Shanghai: Qizhi shudian, 1935), 291.

5. Wang Jingwei, *China's Problems and Their Solution*, 43.

6. Rebecca Karl, *Staging the World: Chinese Nationalism at the Turn of the Twentieth Century* (Durham, NC: Duke University Press, 2002).

7. Kenneth Pomeranz, *The Making of a Hinterland: State, Society, and Economy in Inland North China, 1853–1937* (Berkeley and Los Angeles: University of California Press, 1993). See especially chapter 1 and pp. 138, 201–2.

8. For more details on the Reform Movement and the impact of social Darwinism on it, see James Reeve Pusey, *China and Charles Darwin* (Cambridge, MA: Council on East Asian Studies, Harvard University, 1983), chapter 3; Tang Xiaobing, *Global Space and the Nationalist Discourse of Modernity: The Historical Thinking of Liang Qichao* (Stanford, CA: Stanford University Press, 1996), see especially chapter 2.

9. Arif Dirlik, *Revolution and History: The Origins of Marxist Historiography in China, 1919–1937* (Berkeley and Los Angeles: University of California Press, 1978), 31. See also Tang Xiaobing, *Global Space*.

10. Dirlik, *Revolution and History*, 31; Tang Xiaobing, *Global Space*.

11. Wang Jingwei, *China's Problems and Their Solution*, 13–14.

12. Ibid., 5.

13. Chen Gongbo, *Zhongguo lishishang de geming* (Shanghai: Fudan shudian, 1928), 2–4.

14. Ibid.

15. Chen Gongbo, "Tichang shenme de wenhua," *Minzu zazhi* 2, no. 8 (Aug. 1934).

16. Chen Gongbo, "Tongzhi jingji yu zuzhi," in *Sinian congzhenglu,* by Chen Gongbo (Shanghai: Shangwu yingshuguan, 1936), 175–76. Originally published in *Minzu zazhi,* Nov. 1933. The first half of *Sinian congzhenglu* was written by Chen Gongbo in 1936. The volume also includes an extensive appendix that reprints some of Chen's most important articles from the early 1930s. When referring to the reprinted articles, I specify their titles and original dates of publication. Otherwise, when referring to the material written in 1936, I give only the title of the book.

17. Sun Yat-sen, "Minzu zhuyi" (1924), in *Sun Zhongshan xuanji,* vol. 2, edited by Song Qingling (Beijing: Renmin chubanshe, 1957), 588–602.

18. Wang Jingwei, "An'nei yu rangwai" (talk delivered at the Nationalist government's tenth anniversary), in *Wang Jingwei xiansheng zuijin zhi yanlun,* edited by Lin Bosheng (Shanghai: Zhonghua ribao guan, 1937), 31.

19. Wang Jingwei, *China's Problems and Their Solution,* 45.

20. Ibid., 150.

21. Jiang Jieshi, "Zhengli jundui, tongyi shijun" (talk delivered at the High Military Conference (Apr. 2, 1932), in *Xianzongtong Jiang Gong sixiang yanlun zhongji,* vol. 10, edited by Qing Xiaoyi (Taibei: Zhongguo Guomindang Zhongyang weiyuanhui tangshi weiyuanhui: Zhongyang wenwu gongyingshe jingxiao, 1984), 483.

22. Chen Gongbo, *Sinian congzhenlu,* 7.

23. Chen Gongbo, "Geju de tongzhi jingji," in *Sinian congzhenlu,* 190–91. Originally published in *Minzu zazhi,* Sept. 1934.

24. For a discussion of the use of the term "feudalism" in China, see Dirlik, *Revolution and History,* chapter 4.

25. Fitzgerald, *Awakening China,* 156. The first to theorize the feudal nature of federalism were the Communists in their discussion of Chen Jiongming (the warlord who ruled Guangdong before Chen Jitang). By June 1922 this view had come to be shared by many liberal intellectuals, including Hu Shi, and gained more momentum from the events in Hunan, Yunnan, and Guangdong. For example, Sun Yat-sen hated Chen Jiongming, who had "betrayed" him "because he [Chen] pursued a different dream of national reunification with the same selfless rigor" (Fitzgerald, *Awakening China,* 149).

26. Chen Gongbo, *Sininan congzhenglu,* 7.

27. Chen Gongbo, *Zhongguo lishishang de geming,* 96. Chen's view was very different from that of Fang Xianting (H. D. Fong), a prominent economist at Nankai University who advocated the fragmentation of industrial production in rural areas. See Fang Xianting, "The Cooperative Movement in China," *Nankai University Monthly Bulletin on Economic China* 7, no. 5 (May 1934).

28. Chen Gongbo, *Sinian congzhenglu,* 7; Chen Gongbo, *Zhongguo lishishang de geming,* 2–4.

29. Pomeranz, *Making of a Hinterland,* 4, 47–48, 138, 201–2.

30. Richard H. Tawney, *Land and Labor in China* (Boston: Beacon Press, 1966), 55–56.

31. Fitzgerald, *Awakening China.*

32. Ibid., 174.

33. As quoted in ibid., 185. The Chinese term *guo* used by Sun can be translated as both "state" and "nation." The ambiguity of the term made it easier for Sun to collapse the two notions (state and nation).

34. Ibid., 162.

35. For more information on Chen Jiongming, see Leslie H. Dingyan Chen, *Chen Jiongming and the Federalist Movement;* Tsin, *Nation, Governance, and Modernity in China;* Duara, *Rescuing History from the Nation;* Fitzgerald, *Awakening China.*

36. Chen Jiongming, "Chen Jiongming liangfeng xin" (1932, Shanghai), as quoted in Leslie H. Dingyan Chen, *Chen Jiongming and the Federalist Movement,* 276.

37. Ibid.

38. The Fujian rebellion's leaders ended up looking for allies by proposing federalism. See Fitzgerald, *Awakening China,* 150, 154–56; Eastman et al., *The Nationalist Era in China,* 130–31; Duara, *Rescuing History from the Nation,* 155ff., 194–95.

39. From Chen Jiongming, "Chen Jiongming liangfeng xin," 276.

40. Tsin, *Nation, Governance, and Modernity in China.*

41. Arif Dirlik, "Mass Movements and the Left Kuomintang," *Modern China* 1, no. 1 (Jan. 1975): 46–74.

42. Germaine Hoston, *The State, Identity, and the National Question in China and Japan* (Princeton, NJ: Princeton University Press, 1994), 279–80.

43. Chen Gongbo, *Zhongguo Guomindang suodaibiao de shi shenme?* 3d ed. (Shanghai: Fudan shudian, 1928), chapter 1. See also Hoston, *State, Identity, and the National Question in China and Japan,* 66–80, 279–80.

44. Chen Gongbo, *Zhongguo guomindang suodaibiao de shi shenme?* chapter 1; So, *Kuomintang Left,* 3.

45. Chen Gongbo, *Zhongguo Guomindang suodaibiao de shi shenme?,* introduction.

46. Margherita Zanasi, "Fostering the People's Livelihood: Chinese Political and Economic Thought between Empire and Nation," *Twentieth Century China* 23, no. 1 (Nov. 2004): 6–38; Bergère and Lloyd, *Sun Yat-sen,* see especially chapter 9.

47. Sun Yat-sen, "The Principle of People's Livelihood," in *Sun Zhongshan xuanji,* vol. 2, edited by Song Qingling (Beijing: Renmin chubanshe, 1957).

48. Hoston, *State, Identity, and the National Question in China and Japan,* 279–80; Dirlik, *Revolution and History,* 33.

49. As quoted in Luciano Zani, *Fascismo, autarchia, commercio estero: Felice Guarnieri, un technocrate al servizio dello "stato nuovo"* (Bologna: Il Mulino, 1988), 25.

50. As quoted in Sternhell, *Neither Right nor Left,* 18.

51. Mao Zedong, "Xin minzhu zhuyi," in *Mao Zedong zhuzuo xuandu,* vol. 1 (Beijing: Renmin chubanshe, 1986).

52. Introduction to Chen Gongbo, *Zhongguo Guomindang suodaibiao de shi shenme?;* Dirlik, *Revolution and History.*

53. Introduction to Chen Gongbo, *Zhongguo Guomindang suodaibiao de shi shenme?*

54. Chen Gongbo, *The Communist Movement in China,* edited by Martin Wilbur (New York: Octagon Books, 1966), 63–64.

55. William Lawrence Shirer, *The Rise and Fall of Adolf Hitler* (New York: Random House, 1961), chapter 5.

56. Renzo De Felice, *Mussolini,* vol. 1, *Il rivoluzionario, 1883–1920,* Biblioteca di cultura storica 83 (Turin: Einaudi, 1965), 391–418 and chapter 13.

57. Sun Yat-sen, *Fundamentals of National Reconstruction* (Taibei: China Cultural Service, 1953), 9.

58. Wang Jingwei, "Jianshe," in *Wang Jingwei wencun* (Shanghai: Qizhi shudian, 1935), 276.

59. Chen Gongbo, "Wei shiye jihua gao guoren," in *Sinian congzhenglu,* 160. Originally published in *Minzu zazhi,* Nov. 20, 1933.

60. A tael (*liang*) was roughly the equivalent of one ounce of silver, but its weight and value varied around China. After 1932 the "custom tael" was set at a rate of 1.55 Chinese silver dollars. See Thomas G. Rawski, *Economic Growth in Prewar China* (Berkeley and Los Angeles: University of California Press, 1989), xv.

61. Chen Gongbo, "Wei shiye jihua gao guoren," 160.

62. According to the notion of the Mandate of Heaven, the political legitimacy of a ruler rested on his commitment to see to the welfare of the people. If the ruler failed in this duty, Heaven would withdraw its mandate to rule and manifest its displeasure by sending a series of natural disasters (from floods to droughts) to afflict the empire.

63. Chen Gongbo, "Zhongguo liangshi de ziji," in *Sinian congzhenglu,* 193–94. Originally published in *Minzu zazhi,* June 1935.

64. Wang Jingwei, *China's Problems and Their Solution,* 29, 30.

65. Jiang Jieshi, "Chinese Economic Theory," in *China's Destiny and Chinese Economic Theory,* by Jiang Jieshi (New York: Roy Publishers, 1947), 247–48.

66. Ibid., 248.

67. Ibid., 254.

68. Zhong Xiangcai, *Zhongguo jindai minzu qiyejia jingji sixiang* (Shanghai: Shanghai shehui kexueyuan chubanshe, 1992), 26–32; Chen Yutang, ed., *Zhongguo jinxiandai renwu minghao dacidian* (Hangzhou: Zhejiang guji chubanshe, 1993), 616.

69. Zhong, *Zhongguo jindai minzu qiyejia jingji sixiang,* 32–33.

70. Although an emphasis on foreign trade had already surfaced in earlier economic writings such as those by Wei Yuan and Zheng Guanying, Ma Jianzhong was the first to systematically apply these theories to China. See Hu Jichuang, *A Concise History of Chinese Economic Thought* (Beijing: Foreign Language Press, 1988), 543.

71. Pomeranz, *Making of a Hinterland,* 4, 47–48, 138, 201–2.

72. Polanyi, *Great Transformation,* 3, 19. Polanyi describes the free-exchange system as based on four institutions: balance of power, an international gold standard (a unique organization of world economy), a self-regulating market, and a liberal state.

73. A. James Gregor, *Marxism, China, and Development: Reflections on Theory and Reality* (New Brunswick, NJ: Transaction Publishers, 1995), 154–55; Sun Yat-sen, "Sanmin zhuiyi," in *Sun Zhongshang xuanji,* vol. 2, edited by Song Qingling (Beijing: Renmin chubanshe, 1957); Sun Yat-sen, *Memoirs of a Chinese Revolutionary: A Programme of National Reconstruction for China* (London: Hutchinson and Co., 1927).

74. Polanyi, *Great Transformation,* 20–21.

75. As quoted in Zani, *Fascismo, autarchia, commercio estero,* 48.

76. Chen Gongbo, "Zhongguo liangshi de ziji," 193–94.

77. Chen Gongbo, "Geju de tongzhi jingji," 188.

78. The issue of the impact of foreign imperialism on the Chinese economy has been at the center of a heated debate. See Hou Jiming, *Foreign Investment and Economic Development in China, 1840–1937* (Ann Arbor: Michigan University Press Microfilms International, 1981); Andrew Nathan, "Imperialism's Effect on China," *Bulletin of Concerned Asian Scholars* 4, no. 4 (Dec. 1972); Joseph W. Esherick, "Harvard on China: The Apologetics of Imperialism," *Bulletin of Concerned Asian Scholars* 4, no. 4 (Dec. 1972). The terms of such debate, however, are now beginning to change. Scholars have recently applied a new interpretive framework. Kenneth Pomeranz, for

example, argues that "while people so far apart as 'modernization' and 'dependency' theorists often argue that imperialism's worst political legacy was that it left twentieth-century China (or other Third World countries) with a state incapable of promoting development, it may be more accurate to acknowledge that much was done to develop certain modern sectors and regions and to look instead at how state strategies adopted under foreign pressure shortchanged other policy and geographic areas" (*Making of a Hinterland,* 24). Robert Y. Eng suggests a similar approach: "If we are to understand the modernization process in China and Japan as a whole, we must go beyond citing various internal or external factors that might have facilitated or retarded modernization and even beyond weighing the relative importance of internal versus external factors. Rather, we must try to understand the organic links and dynamic interactions between domestic and foreign forces" (*Economic Imperialism in China: Silk Production and Exports, 1861–1932* [Berkeley: Center for Chinese Studies, University of California, 1986], 11). It is also important to point out here that 1930s Chinese perceptions of imperialist exploitation were mostly the result of Japan's military and economic aggression.

79. Introduction to part 1, "Trade and Investment," in *The Japanese Informal Empire in China, 1895–1937,* edited by Peter Duus, Ramon Hawley Myers, and Mark R. Peattie (Princeton, NJ: Princeton University Press, 1989), 5.

80. Itō Hirobumi, "Tai-Shin shosaku," *Jitsogyō no Nihon* 1, 19:9, as quoted in introduction to part 1, "Trade and Investment," in Duus, Myers, and Peattie, *The Japanese Informal Empire in China,* 5.

81. Introduction to part 1, "Trade and Investment," in Duus, Myers, and Peattie, *The Japanese Informal Empire in China,* 4.

82. Parks M. Coble, "Japan's New Order and the Shanghai Capitalists: Conflict and Collaboration, 1937–1945," in *Chinese Collaboration with Japan, 1932–1945: The Limits of Accommodation,* edited by David P. Barrett and Lawrence N. Shyu (Stanford, CA: Stanford University Press, 2001), 136.

83. In spite of the aggressive stand of the Japanese military, especially the Guangdong (Kwantung) army in Manchuria, the civilian government in Tokyo was not planning to colonize China, a step that would have required investing tremendous resources in terms of military and administrative personnel. Japan preferred to deal with a Chinese government that would cater to Japan's interest. As historian Rana Mitter illustrates in his book *Manchurian Myth,* this was the strategy Japan followed in Manchuria.

84. The Opium War erupted in 1839 between Great Britain and China over Great Britain's illegal smuggling of opium into China. It ended in 1842 in overwhelming victory for Great Britain. This war is generally considered the beginning of large-scale imperialist presence in China.

85. Chen Gongbo, "Xu sinian shiye jihua chugao," in *Sinian congzhenglu,* 42. Originally published in *Minzu zazhi,* Aug. 1933.

86. Duara, *Rescuing History from the Nation,* 36.

87. For an extensive debate on Liang Qichao's views on nationalism, see Tang Xiaobing, *Global Space.*

88. Wang Jingwei, "An'nei yu rangwai," 29, 30.

89. Chen Gongbo, *Sinian congzhenglu,* 58.

90. Chen Gongbo, "Geju de tongzhi jingji," 190–91.

91. Wang Jingwei, *China's Problems and Their Solution,* 31.

92. De Felice, *Mussolini,* vol. 1, *Il rivoluzionario.*

93. Chen Gongbo, "Geju de tongzhi jingji," 188–89.

94. Ibid., 190.

95. Chen Gongbo, *Sinian congzhenglu,* 43.

96. Benito Mussolini, *The Corporate State* (Florence: Vallecchi Editore, 1936), 15.

97. Benito Mussolini, "To the Workers of Milan" (Oct. 16, 1934), in Mussolini, *Corporate State,* 38.

98. Fang Xianting, "Toward Economic Control in China," *Nankai Social and Economic Quarterly* 9, nos. 1–2 (1936): 269.

99. Ibid., 376ff.

100. D. Z. Xu [T. C. Hsu], "Economic Ideas in China's Draft Constitution," *Monthly Bulletin on Economic China* 7, no. 8 (Aug. 1934): 326–27.

101. Jiang Jieshi, "Chinese Economic Theory," 242.

102. For Chinese books focusing on the growth of Chinese *minzu* industrial economy in the late Qing and early Republican periods, see, e.g., Zhong, *Zhongguo jindai minzu qiyejia jingji sixiang;* Wang Wen'an, *Min zu jing ji yu she hui yan jiu* (Beijing: Zhongguo renmin gongan daxue chubanshe, 2001).

103. See, e.g., Zhong, *Zhongguo jindai minzu qiyejia jingji sixiang;* Wang Wen'an, *Min zu jing ji yu she hui yan jiu.*

104. Jiang Jieshi, "Chinese Economic Theory," 248n.

Chapter Two

1. The Jiangnan region comprises the areas south of the lower Yangzi Valley, around the port of Shanghai. This area was historically one of the most economically advanced of China. Rural Jiangnan was, in general, more closely integrated into the newly emerging coastal industrial economy than villages in other regions of China. See, e.g., Bell, *One Industry, Two Chinas.*

2. De Felice, *Mussolini,* vol. 1, *Il rivoluzionario,* 403–18; Sarti, *Fascism and the Industrial Leadership in Italy,* 22–24.

3. Thomas G. Rawski, *Economic Growth in Prewar China* (Berkeley and Los Angeles: University of California Press, 1989), especially 344.

4. Bell, *One Industry, Two Chinas,* 2.

5. Pomeranz, *Making of a Hinterland,* 28 and chapter 1.

6. Tawney, *Land and Labor in China,* 56.

7. "Quangguo jingji weiyuanhui ershisan nianfen shiye jinxing jihua ji jingfei zhi zhibei," attached to the minutes of the third meeting of the Standing Committee of the NEC, 1934, NSHA 44(2)216; Chen Gongbo, *Sinian congzhenglu,* 48.

8. Wang Jingwei, *China's Problems and Their Solution,* 19–20.

9. Chen Gongbo, "Wei shiye jihua gao guoren."

10. Margherita Zanasi, "Far from the Treaty Ports: Fang Xianting and the Idea of Rural Modernity in 1930s China," *Modern China* 30, no. 1 (Jan. 2004): 113–46.

11. See, for example, the discussion of the importance of grain storage in the Qing strategy for stability and security in Pierre-Etienne Will and R. Bin Wong, eds., *Nourish the People: The State Civilian Granary System in China, 1650–1850* (Ann Arbor: University of Michigan Press, 1991).

12. For a discussion of the high status enjoyed by merchants, their appropriation

of Confucian values in their support, and the imperial state's promotion of commerce, see Richard Lufrano, *Honorable Merchants: Commerce and Self-Cultivation in Late Imperial China* (Honolulu: University of Hawai'i Press, 1997); Timothy Brook, *The Confusions of Pleasure: Commerce and Culture in Ming China* (Berkeley and Los Angeles: University of California Press, 1998).

13. Wang Yejian [Wang Yeh-chien], "The Fiscal Importance of the Land Tax during the Ch'ing (Qing) Period," *Journal of Asian Studies* 30, no. 4 (Aug. 1971): 829–42.

14. Brook, *Confusions of Pleasure*; Lufrano, *Honorable Merchants.*

15. Partha Chatterjee, *The Nation and Its Fragments: Colonial and Postcolonial Histories,* Princeton Studies in Culture/Power/History (Princeton, NJ: Princeton University Press, 1993), 6. For an extensive discussion of the "spiritual" and "material" realms in the first stage of nationalism, see Partha Chatterjee, *Nationalist Thought and the Colonial World: A Derivative Discourse* (Minneapolis: University of Minnesota Press, 1993).

16. This formula was first devised by the Confucian scholar and reformer Zhang Zhidong and adopted by most officials and reformers involved in the Self-Strengthening Movement.

17. Zhong Yangcai, *Zhongguo jindai minzu qiyejia jingji sixianshi,* 32.

18. Ibid., 34.

19. Gregor, *Marxism, China, and Development,* 151, 154–55.

20. Myron L. Cohen, "Cultural and Political Inventions in Modern China: The Case of the Chinese 'Peasant,'" *Daedalus* 22, no. 2 (Spring 1993): 151.

21. Susan Mann, "Urbanization and Historical Change in China," *Modern China* 1, no. 1 (Jan. 1984): 87. See also Paul G. Pickowicz, "The Theme of Spiritual Pollution in Chinese Films of the 1930s," *Modern China* 17, no. 1 (Jan. 1991).

22. Alitto, *The Last Confucian,* 78.

23. For more information on Fang Xianting, see Zanasi, "Far from the Treaty Ports."

24. Franklin Lian He, interview by Crystal Lorch Seidman, Oct. 1965 to Aug. 1966, Oral History Project: China, Columbia University, New York, 89.

25. Unfortunately, Fei Xiaotong does not mention the full name of Mr. Chen. It is thus difficult to identify him more specifically.

26. Fei Xiaotong, *Peasant Life in China: A Field Study of Country Life in the Yangtze Valley* (London: Kegan Paul Trench Trubner, 1939), 207–8.

27. Chen Gongbo, "Yinong liguo shi duide ma?" in *Sinian congzhenglu* (Shanghai: Shangwu yingshuguan, 1936), 168. Originally published in *Minzu zazhi,* July 1935.

28. Chen Gongbo, *Sinian congzhenglu,* 32; see also Chen Gongbo, "Yinong liguo shi duide ma?" 168.

29. Wang Jingwei, *China's Problems and Their Solution,* 24.

30. Chen Gongbo, "Yinong liguo shi duide ma?" 168.

31. Ibid., 169.

32. Ibid., 168.

33. Ibid., 168–70.

34. According to Chen Gongbo's data, China lagged behind even India and the Soviet Union. See ibid., 169.

35. Ibid., 170–71.

36. Chen Gongbo, *Zhongguo lishishang de geming,* 96.

37. Chen Gongbo, *Sinian congzhenglu,* 7.

38. Chen Gongbo, "Yinong liguo shi duide ma?" 168.

39. Ibid., 173.

40. "Quangguo jingji weiyuanhui ershisan nianfen shiye jinxing jihua ji jingfei zhi zhibei," attached to the minutes of the third meeting of the Standing Committee of the NEC, 1934, NSHA 44(2)216.

41. Fang Xianting, "Rural Industries in China's Reconstruction," *Monthly Bulletin on Economic China* 7, no. 11 (Nov. 1934): 449.

42. Chen Gongbo, "Yinong liguo shi duide ma?" 171. In Chen Gongbo's writing, the optimum size for a peasant's plot of land remained vague and depended on a balance between the ability of the peasant to work his plot and the capacity of the land to yield enough to support the peasant household.

43. Ibid., 168–71.

44. Ibid., 168–70.

45. Ibid., 169–70.

46. In 1933, when Chen Gongbo was writing this essay, China was recovering from a devastating flood of the Yangzi River that had destroyed the already-shaky agriculture and had necessitated setting priorities for flood relief and prevention.

47. Ibid., 173.

48. Ibid., 171.

49. Mark Elvin, *The Pattern of the Chinese Past* (Stanford, CA: Stanford University Press, 1973), 203.

50. Carl Riskin, "Surplus and Stagnation in Modern China," in *China's Modern Economy in Historical Perspectives,* edited by Dwight Perkins (Stanford, CA: Stanford University Press, 1975); Carl Riskin, *China's Political Economy: The Quest for Development since 1949,* Economies of the World (Oxford: Oxford University Press, 1987); Victor Lippit, *The Economic Development of China* (New York: Armonk, 1987).

51. Tawney, *Land and Labor in China,* 103.

52. Sun Yat-sen, "Minsheng zhuyi," 770–77.

53. Margherita Zanasi, "Fostering the People's Livelihood: Chinese Political and Economic Thought between Empire and Nation," *Twentieth Century China* 23, no. 1 (Nov. 2004): 6–38.

54. Sun Yat-sen, "Sanmin zhuyi," 789, 799–800, 810.

55. Quanguo jingji huiyi mishuchu, ed., *Quanguo jingji huiyi zhuankan* (Shanghai: Quanguo jingji huiyi, 1928).

56. GMDPHC 440/3(19); *Zhongyang ribao,* June 16, 1931; *Zhonghua xunzheng shiqi yuefa,* rules 33–35, in *Shenbao nianjian* (Shanghai: Shenbaoguan, 1933), F2.

57. Tawney, *Land and Labor in China,* 38.

58. "Quangguo jingji weiyuanhui ershisan nianfen shiye jinxing jihua ji jingfei zhi zhibei," attached to the minutes of the third meeting of the Standing Committee of the NEC, 1934, NSHA 44(2)216.

59. Dragoni, *Agricultural Reform,* 173–74.

60. Jiang Jieshi, "Hezuo xunlian zhi yiyi yu mubiao" (Dec. 1, 1932), in *Xianzongtong Jiang Gong sixiang yanlun zhongji,* vol. 10, edited by Qing Xiaoyi (Taibei: Zhongguo Guomindang Zhongyang weiyuanhui tangshi weiyuanhui: Zhongyang wenwu gongyingshe jingxiao), 671–76; Jiang Jieshi, "Zhengli tudi shi women guoji misheng yige shengsi guanjian" (Nov. 15, 1932), in *Xianzongtong Jiang Gong sixiang*

yanlun zhongji, vol. 10, 666–70; Lai Jiancheng, *Jindai Zhongguo de hezuo jingji yundong* (Taibei: Daxue lianshe chuban, 1988), chapter 4; Zhang Li, "Jiangxi noncun fuwu shiye 1934–1945," in *Kangzhan jianguoshi yanjiu Taohui wenji 1937–1945* (Taibei: Zhongyang yanjiuyuan jindaishi yanjiusuo, 1981).

61. Jiang Jieshi, "Chinese Economic Theory," 254.

62. Wang Jingwei, *China's Problems and Their Solution,* 38.

63. In 1931 Chen Guangfu established a joint Sino-British venture, the Baofeng Insurance Firm. See Yao Songling, *Chen Guangfu de yisheng* (Taibei: Zhuanji wenxue chubanshe, 1984), 47–49; Yuan Xijian, "Chen Guangfu de yisheng," *Wenshi ziliao xuanji* 30 (1980): 64–78; Tong Changji, "Chen Guangfu yu Shanghai yinhang," *Wenshi ziliao xuanji* 80 (1980): 138–49; Xu Youchun, *Minguo renwu dacidian,* 1020.

64. Yao Songling, *Chen Guangfu de yisheng,* 40–41; Yuan Xijian, "Chen Guangfu de yisheng," 64–78.

65. Chen Guangfu, "Wuguo jingji gaizao de genben wenti," *Jingji xuekan* 4, no. 4 (Dec. 1933): 118.

66. Ibid.," 118, 117.

67. Ibid., 117.

68. Ibid., 117.

69. Giuseppe Tassinari and Eduardo Cope, *Fascist Economy* (Rome: "Laboremus," 1937), 90.

70. Ibid., 90–91.

71. Vaudagna, "Structural Change in Fascist Italy," 194; Tassinari and Cope, *Fascist Economy,* 91–92.

Chapter Three

1. Zhang Pengyuan and Shen Huaiyu, eds., *Guomin zhengfu zhiguan nianbiao (1925–1949),* vol. 1, *Shiliao Zongshu* (Taibei: Academia Sinica, Modern History Institute, 1987).

2. Wang Jingwei, *China's Problems and Their Solution,* 43.

3. Chen Gongbo, *Sinian congzhenglu,* 57–59.

4. Coble, *Shanghai Capitalists,* 48; Marie-Claire Bergère, *The Golden Age of the Chinese Bourgeoisie, 1911–1937* (Cambridge: Cambridge University Press, 1989), 274. Bergère quotes Jean Monnet, a prominent French businessman and reformer, "It was easy for me to deal with T. V. Soong [Song Ziwen], whose culture was European," from Y. C. Wang, *Chinese Intellectuals and the West.*

5. Wu Jingping, *Song Ziwen pingzhuan* (Fuzhou: Fujian renmin chubanshe, 1992), 69–70.

6. Ibid.

7. The term *trasformismo* (transformism) is used in the context of Italian modern history to describe a system in which political leaders act on the basis of personal contacts and agreements, thus generating a network of clients. This leads to a pragmatic approach to politics that gives political leaders the freedom to change alliances regardless of ideological stands. That is, *trasformismo* refers to the ability to change political color each time opportunities for strategic alliances present themselves (Sarti, *Fascism and the Industrial Leadership in Italy,* 140).

8. Wu Jingping, *Song Ziwen pingzhuan,* 14–20.

9. In 1925 Song had begun unifying Guangdong tax revenue organizations,

bringing all of them under the Ministry of Finance. He hoped to make the administration more efficient, fight malpractice, and control military expenses. See ibid.

10. Quanguo jingji huiyi mishuchu, *Quanguo jingji huiyi zhuankan,* 8.

11. The 1935 reform eliminated the local currencies that were still circulating. Especially during the years of political division following the fall of the imperial system in 1911, local warlords had started issuing their own currencies. This added to the already-fragmented nature of China's monetary situation. For a detailed explanation of currency reform in 1930s China, see Arthur N. Young, *China's Nation Building Effort, 1927–1937: The Financial and Economic Papers* (Stanford, CA: Hoover Institution Press, 1971), 163, 237–38.

12. Pomeranz, *Making of a Hinterland,* 31, 49, 66.

13. Wu Jingping, *Song Ziwen pingzhuan,* 116, 120.

14. Quanguo jingji huiyi mishuchu, ed., *Quanguo jingji huiyi zhuankan.*

15. Coble, *Shanghai Capitalists,* 32–37.

16. Quanguo jingji huiyi mishuchu, ed., *Quanguo jingji huiyi zhuankan,* 7.

17. Exerting and maintaining control over government expenditures would necessitate the creation of a central bank and a central mint and elimination of the tael. See ibid.

18. Wu Jingping, *Song Ziwen pingzhuan,* 78. Song also stated the same point in the official call for the National Economic Conference. See Quanguo jingji huiyi mishuchu, ed., *Quanguo jingji huiyi zhuankan,* 7.

19. Quanguo jingji huiyi mishuchu, ed., *Quanguo jingji huiyi zhuankan,* 23–25; Coble, *Shanghai Capitalists,* 49; Yu Youchun, *Minguo renwu dacidian,* 721.

20. Yao-jun, "Minsheng zhuyi yu caizheng zhuyi," *Xiandao yuekan,* Aug. 15, 1928, as quoted in Coble, *Shanghai Capitalists,* 58.

21. Quanguo jingji huiyi mishuchu, ed., *Quanguo jingji huiyi zhuankan;* Coble, *Shanghai Capitalists,* 49–54. Before participating in the conference, bankers and industrialists held a preparatory meeting where they decided on the position they were going to take vis-à-vis Nanjing.

22. Quanguo jingji huiyi mishuchu, ed., *Quanguo jingji huiyi zhuankan;* Coble, *Shanghai Capitalists,* 50.

23. Quanguo jingji huiyi mishuchu, ed., *Quanguo jingji huiyi zhuankan,* 18.

24. Yao-jun, "Minsheng zhuyi caizheng zhuyi," *Xiandao yuekan,* Aug. 15, 1928, as quoted in Coble, *Shanghai Capitalists,* 58.

25. Coble, *Shanghai Capitalists,* 53.

26. The same fate was also suffered by the Central Financial Reorganization Committee, created on September 2, 1928. This committee also remained mostly inactive. See ibid.; Wu Jingping, *Song Ziwen pingzhuan,* 82–90. Song was also unable to make any significant progress with his demobilization plan, which met with strong opposition both in Beijing, where he met with generals soon after the National Financial Conference, and at the National Military Demobilization Conference in January 1929. Under pressure from strong lobbying by the Shanghai capitalists, the latter conference accepted Song's proposals in principle, but they were never really implemented. Local militarists saw Song's plan of financial unification as a means of curbing their military and economic power bases.

27. Wu Jingping, *Song Ziwen pingzhuan,* 97.

28. Ibid., 96–97.

29. Song Ziwen, *Annual Report,* in *The China Year Book* (Shanghai: North-China

Daily News and Herlad Ltd., 1931), 332–43; Arthur Young, *China's Nation Building Effort,* 291–92.

30. Arthur Young, *China's Nation Building Effort,* 342–43.

31. See Song's telegram to the secretary of the League of Nations announcing that the Chinese government, planning to initiate technical cooperation with the League, had decided to create a National Economic Council: GMDPHC 443/7(2). See also *Zhongyang ribao,* Apr. 29, 1931; Opening Address Delivered at the First Meeting on November Fifteenth in the Twentieth Year of the Republic of China, NSHA 44/589; *Quanguo Jingji Weiyuanhui Jiyao,* Jan. 1933, NSHA 44(2)213.

32. Although Arthur Young, at the time the American financial adviser in Nanjing, wrote that Song seemed to fear that cooperation with the League could bring excessive foreign interference in Chinese affairs, it seems more likely that Song actually was eager to start the new program (Young, *China's Nation Building Effort,* 193).

33. Satoshi Kawai, "Zengoku keizai iinkai no naritachi to sono kaiso o nuguru hichi kōsatsu," *Tōyōshi kenkyū* 40, no. 4 (Mar. 1982): 119–56; *Quanguo gongshang huiyi huibian,* edited by Shiyebu shangyesi (Nanjing: Shiyebu shangyesi, 1931).

34. Sun Yat-sen, "Minsheng zhuyi," 838.

35. China National Flood Relief Commission, *Report of the National Flood Relief Commission, 1931–1932* (Shanghai: Commercial Press 1933), 15–16.

36. *Quanguo jingji weiyuanhui zuzhi tiaoli* and *Quanguo jingji weiyuanhui diyici weiyuan huiyi weiyuanzhang baogaoshu,* NSHA 44(2)213.

37. *Dagongbao,* Apr. 18, 1931; *Quanguo jingji weiyuanhui zuzhi tiaoli,* NSHA 44(2)213.

38. *Quanguo jingji weiyuanhui baogao,* Jan. 1934, NSHA 44(2)69; *Quanguo jingji weiyuanhui huiyi jiyao,* NSHA 44(2)213; Tian Hongmao, *Government and Politics in Kuomintang China,* 141. For more on the Blue Shirts, see chapter 4 below.

39. Opening Address, NSHA 44/589; *Dagongbao,* Apr. 18, 1931; *Quanguo jingji weiyuanhui zuzhi tiaoli,* NSHA 44(2)213.

40. *Quanguo jingji weiyuanhui huiyi jiyao,* 1933, NSHA 44(2)213; Opening Address, NSHA 44/589.

41. *Quanguo jingji weiyuanhui huiyi jiyao,* NSHA 44(2)213; *Quanguo jingji weiyuanhui chengli jiyao,* NSHA 44(2)213; *Quanguo jingji weiyuanhui Congkan diqizhong,* Feb. 1934, NSHA 44(2)213; Zhang Pengyuan and Shen Huaiyuy, eds., *Guomin zhengfu zhiguan nianbiao (1925–1949).*

42. *Quanguo jingji weiyuanhui huiyi jiyao,* NSHA 44(2)213; NEC Preparatory Office to the Administrative Yuan, Aug. 30, 1931, NSHA 44/516.

43. The Executive Yuan chairman and vice-chairman did not hold the chairmanship and vice-chairmanship of the NEC. See rules 2 and 4 of *Xiuzheng quanguo jingji weiyuanhui zhuzhi tiaoli* and "regulations for committees," in *Quanguo jingji weiyuanhui chengli jiyao,* Feb. 1934, NSHA 44(2)213. The new phase of the NEC was also characterized by close collaboration with the Ministry of Industry, headed by Chen Gongbo, the previous Reorganization leader and Wang Jingwei's right hand. The members of the Standing Committee were, as all other members, to be selected by the government, as before.

44. *Quanguo jingji weiyuanhui chengli jiyao,* Feb. 1934, NSHA 44(2)213; Oct. 9, 1993, order for the reorganization of the new NEC on petition from Wang, Sun, and Song, NSHA 44/2426. Wang, Song, and Sun were selected as standing members, and the

organization changed from chairmanship to standing committee. This was the result of the first meeting (Oct. 4) between Wang, Song, and Sun (Oct. 4, 1933, NSHA 44/2426). Records regarding the process that led to the reorganization of the NEC are contradictory and unclear, as are most of the documents left behind by the Nanjing government. In this case the problem rests in the sequence of events. While the regulations appear to be published in September 1931, the approval for the reorganization of the NEC is dated October 4, 1933 (NSHA 44/2426).

45. *Shenbao,* Apr. 26, 1932.

46. Members by office were Huang Shaohong (minister of internal affairs), Gu Mengyu (minister of railways), Zhu Jiahua (minister of communications), Chen Gongbo (minister of industry), Wang Shijie (minister of education), and Zhang Renjie (chairman of the National Reconstruction Commission). Other members were Cai Yuanpei and Shao Yuanchong (who had sided with Jiang's opposition during the political crisis of 1931–32), Wang Kemin, Chen Bozhuang, Chu Minyi, Ye Gongchuo, Yang Ruiliu, and Chen Goufu.

47. Shi Liangcai was the owner of the Shanghai newspaper *Shenbao.*

48. "Quangguo jingji weiyuanhui ershisan nianfen shiye jinxing jihua ji jingfei zhi zhibei," attached to the minutes of the third meeting of the Standing Committee of the NEC, 1934, NSHA 44(2)216; Zhang Pengyuan and Shen Huaiyu, *Guomin zhengfu zhiguan nianbiao.*

49. In addition to Wang at the head of the Executive Yuan and Chen Gongbo at the Ministry of Industry, other members of the previous Reorganization Group held important positions. Gu Mengyu was appointed minister of railways; Chen Shuren, chairman of the Overseas Chinese Affairs Commission; Guo Chuntao, vice-minister of industry; Zeng Zhongmiu, vice-minister of railways; Gan Naiguang, vice-minister of internal affairs; Chen Mingshu, who was also the commander of the Nineteenth Route Army, minister of communications. See Zhang Pengyuan and Shen Huaiyu, eds., *Guomin zhengfu zhiguan nianbiao (1925–1949).* Luo Wengan, who strongly supported Song's anti-Japanese reform plan, was nominated minister of foreign affairs. See Luo Dunwei, *Wushinian huiyilu* (Taibei: Zhongguo wenhua gongyingshe, 1952), 71.

50. Song Ziwen, "Mianmai Jiekuan Jingguo ji banli qingxing baogao," in *Quanguo Jingji Weiyuanhui Huiyi Jiyao,* 7, Mar. 1934, NSHA 44(2)213.

51. Coble, *Shanghai Capitalists,* 126, 137.

52. Song invited Jean Monnet to be the international consortium's chairman. He also invited Thomas W. Lamont, of the J. P. Morgan Company, to head the American group and Sir Charles Addis, of the Hong Kong and Shanghai Banking Corporation, to head the British group. See Coble, *Shanghai Capitalists,* 126–27. In 1920–21 Lamont had been involved in famine relief work for the China International Famine Relief Commission. See Andrew Nathan, *A History of the China International Famine Relief Commission* (Cambridge, MA: Harvard University Press, 1965), 6.

53. Richard Bush, *The Politics of Cotton Textiles in Kuomintang China, 1927–1937* (New York: Garland Publishing, 1982), 213; Coble, *Shanghai Capitalists,* 127; minutes of the third meeting of the NEC's Standing Committee, 1933, NSHA 44(2)216.

54. Coble, *Shanghai Capitalists,* 126; Bush, *Politics of Cotton Textiles,* 216; minutes of the third meeting of the NEC's Standing Committee, NSHA 44(2)216.

55. First meeting of the NEC Standing Committee, NSHA 44/2426.

56. Chen Gongbo, "Xu simian shiye jihua chugao," in *Sinian congzhenglu,* 122–23. Originally published in *Minzu zazhi,* Aug. 1933.

57. The NEC 1934 budget devoted only a relatively small fraction of its resources to industrial development. Of the total 30,000,000 yuan, the budget committed the bulk to road construction (10,000,000 yuan), water navigation (6,000,000 yuan), water conservation (3,700,000 yuan), and public health (1,290,000 yuan). Agriculture was allocated only 710,000 yuan, the cotton industry 1,500,000 yuan, and the silk industry 1,000,000 yuan. The budget also assigned 2,100,000 yuan to construction in Xibei Province, 1,900,000 yuan to construction in Jiangxi Province, 500,000 yuan to geological surveys, and 1,300,000 yuan equally divided between "regular expenses and technological cooperation expenses" and "budget expenses." See NEC, Shiye feizhi peibiao, in "Quanguo jingweiyuanhui ershisan nianfen shiye jinxing jihua ji jingfei," attached to the minutes of the third meeting of the NEC Standing Committee, 1934, NSHA 44(2)216. This budget distribution reflected previous commitments reached with the League of Nations Technical Mission to China, which concerned itself with road construction and public health.

58. "Quanguo jingweiyuanhui ershisan nianfen shiye jinxing jihua ji jingfei," attached to the minutes of the third meeting of the NEC Standing Committee, 1934, NSHA 44(2)216.

59. Minutes of the third meeting of the NEC's Standing Committee, NSHA 44(2)216.

60. *Quanguo jingji weiyanhui chenli jiyao,* 3, Feb. 1934, NSHA 44(2)213. No record is left of the first two meetings held by the three leaders. From a later publication we know that at the first meeting Song, Sun, and Wang, in addition to creating the Cotton Control Commission, reorganized the Secretariat and appointed Qin Fen as its secretary. On November 18, 1933, at the second meeting, they drafted new regulations for the Public Road Commission, the Water Conservancy Commission, the Public Health Commission, the Education Commission, and the Rural Reconstruction Commission.

61. "Quangguo jingji weiyuanhui ershisan nianfen shiye jinxing jihua ji jingfei zhi zhibei," attached to the minutes of the third meeting of the Standing Committee of the NEC, 1934, NSHA 44(2)216.

Chapter Four

1. Chen Gongbo, "Tongzhi jingji yu zuzhi," 174–79.

2. "Quanguo jingji weiyuanhui mianye tongzhi weiyuanhui zanxhing zuzhi tiaoli," in *Quanguo jingji weiyuanhui chengli jiyao,* 34, NSHA 44(2)213.

3. For Song Ziwen's trip to Washington, see Bush, *Politics of Cotton Textiles,* 226; Wu Jingping, *Song Ziwen sixiang yanjiu* (Fuzhou: Fujian renmin chubanshe, 1998), 186–97.

4. Chen Gongbo, *Sinian congzhenglu,* 46–47; Wang Shuhuai, "Mianye tongzhi weiyuanhui de gongzuo chengxiao 1933–1937," in *Kangzhanqian shinina guojia jiansheshi yanjiuhui wenji* (Taibei: Zhongyang yanjiuyuan jindaishi yanjiusuo, 1984).

5. Bush, *Politics of Cotton Textiles,* 226.

6. Song Ziwen, "Weitongzhi mianye gaorenshu," as quoted in Wu Jingping, *Song Ziwen sixiang yanjiu,* 47.

7. Song Ziwen, *Guomin zhoubao,* Oct. 9, 1933, as quoted in Wu Jingping, *Song Ziwen sixiang yanjiu,* 47.

8. The following discussion of the corporativist model is largely taken from Jonathan Unger and Anita Chan, "China, Corporatism, and the East Asian Model," *Australian Journal of Chinese Affairs* 33 (Jan. 1995): 29–53.

9. Ibid., 30, 32.

10. Gregory J. Kasza, *The Conscription Society: Administered Mass Organization* (New Haven, CT: Yale University Press, 1995), 1–2, 19.

11. Unger and Chan, "China, Corporatism and the East Asian Model," 32.

12. Ibid.

13. Joseph Fewsmith, *Party, State, and Local Elites in Republican China: Merchant Organizations and Politics in Shanghai, 1890–1930* (Honolulu: University of Hawaii Press, 1985), 159–66.

14. Kasza, *Conscription Society,* 103.

15. Ibid., 103–4.

16. Philippe Schmitter, "Still the Century of Corporatism?" *Review of Politics* 36, no. 1 (Jan. 1974): 85–131; Unger and Chan, "China, Corporatism and the East Asian Model," 33.

17. "Economic Nationalism," report to the Third Congress of the Nationalist Association (Milan, May 16–18, 1914) presented by the Social Commission (A. Rocco, president; E. Corradini; L. De Prosperi; F. Carli, G. Alessandretti; U. Aillaud), 52–57, as quoted in Carlo Vallauri, *Le radici del corporativismo* (Milan: Bulzoni, 1971), 56.

18. Vallauri, *Radici del corporativismo,* 169–70.

19. Ugo Spirito, *Il corporativismo* (Florence: Sansoni, 1970), 460. A third form of corporativism, rural corporativism (*corporativismo ruralista*), was based on anti-industrialization ideas promoted by Antonio Serpieri, *Dizionario di Politica* (Turin: UTET, 1990).

20. Spirito, *Corporativismo,* 461.

21. Sarti, *Fascism and the Industrial Leadership in Italy,* 72. Representatives of the industrialists met with those of the Fascist government in Vidoni Palace. After a tense confrontation, the industrialists succeeded in imposing their own terms on the regulations of corporations. For the relationship between the Fascist state and the Italian industrialists, see also Piero Melograni, *Gli industriali e Mussolini* (Milan: Longanesi and Co., 1971).

22. Fewsmith, *Party, State, and Local Elites,* 159–66 and chapter 7; Coble, *Shanghai Capitalists,* especially chapters 2, 7–8. Coble does not stress the corporativist nature of Jiang's plan for controlling Shanghai business, but he accurately describes the process followed by the Nanjing government, under Jiang's leadership, to bring it under its strict control.

23. Sun Yat-sen, "Minsheng zhuyi," 778.

24. Duara, *Rescuing History from the Nation;* Fitzgerald, *Awakening China.* Fujian, Hunan, and Guizhou Provinces had remained semiautonomous after the establishment of the Nanjing government in 1927. Fujian had become the center of the Federalist movement. Jiang Jieshi successfully eliminated this pocket of resistance in late 1935 during his pursuit of the Communists on the Long March. At this time the Nationalist army entered Fujian and established its political control over the region.

25. Eastman, *Abortive Revolution,* 42, 82. The Blue Shirts was a GMD military-style organization established in the early 1930s by military officers who were former students of Jiang Jieshi at the Huangpu Military Academy. The organization thus enjoyed Jiang's political and financial support. The Blue Shirts' ideology was strongly influenced by European fascism. This ideological similarity and their function as enforcers of political order from outside the regular police and military forces have

invited inevitable comparisons with the Italian Black Shirts and German Brown Shirts. The Blue Shirts promoted the New Life Movement and were inspired by Jiang's vision of an orderly society devoid of class conflict and characterized by military-like discipline and regimentation. In addition, the Blue Shirts were in charge of the Military Bureau of Investigation and Statistics, a secret police force under Jiang's leadership. See ibid., chapter 3.

26. Anderson, *Imagined Communities.*

27. Wang Jingwei, "Proposal for Economic and Financial Policies," in *Chinese National Revolution: Essays and Documents by Wang Jingwei and Others,* edited by T'ang Leang-li (Beijing: United Press, 1930), 118.

28. Wang Jingwei, *China's Problems and Their Solution,* 30.

29. Wang Jingwei, "Proposal for Economic and Financial Policies," 118.

30. Chen Gongbo, *Zhongguo Guomindang suo daibiaode shi shenme?* 3d ed. (Shanghai: Fudan shudian, 1928); So, *Kuomintang Left,* 72–74.

31. Wang Jingwei, "Jianshe," 277. On "bureaucratic capitalism," see chapter 6.

32. For the Chinese bureaucracy's ability to derail reforms launched by the central government during the Qing dynasty, see Madeleine Zelin, *The Magistrate's Tael: Rationalizing Fiscal Reform in Eighteenth-Century Ch'ing China* (Berkeley and Los Angeles: University of California Press, 1985), especially chapter 6.

33. Wang Jingwei, "Faqi zuzhi guomin jiuguohui tongdian" (Dec. 10, 1931), in *Wang Jingwei wencun* (Shanghai: Qizhi shuju, 1935), 399.

34. Chen Gongbo, "Wei shiye jihua gao guoren," 159.

35. Chen Gongbo, "Tongzhi jingji yu zuzhi," 178–79, 19–20.

36. Chen Gongbo, "Wei shiye jihua gao guoren," 160.

37. Chen Gongbo, "Zhongguo shiye de ziben he zhishu wenti," in *Sinian congzhenglu,* 161. Originally published in *Minzu zazhi* 2, no. 11 (Dec. 1934).

38. Chen Gongbo, *Sinian congzhenglu,* 42–43.

39. Ibid., 49.

40. Ibid., 49–50.

41. Ibid., 49.

42. Ibid., 37, 53; Chen Gongbo, "Tongzhi jingji de xianjue wenti," in *Sinian congzhenglu,* 180. Originally published in *Minzu zazhi,* May 1934.

43. Coble, *Shanghai Capitalists,* 23–25.

44. Bell, "From Compradore to County Magnate," 123–24; Bell, *One Industry, Two Chinas,* 43–45.

45. Bell, *One Industry, Two Chinas,* e.g., 6.

46. Ibid., 154, 170, 252.

47. Bell, "From Comprador to County Magnate," 139.

48. Bell, *One Industry, Two Chinas,* especially chapter 2.

49. Ibid., 156.

50. Chen Gongbo, "Ziji de piping," in *Sinian congzhenglu,* especially 5. In this piece of self-criticism Chen repeatedly complained about the people's mistrust of this four-year industrial plan, the Ministry of Industry's lack of funds, and his inability to mobilize the people. He especially complained that the nationalist spirit he had invoked at a moment of national crisis had not succeeded in mobilizing the people in support of his plan, ultimately making its realization impossible.

51. Bell, "From Comprador to County Magnate," 138–39; Bell, *One Industry, Two Chinas,* 13, 154.

52. Bell, *One Industry, Two Chinas,* 13 and chapter 8. The attempt of private business to integrate itself into the new national body politic was particularly characteristic of the Jiangnan area elite, studied by Bell, since they fell more directly under the control of Nanjing. As the work of Rana Mitter on Manchuria and of Kenneth Pomeranz on Shangdong suggests, more peripheral regions might have continued to rely on strong local authorities who were not compelled to comply with the Nationalist centralizing drive. See Mitter, *Manchurian Myth;* Pomeranz, *Making of a Hinterland.*

53. Bell, *One Industry, Two Chinas,* 187.

54. Zhang Pengyuan and Shen Huaiyu, *Guomin zhengfu zhiguan nianbiao;* Zhong, *Zhongguo jindai minzu qiyejia jingji sixiang,* 140.

55. Yao Songling, *Chen Guangfu de yisheng,* 40–41.

56. Coble, *Shanghai Capitalists,* 30.

57. Ibid., chapter 2.

58. Yao Songling, *Chen Guangfu de yisheng,* 47–49; Xu Youchun, *Minguo renwu dacidian,* 1020.

59. Cheng Linsun, *Banking in Modern China: Entrepreneurs, Professional Managers and the Development of Chinese Banks, 1897–1937* (Cambridge: Cambridge University Press, 2003), 211–14.

60. Chen Guangfu, *Chen Guangfu xiansheng de yanlunji* (Shanghai: Shanghai Savings and Commercial Bank, 1949), 505.

61. Chen Guangfu, "Jingji tongzhi de A B C," *Haiguang yuekan,* June 1933, in *Chen Guangfu xiansheng de yanlunji,* 133.

62. Ibid., 133–34.

63. Ibid., 134.

64. Ron Chernow, *Titan: The Life of John D. Rockefeller, Sr.* (New York: Random House, 1998), 481–82.

65. Miriam Beard, *A History of the Business Man* (New York: Macmillan, 1938), 269; Avraham Barki, *Nazi Economics: Ideology, Theory, and Policy* (New Haven, CT: Yale University Press, 1990), 91–92.

66. Barki, *Nazi Economics,* especially chapter 3. For a discussion of Nazi control over major business and banking groups and of the Nazi war economy, see R. J. Overy, *Goering, the "Iron Man"* (London and Boston: Routledge and Kegan Paul, 1984), chapter 3.

67. Chen Guangfu, "Ziben zhuyi de yitiao xinchulu," *Haiguang yuekan,* Nov. 1933, in *Chen Guangfu xiansheng de yanlunji,* 155. I have been unable to locate the book quoted by Chen Guangfu in this article. I am assuming that Chen is referring to Malcolm Forbes Sr. since he was the most prominent member of the family at the time Chen wrote. Malcolm Forbes Jr. did not take over the reins of the family business until 1954.

68. Bush, *Politics of Cotton Textiles,* 228.

69. GMDPHC 443/7(9); *Shenbao,* Feb. 19, 1934, 9.

70. For more information on Tang Xinhai, see Parks M. Coble, "Chinese Capitalists and the Japanese: Collaboration and Resistance in the Shanghai Area, 1937–45," in *Wartime Shanghai,* edited by Wen-hsin Yeh (New York: Routledge, 1998), 72.

71. Wu Jingping, *Song Ziwen pingzhuan,* 120–21.

72. Xu Youchun, *Minguo renwu dacidian*, 258, 1257, 1282, 1562.

73. Wu Jingping, *Song Ziwen pingzhuan*, 475, 477.

74. *Quanguo jingji weiyuanhui chengli jiyao*, NSHA 44(2)213; Zhang Pengyuan and Shen Huaiyu, *Guomin zhengfu zhiguan nianbiao*, 120–21.

75. Rong Zongjing was also director of the Cotton Mill Owners Association and had played an important role in negotiating the American cotton and wheat loan.

76. Zhang Pengyuan and Shen Huaiyu, *Minguo zhengfu zhiguang nianbiao;* Xu Youchun, *Minguo renwu dacidian*, 378.

77. *Quanguo jingji weiyuanhui zhiyuanlu* (Nanjing: 1937), NSHA 44(2)72; Bush, *Politics of Cotton Textiles*, 228.

78. Wu Xingya was also director of the Social Division of the Shanghai GMD branch; see Xu Youchun, *Minguo renwu dacidian*, 373.

79. Zhang Pengyuan and Shen Huaiyu, *Guomin zhengfu zhiguan nianbiao*, 120–21; Bush, *Politics of Cotton Textiles*, 228. Bush places Lin Yinfu among the government representatives.

80. Xu Youchun, *Minguo renwu dacidian*, 373.

81. Brian Martin, "The Green Gang and the Guomindang Polity in Shanghai, 1927–1937," *Papers on Far Eastern History* 42 (1990): 75; Brian Martin, *The Shanghai Green Gang: Politics and Organized Crime, 1919–1937* (Berkeley and Los Angeles: University of California Press, 1996), 79–82, 114; Frederic E. Wakeman Jr., *Policing Shanghai, 1927–1937* (Berkeley and Los Angeles: University of California Press, 1995), 126.

82. One of these organizations was the Shanghai Citizens Maintenance Association, which had provided administrative, financial, and troop-support functions during the period of conflict instead of the GMD. See Martin, "The Green Gang and the Guomindang Polity in Shanghai," 66. For a list of positions held by Du in Shanghai municipal administration and business organizations, see Xu Youchun, *Minguo renwu dacidian*, 373.

83. Elisabeth Perry, *Shanghai on Strike* (Stanford, CA: Stanford University Press, 1993), 98–99.

84. Coble, *Shanghai Capitalists;* Bergère, *Golden Age of the Chinese Bourgeoisie*.

85. Fewsmith, *Party, State, and Local Elites*, 188–89.

86. Jürgen Habermas, *The Structural Transformation of the Public Sphere: An Inquiry into a Category of Bourgeois Society* (Cambridge, MA: MIT Press, 1991.

87. William Rowe, *Hankou: Commerce and Society in a Chinese City, 1796–1889* (Stanford, CA: Stanford University Press, 1984); William Rowe, *Hankou: Conflict and Community in a Chinese City, 1796–1895* (Stanford, CA: Stanford University Press, 1989); Mary Backus Rankin, *Elite Activism and Political Transformation in China: Zhejiang Province, 1865–1911* (Stanford, CA: Stanford University Press, 1986); David Strand, *Rickshaw Beijing: City People and Politics in the 1920s* (Berkeley and Los Angeles: University of California Press, 1989).

88. Frederic E. Wakeman Jr., "The Civil Society and Public Sphere Debate: Western Reflections on Chinese Politics," *Modern China* 19, no. 2 (Apr. 1993): 108–38.

89. Philip C. C. Huang, "Public Sphere/Civil Society in China? The Third Realm between State and Society," *Modern China* 19, no. 2 (1993): 229, 230.

90. Bush, *Politics of Cotton Textiles*, 296–97.

91. See, for example, the discussion of the 1989 workers' strikes in Elizabeth Perry, "Contradictions under Socialism: Shanghai's Strike Wave of 1957," in *Challenging the*

Mandate of Heaven: Social Protest and State Power in China, by Elizabeth Perry (Armonk, NY: M. E. Sharpe, 2002).

92. See the discussion of "corporatism Chinese style" in Unger and Chan, "China, Corporatism, and the East Asian Model," 37ff.; Bruce J. Dickson, *Red Capitalists in China: The Party, Private Entrepreneurs, and Prospects for Political Change* (Cambridge: Cambridge University Press, 2003), 23–26, 59–69.

Chapter Five

1. Pomeranz, *Making of a Hinterland,* chapter 2.

2. The NEC and the CCC continued to function, although in a reduced capacity, for a few years after the end of the Wang-Jiang coalition. Finally, in 1937, the NEC was closed down and all its functions were transferred to the Ministry of Industry.

3. Philip Huang, *The Peasant Family and Rural Development in the Yangzi Delta, 1350–1988* (Stanford, Calif.: Stanford University Press, 1990), especially chapter 3.

4. "Quanguo jingji weiyuanhui mianye tongzhi weiyuanhui shiye jihua," Jan.–Feb. 1934, NSHA 44(2)216.

5. Peter Duus, "Zaikabō: Japanese Cotton Mills in China, 1895–1937," in *The Japanese Informal Empire in China, 1895–1937,* edited by Peter Duus, Ramon Hawley Myers, and Mark R. Peattie (Princeton, NJ: Princeton University Press, 1989), 65–66; Kuwahara Tetsuya, "The Japanese Cotton Spinners' Direct Investments into China before the Second World War," in *Historical Studies in International Corporate Business,* edited by Alice Teichova, Maurice Lévy-Leboyer, and Helga Nussbaum (Cambridge: Cambridge University Press, 1989), 151–62. This view is challenged by Thomas Rawski, who argues that Chinese cotton mills and products were very competitive vis-à-vis the foreign competition (*Economic Growth in Prewar China,* 7ff.).

6. Duus, "Zaikabō," 66.

7. M. P. Gandhi, *How to Compete with Foreign Cloth: A Study of the Position of Hand-Spinning, Hand-Weaving, and Cotton Mills in the Economics of Cloth-Production in India* (Calcutta: G. N. Mitra, of the Book Company, 1931).

8. Benito Mussolini, speech to the Assemblea dell corporazioni, Mar. 1936 (http://www.fascismoeliberta.net/kf/Discorso23marzo1936.htm). See also Giuseppe Barone, "Dall'agricoltura all'industria: Il cotone nazionale tra le due guerre," *Meridiana* 3, no. 33 (1998): 13–35.

9. Chen Gongbo, "Wei shiye jihua gao guoren," 160.

10. Song Ziwen, *Guomin zhoubao,* 10, no. 4 (Oct. 9, 1933), as quoted in Wu Jingping, *Song Ziwen sixiang yanjiu,* 47.

11. Fang Xianting, "Rural Weaving and the Merchant Employers in a North China District: I," *Nankai Social and Economic Quarterly* 8, no. 1 (Apr. 1935): 75–76.

12. Fang Xianting, "The Growth and Decline of Rural Industrial Enterprise in North China," *Nankai Social and Economic Quarterly* 8, nos. 3–4 (1935–36): 691–92.

13. Zhong Xiangcai, *Zhongguo jindai minzu qiyejia jingji sixiang,* 140.

14. "Quanguo jingji weiyuanhui mianye tongzhi weiyuanhui shiye jihua," Jan.–Feb. 1934, NSHA 44(2)216.

15. Chen Gongbo, "Xu sinian shiye jihua chugao," in *Sinian congzhenglu,* 125–26, and *Sinian congzhenglu,* 46–47.

16. Ibid.

17. "Quanguo jingji weiyuanhui mianye tongzhi weiyuanhui shiye jihua," Jan.–Feb. 1934, NSHA 44(2)216. See also "Quangguo jingji weiyuanhui ershisan nianfen shiye jinxing jihua ji jingfei zhi zhibei," p. 5, 1934, NSHA 44/1679.

18. "Quanguo jingji weiyuanhui mianye tongzhi weiyuanhui shiye jihua," Jan.–Feb. 1934, NSHA 44(2)216.

19. Ibid.

20. Richard A. Kraus, *Cotton and Cotton Goods in China, 1918–1936* (New York: Garland Publishing, 1986), table II.14 (facing p. 52) and p. 52.

21. Hayford, *To the People*, 166–73.

22. For a detailed discussion of the work of the CIFRC, see Nathan, *History of the China International Famine Relief Commission*.

23. J. B. Tayler, CIFRC Pamphlet B-10, as quoted in ibid., 28.

24. Tayler's report also included a study of the Indian cooperative movement based on the Raiffeisen model. This movement began in India in 1904 and had spread widely. See Nathan, *History of the China International Famine Relief Commission*, 29.

25. Wang Shuhuai, "Mianye tongzhi weiyuanhui de gongzuo chengxiao 1933–37," 741–42.

26. Max Brauer and Gaines Liu, *Rural Conditions and Co-operative Movement in Central Shensi* (National Economic Council, National Government of the Republic of China, 1934), 98.

27. Nathan, *History of the China International Famine Relief Commission*, 36–37.

28. Bush, *Politics of Cotton Textiles*, 213; Chen Shuzhu, "Xiandai Zhonghua liusheng zhi nongye jinrong 1927–1937" (M.A. thesis, Taiwan University, 1984), 3.

29. Lai, *Jingdai zhongguo hezuo jingji yundong*, 107–9.

30. Quanguo jingji weiyuanhui mianye tongzhi weiyuanhui, *Quanguo jingji weiyuanhui mianye tongzhi weiyuanhui sannianlai gongzuo baogao* (Shanghai: Quanguo jingji weiyuanhui mianye tongzhi weiyuanhui, 1937), 11. See also Wang Shuhuai, "Mianye tongzhi weiyuanhui de gongzuo chengxiao 1933–37," 743.

31. Wang Shuhuai, "Mianye tongzhi weiyuanhui de gongzuo chengxiao 1933–37," 743–44.

32. Brauer and Liu, *Rural Conditions and Co-operative Movement in Central Shensi*, 96. Other banks invested much smaller amounts: Shaanxi Provincial Bank, 19,000 yuan; Farmers Bank, 5,000 yuan; University of Nanjing, 3,000 yuan; and CIFRC, 2,100 yuan. See ibid.

33. Quanguo jingji weiyuanhui mianye tongzhi weiyuanhui, *Quanguo jingji weiyuanhui mianye tongzhi weiyuanhui sannian lai gongzuo baogao*, 11.

34. Albert Feuerwerker, *Economic Trends in the Republic of China, 1912–1949* (Ann Arbor: Center for Chinese Studies, University of Michigan, 1977), p. 64 and table 18.

35. W. K. H. Campbell, report (title missing), 1935, NSHA 44/1716.

36. W. K. H. Campbell, "Report on Co-operation in Shensi," June–July 1936, NSHA 44/1716.

37. W. K. H. Campbell, "Rural Cooperation," NSHA 44/1716.

38. W. K. H. Campbell, "Report on Co-operation in Shensi," June–July 1936; W. K. H. Campbell, report on Hunan, untitled and undated (early 1936?), NSHA 44/1716.

39. W. K. H. Campbell, report on cooperation in Hunan, untitled and undated (end of 1935 or beginning of 1936), NSHA 44/1716.

40. Xu Zhongdi, "Shaanxi mianhua chanxiao hezuoshe zhi guoqu yu jianglai," *Mianye yuekan* 1, no. 1 (1937): 64–65.

41. Campbell, report on cooperation in Hunan, untitled and undated (early 1936?), NSHA 44/1716.

42. Ibid.

43. W. K. H. Campbell, "Report on Co-operation in Hopei Province," May 1936, p. 13, NSHA 44/1716.

44. Ibid., 13ff.

45. W. K. H. Campbell, "Report on Co-operative Work in China," 1936, p. 33, NSHA 44/1716.

46. CCC work report, no. 8, Apr. 1936, p. 18, NSHA 44(2)230 III.

47. Campbell, report on Hunan, untitled and undated (early 1936?), NSHA 44/1716.

48. Ibid.

49. Nathan, *History of the China International Famine Relief Commission*, 29–30.

50. W. K. H. Campbell, letter to the secretary of the NEC, Qin Fen, May 4, 1936, NSHA 44/1716.

51. Chen Hansheng, *Industrial Capital and Chinese Peasants: A Study of the Livelihood of Chinese Tobacco Cultivators* (New York: Garland Publishing, 1980), 14.

52. Ibid.

53. W. K. H. Campbell, "Some Practical Proposals for the Chinese Co-operatives," *Nankai Social and Economic Quarterly* (Apr. 1937): 100–101.

54. Campbell, "Report on Co-operation in Shensi," June–July 1936, pp. 9–11, NSHA 44/1716.

55. "Quanguo jingji weiyuanhui mianye tongzhi weiyuanhui shiye jihua" (Jan.–Feb. 1934), NSHA 44(2)216.

56. John Fitzgerald, "Warlords, Bullies, and State Building in Nationalist China: The Guangdong Cooperative Movement, 1932–1936," *Modern China* 23, no. 4 (Oct. 1997): 421.

57. Prasenjit Duara, *Culture, Power, and the State: Rural North China, 1900–1942* (Stanford, CA: Stanford University Press, 1988), especially chapter 8 and p. 246.

58. Pomeranz, *Making of a Hinterland*, 101–13.

59. "Quangguo jingji weiyuanhui ershisan nianfen shiye jinxing jihua ji jingfei zhi zhibei," attached to the minutes of the third meeting of the Standing Committee of the NEC, 1934, NSHA 44(2)216.

60. "Quanguo jingji weiyuanhui mianye tongzhi weiyuanhui shiye jihua" (Jan.–Feb. 1934), NSHA 44(2)216; Wang Shuhuai, "Mianye tongzhi weiyuanhui de gongzuo chengxiao 1933–37."

61. "Quanguo jingji weiyuanhui mianye tongzhi weiyuanhui shiye jihua" (Jan.–Feb. 1934), NSHA 44(2)216.

62. "Quanguo jingji weiyuanhui mianye tongzhi weiyuanhui shiye jihua" (Jan.–Feb. 1934), NSHA 44(2)216; "Quangguo jingji weiyuanhui ershisan nianfen shiye jinxing jihua ji jingfei zhi zhibei," 1934, NSHA 44/1679.

63. "Quanguo jingji weiyuanhui mianye tongzhi weiyuanhui shiye jihua" (Jan.–Feb. 1934), NSHA 44(2)216.

64. Brauer and Liu, *Rural Conditions and Co-operative Movement in Central Shensi*, 33–36.

65. "Cotton Cultivation in Shensi," *Chinese Economic Monthly* 3, no. 5 (1926): 200.

66. For a discussion of the role of the local elite in the expansion and improvement of agricultural products for Shanghai industries, see Bell, *One Industry, Two Chinas*. Bell focuses specifically on the silk industry. The picture she draws, however, can easily be extended to cotton, as Kraus's work clearly illustrates (*Cotton and Cotton Goods in China*). See also works describing the lives of Chen Guangfu, Rong Zongjing, and Mu Ouchu and their involvement in cotton improvement: Chen Guangfu, *Chen Guangfu xiansheng de yanlunji*; Shanghai shehui kexue yuanjiuyuan jingjiynajiusuo, ed., *Rongjia qiye shiliao: Mao Xin, Fu Xin, Shen Xinxi tong* (Shanghai: Shanghai renmin chubanshe, 1980); Mu Xiangyue *Ouchu wu shi zi shu* (Shanghai: Shanghai shudian, 1991). For cotton improvement in Hebei, see the work of Fang Xianting published by the Nankai Institute of Economics, including *Cotton Industry and Trade in China*, 2 vols. (Tianjin: Nankai Institute of Economics, 1932); and "Rural Weaving."

67. "Cotton Cultivation in Shensi," 201.

68. Liu Jingshan also claims that he was quite successful in improving public health. Together with Liu Ruiheng he established a Production Assistance School in Xi'an and an Institute for Veterinarian Training and a Serum Manufacturing Institute in Lanzhou. See Liu Jingshan, *Liu Jingshan xiansheng fangwen jilu* (Taibei: Zhongyang yanjiuyuan jindai lishi yanjiusuo, 1987), 99–100.

69. In his memoirs, Liu Jingshan calls the CCC the Cotton Statistical Committee, but he clearly identifies it with the NEC and Chen Guangfu. See ibid., 100.

70. Wang Shuhuai, "Mianye tongzhi weiyuanhui de gongzuo chengxiao 1933–37," 733–34.

71. Kraus, *Cotton and Cotton Goods in China*, 39–40; Pomeranz, *Making of a Hinterland*, 79.

72. Wang Shuhuai, "Mianye tongzhi weiyuanhui de gongzuo chengxiao 1933–37," 738–39.

73. Brauer and Liu, *Rural Conditions and Co-operative Movement in Central Shensi*. In his report Brauer noted that the larger investors in Shaanxi were the Bank of China and the Shanghai Commercial and Savings Bank and that they invested almost exclusively in cooperative societies devoted to cotton cultivation and marketing of cotton. Ibid., 8–9, 11, 98.

74. Wang Shuhuai, "Mianye tongzhi weiyuanhui de gongzuo chengxiao 1933–37," 736. In Henan, the third region on which it concentrated its efforts, the CCC expanded the acreage of land cultivated in higher-quality cotton to 578,345 *mu*. Figures for other regions (Shaanxi, Hubei, Hebei, Gansu) fell sharply (see ibid.).

75. Kraus, *Cotton and Cotton Goods in China*, table VI.1 and p. 42.

76. Wang Shuhuai, "Mianye tongzhi weiyuanhui de gongzuo chengxiao 1933–37," 736; Zou Bingwen, "Miantongzhi mianchan gaijin gongzuo qingkuang," *Mianye yuekan* 1, no. 1 (Jan. 1937): 5; Quanguo jingji weiyuanhui mianye tongzhi weiyuanhui, *Quanguo jingji weiyuanhui mianye tongzhi weiyuanhui sannian lai gongzuo baogao*, 10. Figures for the expansion of acreage in improved cotton in other provinces are 608,760 in Jiangsu, 400,000 in Hebei, 345,533 in Henan, 200,000 in Hubei, 90,000 in Shaanxi, and 4,770 in Gansu (Quanguo jingji weiyuanhui mianye tongzhi weiyuanhui, *Quanguo jingji weiyuanhui mianye tongzhi weiyuanhui sannian lai gongzuo baogao*, 10).

77. Wang Shuhuai, "Mianye tongzhi weiyuanhui de gongzuo chengxiao 1933–37," 739.

78. Kraus, *Cotton and Cotton Goods in China*, 40–42.

79. Wang Shuhuai, "Mianye tongzhi weiyuanhui de gongzuo chengxiao 1933–37," 758.

80. Kraus, *Cotton and Cotton Goods in China,* 40–42.

81. Ibid., 79–94.

82. Ibid., 76.

83. Ibid., table II.14 (facing p. 52), table III.9 (facing p. 76), and pp. 52 and 76; Feuerwerker, *Economic Trends in the Republic of China,* p. 103 and table 28.

84. Inspectorate General of Customs, *Trade of China* (Shanghai: Statistical Department of the Inspectorate General of Customs, 1933), chart 7.

85. Kraus, *Cotton and Cotton Goods in China,* table II.14 (facing p. 52), table III.9 (facing p. 76), and pp. 52, 76; Feuerwerker, *Economic Trends in the Republic of China,* p. 103 and table 28; Leonard Ting, "Recent Developments in China's Cotton Industry," paper presented at the Sixth Conference of the Institute of Pacific Relations, Shanghai, Aug. 1936 (Tianjin: Zhili Press, 1936), 13.

86. Ting, "Recent Developments in China's Cotton Industry," 13; Feuerwerker, *Economic Trends in the Republic of China,* p. 31 and table 10; Kraus, *Cotton and Cotton Goods in China,* table II.14 and p. 52. The importation of cotton peaked in 1931 and 1932 at, respectively, 4.7 and 4.1 million piculs, but then decreased sharply in the following four years, to 2.2 in both 1933 and 1934, 1.1 in 1935, and 0.8 in 1936.

87. Kraus, *Cotton and Cotton Goods in China,* table VI.1 (facing p. 143); Rawski, *Economic Growth in Prewar China,* 96–97.

88. Feuerwerker, *Economic Trends in the Republic of China,* p. 3 and table 10.

89. Chen Hongjin, "Zoushang dianxing zhimindi jingji de zhongguo mianye," *Zhongguo noncun* 2, no. 11 (Oct. 1936): 16–26; Wang Shuhuai, "Mianye tongzhi weiyuanhui de gongzuo chengxiao 1933–37," 714.

90. Chen Hansheng, *Industrial Capital and Chinese Peasants,* 42.

91. Wang Shuhuai, "Mianye tongzhi weiyuanhui de gongzuo chengxiao 1933–37," 746.

92. Ibid., 745; Sun Enlin, "Mianhua yunxiao guoqiu gonzuo zhi jiantao," *Mianye yuekan* 1, no. 4 (Apr. 1937): 467.

93. Campbell, "Report on Co-operation in Shensi," June–July 1936, NSHA 44/1716.

94. Wang Shuhuai, "Mianye tongzhi weiyuanhui de gongzuo chengxiao 1933–37," 745.

95. Ibid.; Wu Huabao, "Zuzhi yunxiao hezuoshi shi liyi ji qi chengbai zhi yinzi," *Mianye yuekan* 1, no. 7 (July 1937): 995–1008.

96. Sun Enlin, "Mianhua yunxiao guoqiu gonzuo zhi jiantao," 488; Wang Shuhuai, "Mianye tongzhi weiyuanhui de gongzuo chengxiao 1933–37," 747.

97. Campbell, "Report on Co-operation in Shensi," June–July 1936, pp. 9–11, NSHA 44/1716.

98. Campbell, "Report on Co-operation in Hopei Province," May 1936, NSHA 44/1716.

99. Sun Enlin, "Mianhua yunxiao guoqiu gongzuo zhi jiantao," 469.

100. Ibid., 469.

101. Ibid.

102. Fang Xianting, "Co-operative Marketing of Cotton in Hobei Province," *Nankai Social and Economic Quarterly* 8, no. 3 (Oct. 1935): 551–77.

103. In 1919 Chinese mills produced 57 percent of the entire production of cotton

yarn (with 43 percent of yarn produced by foreign mills). Chinese yarn production jumped to 67 percent in 1923 and 71 percent in 1933 and 1936. Chinese industrial production of cotton cloth also increased, but foreign production of cloth remained above 50 percent through the 1920s and 1930s (with a high of 64 percent in 1936). The Chinese factory yarn industry, therefore, grew faster than the Japanese one and was able to maintain comparable production levels by the 1930s. This, however, was not the case for cotton cloth. Chinese industrial production of cloth, in spite of its expansion, did not gain over foreign production.

104. Coble, *Facing Japan,* 162.

105. Kong Xiangxi, as minister of finance, immediately resumed the much criticized bond policy, issuing two new bonds secured on customs revenues in June 1934. See Coble, *Shanghai Capitalists,* 132–33, 138, 163.

106. Karl Gerth, *China Made: Consumer Culture and the Creation of the Nation* (Cambridge, MA: Harvard University Asia Center, distributed by Harvard University Press, 2003), 158.

107. Chen Gongbo, "Wei shiye jihua gao guoren," 160.

108. Kraus, *Cotton and Cotton Goods in China,* 126.

109. Ibid., 131; Rawski, *Economic Growth in Prewar China,* 102.

110. Kraus, *Cotton and Cotton Goods in China,* 122–30.

111. Xu Youchun, *Minguo renwu dacidian,* 546.

112. In October 1930 Yang had been appointed chairman of the Shaanxi provincial government.

113. Liu Jingshan, *Liu Jingshan xiansheng fangwen jilu,* 98.

114. Ibid., 98–99.

115. Ibid., 99.

116. Lu Yangyuan and Fang Qingqiu, eds., *Minguo shehui jingjishi* (Beijing: Zhongguo jingji chubanshe, 1991), 450; "Quanguo jingji weiyuanhui chengli jiyao," 1934, NSHA 44(2)213; petition, NSHA 44/516; "Quanguo jingji weiyuanhui choubeichu baogao," NSHA 44/2478; "Kangzhanqian quanguo jingji weiyuanhui de gonglu jianshe (1931–1937)" (master's thesis, Taiwan University, Modern History Institute), 27, NSHA 44/2478; "Quanguo jingji weiyuanhui choubeichu gongzuo baogao," NSHA 44(2)63.

117. The Jiangxi Office was officially established on January 30, 1934, with Xiao Chunjin as director. See "Quanguo jingji weiyuanhui chengli jiyao," NSHA 44(2)213.

118. Third meeting of the NEC's Standing Committee, NSHA 44(2)216.

119. On June 9, 1932, Jiang went to Lushan to launch the anti-Communist campaign. In June he called representatives from Henan, Hubei, Anhui, and Jiangxi Provinces to the Lushan "Communist extermination" meeting. On this occasion he announced the *rangwai bixian an'nei* policy and the beginning of the fourth anti-Communist campaign. See Chen Xuli, *Zhonghua minguoshi dacidian* (Shanghai: Shanghai renmin chubanshe, 1991), 258.

120. Jiang Jieshi, "Gemingjun de zeren shi an'nei rangwai" (May 8, 1933), in *Jiang zongtong ji,* vol. 2 (Taibei: Guofang yanjiuyuan; Zhonghua dianbian suohui, 1970), 622.

121. "Guanyu Jiangxi jianshe shixiang," NSHA 44(2)230.

122. Regulations for these offices were issued at the same time in January 1934; NSHA 44(2)213.

123. Lai, *Jindai Zhongguo de hezuo jingji yundong.*

124. Zhang Li, "Jiangxi noncun fuwu shiye 1934–1945," in *Kangzhan jianguoshi yanjiu Taohui wenji 1937–1945* (Taibei: Zhongyang yanjiuyuan jindaishi yanjiusuo, 1981), 1036.

125. On the recommendation of Kong Xiangxi, Zhang Fulian, the director of the Rural Office of the Chinese National Christian Association, was appointed director of the Administrative Office.

126. Ibid., 1040–41.

127. Ibid. The Cooperation Law was circumvented with a technicality: by appointing the leaders of the Jiangxi Office to the provincial government.

128. NSHA 44/1742; Brauer and Liu, *Rural Conditions and Co-operative Movement in Central Shensi.*

129. Zhang Li, "Jiangxi noncun fuwu shiye 1934–1945," 1042; Lü Fangshang, "Kangzhan qian Jiangxi de nongcun gailiang yu nongcun gaijin shiye," in *Jindai zhongguo nongcun jingjishi lunewenji* (Taibei: Zhongyang yanjiuyuan, jindai yanjiu suo, 1989), 539–42.

130. "Guan yu Jiangxi jianshe shixiang," NSHA 44(2)230.

131. Campbell, report on cooperation in Hunan, untitled and undated (early 1936?), NSHA 44/1716.

132. Ibid.

133. Campbell, "Report on Co-operation in Shensi," June–July 1936, p. 5, NSHA 44/1716; Ting, "Recent Developments in China's Cotton Industry."

134. Chen Guangfu, interview by Julie Lien-Ying How, Dec. 6, 1960, to June 5, 1961, Oral History Project: China, Columbia University, New York.

135. Campbell, "Report on Co-operation in Shensi," June–July 1936, p. 5, NSHA 44/1716.

136. Campbell, "Rural Cooperation," 1936, NSHA 44/1716. Cooperative efforts were mostly carried out in the rural areas. For example, the Provincial Cooperation Commission in Shaanxi dealt only with agricultural cooperation, leaving urban cooperation to the Bureau of Reconstruction. See Campbell, "Report on Co-operation in Shensi," NSHA 44/1716.

137. Campbell, "Some Practical Proposals for the Chinese Co-operatives."

138. The CIFRC had been the first to officially register societies in 1934 and was the largest agency working in Hunan Province, being involved in thirty-two of the seventy-five counties; see Campbell, report on cooperation in Hunan, untitled and undated (early 1936?), NSHA 44/1716. In 1936 the CIFRC managed 564 of the 886 societies in the province.

139. Ibid.; Campbell, "Some Practical Proposals for the Chinese Co-operatives."

140. Campbell, "Rural Cooperation," NSHA 44/1716; Campbell, "Some Practical Proposals for the Chinese Co-operatives," 95–96.

141. Taylor, "Reconstruction Movement in China," 383–84.

142. Campbell, "Some Practical Proposals for the Chinese Co-operatives," 97.

143. Brauer and Liu, *Rural Conditions and Co-operative Movement in Central Shensi,* 84, 114–15.

144. Philip C. C. Huang, *The Peasant Economy and Social Change in North China* (Stanford, CA: Stanford University Press, 1985), especially chapter 3; Rawski, *Economic Growth in Prewar China,* 51–58.

145. CCC, "Gongzuo baogao," NSHA 44/2481; Xu Youchun, *Minguo renwu*

dacidian, 1183. Important members of the NEC and CCC decided to cooperate with the CCP, continuing to work on the development of the cotton industry. Among them were Mao Yisheng, engineer, professor, and director of the Water Conservation Division (irrigation); Feng Zefang, assistant director of the Nanjing Central Cotton Production Improvement Bureau; Zhao Zukang, assistant director of the Road Construction Office (marketing); Jin Baoshan, doctor and professor, assistant director of the Central Experimental Health Station (pest prevention); and Qian Changzhao, economist, member of the NEC Deliberative Committee. See Xu Youchun *Minguo renwu dacidian,* 593, 1319, 503, 1528.

Chapter Six

1. Chernow, *Titan,* 134–35, 153–55.

2. Historian Linsun Cheng makes a similar point in discussing the Jiangnan banking elite. See Linsun Cheng, *Banking in Modern China: Entrepreneurs, Professional Managers and the Development of Chinese Banks, 1897–1937* (New York: Cambridge University Press, 2003), 211–12.

3. Sorgi, "La programmazione e la politica economica nel pensiero economico cinese degli anni venti e trenta," 26; Bush, *Politics of Cotton Textile.*

4. Chen Yutang, *Zhongguo jinxiandai renwu minghao dacidian,* 258.

5. For a discussion of the early development of the Rong family business, see Zhong, *Zhongguo jindai minzu qiyejia jingji sixiang,* 226–32; Shanghai shehui kexue yuanjiuyuan jingjiynajiusuo, *Rongjia qiye shiliao,* chapter 1.

6. Coble, *Shanghai Capitalists,* 221; Zheng Huixin [Cheng Hwei-shing], *Cong touzi gongsi dao "Guanbang shangxing": Zhongguo jianshe yin gongsi de chuangli ji qi jingying huodong* (Hong Kong: Chinese University Press, 2001); Wu Jingping, *Song Ziwen pingzhuan,* 230–39.

7. "Quangguo jingji weiyuanhui ershisan nianfen shiye jinxing jihua ji jingfei zhi zhibei," 1934, NSHA 44/1679.

8. See, for example, the establishment of the Ministry of Industry's central machinery factory and rule 1 of the CCC in "Quanguo jingji weiyuanhui mianye tongzhi weiyuanhui zanxing zuzhi tiaoli," in *Quanguo jingji weiyuanhui chengli jiyao,* 34, NSHA 44(2)213.

9. The research functions of the NEC were to be carried out by four groups, focusing respectively on economics, raw materials, manufacturing, and marketing. Each section was to be staffed with prominent people in the field (ibid., 34).

10. These research centers were the Nantong Academy, the Tianjin Industrial School, and the Jiangsu Provincial Industrial School in Suzhou ("Quangguo jingji weiyuanhui ershisan nianfen shiye jinxing jihua ji jingfei zhi zhibei," 1934, NSHA 44/1679).

11. "Quangguo jingji weiyuanhui ershisan nianfen shiye jinxing jihua ji jingfei zhi zhibei," attached to the minutes of the third meeting of the Standing Committee of the NEC, 1934, NSHA 44(2)216.

12. To compile these statistics the CCC periodically surveyed rainfall, temperature, area under cultivation, and yield per *mu*. See "Quanguo jingji weiyuanhui mianye tongzhi weiyuanhui shiye jihua" (Jan.–Feb. 1934), NSHA 44(2)216.

13. "Quangguo jingji weiyuanhui ershisan nianfen shiye jinxing jihua ji jingfei zhi zhibei," attached to the minutes of the third meeting of the Standing Committee of the NEC, 1934, NSHA 44(2)216. For a more detailed description of the work

carried out by the CCC in managerial training, research on improving the technology of textile production, and compilation of statistics, see Li Shengbo, "Miantonghui gaijin mianfangzhi ye gongzuo gaikuang," *Mianye yuekan* 1, no. 1 (Jan. 1937): 13–18.

14. June 1934 "gongzuo baogao," NSHA 44/2481.

15. "Quangguo jingji weiyuanhui ershisan nianfen shiye jinxing jihua ji jingfei zhi zhibei," 1934, NSHA 44/1679.

16. "Quangguo jingji weiyuanhui ershisan nianfen shiye jinxing jihua ji jingfei zhi zhibei," attached to the minutes of the third meeting of the Standing Committee of the NEC, 1934, NSHA 44(2)216.

17. Ibid.

18. The CCC surveyed the larger Chinese cotton mills and textile factories but not small weaving plants. The survey was divided into three areas: northern China (Shandong and northern Shaanxi, with Tianjin as its center), central China (Jiangsu and Zhejiang, with Shanghai at its center), and southern China (Hubei yarn market, Hunan, Henan, Jiangxi, and Anhui, with Wuhan as its center). The investigation focused on such issues as worker number, efficiency, age, hiring and firing, work and rest hours, wages, food and dormitories, rewards and punishments, bonuses and premiums, injuries and illness, childbirth, savings and insurance, compensation for families of injured workers, retirement, education, associations, and recreation. The survey also investigated issues related to the economic conditions of the factories, including management, assets and properties, debts, and costs incurred. See ibid.

19. "Quanguo jingji weiyuanhui zuijin gongzuo baogao," *Dagongbao,* May 30, 1935; Ting, "Recent Developments in China's Cotton Industry," 38–39.

20. Chen Gongbo, *Sinian congzhenglu,* 8.

21. GMDPHC 443/7 (9); *Zhongyang ribao,* Apr. 2, 1934. The article carries the text of Chen Gongbo's speech, "Tongzhi jingji de xianjue wenti," given at the twentieth meeting of the Central Party Committee.

22. "Quangguo jingji weiyuanhui ershisan nianfen shiye jinxing jihua ji jingfei zhi zhibei," 1934, NSHA 44/1679.

23. GMDPHC 443/7 (9); *Zhongyang ribao,* Apr. 2, 1934.

24. "Quangguo jingji weiyuanhui ershisan nianfen shiye jinxing jihua ji jingfei zhi zhibei," 1934, NSHA 44/1679.

25. Li Shengbo, "Miantonghui gaijin mianfangzhi ye gongzuo gaikuang," 16–17.

26. Bell, *One Industry, Two Chinas,* 166–67.

27. Sarti, *Fascism and the Industrial Leadership in Italy,* 72.

28. Chen Gongbo, *Sinian congzhenglu,* 47, 51–52; Chen Gongbo, "Tongzhi jingji de xianjue wenti," 181.

29. "Zhengli Shenxin Shachan Chuyi," *Dagongbao,* Aug. 15, 1934.

30. Bush, *Politics of Cotton Textiles,* 234. For additional discussion of the Shenxin crisis, see ibid., 233–47; Shanghai shehui kexue yuanjiuyuan jingjiynajiusuo, *Rongjia qiye shiliao,* 408–24.

31. Shanghai shehui kexue yuanjiuyuan jingjiynajiusuo, *Rongjia qiye shiliao,* 413.

32. Ibid., 420.

33. On May 30, 1925, British police fired on Chinese demonstrators in Shanghai. This incident provoked a series of nationalist demonstrations, including boycotts of Japanese goods.

34. Zhong, *Zhongguo jindai minzu qiyejia jingji sixiang,* 227, 229.

35. As quoted in ibid., 230.

36. Bush, *Politics of Cotton Textiles,* 213.

37. Chinese mill owners refused to place orders before Song came back from the United States. But soon it became known that Japanese mills had placed orders while the cotton was in transit. This provoked criticism from the Chinese mill owners who did not want the loan to supply Japanese mills. Rong Zongjing, acting as spokesman for the Chinese cotton industrialists, repeatedly asked the director of the Central Bank, Kong Xiangxi (H. H. Kung), to grant relief loans to the cotton mills. A meeting was finally held on August 29 with Song, Kong, Rong, and the other mill owners attending. The discussion focused on the price of US loan cotton without, however, reaching a solution. The cotton mill owners also asked Song for a "comprehensive solution to the cotton industry's danger" and to consider imposing an import duty and granting tax exemptions to Chinese mills. See ibid., 216–20.

38. NSHA 44(2)216. Song Ziwen's report on the cotton and wheat loan is attached to the minutes of the third meeting of the NEC Standing Committee. For details, see Bush, *Politics of Cotton Textiles,* 224–26. Bush argues that, because of the American loan fiasco and the disagreements on consolidated taxes promoted by Song, Rong Zongjing earned Song's enmity. According to Bush, the loan was a failed attempt by the Shanghai capitalists to get cheaper credit for raw-material purchases. He also argues that the CCC was created to solve the loan problem by starting a "mechanism that could buy up and market elsewhere Shanghai's large yarn inventories [and] place money in the hands of Chinese mill owners" to buy the loan's cotton. However, Bush contends that Song's final resignation was mostly the result of the loan fiasco (ibid., 222).

39. Shanghai shehui kexue yuanjiuyuan jingjiynajiusuo, *Rongjia qiye shiliao,* 413, 420.

40. "Zhengli Shenxin Shachan Chuyi," *Dagongbao,* Aug. 15, 1934.

41. Shanghai shehui kexue yuanjiuyuan jingjiynajiusuo, *Rongjia qiye shiliao,* 428ff.

42. Bush, *Politics of Cotton Textiles,* 241; Bergère, *Golden Age of the Chinese Bourgeoisie,* 283.

43. For the original text of the Shanghai conference agreement that led to the formation of the Wang-Jiang cabinet, see "Yizhou qian guoneiway ashi shuping," *Guowen zhoubao* 8, no. 45 (Nov. 16, 1931): 4–5.

44. Coble, *Shanghai Capitalists,* 111–12.

45. *Shenbao,* June 12, 1932; Coble, *Shanghai Capitalists,* 112.

46. Coble, *Shanghai Capitalists,* 112ff.; *China Weekly Review,* June 18, 1932, 84, 107.

47. *Shenbao,* June 18, 1932. On June 17, soon after Song resigned, Wang Jingwei and Li Shizeng went to Shanghai to invite Song and Chen Minshu to resume office. Wang reported to Song and Chen the results of the Lushan meeting and the new economic and financial directives. Wang also visited Sun Ke. At the Lushan (June 1932) meeting it was decided that a national finance conference was to be held as soon as Song returned to Nanjing (*Shenbao,* June 22, 1934). After Song withdrew his resignation, however, things did not go smoothly. Song remained in Shanghai and did not go to Nanjing to discuss financing the anti-Communist campaign, probably because Jiang was trying not to honor their informal agreement and wanted him to issue a bond to finance his military expedition.

48. In May, on Song's suggestion, the Shanghai Chamber of Commerce, the National Association of Chambers of Commerce, the Shanghai Bankers Association,

and the Shanghai Native Bankers Association formed an Anti–Civil War League supporting Song against Jiang. See Coble, *Shanghai Capitalists,* 113–15.

49. An agreement was also reached on the composition of the commission, which had been a controversial issue since the Shanghai conference. The commission was now to be really representative of economic and financial circles. Members of agricultural, industrial, commercial, and financial circles, as well as financial specialists and economists, were to participate in the NFC (*Shenbao,* June 22, 1932).

50. Song was given special powers among the five members of the NEC Standing Committee. See *Quanguo jingji weiyuanhui disanci weiyuan huiyi jilu,* Jan. 27, 1934, NSHA 442(2)216.

51. Kong immediately resumed the much criticized bond policy, issuing in June 1934 two new bonds secured on customs revenues. See Coble, *Shanghai Capitalists,* 132–33, 137–38, 163.

52. The Ministry of Foreign Affairs also experienced a drastic reversal. In 1933, while Song Ziwen was abroad, Jiang Jieshi sent Luo Wen'gan, minister of foreign affairs and a strong supporter of Song, on a mission to Xinjiang. Actual control of the ministry passed to Wang's pro-Japanese protégé Tang Youren until Wang Jingwei himself took over the position.

53. Jiang Tingfu, interview by Crystal Lorch Seidman, 1965, Oral History Project: China, Columbia University, New York. Weng Wenhao, Wu Dingzhang, and Zhang Jia'ao were also members of the Political Studies Clique. See Tian, *Government and Politics in Kuomintang China.*

54. Coble, *Facing Japan,* 277–78.

55. Bergère, *Golden Age of the Chinese Bourgeoisie,* 290–93; Kirby, *Germany and Republican China,* 209.

56. Bergère, *Golden Age of the Chinese Bourgeoisie,* 290–93.

57. Ibid., 291. Bergère further identifies this group as a "bureaucratic bourgeoisie" that departed from the "liberal bourgeoisie that had been linked to Song Ziwen and NEC (ibid., 285, 292).

58. Jiang Tingfu, interview, 187. Jiang Tingfu was put in charge of reexamining local government, and Weng Wenhao took over the reform of the national government.

59. The National Reconstruction Commission was created at the time of the Hu-Jiang coalition and directed by Hu Hanmin's protégée Zhang Renjie.

60. Wu Dingchang was also a member of the Natural Resource Commission.

61. With the reduction in its responsibilities came a reduction in NEC's budget from 5,933,000 to 5,685,000 yuan. See NSHA 44/680, 1936; Zhongyang yanjiuyuan, Jindaishi yanjiusuo, jingji dangan, 26-01-7-1, June 19, 1936, Economic Archives of the Institute of Modern History of Academia Sinica.

62. Kirby, *Germany and Republican China,* 78.

63. Coble, *Shanghai Capitalists,* 187–92; Bergère, *Golden Age of the Chinese Bourgeoisie,* 287–88.

64. Bergère, *Golden Age of the Chinese Bourgeoisie.*

65. Bell, *One Industry, Two Chinas,* 176.

66. Taylor, "Reconstruction Movement in China," 384; minutes of the tenth meeting of the NEC Standing Committee, 1935, NSHA 44(2)217.

67. T. V. Soong, box 29, China Development Finance Corporation, Hoover Institution Archives.

68. Ibid.

69. Coble, *Shanghai Capitalists,* 221.

70. Ibid., 221–22. For more information on the CDFC, see Zheng Huixin, *Cong touzi gongsi dao "Guanbang shangxing."*

71. Minutes of the tenth meeting of the NEC Standing Committee, 1935, NSHA 44(2)217.

72. Coble, *Shanghai Capitalists,* 216–17.

73. Ibid., 218–19.

74. Taylor, "Reconstruction Movement in China," 384.

75. Information collected in an interview conducted by the author with Professor Shi Quansheng, of the Jiangsu Provincial Archives, in 1992.

76. Bell, *One Industry, Two Chinas,* 178.

77. Sarti, *Fascism and the Industrial Leadership in Italy,* 138.

78. Vaudagna, "Structural Change in Fascist Italy," 181–201.

79. Rawski, *Economic Growth in Prewar China,* 118, 182, 345.

80. Kasza, *Conscription Society,* 103–4; Kirby, *Germany and Republican China,* 95, 209, 262.

Chapter Seven

1. Chen Gongbo, "Banianlai de huiyi," in *Ku xiao lu: Chen Gongpo huiyi (1925–1936),* ed. Wang Ruijiong, Li E, and Zhao Lingyang (Hong Kong: Xianggang daxue yazhou yenjiu zhongxin, 1979), 404, 407. The piece cited here, "Banianlai de huiyi," is also known as "Zibaishu" and was the self-defense document written by Chen at the time of his trial.

2. The use of this expression, *haidu,* denotes an attempt to link the reorganized government with the Nationalist government of the Nanjing Decade, thus implying that Jiang had diverted from the correct political line. The use of the term "reorganized," which echoes the GMD Reorganization Group of 1927, also functioned to show political continuity between the political position of the Wang group in the 1920s and the collaborationist government.

3. Among the many works on collaboration that have been published recently see Mitter, *Manchurian Myth;* Brook, "Collaborationist Nationalism in Occupied China"; Wang Ke-Wen, "Collaborators and Capitalists: The Politics of 'Material Control' in Wartime Shanghai," *Chinese Studies in History* 26, no. 1 (Fall 1992); David Barret and Larry N. Shyu, eds., *Chinese Collaboration: The Limits of Accommodation with Japan, 1932–1945* (Stanford, CA: Stanford University Press, 2001).

4. For a brilliant analysis of the important role played by the discourse on the resistance in postwar France, see Henry Rousso, *The Vichy Syndrome: History and Memory in France since 1944* (Cambridge, MA: Harvard University Press, 1991).

5. See, e.g., Gordon F. Bertram, "The Morphology of the Collaborator: The French Case," *Journal of European Studies* 89, nos. 89–90 (Mar.–June 1993): 1–26; Rousso, *Vichy Syndrome;* Renzo De Felice, *Fascismo, antifascismo, nazione: Note e ricerche* (Rome: Bonacci, 1996); Renzo De Felice and Pasquale Chessa, *Rosso e nero,* 2d ed. (Milan: Baldini and Castoldi, 1995).

6. De Felice and Chessa, *Rosso e nero.*

7. Bertram, "Morphology of the Collaborator"; Brooks, "Collaborationist Nationalism in Occupied China"; Mitter, *Manchurian Myth;* Coble, *Facing Japan.*

8. Chen Gongbo refers here to the 1933 Japanese attack on Hebei that ended with the signing of the Tanggu Truce.

9. Chen Gongbo, "Banianlai de huiyi," 405.

10. Ibid., 411.

11. Jiang Jieshi, "Fuxing zhongguo zhi dao" (Apr. 11, 1932), in *Xianzongtong Jiang Gong sixiang yanlun zhongji, vol.* 10, edited by Qing Xiaoyi (Taibei: Zhongguo Guomindang Zhongyang weiyuanhui tangshi weiyuanhui: Zhongyang wenwu gongyingshe jingxiao, 1984), 489.

12. Jiang Jieshi, "Jiaoyu yu jingji we liguo jiuguo liang yaosu" (Oct. 31, 1932), in *Xianzongtong Jiang Gong sixiang yanlun zhongji,* vol. 10, 660ff.

13. Lyman P. Van Slyke, "Nationalist China during the Sino-Japanese War, 1937–1945," in *The Nationalist Era in China, 1927–1949,* edited by Lloyd Eastman, Jerome Ch'en, Suzanne Pepper, and Lyman P. Van Slyke (Cambridge: Cambridge University Press, 1991), 121.

14. Susan H. Marsh, "Chou Fo-hai: The Making of a Collaborator," in *The Chinese and the Japanese: Essays in Political and Cultural Interactions,* edited by Akira Iriye (Princeton, NJ: Princeton University Press, 1980), 321.

15. Chen Gongbo, report (*bagaoshu*), undated, probably early 1938, unpublished document from the private collection of Chen Kan, p. 8.

16. Gerald E. Bunker, *The Peace Conspiracy* (Cambridge, MA: Harvard University Press, 1972), 4.

17. Wang Jingwei, *Wang Jingwei xiansheng guangyu heping yundong zhi zhongyao yanlun* (China, 1938), 13; Bunker, *Peace Conspiracy,* 2.

18. As quoted in Brook, "Collaborationist Nationalism in Occupied China," 177.

19. Parks M. Coble, *Chinese Capitalism in Japan's New Order: The Occupied Lower Yangzi, 1937–1945* (Berkeley and Los Angeles: University of California Press, 2003), 39.

20. Marsh, "Chou Fo-hai," 319.

21. Coble, *Chinese Capitalism in Japan's New Order,* 35–37.

22. Marsh, "Chou Fo-hai." The Tanggu Truce followed Japan's attack against the Chinese army in Hebei. According to this truce, the northeastern portion of the Hebei region was declared a demilitarized zone. The Japanese army retired to the Great Wall, although it kept the right to maintain a safe approach to Beijing and to fly spotter planes over the region. See Coble, *Facing Japan,* 106–14.

23. Brook, "Collaborationist Nationalism in Occupied China."

24. Mitter, *Manchurian Myth,* 74–77.

25. Chen Gongbo, "Banianlai de huiyi," 413.

26. Ibid., 408.

27. Ibid., 421.

28. Christian Henriot, "Rice, Power, and People: The Politics of Food Supply in Wartime Shanghai (1937–1945)," *Twentieth-Century China* 26, no. 1 (Nov. 2000): 41–84; Wang Ke-Wen, "Collaborators and Capitalists," 46–51; Zhang Genfu, "Wangwei quanguo shangye tongzhi zonghui shulun," *Dangan yu lishi* 3 (June 1997): 41–47.

29. Marsh, "Chou Fo-hai," 318.

30. Coble, "Japan's New Order and the Shanghai Capitalists," 140; Zhang Genfu, "Wangwei quanguo shangye tongzhi zonghui shulun," 41.

31. Marsh, "Chou Fo-hai," 318

32. Zhang Genfu, "Wangwei quanguo shangye tongzhi zonghui shulun," 319.

33. Henriot, "Rice, Power, and People," 48.

34. Michael A. Barnhart, *Japan Prepares for Total War: The Search for Economic Security, 1919–1941* (Ithaca, NY: Cornell University Press, 1987), 91; also quoted in Coble, "Japan's New Order and the Shanghai Capitalists," 138.

35. Henriot, "Rice, Power, and People," 58.

36. Coble, "Japan's New Order and the Shanghai Capitalists," 138.

37. Zhang Genfu, "Wangwei quanguo shangye tongzhi zonghui shulun," 41.

38. Henriot, "Rice, Power, and People," 66–68; Coble, "Japan's New Order and the Shanghai Capitalists," 151–52.

39. Chen Gongbo, "Bainianlai de huiyi," 408.

40. Marsh, "Chou Fo-hai," 319.

41. Coble, "Japan's New Order and the Shanghai Capitalists," 149–50; "Miangangzhiye qingkuang ji chubu fuxing jihua," Apr. 1941, NSHA 2092/76.

42. "Jingji jihua," 1941, NSHA 2092/76; "Qhuangshe guojia gongye yinhang jihua," 1941, NSHA 2092/76. See also "Gongshangye jingji chugao," 1941, NSHA 2092/76.

43. "Diaocha wuzi tongzhi fangan," 1941–42, NSHA 1092/299.

44. Coble, "Japan's New Order and the Shanghai Capitalists," 149–50; NEC "Googzuo baogao," 1943, NSHA 2002/75.

45. Coble, "Japan's New Order and the Shanghai Capitalists," 149.

46. Zhang Genfu, "Wangwei quanguo shangye tongzhi zonghui shulun," 42.

47. As quoted in Henriot, "Rice, Power, and People," 53.

48. Zhang Genfu, "Wangwei quanguo shangye tongzhi zonghui shulun," 42; Yuan Yuquan, "Riben qinlue zhi paozhe de shangtonghui," in *Shanghai wenshi ziliao xuanji* (Shanghai: Shanghai renmin chubanshe, 1987), 555.

49. Yuan Yuquan, "Riben qinlue zhi paozhe de shangtonghui," 555.

50. Henriot, "Rice, Power, and People," 62.

51. Yuan Yuquan, "Riben qinlue zhi paozhe de shangtonghui," 555.

52. "Riben fangweiting zhangshi shibian," in *Huabei zhian zhan* (Tianjin: Renmin chubanshe, 1892), 275, as quoted in Zhang Genfu, "Wangwei quanguo shangye tongzhi zonghui shulun," 42.

53. Yuan Yuquan, "Riben qinlue zhi paozhe de shangtonghui," 105–6.

54. Zhang Genfu, "Wangwei quanguo shangye tongzhi zonghui shulun," 42.

55. Ibid.

56. Ibid.

57. Tang Shoumin had moved to Hong Kong in 1937, where he was under house arrest until he consented to return to Shanghai in December 1941. The Chinese members of the board of directors of the National Merchant Control Association were Yuan Ludeng, Lin Tanghou, Wu Zhenxiu, Ye Fuxiao, Jiang Shangda, Wen Lanting, Lin Kanghou, Rong Desheng, Guo Shun, and, as chairman, Tang Shoumin. In its early period the association received orders mostly from the RNG Ministry of Industry. In May 1943 the association was placed under the control of the Executive Yuan and given additional decision-making and supervisory powers. See Quangguo shangye tongzhi zonghui zanxing tiaoli, NSHA 2002/214; Zhang Genfu, "Wangwei quanguo shangye tongzhi zonghui shulun"; Coble, "Japan's New Order and the Shanghai Capitalists."

58. See, e.g., "Liangshibu zengchan sannian jihua gangan caoan," Aug. 1943, NSHA 2002/26.

59. Zhang Genfu, "Wangwei quanguo shangye tongzhi zonghui shulun," 41, 43–44."

60. "Chen Gongbo zhi daying bianshu," in *Shenxu wangwei hanjian bilu*, vol. 1, edited by Nanjingshi danganguan (Nanjing: Jiangsu guji chubanshe, 1992), 47.

61. Chen Gongbo, "Banianlai de huiyi," 421.

62. Ibid.

63. Marsh, "Chou "Fo-hai."

64. Ibid., 325; Zhu Zijia [Jin Xiongbai], *Wang Zhengquan di kaichan yu shouchang*, vol. 4 (Hong Kong: Chunqiu zazhishe 1959), 90.

65. Wang Jingwei, *Wang Jingwei xiansheng guangyu heping yundong zhi zhongyao yanlun*, 51.

66. Bertram, "Morphology of the Collaborator," 4.

67. Wang Jingwei, *Wang Jingwei xiansheng guangyu heping yundong zhi zhongyao yanlun*, 13; Marsh, "Chou Fo-hai.".

68. Mitter, *Manchurian Myth*.

69. Marsh, "Chou Fo-hai," 319.

70. For a discussion of Vichy and the trial of Marshal Pétain, see Jean-Marc Varaut, *Le process Pétain, 1945–1995* (Paris: Perrin, 1995); Rousso, *Vichy Syndrome*; Bertram, "Morphology of the Collaborator."

71. Caroline Wiedmer, *The Claims of Memory: Representations of the Holocaust in Contemporary Germany and France* (Ithaca, NY: Cornell University Press, 1999), 32–33.

Conclusion

1. Taylor, *Reconstruction Movement in China*, 381, 384.

2. Fitzgerald, *Awakening China*.

3. Peter Nolan and Fureng Dong, *Market Forces in China: Competition and Small Business, the Wenzhou Debate* (London: Zed Books, 1990), 107; Friedman, Pickowicz, and Selden, *Chinese Village, Socialist State*, xxiii.

4. Friedman, Pickowicz, and Selden, *Chinese Village, Socialist State*, xxiii, 280.

5. Ibid.; Nolan and Fureng, *Market Forces in China*, 38. Ultimately both the GMD and the CCP engaged in the kind of high-modernist reforms discussed by James Scott that disregarded local practices and knowledge and imposed socioeconomic reorganization from above often with disastrous results to the local economy. See James C. Scott, *Seeing Like a State: How Certain Schemes to Improve the Human Condition Have Failed* (New Haven, CT: Yale University Press, 1998).

6. Richard Lowenthal, "Development versus Utopia in Communist Policy," in *Change in Communist Systems*, edited by Jeremy R. Azrael and Chalmers A. Johnson (Stanford, CA: Stanford University Press, 1970); Dickson, *Red Capitalists in China*, 7–8.

7. Eastman, *Abortive Revolution*.

8. This is the term Edward Friedman, Paul Pickowicz, and Mark Selden use in their *Chinese Village, Socialist State* (New Haven, CT: Yale University Press, 1991), chapter 5, to describe the early PRC years, before the Communists established a planned economy.

9. On this subject see Douglas Reynolds, "The Chinese Industrial Cooperative Movement and the Polarization of Wartime China, 1938–1945" (Ph.D. diss., Columbia University, 1975).

10. Bell, *One Industry, Two Chinas,* 178.

11. Wang Dong, "Chuangjian zhongguo tese de xiandaihua xinlilun," *Beijing daxue xuebao* 4 (1994): 11–21.

12. Clientelism was also an important feature of everyday life in the Mao years, being the only channel available to common people to improve their access to state-managed resources and attempt to further their interests.

13. Dickson, *Red Capitalists in China,* 61.

14. Ibid., 24, 25 (quotation).

15. Ibid., 19 (quotation), 23.

16. Dorothy Solinger, "Urban Entrepreneurs and the State: The Merger of State and Society," in *State and Society in China: The Consequences of Reform,* edited by Arthur Lewis Rosenbaum (Boulder, CO: Westview Press, 1992).

17. Dickson, *Red Capitalists in China,* 61.

18. David Zweig, *Internationalizing China: Domestic Interests and Global Linkages* (Ithaca, NY: Cornell University Press, 2002), 260, 271.

19. Zheng Yongnian, *Discovering Chinese Nationalism in China: Modernization, Identity, and International Relations* (Cambridge: Cambridge University Press, 1999), 95ff.

20. Peter Hays Gries, *China's New Nationalism: Pride, Politics, and Diplomacy* (Berkeley and Los Angeles: University of California Press, 2004), especially chapter 3.

21. Zheng Yongnian, *Discovering Chinese Nationalism in China,* 3, 52; Zweig, *Internationalizing China,* 272–73.

22. Dickson, *Red Capitalists in China,* 15.

23. Zweig, *Internationalizing China,* 30–31.

24. Ibid., 260, 271.

25. Zheng Yongnian, *Discovering Chinese Nationalism in China,* 86.

26. Zweig, *Internationalizing China,* 273.

BIBLIOGRAPHY

Archives

Archivio storico del Ministero degli Easteri. Rome, Italy.

Economic Archives of the Institute of Modern History of Academia Sinica 經濟檔案, 中央研究院, 近代歷史研究所. Taibei, ROC.

Guomindang Party History Committee (Guomindang dangshihui 國民黨當史會) (GMDPHC). Taibei, ROC.

Hoover Institution Archives, Stanford University, Stanford, CA.

Nanjing Second Historical Archives (Nanjing dier lishi dang'anguan 南京第二歷史檔案館) (NSHA). Nanjing, PRC.

National Historical Archives (Guoshiguan 國史館) (NHA). Taibei, ROC.

Oral History Project: China. Interviews with Chen Guangfu, Franklin Lian He, and Jiang Tingfu. Columbia University, New York, NY.

Chinese Periodicals

Dagongbao 大公保. Tianjing.

Geming pinglun 革命評論. Shanghai.

Jianshe 建設. Nanjing.

Mianye yuekan 棉業月刊. Shanghai.

Minzu zazhi 民族雜誌. Shanghai.

North China Herald. Shanghai.

Shenbao 申報. Shanghai.

Books and Articles

Alitto, Guy. *The Last Confucian: Liang Shu-ming and the Chinese Dilemma of Modernity.* Berkeley and Los Angeles: University of California Press, 1979.

Anderson, Benedict R. O. G. *Imagined Communities: Reflections on the Origin and Spread of Nationalism.* London: Verso, 1983.

Appadurai, Arjun. *Modernity at Large: Cultural Dimensions of Globalization,* vol. 1, *Public worlds.* Minneapolis: University of Minnesota Press, 1996.

Bachman, David. *Bureaucracy, Economy, and Leadership in China: The Institutional Origins of the Great Leap Forward*. Cambridge: Cambridge University Press, 1991.

Barki, Avraham. *Nazi Economics: Ideology, Theory, and Policy*. New Haven, CT: Yale University Press, 1990.

Barnett, Robert W. *Economic Shanghai: Hostage to Politics, 1937–1941*. I.P.R. Inquiry Series. New York: International Secretariat Institute of Pacific Relations, 1941.

Barnhart, Michael A. *Japan Prepares for Total War: The Search for Economic Security, 1919–1941*. Ithaca, NY: Cornell University Press, 1987.

Barone, Giuseppe. "Dall'agricoltura all'industria: Il cotone nazionale tra le due guerre." *Meridiana* 3, no. 33 (1998): 13–35.

Barret, David, and Larry N. Shyu, eds. *Chinese Collaboration: The Limits of Accommodation with Japan, 1932–1945*. Stanford, CA: Stanford University Press, 2001.

Bate, Don. *Wang Ching Wei: Puppet or Patriot*. Chicago: R. F. Seymour, 1941.

Beard, Miriam. *A History of the Business Man*. New York: Macmillan, 1938.

Bell, Lynda Schaefer. "From Comprador to County Magnate: Bourgeois Practice in the Wuxi County Silk Industry." In *Chinese Local Elites and Patterns of Dominance*, edited by Joseph W. Esherick and Mary Backus Rankin. Berkeley and Los Angeles: University of California Press, 1990.

———. *One Industry, Two Chinas*. Stanford, CA: Stanford University Press, 1999.

Bergère, Marie-Claire. *The Golden Age of the Chinese Bourgeoisie, 1911–1937*. Cambridge: Cambridge University Press, 1989.

Bergère, Marie-Claire, and Janet Lloyd. *Sun Yat-sen*. Stanford, CA: Stanford University Press, 1998.

Bertram, Gordon F. "The Morphology of the Collaborator: The French Case." *Journal of European Studies* 89, nos. 89–90 (Mar.–June 1993): 1–26.

Bhabha, Homi K. *Nation and Narration*. London: Routledge, 1990.

Brandt, Loren. *Commercialization and Agricultural Development: Central and Eastern China, 1870–1937*. Cambridge: Cambridge University Press, 1989.

Brauer, Max, and Gaines Liu. *Rural Conditions and Co-operative Movement in Central Shensi*. National Economic Council, National Government of the Republic of China, 1934.

Brook, Timothy. "Collaborationist Nationalism in Occupied China, 1938–1939." In *Nation Work: Asian Elites and National Identities*, edited by Timothy Brook and Andre Schmid. Ann Arbor: University of Michigan Press, 2000.

———. *The Confusions of Pleasure: Commerce and Culture in Ming China*. Berkeley and Los Angeles: University of California Press, 1998.

Bunker, Gerald E. *The Peace Conspiracy*. Cambridge, MA: Harvard University Press, 1972.

Bush, Richard. *The Politics of Cotton Textiles in Kuomintang China, 1927–1937*. New York: Garland Publishing, 1982.

Campbell, W. K. H. "Some Practical Proposals for the Chinese Co-operatives." *Nankai Social and Economic Quarterly* 10, no. 1 (Apr. 1937): 75–103.

Cartier, Carolyn. "Origins and Evolution of a Geographical Idea." *Modern China* 28, no. 1 (2002): 79–136.

Chang, John K. *Industrial Development in Pre-Communist China: A Quantitative Analysis*. Chicago: Aldine, 1969.

Chang, Sidney H., and Ramon H. Myers, eds. *The Storm Clouds over China: The Memoir of Ch'en Li-fu, 1900–1993*. Stanford, CA: Hoover Institution Press, 1994.

Chatterjee, Partha. *The Nation and Its Fragments: Colonial and Postcolonial Histories.* Princeton Studies in Culture/Power/History. Princeton, NJ: Princeton University Press, 1993.

———. *Nationalist Thought and the Colonial World: A Derivative Discourse.* Minneapolis: University of Minnesota Press, 1993.

Chen, Gideon. *Chinese Government Economic Planning and Reconstruction since 1927.* Tianjin: China Institute of Pacific Relations, 1933.

Chen Gongbo. "Banianlai de huiyi." In *Ku xiao lu: Chen Gongpo huiyi (1925–1936),* edited by Wang Ruijiong, Li E, and Zhao Lingyang. Hong Kong: Xianggang daxue yazhou yenjiu zhongxin, 1979.

———. "Chen Gongbo yuzhong riji." Edited by Jia Guangguan and Di Gongbing. In *Minguo dang'an,* vol. 4, 57–64. Nanjing: "Minguo dangan" bianjibu, 1991.

———. *Chen Gongbo zizhuan.* Bincheng: Nanguo chubanshe, 1957.

———. *Ch'en ni Kung-po yu chung jih chi.* Shanghai: Dafengshe, 1946.

———. *The Communist Movement in China.* Edited by Martin Wilbur. New York: Octagon Books, 1966.

———. *Gongdang yundong zai zhongguo.* Taibei: Sifa xingzhengbu diaochaju, 1962. (A Chinese translation of Chen Gongbo's M.A. thesis, Columbia University, 1924.)

———. "Guomin geming de weiji." *Geming pinglun (quanji)* 8 (1928).

———. *Hanfengji.* Vol. 99, *Minguo congshu.* Shanghai: Shanghai shudian, 1945.

———. "Heyi haiyou lianbanglun." *Minzu zazhi* 2, no. 6 (June 1934): 797–805.

———. "Jinhou de Guomindang." *Geming pinglun (quanji)* 1 (1928): 1–14.

———. *Sinian congzhenglu.* Shanghai: Shangwu yingshuguan, 1936.

———. "Tichang shenme de wenhua." *Minzu zazhi* 2, no. 8 (Aug. 1934).

———. "Tongzhi jingji de xianjue wenti" (May 1934). In *Sinian congzhenglu.* Shanghai: Shangwu yingshuguan, 1936. (First published in *Minzu zazhi,* May 1933.)

———. "Tongzhi jingji yu zuzhi" (Nov. 1933). In *Sinian congzhenglu.* Shanghai: Shangwu yingshuguan, 1936.

———. "Wei shiye jihua gao guoren" (Dec. 1933). In *Sinian congzhenglu.* Shanghai: Shangwu yingshuguan, 1936.

———. "Xu sinian shiye jihua chugao" (Aug. 1933). In *Sinian congzhenglu.* Shanghai: Shangwu yingshuguan, 1936.

———. "Yinong liguo shi duide ma?" (July 1935). In *Sinian congzhenglu.* Shanghai: Shangwu yingshuguan, 1936.

———. "Zailun disandang." *Geming pinglun (quanji)* 8 (1928).

———. *Zhongguo Guomindang suodaibiaode shi shenme?* 3d ed. Shanghai: Fudan shudian, 1928.

———. "Zhongguo liangshi de ziji" (June 1935). In *Sinian congzhenglu.* Shanghai: Shangwu yingshuguan, 1936.

———. *Zhongguo lishishang de geming.* Shanghai: Fudan shudian, 1928.

———. "Zhongguo shiye de ziben he zhishu wenti" (Dec. 1934). In *Sinian congzhenglu.* Shanghai: Shangwu yingshuguan, 1936.

"Chen Gongbo zhi daying bianshu." In *Shenxu wangwei hanjian bilu,* vol. 1, edited by Nanjingshi danganguan. Nanjing: Jiangsu guji chubanshe, 1992.

Chen Guangfu. *Chen Guangfu xiansheng de yanlunji.* Shanghai: Shanghai Savings and Commercial Bank, 1949.

———. "Jingji tongzhi de A B C." In *Chen Gungfu xiansheng de yanlunji*. Shanghai: Shanghai Savings and Commercial Bank.

———. "Wuguo jingji gaizao de genben wenti." *Jingji xuekan* 4, no. 4 (Dec. 1933): 142–54. (Inauguration speech for the tenth meeting of the Chinese Economic Studies Society.)

———. "Ziben zhuyi de yitiao xinchulu." In *Chen Gungfu xiansheng de yanlunji*. Shanghai: Shanghai Savings and Commercial Bank, Nov. 1933.

Chen Hai. "Chen Guangfu yu Shanghai yinhang." In *Jindai zhongghuo gongshang jingji congshu*. Beijing: Zhongguo wenshi chubanshe.

Chen Hansheng. *Industrial Capital and Chinese Peasants: A Study of the Livelihood of Chinese Tobacco Cultivators*. New York: Garland Publishing, 1980. (First published in 1939.)

Chen Hongjin. "Zoushang dianxing zhimindi jingji de zhongguo mianye." *Zhongguo noncun* 2, no. 11 (Oct. 1936).

Chen, Leslie H. Dingyan. *Chen Jiongming and the Federalist Movement*. Ann Arbor: Center for Chinese Studies, University of Michigan, 1999.

Cheng Linsun. *Banking in Modern China: Entrepreneurs, Professional Managers and the Development of Chinese Banks, 1897–1937*. Cambridge: Cambridge University Press, 2003.

Chen Shuzhu. "Xiandai Zhonghua liusheng zhi nongye jinrong 1927–1937." M.A. thesis, Taiwan University, 1984.

Chen Xuli. *Zhonghua minguoshi dacidian*. Shanghai: Shanghai renmin chubanshe, 1991.

Chen Yutang, ed. *Zhongguo jinxiandai renwu minghao dacidian*. Hangzhou: Zhejiang guji chubanshe, 1993.

Chernow, Ron. *Titan: The Life of John D. Rockefeller, Sr*. New York: Random House, 1998.

China National Flood Relief Commission. *Report of the National Flood Relief Commission, 1931–1932*. Shanghai: Commercial Press, 1933.

The China Year Book. Shanghai: North-China Daily News and Herlad Ltd., 1931.

Chu, Samuel C., and Kwang-ching Liu. *Li Hung-chang and China's Early Modernization*. Armonk, NY: M. E. Sharpe, 1994.

Coble, Parks M. *Chinese Capitalism in Japan's New Order: The Occupied Lower Yangzi, 1937–1945*. Berkeley and Los Angeles: University of California Press, 2003.

———. "Chinese Capitalists and the Japanese: Collaboration and Resistance in the Shanghai Area, 1937–45." In *Wartime Shanghai*, edited by Wen-hsin Yeh. New York: Routledge, 1998.

———. *Facing Japan: Chinese Politics and Japanese Imperialism, 1931–1937*. Harvard East Asian Monographs, no. 135. Cambridge, MA: Council on East Asian Studies, Harvard University; distributed by Harvard University Press, 1991.

———. "Japan's New Order and the Shanghai Capitalists: Conflict and Collaboration, 1937–1945." In *Chinese Collaboration with Japan, 1932–1945: The Limits of Accommodation*, edited by David P. Barrett and Lawrence N. Shyu. Stanford, CA: Stanford University Press, 2001.

———. *The Shanghai Capitalists and the Nationalist Government, 1927–1937*. Cambridge, MA: Council on East Asian Studies, Harvard University, 1980.

Cohen, Myron L. "Cultural and Political Inventions in Modern China: The Case of the Chinese 'Peasant.'" *Daedalus* 22, no. 2 (Spring 1993): 151–70.

"Cotton Cultivation in Shensi." *Chinese Economic Monthly* 3, no. 5 (1926): 197–201.

De Felice, Renzo. *Fascismo, antifascismo, nazione: Note e ricerche*. Rome: Bonacci, 1996.

———. *Gabriele D'Annunzio*. Bologna: M. Boni, 1978.

———. *Mussolini*. Vol. 1, *Il rivoluzionario, 1883–1920*. Biblioteca di cultura storica 83. Turin: Einaudi, 1965.

———. *Mussolini*. Vol. 2, pt. 1, *Il fascista*. Vol. 2, pt. 2, *La conquista del potere, 1921–1925*. Biblioteca di cultura storica 92 and 126. Turin: Einaudi, 1965.

De Felice, Renzo, and Pasquale Chessa. *Rosso e nero*. 2d ed. Milan: Baldini and Castoldi, 1995.

Dickson, Bruce J. *Red Capitalists in China: The Party, Private Entrepreneurs, and Prospects for Political Change*. Cambridge: Cambridge University Press, 2003.

Dirlik, Arif. *Anarchism in the Chinese Revolution*. Berkeley and Los Angeles: University of California Press, 1991.

———. "Chinese History and the Question of Orientalism." *History and Theory* 35, no. 4 (1996): 96–118.

———. "Mass Movements and the Left Kuomintang." *Modern China* 1, no. 1 (Jan. 1975): 46–74.

———. *Revolution and History: The Origins of Marxist Historiography in China, 1919–1937*. Berkeley and Los Angeles: University of California Press, 1978.

Dragoni, Mario. *Agricultural Reform and Development in China*. Shanghai: National Economic Council, National Government of the Republic of China, 1933.

Duara, Prasenjit. *Culture, Power, and the State: Rural North China, 1900–1942*. Stanford, CA: Stanford University Press, 1988.

———. *Rescuing History from the Nation*. Chicago: University of Chicago Press, 1995.

Duus, Peter. "Zaikabo: Japanese Cotton Mills in China, 1895–1937." In *The Japanese Informal Empire in China, 1895–1937*, edited by Peter Duus, Ramon Hawley Myers, and Mark R. Peattie. Princeton, NJ: Princeton University Press, 1989.

Duus, Peter, Ramon Hawley Myers, and Mark R. Peattie, eds. *The Japanese Informal Empire in China, 1895–1937*. Princeton, NJ: Princeton University Press, 1989.

———, eds. *The Japanese Wartime Empire, 1931–1945*. Princeton, NJ: Princeton University Press, 1996.

Eastman, Lloyd E. *The Abortive Revolution: China under Nationalist Rule, 1927–1937*. Cambridge, MA: Harvard University Press, 1974.

———. "Fascism in Kuomintang China: The Blue Shirts." *China Quarterly* 49 (1972): 1–31.

Eastman, Lloyd E., et al. *The Nationalist Era in China, 1927–1949*. Cambridge: Cambridge University Press, 1991.

Elvin, Mark. *The Pattern of the Chinese Past*. Stanford, CA: Stanford University Press, 1973.

Eng, Robert Y. *Economic Imperialism in China: Silk Production and Exports, 1861–1932*. Berkeley: Center for Chinese Studies, University of California, 1986.

Esherick, Joseph W. "Harvard on China: The Apologetics of Imperialism." *Bulletin of Concerned Asian Scholars* 4, no. 4 (Dec. 1972): 9–16.

———. *Reform and Revolution in China: The 1911 Revolution in Hunan and Hubei*. Berkeley and Los Angeles: University of California Press, 1976.

Fang Xianting. "Co-operative Marketing of Cotton in Hobei Province." *Nankai Social and Economic Quarterly* 8, no. 3 (Oct. 1935): 551–77.

———. "The Cooperative Movement in China." *Nankai University Monthly Bulletin on Economic China* 7, no. 5 (May 1934): 179–208.

———. *Cotton Industry and Trade in China*. 2 vols. Tianjin: Nankai Institute of Economics, 1932.

———. "The Growth and Decline of Rural Industrial Enterprise in North China." *Nankai Social and Economic Quarterly* 8, nos. 3–4 (1935–36): 691–772.

———. "Rural Industries in China's Reconstruction." *Monthly Bulletin on Economic China* 7, no. 2 (Nov. 1934): 449–55.

———. "Rural Weaving and the Merchant Employers in a North China District: I." *Nankai Social and Economic Quarterly* 8, no. 1 (Apr. 1935): 75–120.

———. "Toward Economic Control in China." *Nankai Social and Economic Quarterly* 9, nos. 1–2 (1936): 269–397.

Fei Xiaotong. *Peasant Life in China: A Field Study of Country Life in the Yangtze Valley*. London: Kegan Paul Trench Trubner, 1939.

Feuerwerker, Albert. *The Chinese Economy, 1870–1949*. Ann Arbor: Center for Chinese Studies, University of Michigan, 1995.

———. *Economic Trends in the Republic of China, 1912–1949*. Ann Arbor: Center for Chinese Studies, University of Michigan, 1977.

Fewsmith, Joseph. *Party, State, and Local Elites in Republican China: Merchant Organizations and Politics in Shanghai, 1890–1930*. Honolulu: University of Hawaii Press, 1985.

Fitzgerald, John. *Awakening China: Politics, Culture, and Class in the Nationalist Revolution*. Stanford, CA: Stanford University Press, 1996.

———. "Warlords, Bullies, and State Building in Nationalist China: The Guangdong Cooperative Movement, 1932–1936." *Modern China* 23, no. 4 (Oct. 1997): 420–58.

Friedman, Edward. "Reconstructing China's National Identity: A Southern Alternative to Mao-Era Anti-imperialist Nationalism." *Journal of Asian Studies* 53, no. 1 (Nov. 1994): 67–91.

Friedman, Edward, Paul Pickowicz, and Mark Selden. *Chinese Village, Socialist State*. New Haven, CT: Yale University Press, 1991.

Furet, François. *The Passing of an Illusion: The Idea of Communism in the Twentieth Century*. Chicago: University of Chicago Press, 1999.

Gandhi, M. P. *How to Compete with Foreign Cloth: A Study of the Position of Hand-Spinning, Hand-Weaving, and Cotton Mills in the Economics of Cloth-Production in India*. Calcutta: G. N. Mitra, of the Book Company, 1931.

Gao Bai. "Arisawa Hiromi and His Theory for a Managed Economy." *Journal of Japanese Studies* 20, no. 1 (Winter 1994): 115–53.

Gates, Hill. *China's Motor: A Thousand Years of Petty Capitalism*. Ithaca, NY: Cornell University Press, 1996.

Gerschenkron, Alexander. *Economic Backwardness in Historical Perspective*. Cambridge, MA: Belknap Press of Harvard University Press, 1962.

Gerth, Karl. *China Made: Consumer Culture and the Creation of the Nation*. Harvard East Asian Monographs, no. 224. Cambridge, MA: Harvard University Asia Center, distributed by Harvard University Press, 2003.

Godley, M. R. "Fascismo e nazionalismo cinese, 1931–1938: Note preliminari allo studio dei rapporti italo-cinese durante il periodo fascista." *Storia contemporanea*, Anno 4, no. 4 (Dec. 1973): 739–77.

Goodman, Bryna. *Native Place, City, and Nation: Regional Networks and Iden-tities in Shanghai, 1853–1937*. Berkeley and Los Angeles: University of California Press, 1995.

Gordon, Bertram M. "The Morphology of the Collaborator: The French Case." *Journal of European Studies* 89, nos. 89–90 (Mar.–June 1993): 1–26.

Gourgouris, Stathis. *Dream Nation: Enlightenment, Colonization, and the Ins-titution of Modern Greece*. Stanford, CA: Stanford University Press, 1996.

Greenfeld, Liah. *The Spirit of Capitalism: Nationalism and Economic Growth*. Cambridge, MA: Harvard University Press, 2001.

Gregor, A. James. *The Ideology of Fascism: The Rationale of Totalitarianism*. New York: Free Press, 1969.

———. *Marxism, China, and Development: Reflections on Theory and Reality*. New Brunswick, NJ: Transaction Publishers, 1995.

———. *A Place in the Sun: Marxism and Fascism in China's Long Revolution*. Boulder, CO: Westview Press, 2000.

Gries, Peter Hays. *China's New Nationalism: Pride, Politics, and Diplomacy*. Berkeley and Los Angeles: University of California Press, 2004.

Guarnieri, Felice. *Autarchia e commercio estero: Discorso pronunciato al Convegno per l'Autarchia*. Turin: La libreria dello stato, 1938.

Habermas, Jürgen. *The Structural Transformation of the Public Sphere: An Inquiry into a Category of Bourgeois Society*. Translated by Thomas Burger with the assistance of Frederick Lawrence. Cambridge, MA: MIT Press, 1991. (First published in 1989.)

Hayford, Charles Wishart. *To the People: James Yen and Village China*. The United States and Pacific Asia Studies in Social, Economic, and Political Interactions. New York: Columbia University Press, 1990.

He, Franklin Lian [Franklin Ho]. *Rural Economic Reconstruction in China*. Shanghai: China Institute of Pacific Relations, 1936.

Henriot, Christian. "Rice, Power, and People: The Politics of Food Supply in Wartime Shanghai (1937–1945)." *Twentieth-Century China* 26, no. 1 (Nov. 2000): 41–84.

Hevia, James Louis. *Cherishing Men from Afar: Qing Guest Ritual and the Macartney Embassy of 1793*. Durham, NC: Duke University Press, 1995.

Higgins, Benjamin, and Jean Downing Higgins. *Economic Development of a Small Planet*. New York: W. W. Norton, 1979.

Hobsbawm, E. J. *Nations and Nationalism since 1780: Programme, Myth, Reality*. Canto ed. Wiles Lectures Given at the Queen's University of Belfast. Cambridge: Cambridge University Press, 1991.

Hobsbawm, E. J., and T. O. Ranger, eds. *The Invention of Tradition*. 1st pbk. ed. Past and Present Publications. Cambridge: Cambridge University Press, 1984.

Hoston, Germaine. *The State, Identity, and the National Question in China and Japan*. Princeton, NJ: Princeton University Press, 1994.

Hou Jiming. *Foreign Investment and Economic Development in China, 1840–1937*. Ann Arbor: Michigan University Press Microfilms International, 1981.

Hu Jichuang. *A Concise History of Chinese Economic Thought*. Beijing: Foreign Language Press, 1988.

Hu Shih, Lin Yu-tang, and Wang Ching-wei. *China's Own Critics: A Selection of Essays.* New York: Paragon Book Reprint Corp., 1969.

Huang, Philip C. C. *The Peasant Economy and Social Change in North China.* Stanford, CA: Stanford University Press, 1985.

———. *The Peasant Family and Rural Development in the Yangzi Delta, 1350–1988.* Stanford, Calif.: Stanford University Press, 1990.

———. "Public Sphere/Civil Society in China? The Third Realm between State and Society." *Modern China* 19, no. 2 (1993): 216–40.

Inspectorate General of Customs. *Trade of China.* Shanghai: Statistical Department of the Inspectorate General of Customs, 1933.

Jameson, Fredric. *Postmodernism.* Durham, NC: Duke University Press, 1991.

Jeans, Roger B. "In Search of the Middle Way: Chang Chun-mai and the Debate over Democracy and Dictatorship in the 1930s." *Republican China* 10, no. 3 (June 1985): 27–43.

———. "Third Force: Zhang Junmai (Carsun Chang) and the National Socialist Party of China, 1932–1937." *Republican China* 19, no. 1 (Nov. 1993): 113–45.

Jiang Jieshi [Chiang Kai-shek]. "Chinese Economic Theory." In *China's Destiny and Chinese Economic Theory,* by Jiang Jieshi. New York: Roy Publishers, 1947.

———. "Gemingjun de zeren shi an'nei rangwai" (May 8, 1933). In *Jiang zongtong ji,* vol. 2, 622–26. Taibei: Guofang yanjiuyuan; Zhonghua dianbian suohui, 1970.

———. "Fuxing zhongguo zhi dao" (Apr. 11, 1932). In *Xianzongtong Jiang Gong sixiang yanlun zhongji,* vol. 2, edited by Qing Xiaoyi, 489. Taibei: Zhongguo Guomindang Zhongyang weiyuanhui tangshi weiyuanhui: Zhongyang wenwu gongyingshe jingxiao, 1984.

———. "Hezuo xunlian zhi yiyi yu mubiao" (Dec. 1, 1932). In *Xianzongtong Jiang Gong sixiang yanlun zongji,* vol. 10, edited by Qing Xiaoyi, 671–76. Taibei: Zhongguo Guomindang Zhongyang weiyuanhui tangshi weiyuanhui: Zhongyang wenwu gongyingshe jingxiao, 1984.

———. "Jiaoyu yu jingji we liguo jiuguo liang yaosu" (Oct. 31, 1932). In *Xianzongtong Jiang Gong sixiang yanlun zhongji,* vol. 10, edited by Qing Xiaoyi, 655–65. Taibei: Zhongguo Guomindang Zhongyang weiyuanhui tangshi weiyuanhui: Zhongyang wenwu gongyingshe jingxiao, 1984.

———. "Xiuming neizheng yu zhengchi lizhi" (Dec. 14, 1932). In *Xianzongtong Jiang gong sixiang yanlun zhongji,* vol. 10, edited by Qing Xiaoyi, 677–86. Taibei: Zhongguo Guomindang Zhongyang weiyuanhui tangshi weiyuanhui: Zhongyang wenwu gongyingshe jingxiao, 1984.

———. "Zhengli jundui, tongyi junshi" (Apr. 2, 1932). In *Xianzongtong Jiang Gong sixiang yanlun zhongji,* vol. 10, edited by Qing Xiaoyi, 483–85. Taibei: Zhongguo Guomindang Zhongyang weiyuanhui tangshi weiyuanhui: Zhongyang wenwu gongyingshe jingxiao, 1984.

———. "Zhengli tudi shi women guoji misheng yige shengsi guanjian" (Nov. 15, 1932). In *Xianzongtong Jiang Gong sixiang yanlun zhongji,* vol. 10, edited by Qing Xiaoyi, 666–70. Taibei: Zhongguo Guomindang Zhong-yang weiyuanhui tangshi weiyuanhui: Zhongyang wenwu gongyingshe jingxiao, 1984.

Jiang Yongjing. "Guomindang sanjutou Hu Wang Jiang de fenhe." *Zhuanji wenxue* 62, no. 3 (Mar. 15, 1993): 15–24.

Johnson, Chalmers A. *MITI and the Japanese Miracle: Growth of Industrial Policy, 1925–1975.* Stanford, CA: Stanford University Press, 1982.

———. *Peasant Nationalism and Communist Power: The Emergence of Revolutionary China*. Stanford, CA: Stanford University Press, 1962.

Jordan, Donald A. *China's Trial by Fire: The Shanghai War of 1932*. Ann Arbor: University of Michigan Press, 2001.

Karl, Rebecca. *Staging the World: Chinese Nationalism at the Turn of the Twentieth Century*. Durham, NC: Duke University Press, 2002.

Kasza, Gregory J. *The Conscription Society: Administered Mass Organization*. New Haven, CT: Yale University Press, 1995.

Keating, Pauline. "The Yan'an Way of Co-operativization." *China Quarterly* 144 (1994): 1025–51.

Kirby, William C. "Engineering China: Birth of the Developmental State, 1928–1937." In *Becoming Chinese: Passages to Modernity and Beyond*, edited by Wen-hsin Yeh. Berkeley and Los Angeles: University of California Press, 2000.

———. *Germany and Republican China*. Stanford, CA: Stanford University Press, 1984.

Kraus, Richard A. *Cotton and Cotton Goods in China, 1918–1936*. New York: Garland Publishing, 1980.

Lai Jiancheng. *Jindai Zhongguo de hezuo jingji yundong*. Taibei: Daxue lianshe chuban, 1988.

Lenin, Vladimir Il'ich. "Preliminary Draft Theses on the National and Colonial Question" (July 1920). In *Collected Works*, vol. 31, 144–51. Moscow: Progress Publisher, 1966.

Levenson, Joseph Richmond. *Confucian China and Its Modern Fate: A Trilogy*. Berkeley and Los Angeles: University of California Press, 1968.

Li Shengbo. "Miantonghui gaijin mianfangzhi ye gongzuo gaikuang." *Mianye yuekan* 1, no. 1 (Jan. 1937): 13–18.

Lippit, Victor. *The Economic Development of China*. New York: Armonk, 1987.

Liu Dazhun. *The Growth and Industrialization of Shanghai*. Shanghai: China Institute of Pacific Relations, 1936.

Liu Jingshan. *Liu Jingshan xiansheng fangwen jilu*. Taibei: Zhongyang yanjiuyuan jindai lishi yanjiusuo, 1987.

Lowenthal, Richard. "Development versus Utopia in Communist Policy." In *Change in Communist Systems*, edited by Jeremy R. Azrael and Chalmers A. Johnson. Stanford, CA: Stanford University Press, 1970.

Lü Fangshang. "Kangzhan qian Jiangxi de nongcun gailiang yu nongcun gaijin shiye." In *Jindai Zhongguo nongcun jingjishi lunewenji*, 517–56. Taibei: Zhongyang yanjiuyuan, jindai yanjiu suo, 1989.

Lu Yangyuan and Fang Qingqiu, eds. *Minguo shehui jingjishi*. Beijing: Zhongguo jingji chubanshe, 1991.

Lubot, Eugene. *Liberalism in an Illiberal Age: New Culture Liberals in Republican China, 1919–1937*. Westport, CT: Greenwood Press, 1982.

Lufrano, Richard. *Honorable Merchants: Commerce and Self-Cultivation in Late Imperial China*. Honolulu: University of Hawai'i Press, 1997.

Luo Dunwei. *Wushinian huiyilu*. Taibei: Zhongguo wenhua gongyingshe, 1952.

Mann, Susan. "Urbanization and Historical Change in China." *Modern China* 1, no. 1 (Jan. 1984): 79–113.

Mao Zedong. "Xin minzhu zhuyi." In *Mao Zedong zhuzuo xuandu*, vol. 1. Beijing: Renmin chubanshe, 1986.

Marsh, Susan H. "Chou Fo-hai: The Making of a Collaborator." In *The Chinese and the Japanese: Essays in Political and Cultural Interactions,* edited by Akira Iriye. Princeton, NJ: Princeton University Press, 1980.

Martin, Brian. "The Green Gang and the Guomindang Polity in Shanghai, 1927–1937." *Papers on Far Eastern History* 42 (1990): 59–96.

———. *The Shanghai Green Gang: Politics and Organized Crime, 1919–1937.* Berkeley and Los Angeles: University of California Press, 1996.

Mason, Tim. "Italy and Modernization: A Montage." *History Workshop* 25 (1988): 110–47.

Melograni, Piero. *Gli industriali e Mussolini.* Milan: Longanesi and Co., 1971.

Mitter, Rana. *The Manchurian Myth: Nationalism, Resistance, and Collaboration in Modern China.* Berkeley and Los Angeles: University of California Press, 2000.

Mu Xiangyue. *Ouchu wu shi zi shu.* Shanghai: Shanghai shudian, 1991. (First published in 1926.)

Mussolini, Benito. *The Corporate State.* Florence: Vallecchi Editore, 1936.

Nathan, Andrew. *A History of the China International Famine Relief Commission.* Cambridge, MA: Harvard University Press, 1965.

———. "Imperialism's Effect on China." *Bulletin of Concerned Asian Scholars* 4, no. 4 (Dec. 1972): 3–8.

National Flood Relief Commission. *Report of the National Flood Relief Commission, 1931–1932.* Shanghai: [Govt.] Comacrib Press, 1933.

Nolan, Peter, and Fureng Dong. *Market Forces in China: Competition and Small Business, the Wenzhou Debate.* London: Zed Books, 1990.

Overy, R. J. *Goering, the "Iron Man."* London and Boston: Routledge and Kegan Paul, 1984.

Patriarca, Silvana. *Numbers and Nationhood: Writing Statistics in Nineteenth-Century Italy.* Cambridge: Cambridge University Press, 1996.

Pepper, Suzanne. *Civil War in China: The Political Struggle, 1945–1949.* Berkeley and Los Angeles: University of California Press, 1978.

Perfetti, Francesco. *La camera dei fasci e delle corporazioni.* Rome: Bonacci, 1991.

Perry, Elizabeth. "Contradictions under Socialism: Shanghai's Strike Wave of 1957." In *Challenging the Mandate of Heaven: Social Protest and State Power in China,* by Elizabeth Perry. Armonk, NY: M. E. Sharpe, 2002.

———. *Shanghai on Strike.* Stanford, CA: Stanford University Press, 1993.

Pickowicz, Paul G. "The Theme of Spiritual Pollution in Chinese Films of the 1930s." *Modern China* 17, no. 1 (Jan. 1991): 38–75.

Pietz, David. *Engineering the State: The Huai River and Reconstruction in Nationalist China, 1927–37.* New York: Routledge, 2002.

Polanyi, Karl. *The Great Transformation.* Boston: Beacon Press, 1957.

Pomeranz, Kenneth. *The Making of a Hinterland: State, Society, and Economy in Inland North China, 1853–1937.* Berkeley and Los Angeles: University of California Press, 1993.

———. "Ritual Imitation and Political Identity in North China: The Late Imperial Legacy and the Chinese National State Revisited." *Twentieth-Century China* 22, no. 1 (1997): 1–30.

Pusey, James Reeve. *China and Charles Darwin.* Cambridge, MA: Council on East Asian Studies, Harvard University, 1983.

Quanguo gongshang huiyi huibian. Edited by Shiyebu Shangyesi. Nanjing: Shiyebu Shangyesi, 1931.

Quanguo jingji huiyi mishuchu bianji. *Quanguo jingji huiyi zhuankan.* Shanghai: Caizhengbu zhuhu banshichu, 1928.

Quanguo jingji weiyuanhui mianye tongzhi weiyuanhui. *Quanguo jingji weiyuanhui mianye tongzhi weiyuanhui sannianlai gongzuo baogao.* Shanghai: Quanguojingji weiyuanhui mianye tongzhi weiyuanhui, 1937.

Rankin, Mary Backus. *Elite Activism and Political Transformation in China: Zhejiang Province, 1865–1911.* Stanford, CA: Stanford University Press, 1986.

Rawski, Thomas G. *China's Transition to Industrialism: Producer Goods and Economic Development in the Twentieth Century.* Ann Arbor: University of Michigan Press, 1980.

———. *Economic Growth and Employment in China.* New York: Oxford University Press, for the World Bank, 1979.

———. *Economic Growth in Prewar China.* Berkeley and Los Angeles: University of California Press, 1989.

Reynolds, David C. "The Advancement of Knowledge and the Enrichment of Life: The Science Society of China and the Understanding of Science in the Early Republic, 1914-1930." Ph.D. diss., University of Wisconsin, 1986.

Reynolds, Douglas. "The Chinese Industrial Cooperative Movement and the Polarization of Wartime China, 1938–1945." Ph.D. diss., Columbia University, 1975.

Riskin, Carl. *China's Political Economy: The Quest for Development since 1949.* Economies of the World. Oxford: Oxford University Press, 1987.

———. "Surplus and Stagnation in Modern China." In *China's Modern Economy in Historical Perspectives,* edited by Dwight Perkins. Stanford, CA: Stanford University Press, 1975.

Rousso, Henry. *The Vichy Syndrome: History and Memory in France since 1944.* Cambridge, MA: Harvard University Press, 1991.

Rowe, William. *Hankou: Commerce and Society in a Chinese City, 1796–1889.* Stanford, CA: Stanford University Press, 1984.

———. *Hankou: Conflict and Community in a Chinese City, 1796–1895.* Stanford, CA: Stanford University Press, 1989.

Scott, James C. *Seeing Like a State: How Certain Schemes to Improve the Human Condition Have Failed.* New Haven, CT: Yale University Press, 1998.

Said, Edward W. *Orientalism.* New York: Vintage Books, 1979.

Sarti, Roland. *Fascism and the Industrial Leadership in Italy, 1919–1940.* Berkeley and Los Angeles: University of California Press, 1971.

Satoshi Kawai. "Zengoku keizai iinkai no naritachi to sono kaiso o nuguru hichi kosatsu." *Toyoshi kenkyu* 40, no. 4 (Mar. 1982): 119–56.

Schmitter, Philippe. "Still the Century of Corporatism?" *Review of Politics* 36, no. 1 (Jan. 1974): 85–131.

Shanghai shehui kexue yuanjiuyuan jingjiynajiusuo, ed. *Rongjia qiye shiliao: Mao Xin, Fu Xin, Shen Xinxi tong.* Shanghai: Shanghai renmin chubanshe, 1980.

Shenbao nianjian. Shanghai: Shenbaoguan, 1933.

Shenxu wangwei hanjian bilu. Edited by Nanjingshi danganguan. 2 vols. Nanjing: Jiangsu guji chubanshe, 1992.

Shirer, William Lawrence. *The Rise and Fall of Adolf Hitler.* New York: Random House, 1961.

Shou Miancheng. "Chen Guofu yu Guomindang de Hezuo Yundong." *Wenshi ziliao xuanji* 80, no. 29 (1980).

Skinner, William. "Marketing and Social Structure in Rural China (Parts I, II, III)." *Journal of Asian Studies* 24, nos. 1–3 (1964–65): 3–43, 195–228, 363–99.

So Wai-chor. *The Kuomintang Left in the National Revolution, 1924–1931*. East Asian Historical Monographs. Hong Kong: Oxford University Press, 1991.

Solinger, Dorothy. "Urban Entrepreneurs and the State: The Merger of State and Society." In *State and Society in China: The Consequences of Reform,* edited by Arthur Lewis Rosenbaum. Boulder, CO: Westview Press, 1992.

Sorgi, Alberto. "La programmazione e la politica economica nel pensiero economico cinese degli anni venti e trenta." Ph.D. diss., Università degli studi di Roma "La Sapienza," Rome, 2002.

Spirito, Ugo. *Il corporativismo*. Florence: Sansoni, 1970.

Sternhell, Zeev. *The Birth of Fascist Ideology*. Translated by David Maisel. Princeton, NJ: Princeton University Press, 1994. (First published in 1989.)

———. *Neither Right nor Left: Fascist Ideology in France*. Translated by David Maisel. Berkeley and Los Angeles: University of California Press, 1986. (First published in 1983.)

Strand, David. *Rickshaw Beijing: City People and Politics in the 1920s*. Berkeley and Los Angeles: University of California Press, 1989.

Sun Enlin. "Mianhua yunxiao guoqiu gonzuo zhi jiantao." *Mianye yuekan* 1, no. 4 (Apr. 1937): 465–676.

Sun Yat-sen. *Fundamentals of National Reconstruction*. Taibei: China Cultural Service, 1953. (First published in 1923.)

———. *Memoirs of a Chinese Revolutionary: A Programme of National Recon-struction for China*. London: Hutchinson and Co., 1927.

———. "Minsheng zhuyi" (1924). In *Sun Zhongshan xuanji,* vol. 2, edited by Song Qingling. *Beijing: Renmin chubanshe, 1957.*

———. "Minzu zhuyi" (1924). In *Sun Zhongshan xuanji,* vol. 2, edited by Song Qingling. Beijing: Renmin chubanshe, 1957.

———. "Minquan zhuyi." In *Sun Zhongshang xuanji,* vol. 2, edited by Song Qingling. Beijing: Renmin chubanshe, 1957.

———. *Sun Zhongshan xuanji*. 2 vols. Edited by Song Qingling. Beijing: Renmin chubanshe, 1957.

Tang Han. *Jiang, Song, Kong, Chen: Sida jiazu*. Beijing: Jingcheng chubanshe, 1998.

Tang Xiaobing. *Global Space and the Nationalist Discourse of Modernity: The Historical Thinking of Liang Qichao*. Stanford, CA: Stanford University Press, 1996.

Tassinari, Giuseppe, and Eduardo Cope. *Fascist Economy*. Rome: "Laboremus," 1937.

Tawney, Richard H. *Land and Labor in China*. Boston: Beacon Press, 1966. (First published 1932.)

Tayler, J. B. "The Organisation of Cooperation: Integrated Society or Integrated Movement?" *Nankai Social and Economic Quarterly* 9, no. 4 (Jan. 1937): 893–916.

Taylor, George E. "The Reconstruction Movement in China." In *Problems of the Pacific, 1936,* edited by W. L. Holland and Kate Mitchell. Chicago: University of Chicago Press, 1936.

Tetsuya, Kuwahara. "The Japanese Cotton Spinners' Direct Investments into China before the Second World War." In *Historical Studies in International Corporate Business,* edited by Alice Teichova, Maurice Lévy-Leboyer, and Helga Nussbaum. Cambridge: Cambridge University Press, 1989.

Thompson, Doug. *State Control in Fascist Italy: Culture and Conformity, 1925–43.* Manchester, UK: Manchester University Press, 1991.

Tian Hongmao [Tien Hung-mao]. *Government and Politics in Kuomintang China, 1927–1937.* Stanford, CA: Stanford University Press, 1972.

Ting, Leonard. "Recent Developments in China's Cotton Industry." Paper presented at the Sixth Conference of the Institute of Pacific Relations, Shanghai, Aug. 1936. Tianjin: Zhili Press, 1936.

Tong Changji. "Chen Guangfu yu Shanghai yinhang." *Wenshi ziliao xuanji* 80 (1980): 138–49.

Tsin, Michael. *Nation, Governance, and Modernity in China: Canton, 1900–1927.* Stanford, CA: Stanford University Press, 1999.

Unger, Jonathan, and Anita Chan. "China, Corporatism, and the East Asian Model." *Australian Journal of Chinese Affairs* 33 (Jan. 1995): 29-53.

Vallauri, Carlo. *Le radici del corporativismo.* Milan: Bulzoni, 1971.

Van Slyke, Lyman P. "Nationalist China during the Sino-Japanese War, 1937–1945." In *The Nationalist Era in China, 1927–1949,* edited by Lloyd Eastman, Jerome Ch'en, Suzanne Pepper, and Lyman P. Van Slyke. Cambridge: Cambridge University Press, 1991.

Varaut, Jean-Marc. *Le process Pétain, 1945–1995.* Paris: Perrin, 1995.

Vaudagna, Maurizio. "Structural Change in Fascist Italy." *Journal of Economic History* 38, no. 1 (1978): 181–201.

Wakeman, Frederic E., Jr. "The Civil Society and Public Sphere Debate: Western Reflections on Chinese Politics." *Modern China* 19, no. 2 (Apr. 1993): 108–38.

———. *Policing Shanghai, 1927–1937.* Berkeley and Los Angeles: University of California Press, 1995.

———. "A Revisionist View of the Nanjing Decade: Confucian Fascism." *China Quarterly* 150 (1997): 395–432.

Wang Dong. "Chuangjian zhongguo tese de xiandaihua xinlilun." *Beijing daxue xuebao* 4 (1994): 11–21.

Wang Jingwei [Wang Ching-wei]. "An'nei yu rangwai." In *Wang Jingwei xiansheng zuijin zhi yanlun,* edited by Lin Bosheng. Shanghai: Zhonghua ribao guan, 1937.

———. *China's Problems and Their Solution.* China To-day series, no. 2. Shanghai: United Press, 1934.

———. "Faqi zuzhi guomin jiuguohui tongdian" (Dec. 10, 1931). In *Wang Jingwei wencun.* Shanghai: Qizhi shuju, 1935.

———. "Jianshe." In *Wang Jingwei wencun.* Shanghai: Qizhi shudian, 1935.

———. "Minzu de guomin" (1905). In *Wang Jingwei xiansheng wenji.* Shanghai: Dahan Ribao, 1910.

———. "Proposal for Economic and Financial Policies." In *The Chinese National Revolution: Essays and Documents by Wang Jingwei and Others,* edited by T'ang Leang-li. Beijing: United Press, 1930.

———. *Wang Jingwei wenxuan.* Shanghai: Fanggu shudian, 1936.

———. *Wang Jingwei xiansheng guangyu heping yundong zhi zhongyao yanlun.* China, 1938.

———. "Women yao jianshe zenmeyang de guojia" (July 1927). In *Wang Jingwei wencun.* Shanghai: Qizhi shudian, 1935.

Wang Jingwei [Wang Ching-wei], and Jiang Jieshi [Chiang Kai-shek]. *China's Leaders and Their Policies: Messages to the Chinese People*. China Recon- struction series, no. 2. Shanghai: China United Press, 1935.

Wang Jingwei, I. Sen Teng, and John Nind Smith. *China and the Nations; Being the Draft of the Report on International Problems Prepared for the International Problems Committee of the People's Conference of Delegates at Peking in April, 1925*. London: Martin Hopkinson, 1927.

Wang Ke-Wen. "Collaborators and Capitalists: The Politics of 'Material Control' in Wartime Shanghai." *Chinese Studies in History* 26, no. 1 (Fall 1992): 42–62.

Wang Shuhuai. "Mianye tongzhi weiyuanhui de gongzuo chengxiao 1933–37." In *Kangzhanqian shinina guojia jiansheshi yanjiuhui wenji*. Taibei: Zhongyang yanjiuyuan jindaishi yanjiusuo, 1984.

Wang Wen'an. *Min zu jing ji yu she hui yan jiu*. Beijing: Zhongguo renmin gongan daxue chubanshe, 2001.

Wang Yejian [Wang Yeh-chien]. "The Fiscal Importance of the Land Tax during the Ch'ing (Qing) Period." *Journal of Asian Studies* 30, no. 4 (Aug. 1971): 829–42.

White, Lynn, and Li Cheng. "China Coast Identities: Regional, National, and Global." In *China's Quest for National Identity*, edited by Lowell Dittmer and S. Samuel Kim. Ithaca, NY: Cornell University Press, 1993.

Wiedmer Caroline. *The Claims of Memory: Representations of the Holocaust in Contemporary Germany and France*. Ithaca, NY: Cornell University Press, 1999.

Will, Pierre-Etienne, and R. Bin Wong, eds. *Nourish the People: The State Civilian Granary System in China, 1650–1850*. Ann Arbor: University of Michigan Press, 1991.

Wilson, Rob, and Wimal Dissanayake, eds. *Global/Local: Cultural Production and the Transnational Imaginary*. Durham, NC: Duke University Press, 1996.

Wu Huabao. "Zuzhi yunxiao hezuoshi shi liyi ji qi chengbai zhi yinzi." *Mianye yuekan* 1, no. 7 (July 1937): 995–1008.

Wu Jingping. *Song Ziwen pingzhuan*. Fuzhou: Fujian renmin chubanshe, 1992.

———. *Song Ziwen sixiang yanjiu*. Fuzhou: Fujian renmin chubanshe, 1998.

Xu, D. Z. [Hsu, T. C.]. "Economic Ideas in China's Draft Constitution." *Monthly Bulletin on Economic China* 7, no. 8 (Aug. 1934): 325–40.

Xu Youchun, ed. *Minguo renwu dacidian*. Shijiazhuang: Hebei renmin chubanshe, 1991.

Xu Zhongdi. "Shaanxi mianhua chanxiao hezuoshe zhi guoqu yu jianglai." *Mianye yuekan* 1, no. 1 (1937): 56–73.

Yang, Mingzhe. "Guomin ershinian changjiang dashuizai zhi yanjiu." Ph.D. diss., Zhengzhi University, Taibei, Taiwan, 1987.

Yao Songling. *Chen Guangfu de yisheng*. Taibei: Zhuanji wenxue chubanshe, 1984.

Young, Arthur N. *China's Nation Building Effort, 1927–1937: The Financial and Economic Papers*. Stanford, CA: Hoover Institution Press, 1971.

Young, Ernest. *The Presidency of Yuan Shi-kai*. Ann Arbor: University of Michigan Press, 1977.

Young, Louise. *Japan's Total Empire: Manchuria and the Culture of Wartime Imperialism*. Twentieth-Century Japan 8. Berkeley and Los Angeles: University of California Press, 1998.

Yuan Xijian. "Chen Guangfu de yisheng." *Wenshi ziliao xuanji* 30 (1980): 64–78.

Yuan Yuquan. "Riben qinlue zhi paozhe de shangtonghui." In *Shanghai wenshi ziliao xuanji*. Shanghai: Shanghai renmin chubanshe, 1987.

Zanasi, Margherita. "Far from the Treaty Ports: Fang Xianting and the Idea of Rural Modernity in 1930s China." *Modern China* 30, no. 1 (Jan. 2004): 113–46.

———. "Fostering the People's Livelihood: Chinese Political and Economic Thought between Empire and Nation." *Twentieth Century China* 23, no. 1 (Nov. 2004): 6–38.

Zani, Luciano. *Fascismo, autarchia, commercio estero: Felice Guarnieri, un technocrate al servizio dello "stato nuovo."* Bologna: Il Mulino, 1988.

Zarrow, Peter Gue. *Anarchism and Chinese Political Culture*. New York: Columbia University Press, 1990.

———. "Political Ritual in the Early Republic of China." In *Constructing Nationhood in Modern East Asia,* edited by Kai-wing Chow, Kevin M. Doak, and Poshek Fu. Ann Arbor: University of Michigan Press, 2001.

Zelin, Madeleine. *The Magistrate's Tael: Rationalizing Fiscal Reform in Eighteenth-Century Ch'ing China*. Berkeley and Los Angeles: University of California Press, 1985.

Zhang Genfu. "Wangwei quanguo shangye tongzhi zonghui shulun." *Dangan yu lishi* 3 (June 1997): 41–47.

Zhang Li. *Guoji hezuo zai zhonggho*. Taibei: Zhongyang yanjiuyuan jindaishi yanjiusuo, 1999.

———. "Jiangxi noncun fuwu shiye 1934–1945." In *Kangzhan jianguoshi yanjiu Taohui wenji 1937–1945*. Taibei: Zhongyang yanjiuyuan jindaishi yanjiusuo, 1981.

Zhang Pengyuan, and Shen Huaiyu, eds. *Guomin zhengfu zhiguan nianbiao (1925–1949)*. Vol. 1, *Shiliao Zongshu*. Taibei: Zhongyang yanjiuyuan jinshisuo, 1987.

Zhang Shuguang. *Mao's Military Romanticism: China and the Korean War, 1950–1953*. Lawrence: University Press of Kansas, 1995.

Zheng Guanying. *Sheng shi wei yan*. Zhengzhou: Zhongzhou guji chubanshe, 1988.

Zheng Huixin [Cheng Hwei-shing]. *Cong touzi gongsi dao "Guanbang shangxing": Zhongguo jianshe yin gongsi de chuangli ji qi jingying huodong*. Hong Kong: Chinese University Press, 2001.

Zheng Yongnian. *Discovering Chinese Nationalism in China: Modernization, Identity, and International Relations*. Cambridge: Cambridge University Press, 1999.

Zhi Xisheng [Chi Hsi-sheng]. *The Chinese Warlord System, 1916–1928*. Washington, DC: American University Center for Research in Social Systems, 1969.

———. *Warlord Politics in China, 1916–1928*. Stanford, CA: Stanford University Press, 1976.

Zhong Xiangcai. *Zhongguo jindai minzu qiyejia jingji sixiang*. Shanghai: Shanghai shehui kexueyuan chubanshe, 1992.

Zhu Zijia [Jin Xiongbai]. *Wang Zhengquan di kaichan yu shouchang*. Hong Kong: Chunqiu zazhishe, 1959.

Zou Bingwen. "Miantongzhi mianchan gaijin gongzuo qingkuang." *Mianye yuekan* 1, no. 1 (Jan. 1937): 1–12.

Zweig, David. *Agrarian Radicalism in China, 1968–1981*. Cambridge, MA: Harvard University Press, 1989.

———. *Internationalizing China: Domestic Interests and Global Linkages*. Ithaca, NY: Cornell University Press, 2002.

INDEX